FROM A FISHING TRIP IN PATMOS

THE DISCIPLEMAKER'S EDITION

Michael Donaldson

Shepard's
Ink
Publishing
Live to read – read to Live

All rights reserved.

No part of this publication may be reproduced or transmitted in any form or by any means electronic or mechanical, including photocopy, recording, or any information storage and retrieval system, without permission in writing from both the copyright owner and the publisher. All scriptures and quotations used by permission.

Requests for permission to make copies of any part of this work should be mailed to Permissions Department, Shepard's Ink P.O. Box 78211 Nashville, Tn. 37207. Shepard's Ink Publishing is a proud member of Ashara Ministries.

Copyright 2005   Michael L. Donaldson
ISBN: 0-9764645-5-1

Dedication

I DEDICATE <u>FROM A FISHING TRIP IN PATMOS</u>, TO MY TWO FATHERS. THEY GAVE ME THE TWO GREATEST GIFTS THAT ANY SON COULD RECIEVE. ELWOOD DONALDSON, MY EARTHLY FATHER TAUGHT ME HOW TO THINK AND BE FREE AND MY HEAVENLY **FATHER,** WHO IS STILL TEACHING ME WHAT TO THINK AND WHAT TO DO WITH THAT FREEDOM.

Table of Contents

PART I

ACKNOWLEDGEMENTS

ABOUT THE DISCPLE MAKER'S EDITION…………………..3

ABOUT THE AUTHOR AND THIS EDITION…...…………….4

SALUTATIONS……………………………………………....……6

LETTER I ≈ A LETTER TO ME……………………….....……10

LETTER II ≈ THE TRUE SYMBOL OF CHRISTIANITY…..14
WORK AREA…………………………………………………....26

LETTER III ≈ FISHERS OF MEN……………………….....…36
WORK AREA………………………………………………..…..69

LETTER IV ≈ TO CATCH THE FISH……………………….78
WORK AREA…………………………………………..………..84

LETTER V ≈ LURE, BAIT & TACKLE & BEST WATERS …92
WORK AREA……………………………………………………106

LETTER VI ≈ CLEANING & SCALING……………………114
WORK AREA…………………………………………………..136

LETTER VII ≈ A TALE OF A WHALE…………………….144
WORK AREA…………………………………………………..159

Table of Contents

PART II ...ALMOST A CHURCH

LETTER VIII ≈ ME AND MRS BONES........................170
WORK AREA..188

LETTER IX ≈ SINK OR SWIM (BAPTISM) 197
WORK AREA..205

LETTER X ≈ YOUR PLACE OR MINE (COMPETITION)...213
WORK AREA..223

LETTER XI ≈ TWO DRINK MINIMUM.......................232
WORK AREA..238

LETTER XII ≈ THE OTHER WHITE MEAT................247
WORK AREA..262

LETTER XIII ≈ THE MYSTERY OF THE MINISTRIES......269
WORK AREA..286

LETTER XIV ≈ THE 13TH TRIBE (TRIBE OF JUDAS)......295
WORK AREA..314

LETTER XV ≈ ETERNAL AFFAIRS (AUTHORITY).........322
WORK AREA..339

LETTER XVI ≈ LET MY PEOPLE KNOW....................347
WORK AREA..371

LETTER XVII ≈ A LETTER TO YOU..........................383
WORK AREA..389

Table of Contents

PART III... DISCIPLESHIP BASICS

DISCIPLESHIP BASICS - A BASIC OVERVIEW OF FIRST CONTACT METHODS EXEMPLIFIED BY THE MASTER..395

THE STRUCTURE OF A SAINTLY ARMY......................399

SPIRITUAL WARFARE: THE WEAPONS 400
- Loin...403
- Breastplate...405
- Boots..407
- Shield...409
- Helmet...414
- Sword...416
- Prayer..418
- Alertness...421

SPIRITUAL WARFARE: THE THREE MAIN COMPONENTS OF A SUCCESSFUL SPIRITUAL CAMPAIGN................424
- Dedication..426
- Inspiration...428
- Education...430

GLOSSARY...432

SYMBOLIC LANGUAGE USED IN THE BIBLE...............433

INDEX..435

Acknowledgements

I would like to take the opportunity to acknowledge each and everyone one that purchased this book. Not because I need the money but because you realize you need the Lord. For that both He and I rejoice.

Foreword

From A Fishing Trip in Patmos is a very complete book. It tells about the personal experiences of the author. It relates passages of scripture to the very events that are our lives. It explains scriptures and explores the meanings of scriptures. The author has lived a lot; the author has seen a lot. The author takes you there, weaving the lessons of the ancient writings into the realities of modern living. Some people take the spiritual journey alone; eventually all must walk the path to their own enlightenment at their own speeds and by their own routes. But all the seekers benefit from road maps, tour guides, and lamps to light their way. From A Fishing Trip in Patmos will assist and ease the journey.

Jan A. Bossing Nashville D.A.'s Office (ret)

About the author and this Edition

The author Michael Donaldson was born in Nassau, Bahamas. On that island, he grew up in a Methodist school and a Pentecostal church; he accepted Christ when he was 14yrs old. After leaving home at age sixteen and experiencing college at that tender age, he came to the following conclusion: Kids do not have a clue. "The biggest mistake in my life was ignoring my parents and leaving home at 16, I had no idea what real life was like."

He moved to Tennessee in 1988 where for the next seven years he contributed precious little to the Kingdom of Heaven. He proudly served in the United States Marine Corps Res. Where he learned indispensable lessons in warfare and weaponry.

After returning to Kingdom service in 1995 he spent the last 10 years teaching Spiritual Warfare, and making disciples. He is founder and CEO of Ashara Outreach Ministries. The motto of Ashara is, "Building people not churches." Under that mission, Ashara has developed numerous programs to reach the lost sheep. The great joy in Kingdom work manifested itself in his life through prison outreach and working with the Police and Sheriff's departments in Nashville.

According to the author, "There is beauty in all of God's children which manifests itself in their expression of His love. The only true church of Christ is found in the heart's of people. The edifices we build fail in comparison to give glory and honor to the Lord God almighty. The love of God shows itself in the hearts of people, and only this love lasts forever. This is not because man last forever, it is because God does. Remember, only what you do for Christ will last."

His education consists of tenure at Tennessee State University, which resulted in a B.S. in Political Science, being a member of Pres. Dorm Council, Student Union Board of Governors, Food Services Committee, Student Court, and spending numerous semesters on the Nat'l Dean's List. From there he attained a Master's of Science in Public Administration, - policy, and planning from Cumberland University, where he was inducted into Pi Gamma Mu Int'l Honor Society in Social Science. He also has studied and attained a Certificate of Theology from Falwell University.

Michael worked thirteen years in the Metro-Nashville Police department during which he has been decorated nine times and received numerous awards and certificates. He also instructed the following topics; Strategic Planning Committee, Involvement in community activities, Neighborhood policing. Interacting/briefing with the Mayor and Judges to inform them of recent changes in Crime trends. Case management, management of confidential informants and witnesses, Coordinating inter-agency raids. Counter Terrorism, Courtroom testimony, Booking and property procedures, Street level drug buys and arrests, Designer drugs and Rave parties, Undercover living and concerns. In addition, he has done consultation for the Crime Commission Commonwealth of the Bahamas regarding crime prevention and community policing.

Eight of the thirteen years as policeman were spent in the Vice division buying, selling and distribution drugs, dealing with prostitutes and sex crimes. In those eight years, the untold stories of human suffering and misery troubled and frightened him. More than being frightened, exposure to this suffrage moved Donaldson to try to do something to increase awareness and alleviate some of the sorrow.

Donaldson is also the developer of Jesuka Martial Arts discipline - The art of physical-spirituality. He has spent the last 10 years teaching various topics ranging from Rape prevention to preventing kids from becoming sexually active. His list of published works consists of From a Fishing Trip in Patmos, From a Fishing Trip in Patmos: Disciple-maker's Edition, Black Coffee, The Butterfly Veil. In addition, the following works Apologies from Patmos, Famine in Patmos and The Jesuka: The Art of Physical Spirituality, to come out in 2006.

The afore mentioned qualifications give more information about the author; not to validate the author. The purpose of the information is to give an example of some basic signs of effort that we should look for in all God's servants. The credentials do not indicate level of spirituality, but the level of stewardship and dedication. Credentials only matter when the Sprit is not present, in His presence we all dim and must kneel.

The components of the Disciple-maker's edition form one of the most useful tools of disciple making I have encountered. This book asks numerous potent questions which when answered give an excellent platform from which to fish for sheep.

Also included in the disciple's edition are;

1) Discipleship Basics - A basic overview of first contact methods exemplified by The Master.

2) Spiritual Warfare: The Weapons and three main components of a successful Spiritual Campaign.

3) Three main components of a successful Spiritual campaign.

This edition also has an index and a list of symbolic language used in the bible; both of these I am sure you will find make this book more user friendly.

Capitalized, italicized text indicates words spoken by the Lord our God. Bold and italics indicate words spoken by the Father or by Jesus. All areas enclosed by the ' ≈ ' and emphasized by the **Berlin Sans fb demi** font indicate scripture. All scriptures used are King James version unless otherwise indicated.

Due to an overwhelming response to the poems included in the original version I have abridged the poems in this work. The abridged poems and many more can be found in Black Coffee.

Feel free to contact me at Shepardsink@yahoo.com with questions or comments.

Salutations

≈ **And therefore will the Lord wait, that He may be gracious unto you, and therefore will He be exalted, that He may have mercy upon you: for the Lord is a God of judgment: blessed (are) all they that wait for Him. For the people shall dwell in Zion at Jerusalem: thou shalt weep no more: He will be very gracious unto thee at the voice of thy cry; when He shall hear it, He will answer thee. And (though) the Lord give you the bread of adversity, and the water of affliction, yet shall not thy teachers be removed into a corner any more, but thine eyes shall see thy teachers: And thine ears shall hear a word behind thee, saying, This (is) the way, walk ye in it, when ye turn to the right hand, and when ye turn to the left.** ≈ (Isa 31:18-21)

SALUTATIONS

Growing up in Nassau, Bahamas fish and fish stories constantly surrounded me; living on an island is like that. One day my brother and I went on a great outing. My father took us fishinin (the use of the "ing" ending has not been perfected in my country). Popeil manufactured a pocket fisherman at that time; a football sized self-contained apparatus. When we got to the dock, my father put a piece of bacon on the hook and began to cast (throw the line).

In order to get extra leverage, he came from behind his head. As he threw the line, the hook flew and caught a great catch…it caught him! The self-proclaimed fisherman was standing on the dock with his two sons looking and laughing and a fishing hook embedded in his back.

It took a few minutes to free the hook, it was much trickier than we expected. After the first failed attempt, he cast again and this time it flew true and went into the water. After a few short moments, a nibble at the hook resulted in the capturing of the only fish I have ever seen my father catch. The fish was about the size of a chocolate bar and was rather ugly. Dad took it home, scaled (cleaned) it, and then cooked it. The fish was just enough for one child but my father ate it anyway.

Greetings to you brothers and Sisters, I write to you from the sanctuary of my exile. Patmos is the Isle the writer of Revelations John was exiled to in Revelations 1:9. Unlike most sanctuaries; this sanctuary is the paradise of solitude with the Father. Unlike our fleshly nature, which is to congregate for purposes of safety and belonging, within this sanctuary lays the true blessing; the time spent alone in God's bosom.

This work is a series of letters bound together, not a novel, but more so an anthology of individual letters. Although they do share a common thread, they are not congruous chapters. Each is prepared to cover a particular topic without regard to the topic covered in any other letter. I pray that they be used to aid believers in their Christian walk, to edify and to exhort.

This work is an adventure in the study of God's word and several principles therein. Freemasonry[2] teaches two types of lessons, objective

---

[2] I am no longer an active mason but the things God allowed me to glean from that experience have only made me a better Christian. God ordains all things and I have no cause to speak evil of the Masons. I am not qualified to judge them nor are they on trial here. Let the Spirit be your guide in what you do and whom you do it with.

and speculative. The objective lesson is the practical, tangible messages (i.e. a reference to a hammer actually means a hammer.) In speculative masonry, the same reference might mean a powerful thought, some type of force or even anger.

Many passages of the bible are also written this way serving two very important purposes. One is that in the present tense it has its seemly practical application. Secondly, in order that God's word last throughout time it had to also have the speculative quality. This turns the principle, into the lesson, and so we are not caught up simply in semantics. This is most often done with Old Testament scriptures.

The speculative lesson in my father's story is when you call yourself to be a fisherman (fisher of men) you go forth at your own peril. The result of your action is always death. How many fish have been devoured in this way by self-proclaimed fishers of men. Men that have harvested them while they were still young and unprepared then served them as appetizers to the devourer of souls--Satan.

Without the proper training and the call from God, the inevitable result is to catch the wrong thing. This could be the wrong spirit, or it could be that you get caught up yourself. However, either way it is not God's way, so there is no eternal reward and the only thing you may be spreading is damnation.

Another short example of the need for the proper call and training occurred in my country. Six Mothers of Zion (The older women that wear all white to church and sit in the pulpit) took a new convert to the ocean to baptize her. Baptism according to the Word of God is unto eternal life of Christ but in her case, it was unto death. There happened to be a Marine on vacation sitting on the beach that day. As he watched the baptism, he observed what too many sinners observe and fear, the death caused by false fishers.

As in every true baptism, the initiate is submerged and then raised anew. In this instance however, the Mothers held the girl under until she thrashed. As the thrashing grew worse, the other Mothers assisted in holding the girl under until the most horrible thing happened--all motion in the girl stopped...the girl was dead. When questioned by the authorities as to why they drowned the girl, the Mothers (who by the way are still in jail) answered honestly. The women thought the girl had demons that were resisting, and they were trying to cast the demons out.

Sadly, this too often is the case wherein the lost destroy the innocent and helpless. The real blame however, is on the church that gave these obviously demented ladies the authority to kill and destroy God's fish. What a marring event to associate with one of the greatest privileges a believer can have; to be covered by the Blood of Jesus. Even worse, (or at least just as bad) what do you think that that marine thought seeing these women of God drown a young girl that unfortunately trusted them. How many have been scared away in this manner and how many more murdered? How many murdered by the church? By those of us who claim to be servants of a Master who said, **(I CAME THAT YOU MIGHT HAVE LIFE AND IT MORE ABUNDANTLY.)**

These letters deal with allegory and principles that the Holy Spirit uses to make various points. I have also enclosed my spiritual resume, something that I admonish all church leaders to be required to have. For too long have we allowed the willing to hold office in God's church, although willingness is important, qualifications and "the call" were the two criterion required for elders and deacons. If a person has attended church for 20 years and is still drinking milk, how then can they be qualified to teach meat eaters? I do not know about you but when it comes to God's Word, I am a carnivore.

Letters <u>From a Fishing Trip in Patmos</u> resulted from years in spiritual exile being prepared by the Holy Spirit. I pray that they find you in health and may peace be unto you and your households.

LETTER I

≈

A LETTER TO ME!

"It is the Father's good pleasure to give you the keys to the kingdom; the way to enter His presence, how to praise and receive from Him, the assurance that every one of your prayers has been heard. But if you come to Him, you must believe that He is! And that He is a rewarder of those who diligently, respectfully, willfully and dedicatedly seek Him.

I WILL REVEAL MYSELF TO YOU BUT YOU MUST BE QUIET ENOUGH IN YOUR RESTLESSNESS TO OPEN YOUR HEART AND MIND TO ME. TRAIN YOURSELF; YOU BELIEVE IN TRAINED PERFECTION, PRACTICE COMING BEFORE ME TO WAIT UNTIL IT BECOMES A DAILY PRACTICED DISCIPLINE OF YOURS. I HAVE BEEN WAITING ON YOU FOR A LONG TIME--YOUR RESPECT FOR ME, FOR MY PEOPLE, FOR MY WORD (PRAISE, SINGING, AND TITHING). YOU MUST MAKE THE DECISION FOR YOURSELF TO DO THINGS MY WAY AND ACCORDING TO MY WORD. YOU ARE STUBBORN AND THAT HINDERS ME. I HAVE VISITED YOU SO OFTEN BUT YOU ALWAYS TURN INTO SOMETHING ELSE. ABOVE EVERYTHING ELSE, I AM A PRESENCE AND I AM MY WORD. YOUR WEAPON IS AIMED IN THE WRONG DIRECTION. DRAW BACK YOUR ARROWS, LIFT YOUR HEAD, AND LOOK TO THE HEAVENS AND RECEIVE FROM ME!

Thus said the Lord. (April 4, 2000)"

LETTER I ≈ A LETTER TO ME!

My mother read this letter to me after I complained to her about my unhappiness and disdain with church. I went to work and left her sitting in a chair praying. When I returned, she asked me to sit with her and read the above letter to me.

I felt rather stupid afterwards, but the letter addressed my chief complaint; namely God would not talk to me. After receiving this letter (actually she read it because I cannot read her handwriting) we prayed, and I went about my merry way, still confused and dismayed.

Several weeks later, while driving down the road the Holy Spirit finally revealed to me my purpose in the Kingdom.[4] Ironically, it came right after reading Sorge's book <u>Dealing with the Rejection and Praise of Man</u>, and it made my heart soar.[5] Much like Peter, I set out on my mission lopping off spiritual ears, and I had far more than one sword![6] Much as the loving father reproaches his children when they do silly things, He corrected me.

Correction came in several forms the first was a joke. I stopped to assist a man kneeling behind his car, assuming that he needed my help. When I got closer, it turned out that the man was Islamic and was praying. When I got back into my vehicle, the Holy Spirit asked me a question; {DO YOU KNOW WHY YOU DID NOT RECOGNIZE IT?} The Holy Spirit then answered, {IT IS BECAUSE YOU DO NOT SPEND ENOUGH TIME DOING IT!}

Next, the Holy Spirit answered a question that had plagued me for years. Why He left me confused for such a long time and without guidance? I referred to the years I spent studying and practicing the various religions of the world. I studied their philosophies and their beliefs and prayed in vain to their false gods. {I HAVE ALWAYS GUIDED YOUR HAND! YOU WERE NEVER LOST. I TOOK YOU ON A JOURNEY TO PREPARE YOU FOR MY TASK. YOU SPENT TIME IN THE DARKNESS LOOKING FOR ME AND I WAITED UNTIL YOU WERE READY TO DO MY BIDDING. I PLACED YOU OUTSIDE THE NEED TO BE PRAISED AND ACCEPTED BY MEN

---

[4] Not all of the contents will be discussed here, as they are all not pertinent.
[5] That should have been my first clue that I misunderstood what the Father was saying.
[6] Luke 22:36.

FOR MY WORKS. YOU WILL NEVER BE ACCEPTED AND YOU WILL ALWAYS BE OUTSIDE OF THEIR CIRCLES, SO PREPARE YOURSELF}.

This came to me as I was driving and praising the Lord, I had to pull over and stop. Curiously, the part of His words that stuck out the most was the end. I was tired of being an outcast, and it crushed me so that I had to sit still and compose myself.

The years of silent tears had finally made their purpose known and the answer vexed me. It took a few weeks for my anger to subside; time they say heals all wounds. Actually, I was simply pouting and I was unhappy about the task God gave me. The fact of the matter is that it is usually the thing that we least want to do that God assigns to us. Only the flesh does what it wants to do, the spirit obeys the Father. At least I knew now that God heard me, and I was not doing it all in vain. It did not hurt less, but it at least gave my pain purpose. There were years of study needed to complete His good works. Much like a child I laid around for a while pouting, and completely overlooking the fact that I was chosen to do a good work for the Lord. I even forgot what He initially told me to do. Thank God, He stopped me because I was way off the track He laid. I misunderstood what He said, like Peter in the garden when Jesus told him;

≈ **HE THAT HATH NO SWORD, LET HIM SELL HIS GARMENT, AND BUY ONE.** ≈

Peter assumed that Jesus spoke literally, and in his misplaced zeal, he lopped off the soldier's ear. What Jesus actually meant was that He had provided for their every need thus far, and if they needed to do it a way other than His, it would take a lot more than they had to fight His battles. Fortunately, the Father was gracious enough to give me clarity as to what my task was.

When seeking help from the Lord, do not ask for signs ask for guidance. Only unbelievers need signs. When we pray, ask God to speak directly to us. We need to be specific, and we should always ask for clarity. Ask not for the purpose of knowing the whole plan or debating, but for receiving His responses in an understandable manner. Even, if we do not obey at least His instructions were clear.

From a fishing trip in Patmos is a series of letters the Holy Spirit has led me to share. Try everything by the Spirit and the word. This requires that we read the Word. The only way to try something by the

Word is to first know the Word. Be careful not to let your pride stand in God's way. The word tells that a man's pride brings him low[7].

Moreover, I pray that you will always be cognizant of the words we use. Words are also Lucifer the silver tongue's weapons against us. The slightest scriptulaton[8], or misinterpretation can take a whole nation to hell with it.

≈ **AMEN** ≈

---

[7] Prov. 29:23.
[8] Defined by the author as scriptural manipulation.

LETTER II

≈

THE TRUE SYMBOL OF CHRISTIANITY

"Consider how Aristotle describes the Christians to the Roman Emperor Hadrian: They love one another. They never fail to help widows: they save orphans from those who would hurt them. If they have something, they give freely to the man who has nothing; if they see a stranger, they take him home, and are happy, as though he were a real brother. They don't consider themselves brothers in the usual sense, but brothers through the Spirit, in God.[9] "

---

[9] Loving God (p.176).

LETTER II ≈ THE TRUE SYMBOL OF CHRISTIANITY

Believers let us begin this letter by dispelling a common fallacy. The symbol of the fish although used, has never and in no way represents Christ. Although it a one time was a secret symbol among Christians in the first century A.D., Christ neither approved nor condoned the fish symbol. In researching the symbol of the fish I found several things:

1. The initial letters of the Greek phrase "Jesus Christ, Son of God, Savior" form the Greek word ICHTHUS, which means "fish." This symbol was used by believers in the early days of persecution as a secret sign of their shared faith. One person would draw an arc in the sand, and the other would complete the sign to show his brotherhood in Christ[7].

Three fish represent Jesus as a member of the Trinity[10]

---

[10] <u>Symbols in Christian Art and Architecture.</u> Gast, Walter. http://home.att.net/~wegast/symbols/headline.htm.

2. The dolphin is one of the most common "fish" (the dolphin is actually a mammal) found in Christian art. Because dolphins are often seen to swim alongside ships, they came to represent Christ, who guides believers to heaven. In this sense a dolphin usually shown together with an anchor or a boat. Dolphins were the fish often used to portray the story of Jonah, and by extension came to be symbolic of the Resurrection. Because they are strong, swift swimmers, they are sometimes shown bearing the souls of the dead to the world beyond the sea[7].

3. The symbol of the fish existed long before Jesus came on the scene.

4. The fish has long been a symbol of the great mother, which has two distinctly anti- Christian aspects. A: Mother is feminine character and although Jesus gave birth to what we call Christianity God always refers to Him in a male persona. He would be more of a Father of Christianity than a mother. B: The great mother controverts our Trinity, which consists of Father, Son, and Holy Ghost.

5. The fish in Egyptian, African, Chinese, Indian, and Greek mythology was a symbol of maternity, (the womb and its ability to give life).

6. According to the Encyclopedia of Myths[11], the *yoni* was a worldwide symbol of the great mother. The yoni was a pointed oval sign known as *vesica piscis, vessel of the fish* (which is also where the zodiac sign Pisces came from.) Fish and womb were synonymous in Greek; *delphos* meant both. The Catholic Church inherited the pagan custom of Friday fish-eating and pretending it was a holy fast; Friday was *dies veneres* in Latin, the Day of Venus, or of lovemaking. The Christian fish-sign was the same as that of the Goddess's *yoni*, two crescent moons forming a *vesica piscis*. Sometimes the Christ child was portrayed inside the vesica, which was super-imposed on Mary's stomach obviously to represent her womb, just as the goddess *yoni* symbol did.

7. The word "Ichthys" which is Greek for fish was considered an acronym for Jesus Christ, Son of God.

---

[11] See The Women's Encyclopedia of Myths and Secrets. Walker, Barbara. Harper Collins, San Francisco. 1983 pg. 313 - 314.

8. According to the Woman' <u>Dictionary of Symbols & Sacred Objects</u>, *Ichthys* was the name of a son of the ancient Sea-goddess Atargatis, whose name meant both "womb" and "dolphin." The fish sign consists of two crescent moons, the conventional representation of the goddess as the source of all the water of the earth.

According to the Bible, the articulated symbol/sign of Jesus and His believers is "love." (John 13:34, 35) ≈ **A NEW COMMANDMENT I GIVE UNTO YOU, THAT YE LOVE ONE ANOTHER; AS I HAVE LOVED YOU, THAT YE ALSO LOVE ONE ANOTHER. BY THIS SHALL ALL (MEN) KNOW THAT YE ARE MY DISCIPLES, IF YE HAVE LOVE ONE TO ANOTHER.** ≈ Incidentally, Jesus in the tradition of the Jews was a carpenter like His father.

Jesus states: ≈ **I AM THE GOOD SHEPHERD; AND KNOW MY OWN, AND MY OWN KNOW ME.**[12] ≈ (John 10:14) Here again, there is no tangible symbol associated with identifying Christ.

Jesus articulates another sign, which He called the sigh of Jonah[13], covered in a biblical portion subtitled "The Desire for Signs." Based on Jesus' characterization of the type of people requiring signs, believers should pray that they do not fall into either category. ≈ **But He answered and said unto them, AN EVIL AND ADULTEROUS GENERATION SEEKETH AFTER A SIGN; AND THERE SHALL NO SIGN BE GIVEN TO IT, BUT THE SIGN OF THE PROPHET JONAH.** ≈ (Matt.12: 39)

≈ **Now the Lord had prepared a great fish to swallow up Jonah. And Jonah was in the belly of the fish three days and three nights.** ≈

The book of Deuteronomy (4:15-24) also discusses signs and symbols in ≈ **Take ye therefore good heed unto yourselves; for ye saw no manner of similitude on the day (that) the Lord spake unto you in Horeb out of the midst of the fire: Lest ye corrupt yourselves and make a graven image, the similitude of any figure, the likeness of male or female, likeness of any beast that (is) on the earth, the likeness of any winged fowl that flieth in the air, The likeness of any thing that creepeth on the ground, the likeness of any fish that (is) in the waters beneath the earth: And lest thou lift up thine eyes unto heaven, and when thou seest the sun, and the moon, and the stars, (even) all the host of heaven, shouldest be**

---

[12] Words spoken by Jesus or God the Father will be in capital letters, and unless indicated all scripture references are from the King James Version.
[13] Jonah 1:17.

driven to worship them, and serve them, which the Lord thy God hath divided unto all nations under the whole heaven Take heed unto yourselves, lest ye forget the covenant of the Lord your God, which he made with you, and make you a graven image, (or) the likeness of any (thing), which the Lord thy God hath forbidden thee. For the Lord thy God (is) a consuming fire, (even) a jealous God. ≈

Believers, I outline the main reason for not using the fish or any other symbol to represent Christ or the church in the following scriptures; (Exodus 20:4-6) ≈ **THOU SHALT NOT MAKE UNTO THEE ANY GRAVEN IMAGE, OR ANY LIKENESS (OF ANY THING) THAT (IS) IN HEAVEN ABOVE, OR THAT (IS) IN THE EARTH BENEATH, OR THAT (IS) IN THE WATER UNDER THE EARTH: THOU SHALT NOT BOW DOWN THYSELF TO THEM, NOR SERVE THEM: FOR I THE LORD THY GOD (AM) A JEALOUS GOD, VISITING THE INIQUITY OF THE FATHERS UPON THE CHILDREN UNTO THE THIRD AND FOURTH (GENERATION) OF THEM THAT HATE ME** ≈ Notice again the concept of love used as a sign, for the Father says that those who build graven images do not love Him. Combining Exodus 20:4-6 with (Matt. 5:17) Jesus could not have given any tangible signs for believers. ≈ **THINK NOT THAT I AM COME TO DESTROY THE LAW OR THE PROPHETS: I AM NOT COME TO DESTROY, BUT TO FULFIL.** ≈ Simply put Jesus could not leave, authorize, ordain or suggest any signs because it was contrary to the law of God.

One day whilst preparing a Discipleship course the Lord shared something with me. The Lord shared an obscure passage of scripture, but so very appropriate for the Modern Church. Luke 2: 41-45 relates the story of Jesus and His parents going to the Feast of the Passover in Jerusalem. ≈ **Now His parents went to Jerusalem every year at the feast of the Passover. And when He was twelve years old, they went up to Jerusalem after the custom of the feast. And when they had fulfilled the days, as they returned, the child Jesus tarried behind in Jerusalem; and Joseph and His mother knew not (of it). But, they, supposing Him to have been in the company, went a day's journey; and they sought him among (their) kinsfolk and acquaintance. And when they found Him not, they turned back again to Jerusalem, seeking Him.** ≈ Mary and Joseph made the same mistake that many believers fall prey to, and ALL believers who need, crave, watch for, or create signs make. ≈ **...but supposed Him to be in the caravan, and went a days journey; and they began looking for**

Him. ≈ They assumed that because they believed a thing to be so that it had to be true.

The moral of the story is this; many of us have started churches, hosted revivals, raised children, coined symbols and signs, operating under the assumption that Jesus was not only for it, but also in it. As indicated by the scripture too many of us have left Jesus behind and gone out to face Satan alone; unguarded and without backup.

A common practice we need to adapt is a constant check of our Jesources (Resources of\from Jesus) assuming He is with us is far worse than going out without Him intentionally. Can you imagine being a policeman and trying to stop an armed robber, but you left your gun at home? It would be fine for a parade, but Satan is a roaring lion wish you to face him unarmed? Why even bother to fight then? Lastly, but no less important, is that the Bible warns that symbols easily become idols.

Again, from (Deut. 4:15&16) we find a warning about signs and symbols that reiterates make no images of anything to represent God.

≈ **Take ye therefore good heed unto yourselves; for ye saw no manner of similitude on the day (that) the Lord spake unto you in Horeb out of the midst of the fire: Lest ye corrupt (yourselves), and make you a graven image, the similitude of any figure, the likeness of male or female.** ≈ This passage implicitly tells us that there was "no symbol" when God spoke!

In everything, we need to seek not only God's council but also His presence in our lives. If nothing else, it is one sure way of understanding and making sure, that God is talking to you. Not only do you hear His voice but you also confirm it with His presence. Brother Lawrence would remind us to practice the presence of God[14]. Is it not peculiar that much like spoiled children we opt to create symbols of our own design instead of living the lifestyle by which He said we should be identified.

We find that the danger of symbols is that they cause us to loose our focus. We choose which commandments to follow and which part of the Bible we want to believe. No matter how we slice it, unless we resign ourselves to live by His rules, whatever we do is for naught. In a training scene from the movie, Enter the Dragon, Bruce Lee instructs a student. As he is pointing to the sky to make a point, he notices the student looking at his finger. The master slaps the student atop his head and says these words, *"Don't concentrate on the finger or you will miss all that heavenly glory."* The object lesson, which so many of us miss, is precisely the same.

---

[14] The Practice of the presence of God, Brother Lawrence

We get so caught up on what is right here, right now, that we also miss all the heavenly glory. When I think of the glory of God all I can think is wonderful, wonderful, most wonderful!

In this venue, sex is the aspect Paul is talking about, but in Exodus, it was a cow. The true travesty in Exodus was that the golden calf they were worshiping was not even from their own culture or religion, it was a deity from their enslavers. When Moses returned, they were amidst a sex-oriented celebration in honour of a foreign goddess of fertility. The golden calf that the children of Israel formed represented Hathor, a manifestation of Isis the Egyptian Mother. In the Egyptian ritual, she was called the *great cow who gives birth to the Sun*. Considering the prevalence of Sun worship amongst the Egyptians, it is easy to understand how after several renditions (commonly called versions) the phrase Son of God became sun of god[15].

Is this not true of so many of our symbols (synthesized symbols), they are taken from someone or somewhere else. Sadly enough, however, we use and accept symbols without finding out from whence they came. Not only is this dangerous but anyone who believes in symbols has to concede that it is virtually impossible to divorce the symbol from its original meaning. This can be very dangerous, as a person can very easily be worshipping gods of evil and not know it.

When I was about sixteen years old, I walked up behind my mother as she was washing dishes and ran my finger down the center of her back. She in turn spun and slapped me. When the soap cleared from my eyes, I asked her why she smacked me. She explained that in her days (whenever they were) that was a proposition, a request for sex.

Obviously, that was not my intention. I was trying to tickle her I thought as I had seen my aunt laughing when my uncle did it. Now I know why! The lesson here should be obvious…despite my naiveté the spirit of the symbol did not die. Nor was I completely able to erase the old connotation; and I will never be able to as long as someone lives that knows the symbol as it was previously used. In addition, we do not want to give false gods credence in God's eyes, or credit for His works for He is a jealous God!

Even things like the christmas[16] tree, were borrowed from pagan tree worship. Wherein the Evergreen/pine is a symbol of everlasting youth

---

[15] Not to assert that believers still worship Hathor, but symbol synthesis often takes place in exactly this way.

[16] Lowercase used in maintenance of the point, no disrespect intended.

in deference to the season's change, and to God (as God changes the seasons.)[17] The Easter bunny was borrowed from the pagan festival of the Goddess Eostre, who laid golden eggs for children to eat[18]. Even the church steeple is an imitation of the Egyptian obelisk a known phallic symbol. There are two honoured days in witchcraft; birthdays and Halloween. Yes, this word "Halloween" should be familiar to you; the root can be found in (Matt 6:9), the Lord's Prayer. The word Hallowed means, "blessed above all others, beyond or without compare or equal." This Eve was All Hallows-eve (now Halloween), which was Christianized into "All Saints," but it used to be the Festival of the Dead. As we know, sainthood has in it a prerequisite of death.

It is just that easy for symbols, words, or graphics to become corrupted. However, love is another thing; only the sin of rebellion can corrupt love. Of all things that grieve the Father, rebellion is His least favorite. The parable of the "Lost" sheep was about a lost sheep not a rebellious sheep. If you choose to stay lost as the Prodigal son did the Father **will** not go looking for you! Nevertheless, He said He would leave 99 to go and find the "Lost" one. Other synonyms for lost include, missing, off track, confused, forfeited and destroyed, which are terms that imply a need for help. Notice, neither choice, rebellious, nor deceitful is mentioned. Paul tells us that if we desire to be apart from God once we have been given the truth then, He gives us up giving us over to our reprobate minds. (Rom 1:28) ≈ **And even as they did not like to retain God in (their) knowledge, God gave them over to a reprobate mind, to do those things which are not convenient;** ≈

I encourage you to research all the symbols in your church and the ones you use and confide in. Most importantly, pay attention to the words you read in your Bible[19]. The Holy Spirit has a plan for each of us but different translations often cause confusion and the Holy Spirit is our

---

[17] See <u>Women's Dictionary of Symbols and Scared Objects</u>. Walker, Barbara. Harper Collins, San Francisco. 1988 pg. 462.

[18] See <u>Women's Dictionary of Symbols and Scared Objects</u>. Walker, Barbara. Harper Collins, San Francisco. 1983 pg. 26.

[19] When I say your Bible, pick one version/translation and stick with that one for consistency and ease of reading. Too often confusion is the result of too many versions of the Good Book. "The versions of Scripture we read, whether they are in original languages or translations in other languages, shape what we hear. Translations are coloured by translators, who shape the presentation of the text, their personalities, interests, prayers, and the times and cultures in which they live influence their work, even when they intend to remain objective and communicate only what is present in the original scripts. (<u>Holy Invitations</u>, Bakke. J, Baker Books, Grand Rapids, MI. 2000)".

teacher. There is no need for easier translations – Jesus Himself told us that the word is for believers, sinners are not supposed to understand the mysteries of the Kingdom. (Mark 4:11&12) ≈ **And He said unto them, UNTO YOU IT IS GIVEN TO KNOW THE MYSTERY OF THE KINGDOM OF GOD: BUT UNTO THEM THAT ARE WITHOUT, ALL (THESE) THINGS ARE DONE IN PARABLES: THAT SEEING THEY MAY SEE, AND NOT PERCEIVE; AND HEARING THEY MAY HEAR, AND NOT UNDERSTAND; LEST AT ANY TIME THEY SHOULD BE CONVERTED, AND (THEIR) SINS SHOULD BE FORGIVEN THEM.** ≈

(Deut 29:29) ≈ **The secret (things belong) unto the Lord our God: but those (things which are) revealed (belong) unto us and to our children forever, that (we) may do all the words of this law.** ≈

The word also tells us that believers are destroyed for lack of knowledge. Never be afraid to study and never be afraid to hear from God unlike the Children of Israel[20]. Also consider John 8:23 ≈ **AND YE SHALL KNOW THE TRUTH, AND THE TRUTH SHALL MAKE YOU FREE.** ≈ Where the word "know" is used. The Bible says this knowledge (the root word in the word knowledge) shall set us free. There are two ways to acquire knowledge; study or as a gift from the Holy Spirit. ≈ **Then said Jesus unto them, WHEN YE HAVE LIFTED UP THE SON OF MAN, THEN SHALL YE KNOW THAT I AM (HE), AND (THAT) I DO NOTHING OF MYSELF; BUT AS MY FATHER HATH TAUGHT ME, I SPEAK THESE THINGS.** ≈ To believers this means that the life saving knowledge of God will either come in the form of revelation or in the gift of wisdom from above.

However, let us transition back to love as the symbol of Jesus' people. Love is a very nebulous term, which seems to escape most people especially the young. Let us see what the good book has to say about love. (I John 4:8) ≈ **He that loveth not knoweth not God; for God is love.** ≈ states clearly that, "…God is Love." This means among other things, that love is not stupid, manipulative, hateful, or destructive. On the contrary, the word says love is a host of things – all good. (1 Cor 13:3-8) ≈ **And though I bestow all my goods to feed (the poor), and though I give my body to be burned, and have not love, it profiteth me nothing.**

---

[20] (Hos 4:6) ≈ **MY PEOPLE ARE DESTROYED FOR LACK OF KNOWLEDGE: BECAUSE THOU HAST REJECTED KNOWLEDGE, I WILL ALSO REJECT THEE, THAT THOU SHALT BE NO PRIEST TO ME: SEEING THOU HAST FORGOTTEN THE LAW OF THY GOD, I WILL ALSO FORGET THY CHILDREN.** ≈

Love suffereth long, (and) is kind; love envieth not; love vaunteth not itself, is not puffed up, Doth not behave itself unseemly, seeketh not her own, is not easily provoked, thinketh no evil. Rejoiceth not in iniquity, but rejoiceth in the truth; Beareth all things, believeth all things, hopeth all things, endureth all things. Love never faileth: but whether (there be) prophecies, they shall fail; whether (there be) tongues, they shall cease; whether (there be) knowledge, it shall vanish away. ≈

According to the word of God, love is so important to God (John 3:16) that He gave His only begotten Son, as well, it says perfect love casteth out fear. John (Yochanan in Hebrew) says that no greater love hath a man he lay down his life for a friend. Jesus (Yeshua is Jesus in Hebrew) laid His life down while we were yet sinners, most of whom He never saw – what a picture of love and virtue. If only we could emulate even a small portion of this type of love, we could make the world a better place. In his song Man in the mirror – Michael Jackson says, "*If you wanna make the world a better place, take a look at yourself and make a change.*"

A most destructive; fallacious teaching, one that which hath brought about a moral decay in the body of Christ reminiscent of the old church at Corinth is Unconditional love. The word of God does saysthat His love for us fadeth not[21]. However, the change came with the teaching of unconditional acceptance; the scripture proves repeatedly that this concept is a lie. The New Testament words (Heb. 10:26) thusly; ≈ **For if we sin wilfuly after that we have received the knowledge of the truth, there remaineth no more sacrifice for sins.** ≈ Also, see (2 Peter 2:20-22): ≈ **For if after they have escaped the pollutions of the world through the knowledge of the Lord and Saviour Jesus Christ, they are again entangled therein, and overcome, the latter end is worse with them than the beginning. For it had been better for them not to have known the way of righteousness, than, after they have known (it), to turn from the Holy commandment delivered unto them. But it is happened unto them according to the true proverb, The dog (is) turned to his own vomit again; and the sow that was washed to her wallowing in the mire.** ≈

---

[21] (Isa 54: 10) ≈ **FOR THE MOUNTAINS SHALL DEPART, AND THE HILLS BE REMOVED; BUT MY KINDNESS SHALL NOT DEPART FROM THEE, NEITHER SHALL THE COVENANT OF MY PEACE BE REMOVED,** saith the Lord that hath mercy on thee. ≈

Also, (Hebrews 6:4-6) again referring to the Living New Testament it reads thus; ≈ **For it is impossible for those who were once enlightened, and have tasted of the heavenly gif, and were made partakers of the Holy Ghost, and have tasted the good word of God, and the powers of the world to come, If they fall away, to renew them again unto repentance: seeing they crucify to themselves the Son of God afresh, and put *Him* to an open shame.** ≈ Again in 1 Cor 6:9-11 we see that the unrepentant shall not inherit the Kingdom of God, despite His love for us only those qualified[22] will be able to enter and inherit the Kingdom. ≈ **Know ye not that the unrighteous shall not inherit the kingdom of God? Be not deceived: neither fornicators, nor idolaters, nor adulterers, nor effeminate, nor abusers of themselves with mankind. Nor thieves, nor covetous, nor drunkards, nor revilers, nor extortioners, shall inherit the kingdom of God. And such were some of you: but ye are washed, but ye are sanctified, but ye are justified in the name of the Lord Jesus, and by the Spirit of our God.** ≈

Obviously, God in His grace and wisdom loves us beyond our ability to understand and it is because of His love for us He is just. (2 Peter 2:4-9) ≈ **For if God spared not the angels that sinned, but cast (them) down to hell, and delivered (them) into chains of darkness, to be reserved unto judgment; And spared not the old world, but saved Noah the eighth (person), a preacher of righteousness, bringing in the flood upon the world of the ungodly; And turning the cities of Sodom and Gomorrah into ashes condemned (them) with an overthrow, making (them) an example unto those that after should live ungodly; And delivered just Lot, vexed with the filthy conversation of the wicked: For that righteous man dwelling among them, in seeing and hearing, vexed (his) righteous soul from day to day with (their) unlawful deeds; The Lord knoweth how to deliver the Godly out of temptations, and to reserve the unjust unto the day of judgment to be punished.** ≈

Although God loves us unconditionally and this gift was freely given (Eph. 5:2), Life does not exempt us from loving righteously. To preach unconditional acceptance is not accurate. God accepts us in whatever state we come to Him in, however, not only does He expect a change He requires it. God's acceptance is of our lives before salvation,

---

[22] Saved by His grace and living in repentance.

not afterwards. To teach that this acceptance is ongoing is to spread death and to block believers from the kingdom of heaven.

God's justice proves His love, because for He gave us a choice. The choice He gives us allows us to decide whether to obey and share in His rewards or alternatively, disobey and encounter His judgment. The term judgment implies authority and compassion. Without these two traits, God would simply be wrathful. In addition, although God's judgment is swift and permanent, it is just. God's judgment differs from His wrath in that He forewarns those whom He judges; He allows them to choose. Wrath is not always forewarned[23] although it can be just as severe.

The Almighty is a doting Father and He wishes to be loved and served. He is not keen on slaves; Otherwise, He would revoke our choice. It is only in His giving us a choice and in our choosing to obey that His true glory is revealed.

> ≈ **For God so loved the world that he gave his only begotten Son that whosoever believeth in him should not perish, but have everlasting life.** ≈

---

[23] Genesis 12: 11-20.

WORK AREA LETTER II

≈

THE TRUE SYMBOL OF CHRISTIANITY

Topical Scriptures

(John 10:14) (Matt.12: 39) (Jonah 1:17) (4:15-24) (Exod 20:4-6) (Matt. 5:17) (Luke 2: 41-45) (Deut. 4:15&16) (Matt 6:9) (Rom 1:28) (Mark 4:11&12) (Deut 29:29) (I John 4:8) (1 Cor 13:3-8) (John 3:16) (Is54: 10) (Heb. 10:26) (2 Peter 2:20-22) (Heb 6:4-6) (1 Cor 6:9-11) (2 Peter 2:4-9) (Eph. 5:2) (Luke 22:36) (Luke 22:35) (Prov. 29:23) (John 13:34 &35)

1. WHAT IS A CHRISTIAN?

2. WHY DO PEOPLE USE SYMBOLS?

3. LIST ALL POSITIVE AND NEGATIVE ASPECTS OF SYMBOLS.

4. WHY IS LOVE S IMPORTANT TO GOD?

5. WHY IS LOVE SO CONFUSING?

6. WHAT IS A SIMPLE DEFINITION OF LOVE? CITE SCRIPTURES.

7. WHY DOES THE BIBLE WARN AGAINST IDOLS?

8. DEFINE THE FOLLOWING; A) IDOL. B) SYMBOL. C) PARAPHERNALIA. D) RELIC.

9. CAN YOU LOVE SOMEONE AND NOT LIKE THEM?

10. WHY DID MOSES PERMIT DIVORCE, WHY DOES JESUS NOT PERMIT DIVORCE? CITE SCRIPTURES AND EXPLAIN THE CONSEQUENCES.

11. READ JOHN 14:15 AND THEN WRITE IN YOUR OWN WORDS WHY CHRISTIANS SIN CONTINUALLY.

ADDITIONAL NOTES FOR THIS CHAPTER

LETTER III

≈

FISHERS OF MEN

≈ AGAIN, THE KINGDOM OF HEAVEN IS LIKE UNTO A DRAGNET, THAT WAS CAST INTO THE SEA, AND GATHERED OF EVERY KIND: WHICH, WHEN IT WAS FULL, THEY DREW TO SHORE, AND SAT DOWN, AND GATHERED THE GOOD INTO VESSELS, BUT CAST THE BAD AWAY. ≈ (Matt. 13:47 & 48)

LETTER III ≈ FISHERS OF MEN

Matt 13:47 & 48, the Master likens believers to fish, and consequently those who bring them unto Him must be fishers of men. The Master uses several metaphors in His parable and each taken in depth all paint the picture of His grace and the magnitude of His mercy.

The word <u>Dragnet</u> is used; a dragnet is dragged behind a fishing boat. This term implies several things; one of which is that the boat has a great storage capacity; otherwise, they would use smaller nets. The other thing this implies is that there is expected to be a great haul. The greatness of the haul is not only its sheer size but also it is the fact that the net will be dragged from Adam to the last instant before judgment.

The word <u>Sea</u> is used because it contains fish, but also because it covers most of the Earth (75%). Water has long since been synonymous with time and God's grace has covered all time through our Lord Jesus Christ. (Rev 15:2) ≈ **And I saw as it were a sea of glass mingled with fire: and them that had gotten the victory over the beast, and over his image, and over his mark, (and) over the number of his name, stand on the sea of glass, having the harps of God.** ≈

The phrase <u>Every kind</u> implies that those gathered will be both Jew and Gentile male and female. (Luke 2:30. -32) ≈ **For mine eyes have seen Thy salvation, which Thou hast prepared before the face of all people; A Light to lighten the Gentiles, and the glory of thy people Israel.** ≈

The word <u>Full</u> implies that the fishing did not stop until the net was full it was dragged throughout the shimmering Glass Sea until the harvest was complete. (2 Peter 3:9) ≈ **The Lord is not slack concerning His promise, as some men count slackness; but is longsuffering to us-ward, not willing that any should perish, but that all should come to repentance.** ≈

The word <u>Gathered</u> implies that they will be brought together from all places and times. There will be a concerted effort to bring forth, lay hold, and reclaim those claimed by the grave, lost in sin and those who died before Jesus came. (John 12:32) ≈ **AND I, IF I BE LIFTED UP FROM THE EARTH, WILL DRAW ALL (MEN) UNTO ME.** ≈

The word <u>Vessels</u> (John 14:2) tells us of the vessels prepared for good fish. The vessels are houses for the righteous that have been rewarded for their fidelity. ≈ **IN MY FATHER'S HOUSE ARE MANY MANSIONS: IF (IT WERE) NOT (SO), I WOULD HAVE TOLD YOU. I GO TO PREPARE A PLACE FOR YOU.** ≈

To be <u>Cast</u> indicates judgment and the results of the determination of the level of sin and disobedience in your life. (Rev 14 19) ≈ **And the angel thrust in his sickle into the earth, and gathered the vine of the earth, and cast (it) into the great winepress of the wrath of God.** ≈

(Matt 3:12) ≈ **Whose fan (is) in His hand, and He will thoroughly purge his floor, and gather His wheat into the garner; but He will burn up the chaff with unquenchable fire.** ≈

(Matthew 4:18-22) Chronicles that Kefa (Peter in Hebrew) and Andrew were going about their business casting nets, as they were fishermen. ≈ **And Jesus, walking by the Sea of Galilee, saw two brethren, Simon called Peter, and Andrew his brother, casting a net into the sea: for they were fishers. And He saith unto them, FOLLOW ME AND I WILL MAKE YOU FISHERS OF MEN. And they straightway left (their) nets, and followed Him. And going on from thence, He saw other two brethren, James (the son) of Zebedee, and John his brother, in a ship with Zebedee their father, mending their nets; and He called them. And they immediately left the ship and their father, and followed Him. And Jesus went about all Galilee, teaching in their synagogues, and preaching the gospel of the kingdom, and healing all manner of sickness and all manner of disease among the people.** ≈ This is the case with so many pastors/fishermen; they are self-proclaimed just like my father. In addition, just like my father they do so many things wrong.

Then it says that Jesus said to them, ≈ **FOLLOW ME AND {I} (emphasis mine) WILL MAKE YOU FISHERS OF MEN.** ≈ Notice the first thing Jesus did was to call them away from their self-proclaimed or self-anointed status as fishermen. Obviously, the first criterion for service is to leave whatever it is you called yourself to be and heed the call of Christ. (Matt 11: 29) ≈ **TAKE MY YOKE UPON YOU, AND LEARN OF ME; FOR I AM MEEK AND LOWLY IN HEART: AND YE SHALL FIND REST UNTO YOUR SOULS. FOR MY YOKE (IS) EASY, AND MY BURDEN IS LIGHT.** ≈ Here again, Jesus asserts Mastery when He tells us to take His yoke. The yoke is a collar that oxen or beasts of burden wear in order to maintain control and obedience over them. Jesus tells us that His burden is light. It is light because as soon as you allow Him to put it on you He carries all the weight, and bears your weaknesses.

Next, He instructed us to learn from Him for He is *gentle and humble in heart*. Then He tells the two men that He will make of them (create, fashion, frame, mould) fishers of men. Jesus asserts Himself as the teacher this time. Thus far, He has chosen these men, and then called these men. Now He is undertaking teaching these men. These are the steps All servants of God must undergo ~ who else can be His lest He chooses us. John 6:37 reasserts that we belong to Jesus. ≈ **ALL THAT THE FATHER GIVETH ME SHALL COME TO ME; AND HIM THAT COMETH TO ME I WILL IN NO WISE CAST OUT.**[24] ≈ Jesus then told, them that He would make of them fishers of men notice again that He did not say fishermen. Pay heed to the most important single phrase in the story, (Matt 4:19) ≈ And He saith unto them, **FOLLOW ME, AND I WILL MAKE YOU FISHERS OF MEN.** ≈ Jesus states, "**I WILL MAKE YOU**..."

Why is this so important us as a body of believers? When I was a young lad, my family had to move from our promised land into the wilderness, (some of us are still in exile). We moved into a neighborhood, which was about two miles from the beach. I would get on a bicycle toting a plastic gallon jug. At or about early evening (low tide) I would go to the beach and go near the reefs. When the tide went out, it would leave many fish stranded in the small pools until the next high tide. I simply would pick them up either by hand or with my net and put them in my jug to carry home.

When I got home, I put them in my 20-gallon tank, which I had prepared for them. This tank contained gravel and plastic plants and an air pump, it was quite pretty. I even filled it up with salt water and a heater. Everyday my family would remark at how beautiful and colorful the new fish were. I was so proud of the environment, which I had created for them, my little children.

Although the tank was warm, beautiful, and salty the fish would die within a day or two. I would scoop them out before they stunk and get rid of them. They were of no use to me and they made the tank ugly. I buried them in the usual way, the eulogy characterized by a very audible flush. Then, off I went to gather more. This process went on for several months. I had nothing better to do and there were plenty of fish-what did it matter to me if they died.

---

[24] The Fisher story appears in the Gospels of Maitiyahu (Matthew in Hebrew) (4:18), Mark (1:16), and Luke (5:2).

One day whilst visiting my friend Peter Lunn, we went to Modernistic Gardens, a pet store to look at the fish. When we got there, I saw and immediately fell in love with a Lionfish. I asked the clerk how much the fish was in the window. He told me $75.00 for the fish and $189.00 for the tank and another $50 in coral $45 in filters. The 55-gallon tank was the smallest recommended size for the proper ecosystem. He then explained to me that the ecosystem was very delicate and it was very easily destroyed. The clerk told me that the fish was guaranteed for three days as they often die in transit, as they are very susceptible to shock because of a change in their environment.

After the very informative lesson, I went back home and did what any self-respecting teenager would do. I got on my bike and went to get more free fish. I was neither prepared nor willing to get the necessary tools to begin the tank, nor was I sincere enough to maintain the tank--I just wanted some pretty fish. It was not until my father told me that I should not be so callous in the treatment of other life forms, even the lower life forms that I stopped.

How long and how many times will the Father have to remind us of the same? How long before we become what is needed and treat sinners the way they should be treated? Proper teaching/preparation is very important to ensure success in any endeavor. Knowledge is just as important to a mission, but the key to successfully mastering any task is love/desire. Without love, the traits perseverance and patience revert to simple tolerance. If I loved having a tank, really loved it, before I ever bought those beautiful--not to mention expensive fish, I would have prepared myself.

Firstly, I would have gotten a job so I could afford the tools needed. Secondly, I would have acquired all the parts necessary to prepare the environment. I would have learned how to prepare their environment for their new lives and how to maintain it. All this would have been done well before adding the water.

The next phase is to assemble the tank itself. The gravel or sand goes in on top of the underground filtration system, then the rocks and coral. Wooden air stones (not like the ugly blue ones brought from department stores) are strategically placed and hidden by the plants and coral--notice no fish have even been mentioned yet!

After you meet the basic needs, water is added, adjusted to the correct pH[25], and temperature. You have to understand that almost everything in a salt-water tank is alive. There is a need for bacteria to sustain the plants, coral, as well as the fish. The bacteria is also food and a filter for the tank. All of the components must be considered--they depend on each other. After the water has been sitting for about three days, you do another pH check.

If everything is up to snuff, it is time to add fish (not the expensive fish however,) to our biosphere. This is probably the most important yet confusing part of the process. There are these beautiful fish called Blue Damsels, some of the prettiest fish in the store. They also happen to be the least expensive saltwater fish in the store.

Sadly, you purchase these fish for the sole purpose of dying. It is not until they die that the tank becomes alive and ready to support life. It is only through their dying that the tank is brought to life. When the fish die their bodies release chemicals necessary for the life of the tank. These chemicals are not bought nor man-made, they are the keys to life.

Peculiar as it is, any other fish, which die in the tank after it has been established; must be removed immediately or else they will poison the tank and kill the other fish? The environment is so delicate that after the first fish die anymore death destroys the tank for the other fish. Is it not amazing how delicate the salt-water tank is[26]! After the pH is checked again (it is usually perfect by now) one considers acquiring the other fish.

Even this takes time, as there are three types of fish. Top feeders, middle feeders and bottom feeders, and all three are needed to support the life of the tank.

Top feeders eat at the top of the tank as soon as the food is dropped in and they get first pick of the food and first results of its nutrients. The heaviest food keeps falling and is consumed by the others. The middle feeders catch the food as it falls and much to their dismay, not all of the

---

[25] PH includes Nitrogen, Oxygen, Salt and several other chemicals needed to support life itself.

[26] Much like Jesus; only through His death did we gain the gift of life. No one else could have bought life with their death. In the tank, all other death causes poison. This is because the death of the other fish releases toxins into the water. These toxins in perfect balance sustain life, but any excess causes death. Only Jesus' death could bring about life because His body was without sin (toxins). The carcasses of man release sin into the environment. Jesus sin free body released His spirit and therefore life. Not only life but also eternal life comes through the death of Christ.

falling morsels are food. The top feeders excrete as they eat so excrement also falls with the food and is often gobbled by the middle guys.

The bottom feeders catch all the hell; you see it is at the bottom that all the excrement, fungus and unwanted food falls. The bottom feeders are scavengers and they consume the things in the tank that are unwanted, distasteful, and would kill the other fish. They eat the old food as well as the excrement. In addition, what they excrete is not even partially as rich as the top feeders nor is it as toxic.

When it comes to feeding you will almost never see a top feeder eat on the bottom, guys in the middle visit periodically but rarely eat below the tops of the coral. The bottom feeders can eat anywhere in the tank they want to and are often seen coming to the surface. Ironically, they come to the surface to eat the algae there instead of the food. Here is the kicker, when you buy food for the tank, which is the best type of food to buy, food that floats, or food that sinks? The best type of food to buy for the system is food, which sinks slowly; if not, the bottom feeders' die. Without them, the ecosystem becomes filthy and contaminated and all the other fish die. The bottom feeder can live a lot longer in the tank alone than the other two types of fish. Once everything is in place and the system is running it usually runs quite easily though it is very delicate.

Reading this entire process, do you really believe that without passion a saltwater tank would last very long? No! That is why Goldfish and Beta's are so popular. Anyone can care for them, they are cheap, and the tank is easy to maintain.

Is not God great? In this world, even the animals still obey Him. The fish never forget their station in life and they accept whatever that station is. They operate without malice and resentment; even the ones who eat the other fish do so out of obedience. As soon as the big fish eat, the other fish no longer run from them but resume the tranquility of life. It is a shame that we who claim to be so intelligent fail to understand and obey our simple call in life: Be what God told you to be!

However, going back to the story, I was like many believers--a self-proclaimed fisherman. I received no real training in saltwater tanks and ecosystems, though I did have some knowledge of aquariums. Nevertheless, it was my inadequate knowledge and the use thereof that resulted in the destruction of the fish, the modern church functions the same way.

Christians who were in adequately trained and taught have destroyed too many fish (lost sheep) or even worse lived a life contrary to the word. For too long have, we represented God with mediocrity and lethargy. We are His chosen people and have been promised joy unspeakable...but most of us live as though it was joy unattainable, unshareable and undesirable.

The word differentiates the four-fold ministry in (1 Eph. 4:11 &12) and if you notice, they are listed in a certain order. This is God's ecosystem. (Gecosystem). In it we are given to be different types of fish none more important than the other nor are they independent of each other. It is to this Paul the Apostle spoke saying: (Rom 12:4-7) ≈ **For as we have many members in one body, and all members have not the same office. So we, (being) many, are one body in Christ, and every one members one of another. Having then gifts differing according to the grace that is given to us, whether prophecy, (let us prophesy) according to the proportion of faith; Or ministry, (let us wait) on (our) ministering or he that teacheth, on teaching.** ≈ In the ecosystem of the church however, for far too long we have tried to be other types of fish.

Of course, no one wants to be a bottom feeder, but they make the whole thing work. There are many types of fish in the great Aquarium (body of Christ), some beautiful and some downright ugly. Some graceful like my Lionfish and others ugly like the rockfish, but it is still God's aquarium. Since we are called the salt of the Earth, it must be a salt-water aquarium (Matt 5:13) ≈ **YE ARE THE SALT OF THE EARTH: BUT IF THE SALT HAVE LOST HIS SAVIOUR, WHEREWITH SHALL IT BE SALTED? IT IS THENCEFORTH GOOD FOR NOTHING, BUT TO BE CAST OUT, AND TO BE TRODDEN UNDER FOOT OF MEN.** ≈

Only the ignorant attempt to be other types of fish. All one can ever truly be is what they were created to be. Covetousness and rebellion make us want to be what we are not called to be, can be, or should be. Much like my daddy in my first story, we are hung up on aspects of life. Like my fathers preoccupation with casting, we often ourselves get hooked by whatever appeals to us. It usually then takes others to untangle us. Some hooks are so treacherous that only the Holy Spirit can remove them, for they are beyond our understanding.

Unlike real fish, believers desire to be something else and they desire understand all of the Gecosystem^. There are at least two problems with that. Firstly, God reveals to us what He wants, to whom He wants without having to explain Himself. This leaves a lot of dissatisfied, grumbling fish. Fish who if they are not careful will have this railing judgment placed on them, as it was with the Children of Israel in Moses' time. (Deut 1) ≈ **And the Lord heard the voice of your words, and was wroth, and sware, saying, SURELY THERE SHALL NOT ONE OF THESE MEN OF THIS EVIL GENERATION SEE THAT GOOD LAND, WHICH I SWARE TO GIVE UNTO YOUR FATHERS.** ≈ As for the shepherds of those flocks, ≈ **Also the Lord was angry with me for your sakes, saying, THOU ALSO SHALT NOT GO IN THITHER.** ≈

Secondly, in trying to be other fish we forget that fish have functions in the Gecosystem, and when too many fish fail to function the system breaks down and death is always the result.

The Lionfish that I mentioned is gorgeous with its orange, white, and black markings. Though coloured like a Tiger, it appears to have a mane, probably where it got its name. Moreover, it swims around majestically like the king of its domain. What I did not know until a few years ago was that the Lionfish has a very ugly cousin. It has the exact same physical make up, but its colors are brown and black. Although it is not as beautiful as its cousin is it is still happy, and functions well in its place.

The orange and white fish uses poison and speed to kill whereas its counterpart uses stealth and camouflage. Why are there two types or methods for these fish? First, it is God's ecosystem, and secondly the bright fish cannot hide because of its bright colors. Therefore, it was adapted to hunt another way. The darker fish is neither as fast nor is it poisonous, so it uses camouflage to conceal itself and its true intention, by the time that the prey finds out dinner is served.

Too many of us want to be Saulfish^. (1 Sam 9:2) ≈ **And he had a son, whose name (was) Saul, a choice young man, and a goodly: and (there was) not among the children of Israel a goodlier person than he: from his shoulders and upward (he was) higher than any of the people.** ≈ However, the vain fall from grace quickly. Before Saul fell from grace, he endeared many to him. Although Saul was chosen he was chosen to actually punish the Children of Israel (1 Sam 8:6-9) ≈ **But the thing displeased Samuel, when they said, Give us a king to judge us. And Samuel prayed unto the Lord. And the Lord said unto Samuel, HEARKEN UNTO THE VOICE OF THE PEOPLE IN ALL THAT THEY SAY UNTO THEE: FOR THEY HAVE NOT REJECTED THEE, BUT THEY HAVE REJECTED ME, THAT I SHOULD NOT REIGN OVER THEM. ACCORDING TO ALL THE WORKS WHICH THEY HAVE DONE SINCE THE DAY THAT I BROUGHT THEM UP OUT OF EGYPT EVEN UNTO THIS DAY, WHEREWITH THEY HAVE**

FORSAKEN ME, AND SERVED OTHER GODS, SO DO THEY ALSO UNTO THEE. NOW THEREFORE HEARKEN UNTO THEIR VOICE: HOWBEIT YET PROTEST SOLEMNLY UNTO THEM, AND SHEW THEM THE MANNER OF THE KING THAT SHALL REIGN OVER THEM. ≈

God gave the Children of Israel a warning about what their new king would do. They heeded not! Verily I say unto you be very weary of Saulfish who in their own fleshly desires serve God for their own ends, constantly misinterpret Him and inevitably bring sadness and death. Saulfish are those of us who after being called become puffed up about our position and tasks and loose sight of who the Taskmaster is.

Saulfish are also dangerous for these other reasons, (1 Samuel 8:10-22) tells us why. ≈ **And Samuel told all the words of the Lord unto the people that asked of him a king. And he said, this will be the manner of the king that shall reign over you: He will take your sons, and appoint (them) for himself, for his chariots, and (to be) his horsemen; and (some) shall run before his chariots. And he will appoint him captains over thousands, and captains over fifties; and (will set them) to ear his ground, and to reap his harvest, and to make his instruments of war, and instruments of his chariots. And he will take your daughters (to be) confectioneries, and (to be) cooks, and (to be) bakers. And he will take your fields, and your vineyards, and your olive yards, (even) the best (of them), and give (them) to his servants. And he will take the tenth of your seed, and of your vineyards, and give to his officers, and to his servants. And he will take your menservants, and your maidservants, and your goodliest young men, and your Asses, and put (them) to his work. He will take the tenth of your sheep: and ye shall be his servants. And ye shall cry out in that day because of your king, which ye shall have chosen you; and the Lord will not hear you in that day. Nevertheless the people refused to obey the voice of Samuel; and they said, Nay; but we will have a king over us; That we also may be like all the nations; and that our king may judge us, and go out before us, and fight our battles. And Samuel heard all the words of the people, and he rehearsed them in the ears of the Lord. And the Lord said to Samuel, *HEARKEN UNTO THEIR VOICE*, and makes them a king. And Samuel said unto the men of Israel, Go ye every man unto his city.** ≈

Expounding on this and relating it to the Saulfish, the spesson is that Saulfish appoint people to serve them and glorify themselves. They choose yes men and women to pander, support, and sing their praises. They take the riches God has given them (i.e. lost sheep, wealth etc.), and store them for their own glory, claiming these trophies as their own work. They use the women and the faithful to stock their ego and disguise it by giving title and notoriety to it; I believe it is called Pastoral care. Saulfish feed his friends, family, and colleagues off the tithes and offerings of good and faithful sheep. He has the best of material things and calls it God's favour when it is the toil and sweet of the believers. He chooses the most eager (often young foundationless Christians) to do the legwork while sitting back and using clever scriptulation,[27]^ to solicit more than the required 10% tithe and regular offering. Some Saulfish even get "love" offerings as though they should be loved more than any other men should. The Master says this to us about Saulfish (Matt 23:8-10) ≈ **BUT BE NOT YE CALLED RABBI: FOR ONE IS YOUR MASTER, (EVEN) CHRIST; AND ALL YE ARE BRETHREN. AND CALL NO (MAN) YOUR FATHER UPON THE EARTH: FOR ONE IS YOUR FATHER, WHICH IS IN HEAVEN. NEITHER BE YE CALLED MASTERS: FOR ONE IS YOUR MASTER, (EVEN) CHRIST. BUT HE THAT IS GREATEST AMONG YOU SHALL BE YOUR SERVANT.** ≈

Referring to Matt 11:11 ≈ **VERILY I SAY UNTO YOU, AMONG THEM THAT ARE BORN OF WOMEN THERE HATH NOT RISEN A GREATER THAN JOHN THE BAPTIST: NOTWITHSTANDING HE THAT IS LEAST IN THE KINGDOM OF HEAVEN IS GREATER THAN HE.** ≈

Another favorite scripulation is, ≈…**the mule is worth his hire.** ≈ For big tasks however, a mule team is used. They are not all worthy of hire; apparently, for in most teams the other mules are expected to volunteer their time and labour. However, if the team is working to the uplifting of the kingdom are they too not worthy? Matt 10:6-16 gives instructions for disciple service, starting at verse six. ≈ **BUT GO RATHER TO THE LOST SHEEP OF THE HOUSE OF ISRAEL. AND AS YE GO, PREACH, SAYING, THE KINGDOM OF HEAVEN IS AT HAND. HEAL THE SICK, CLEANSE THE LEPERS, RAISE THE DEAD, AND CAST OUT DEVILS: FREELY YE HAVE RECEIVED, FREELY GIVE. PROVIDE NEITHER GOLD, NOR SILVER, NOR BRASS IN YOUR PURSES, NOR SCRIP FOR (YOUR) JOURNEY, NEITHER TWO COATS, NEITHER SHOES, NOR YET STAVES: FOR THE WORKMAN IS WORTHY OF HIS**

Manipulation of scripture.

MEAT. AND INTO WHATSOEVER CITY OR TOWN YE SHALL ENTER, ENQUIRE WHO IN IT IS WORTHY; AND THERE ABIDE TILL YE GO THENCE. AND WHEN YE COME INTO A HOUSE, SALUTE IT. AND IF THE HOUSE BE WORTHY, LET YOUR PEACE COME UPON IT: BUT IF IT BE NOT WORTHY, LET YOUR PEACE RETURN TO YOU. AND WHOSOEVER SHALL NOT RECEIVE YOU, NOR HEAR YOUR WORDS, WHEN YE DEPART OUT OF THAT HOUSE OR CITY, SHAKE OFF THE DUST OF YOUR FEET. VERILY I SAY UNTO YOU, IT SHALL BE MORE TOLERABLE FOR THE LAND OF SODOM AND GOMORRAH IN THE DAY OF JUDGMENT, THAN FOR THAT CITY. BEHOLD, I SEND YOU FORTH AS SHEEP IN THE MIDST OF WOLVES: BE YE THEREFORE WISE AS SERPENTS, AND HARMLESS AS DOVES. ≈ Most churches spend a meager portion of their uptake on missions and evangelism. It is obvious that they do not intend to go anywhere as they erect huge buildings with huge parking lots and have service at select times, most of them by the way are not conducive to the lost sheep coming.

Spending time sitting in offices, going to luncheons, and hobnobbing is not exactly what the lost sheep need. The fact of the matter is that fishers of men have to follow the example of Jesus and go out to the lost sheep for a variety of reasons:

First, the sheep is lost! This seems a simple concept but the truth of it is that this is the most important piece of information for it implies many things. Being lost also implies the ability to be found and there are really only four sets of people who seem irrevocably bound for hell:

A) The damned (Matt 12:30-32) ≈ **HE THAT IS NOT WITH ME IS AGAINST ME; AND HE THAT GATHERETH NOT WITH ME SCATTERETH ABROAD. WHEREFORE I SAY UNTO YOU, ALL MANNERS OF SIN AND BLASPHEMY SHALL BE FORGIVEN UNTO MEN: BUT THE BLASPHEMY (AGAINST) THE (HOLY) GHOST SHALL NOT BE FORGIVEN UNTO MEN. AND WHOSOEVER SPEAKETH A WORD AGAINST THE SON OF MAN, IT SHALL BE FORGIVEN HIM: BUT WHOSOEVER SPEAKETH AGAINST THE HOLY GHOST, IT SHALL NOT BE FORGIVEN HIM, NEITHER IN THIS WORLD, NEITHER IN THE (WORLD) TO COME.** ≈

B) Those who choose to go. (Rom 1:28) ≈ **And even as they did not like to retain God in (their) knowledge, God gave them over to a reprobate mind, to do those things which are not convenient;** ≈

C) The supporters of those who choose to go. (Rom 1:32) ≈ **Who knowing the judgment of God, that they which commit such things are worthy of death, not only do the same, but have pleasure in them that do them.** ≈

D) Those who were not called of God. (Rom 9:22) ≈ **(What) if God, willing to shew (His) wrath, and to make His power known, endured with much longsuffering the vessels of wrath fitted to destruction: And that He might make known the riches of his glory on the vessels of mercy, which He had afore prepared unto glory.** ≈

Although Romans 1:28, refers specifically to homosexuality. If one reads it properly, you will discover that there are different hues of this affliction. It is those who have undergone a complete heart change that are given up. Their lifestyle is a manifestation of this heart change, God does not curse or damn birth defects, so the change of heart must then be a voluntary one. Which then stands to reason that the lifestyle therefore is also voluntary? (Rom 1:24 & 25) ≈ **Wherefore God also gave them up to uncleanness through the lusts of their own hearts, to dishonour their own bodies between themselves: Who changed the truth of God into a lie, and worshipped and served the creature more than the Creator, who is blessed for ever. Amen.** ≈

Those in the earlier verse do not come under this decision of the Father to turn them up. Turning them up is what makes them beyond redemption. At this stage, the Father turns them up, because they are in a state of complete and utter rebellion to God. They choose to serve Satan and sex (the creature) and hate God the creator. Therefore, it is not the sin of homosexuality by itself that causes the cleavage from God. They choose to leave and God in essence releases them. Although not stated one must infer one of two things. The change either is irreversible, or at a point God grows angry as He did with Lucifer and the angels and spews them out as unfit to ever share in His Glory (Exod 20:5). Even in this God show's His mercy. He allows them to continue to live and to choose. Unlike an earthy leader who would punish this degree of treason with mandatory death.

One also must consider the following scriptures when debating redemption (Matt 15:17-20) ≈ **DO NOT YE YET UNDERSTAND, THAT WHATSOEVER ENTERETH IN AT THE MOUTH GOETH INTO THE BELLY, AND IS CAST OUT INTO THE DRAUGHT? BUT THOSE THINGS, WHICH PROCEED OUT OF THE MOUTH, COME FORTH FROM THE HEART; AND THEY DEFILE THE MAN. FOR OUT OF THE HEART PROCEED EVIL THOUGHTS, MURDERS, ADULTERIES,**

FORNICATIONS, THEFTS, FALSE WITNESS, BLASPHEMIES: THESE ARE (THE THINGS) WHICH DEFILE A MAN: BUT TO EAT WITH UNWASHEN HANDS DEFILETH NOT A MAN. ≈

(Gen 3:3) ≈ **But of the fruit of the tree which (is) in the midst of the garden, God hath said, YE SHALL NOT EAT OF IT, NEITHER SHALL YE TOUCH IT, LEST YE DIE.** ≈ **(Matt 10:28)** ≈ **AND FEAR NOT THEM, WHICH KILL THE BODY, BUT ARE NOT ABLE TO KILL THE SOUL: BUT RATHER FEAR HIM WHICH IS ABLE TO DESTROY BOTH SOUL AND BODY IN HELL.** ≈ And (John 8:41) ≈ **YE DO THE DEEDS OF YOUR FATHER. THEN SAID THEY TO HIM, WE BE NOT BORN OF FORNICATION; WE HAVE ONE FATHER, (EVEN) GOD.** ≈ This seems to indicate that it is more of attitudinal \rebellious sin in the soul of man that brings about disdain from God. The lost sheep need guidance and redemption. Those who choose to go to hell have free access. As John indicates, there are some sins which lead to death--they are without forgiveness and others we are forgiven for. Make no mistake all unrepented sin leads to death, but there are some sins that one cannot repent from.

This clarification is also because to preach that all homosexuals are damned is erroneous according to scripture. To pretend/assert or even preach that no homosexuals are going to heaven is also wrong. NO UNREPENTED SINNER IS GOING TO INHERIT THE KINGDOM. But if anyone repents, having been forgiven, and recognizing uprightness come away from the death of sin and into the life of Christ--they will be saved! Thus, says the word of God.

The word "Lost" means that intent is missing and hence the lost sheep are immune to our judgment. Jude 9 ≈ Yet Michael the archangel, when contending with the devil he disputed about the body of Moses, durst not bring against him a railing accusation, but said, The Lord rebuke thee. ≈ tells us that even the archangel Michael dared not judge but only rebuked in the name of the Lord. Again in (Matt 7:1-5) ≈ **JUDGE NOT, THAT YE BE NOT JUDGED FOR WITH WHAT JUDGMENT YE JUDGE, YE SHALL BE JUDGED: AND WITH WHAT MEASURE YE METE, IT SHALL BE MEASURED TO YOU AGAIN. AND WHY BEHOLDEST THOU THE MOTE THAT IS IN THY BROTHER'S EYE, BUT CONSIDERS NOT THE BEAM THAT IS IN THINE OWN EYE? OR HOW WILT THOU SAY TO THY BROTHER, LET ME PULL OUT THE MOTE OUT OF THINE EYE; AND, BEHOLD, A BEAM (IS) IN THINE OWN EYE? THOU HYPOCRITE, FIRST CAST OUT THE BEAM OUT OF THINE OWN EYE; AND THEN SHALT THOU SEE CLEARLY TO CAST**

OUT THE MOTE OUT OF THY BROTHER'S EYE. ≈ The Master warns against judgment. (1 Sam:) says ≈ **...now appoint a king for us to judge us like all the nations.** ≈ Therefore, the second main reason not to judge is that the scale by which we use to judge others, no matter how faulty, is that same scale God will use against us.

Third, as indicated judgment requires authority, we have not been called to judge anyone, but to correct them with the love of the Father. Additionally, it also means that once found the sheep could rejoin the flock.

Sometimes the sheep get lost because they stray, but on occasion (Jim Jones is a perfect example) the flock strays away from the sheep. It is imperative not to render judgment for just as the blind cannot lead, the lost can neither find nor judge the lost. Worst of all too many sheep are lost because of the rest of the flock. *"I would have become a Christian were it not for Christians,"*(Gandhi) which is a railing accusation against us as believers. Many have become too much like the Pharisees and chase the lost sheep away. Jesus made no mystery of God's attitude towards those who chase away His sheep. Matt. 18:6 explicitly warns us about consequences of hurting God's sheep. ≈ **BUT WHOSO SHALL OFFEND ONE OF THESE LITTLE ONES, WHICH BELIEVE IN ME, IT WERE BETTER FOR HIM THAT A MILLSTONE WERE HANGED ABOUT HIS NECK AND (THAT) HE WERE DROWNED IN THE DEPTH OF THE SEA** ≈ Although intent is often a mitigating factor in determination of guilty no deference is made here, so beware! Perhaps more churches should teach swimming to their parishioners just in case!

Jesus also dealt with the Pharisees about this. The words God and Jesus will be used interchangeably concerning New Testament references to God's attitude. Spoken by Jesus who said, ≈ **I AND THE FATHER ARE ONE.** ≈ (Matt 23:8).

Let us dwell here for a while; the attitude of the church towards the word of God vexed Jesus at least twice. One of the most famous instances is found in (Mark 11:15-18) ≈ **And they come to Jerusalem: and Jesus went into the temple, and began to cast out them that sold and bought in the temple, and overthrew the tables of the moneychangers, and the seats of them that sold doves; Would not suffer that any man should carry (any) vessel through the temple. And He taught, saying unto them, IS IT NOT WRITTEN, MY HOUSE SHALL BE CALLED OF ALL NATIONS THE HOUSE OF PRAYER? BUT YE HAVE MADE IT A DEN OF THIEVES. And the scribes and chief**

priests heard (it), and sought how they might destroy him: for they feared him, because all the people were astonished at His doctrine. ≈ Jesus goes to the temple of Solomon and finds that it has become a market place buying, selling, and trading.

Today's church has declined to the same level. Our churches imitate the world's music calling it crossover music. Although many singers do sing true praise and worship songs, many sing simply popular music, which often makes no mention of God and His word.

We use in our movies the same people the world does and in both instances success and appeal being based on profit and sales. The business of God is still souls. God does not make men rich simply to make them rich. All of God's gifts have purpose and to whom ever much is given, much is expected. One will become rich if they do the will of God. It cannot be helped if you are doing great works--you need great tools to do the job. You will have access to all of God's gifts -- but the greatest gift given to us died on the cross for our sins and allowed us the opportunity to have everlasting life.

Delving further, we traded the true harsh truth of God for mediocrity. Jesus told us what He thought about middle dwellers; let us see what He said. (Rev 3:15-16) ≈ **I KNOW THY WORKS, THAT THOU ART NEITHER COLD NOR HOT: I WOULD THOU WERT COLD OR HOT. SO THEN BECAUSE THOU ART LUKEWARM, AND NEITHER COLD NOR HOT, I WILL SPUETHEE OUT OF MY MOUTH.** ≈ This is the posture of too many churches, and God is spewing them out all over the world.

By spewed out or spit out what does He mean? Churches are going bankrupt and music ministries are failing. Gay marriages are being recognized and ordained homosexuals are in charge of flocks, ministers are being arrested and exposed in various crimes. People are walking into churches, shooting, and robbing them. These churches have been brought to the light of the truth of God -- Who told us what we do in the dark He will bring to light. A wise man once told me that the only thing one gets from straddling the fence is a sore crotch. Perhaps that is why so many churches are prostrate, broken, and bending over and tiptoeing in their walk with God: They have sore crotches!

Unlike the lukewarm water simply being spewed out, Jesus actively whipped the people out of His Father's house in one of the most famous acts of passion in history. The Groom came home and found His bride defiled and committing unnatural acts with other men; and thus, the Bridegroom was enraged and drove the men away from His bride.

Revelations talks about the whore of Babylon committing fornication, numerous references are made about adultery robbing both the men and women of their virtue.

Judah, one of Joseph's brothers, (the one who stopped the brothers from killing Joseph) went into town and saw a beautiful woman, thinking her a harlot decided he had to lay with her (Gen 38:13-25). She required a sheep as payment[28]. Until he could bring the sheep; he left her his staff, his cord and his seal. The bible refers to his seal as his virtue. Why is the seal called his virtue? It was this seal that gave him his authority and place in society, it was who he was and what he was, and it was in essence his power.

How hurt he was when he returned and the woman had gone taking with her his virtue/power/identity whatsoever term you desire to use. His initial thought was about how he was going to be able to still conduct his fathers business without proof of who he was -- His staff was also gone, his means to guide and protect both himself and his sheep. The man had nothing! Many pastors find themselves in the same position after they are caught up in the flesh. They too are without virtue and loose their ability to guide the flock.

Another incident confirming that virtue and power are synonymous occurred when Jesus was walking a woman touched Him. (Mark 5:30-31) ≈ **And Jesus, immediately knowing in Himself that virtue had gone out of Him, turned Him about in the press, and said, WHO TOUCHED MY CLOTHES? And His disciples said unto Him, Thou seest the multitude thronging Thee, and sayest Thou, Who touched me? And He looked round about to see her that had done this thing.** ≈ The disciples said You are in a crowd of course someone touched You. Jesus replies that His virtue had left Him. It was this virtue/power that ebbed from Him which cured the woman and so many others.

When the bride of Christ commits adultery with the world[29], we stand in adultery. Some churches have become almost as bold as the whore of Babylon. When we do this, we also give up our virtue and power to heal, cast out devils, and do God's work. Although we have been redeemed, too many brides have again become adulterous and unfaithful. Is it a wonder that the Groom was angry-beautiful as He thought His bride

---

[28] What have we paid the world with thus far but the lost, saddened and hurting sheep; The very same sheep that He came to save and die for.
[29] Rev 17:1-3.

was, sleeping with another man? Probably telling him how great he was for being so good to her, taking all his sins into her and their recompense. Bearing his bastard--children, enjoying it and flaunting it before God and the world--what an adulteress!

What does God's word say of what the "Modern Church" has become? Consult the word as to whores, adulterers and whoremongers. Prov 6:23-29 ≈ **For the commandment (is) a lamp; and the law (is) light; and reproofs of instruction (are) the way of life. To keep thee from the evil woman, from the flattery of the tongue of a strange woman. Lust not after her beauty in thine heart; neither let her take thee with her eyelids. For by means of a whorish woman (a man is brought) to a piece of bread: and the adulteress will hunt for the precious life. Can a man take fire in his bosom, and his clothes not be burned? Can one go upon hot coals, and his feet not be burned? So he that goeth in to his neighbour's wife; whosoever toucheth her shall not be innocent.** ≈

Prov 7:11-27) ≈ She (is) loud and stubborn; her feet abide not in her house: Now (is she) without, now in the streets, and lieth in wait at every corner.) So she caught him, and kissed him, (and) with an impudent face said unto him, (I have) peace offerings with me; this day have I payed my vows. Therefore came I forth to meet thee, diligently to seek thy face, and I have found thee. I have decked my bed with coverings of tapestry, with carved (works), with fine linen of Egypt. I have perfumed my bed with myrrh, aloes, and cinnamon. Come, let us take our fill of love until the morning: let us solace ourselves with loves. For the goodman (is) not at home, he is gone a long journey: He hath taken a bag of money with him, (and) will come home at the day appointed. With her much fair speech she caused him to yield, with the flattering of her lips she forced him. He goeth after her straightway, as an ox goeth to the slaughter, or as a fool to the correction of the stocks; till a dart strike through his liver; as a bird hasteth to the snare, and knoweth not that it (is) for his life. Hearken unto me now therefore, O children, and attend to the words of my mouth. Let not thine heart decline to her ways; go not astray in her paths. For she hath cast down many wounded: yea, many strong (men) have been slain by her. Her house (is) the way to hell, going down to the chambers of death. ≈

For too many years the church or better yet Mrs. Jesus Christ, (the bride always takes the name of the husband), has been unlike the virtuous bride. According to the word, anyone who lies with (partners with) an adulteress themselves becomes an adulterer. (1 Cor 6:16) ≈ **What? Know ye not that he which is joined to an harlot is one body? For two, saith he, shall be one flesh.** ≈

Be careful with which ministries you collaborate, and pray for the ministries built out of wedlock. All we can do is pray and intercede for them and hope they will be allowed in as adoptees to the Banquet of the Lamb.

At a meeting with several church leaders, one of them told a joke. "On a desert island a man had been shipwrecked for several years and lived there all alone. After about 10 years, a ship was passing by and after seeing three huts on the beach they stopped. The man ran up to them saying I am so glad to see you, I have not seen a soul in 10 years. So, the sailors asked why then are there three huts? The man said I am a pastor; that hut is my house that one is my first church and the other one is my new church!"

Although this quip is humorous, it is indicative of the attitudes that have always been prevalent in the body. The covetousness, competition, backstabbing, and sheep stealing that goes on in the church (ironic is it not that they quibble over that which does not belong to them.) This is why putting God in the right place in His ministry is so important. In the book <u>Spiritual Leadership</u>[31] one of the most profound assertions that the author makes is that the main criterion for being a Spiritual Leader is being Spirit filled. I dare say filled with the Holy Spirit, and this is so that there will be no room for any other spirits. (Matt 12:45) ≈ **THEN GOETH HE, AND TAKETH WITH HIMSELF SEVEN OTHER SPIRITS MORE WICKED THAN HIMSELF, AND THEY ENTER IN AND DWELL THERE: AND THE LAST (STATE) OF THAT MAN IS WORSE THAN THE FIRST. EVEN SO SHALL IT BE ALSO UNTO THIS WICKED GENERATION.** ≈

The words in this verse also explain why the name of the Spirit is important because there are so many. In the church, there are many sprits too; they are not all of God. (Mark 1:22-26) ≈ **And they were astonished at His doctrine: for He taught them as one that had authority, and not as the scribes. And there was in their synagogue**

---

[31] Oswald Saunders.

a man with an unclean spirit; and he cried out, Saying, Let (us) alone; what have we to do with thee, thou Jesus of Nazareth? Art thou come to destroy us? I know thee who thou art, the Holy One of God. And Jesus rebuked him, saying, HOLD THY PEACE, AND COME OUT OF HIM. And when the unclean spirit had torn him, and cried with a loud voice, he came out of him.** ≈

Many positions in the church are filled with the willing and not the Spirit filled, even those positions for which it is required (Titus 1:5-16, Tim 3). There is definitely a place in the Kingdom for the willing, for the body could not function without them but leadership is not it! The simple fact is that willingness and ability are not the same thing, and in this passage, the point is made clear. (Acts 19:13-15) ≈ **Then certain of the vagabond Jews, exorcists, took upon them to call over them which had evil spirits the name of the Lord Jesus, saying, We adjure you by Jesus whom Paul preacheth. There were seven sons of (one) Sceva, a Jew, (and) chief of the priests, which did so. And the evil spirit answered and said, Jesus I know, and Paul I know; but who are ye?** ≈

In God's workforce there are those led[32] by the Spirit and those who are not--although they hold positions. Let us remember that man created these positions not God, and men not God appointed these people.

If you go to the dock or watch a fishing show, you will notice that there are different types of fishermen. As so, in the church there are different types of fishers of men, and I have written to you about four. The prototype Jesus has been covered already so there is no real need to address the good fishers for if they follow Jesus and have allowed Him to teach them their reward shall be just. (1 Cor 3:7 & 8) ≈ **So then neither is he that planteth any thing, neither he that watereth; but God that giveth the increase. Now he that planteth and he that watereth are one: and every man shall receive his own reward according to his own labour.** ≈

The latter four types will also receive their just rewards, but verily I say unto you that with your reward you will not be happy. Your reward shall come first in the form of these words found in (Matt 7:22 & 23) ≈ **MANY WILL SAY TO ME IN THAT DAY, LORD, LORD, HAVE WE NOT PROPHESIED IN THY NAME? AND IN THY NAME HAVE CAST OUT DEVILS? AND IN THY NAME DONE MANY WONDERFUL**

---

[32] Many of us have to be led by the Spirit instead of spoken to because so often we will not shut up long enough to hear His still small voice.

WORKS? AND THEN WILL I PROFESS UNTO THEM, I NEVER KNEW YOU: DEPART FROM ME, YE THAT WORK INIQUITY. ≈ There is no need to continue describing their reward for if they still hold their hands out there is nothing that can be said to them that would make a difference.

I will make a quick reference to *Trawlers*, the true fishers.[33] I refer to them because in another letter the same scripture is used to explain the power the kingdom of Heaven has to capture/win souls and this same dragnet is what Trawlers use. It is by the use of these people that the 9,000 were fed. By the use of good, obedient fishers who allowed themselves to be shared amongst the hungry to help feed the starving lost souls.

(Matt 15:32-38) ≈ **Then Jesus called His disciples (unto Him), and said, I HAVE COMPASSION ON THE MULTITUDE, BECAUSE THEY CONTINUE WITH ME NOW THREE DAYS, AND HAVE NOTHING TO EAT: AND I WILL NOT SEND THEM AWAY FASTING, LEST THEY FAINT IN THE WAY. And His disciples say unto Him, Whence should we have so much bread in the wilderness, as to fill so great a multitude? And Jesus saith unto them, HOW MANY LOAVES HAVE YE? And they said Seven[34], and a few little fishes. And he commanded the multitude to sit down on the ground. And He took the seven loaves and the fishes, and gave thanks, and brake (them), and gave to His disciples, and the disciples to the multitude. And they did all eat, and were filled: and they took up of the broken (meat) that was left seven baskets full. And they that did eat were four thousand men, beside women and children.** ≈

(Mark 6:33-44) ≈ **And the people saw them departing, and many knew Him, and ran afoot thither out of all cities, and out went them, and came together unto him. And Jesus, when he came out, saw much people, and was moved with compassion toward them, because they were as sheep not having a shepherd: and He began to teach them many things. And when the day was now far spent, His disciples came unto Him, and said, This is a desert place, and now the time (is) far passed: Send them away, that they may go into the country round about, and into the villages, and buy themselves bread: for they have nothing to eat. He answered and said unto them, GIVE YE THEM TO EAT. AND THEY SAY UNTO**

---

[33] Unless otherwise noted the fishers in the latter part of this letter refers to church bodies as a whole not just the pastor.

[34] According to The book of Numerology, the number 7 is the number of completion.

HIM, SHALL WE GO AND BUY TWO HUNDRED PENNYWORTH OF BREAD, AND GIVE THEM TO EAT? He saith unto them, HOW MANY LOAVES HAVE YE? GO AND SEE. And when they knew, they say, Five and two fishes. And He commanded them to make all sit down by companies upon the green grass. And they sat down in ranks, by hundreds, and by fifties. And when He had taken the five loaves and the two fishes, He looked up to heaven, and blessed, and brake the loaves, and gave (them) to His disciples to set before them; and the two fishes divided he among them all. And they did all eat, and were filled. And they took up twelve baskets full of the fragments, and of the fishes. And they that did eat of the loaves were about five thousand men. ≈

For you see, much like in Luke when the boat became full Peter called other fishermen to assist. After 9,000 were fed there was plenty left over for anyone else who needed to be fed. This means we ought not to be limiting the gifts God has given to us, and even worst withholding them from those He wants to bless. If one claims to be gifted by God, then one should be readily available to share this gift more than two or three sermons (1-1.5 hrs long) per week.

Just like the fish after feeding your flock at your church there should be plenty left over to feed anyone else who hungers and thirsts for Jesus. After all the real work is done in the spirit by the Spirit, if we tire easily it is because we are still working in the flesh. When the Almighty gives you a gift and you are a good steward, you will not be able to contain it. People only had to touch Jesus to be healed; Paul's clothes healed people. (Acts 19:12)

This characteristic of giving glory to God for the good things He has done is what made these men great fishers of men. Jesus, Paul, and Peter in the following scriptures exemplify why they were successful fishers. (Matt 28:18) ≈ **And Jesus came and spake unto them, saying, ALL POWER IS GIVEN UNTO ME IN HEAVEN AND IN EARTH.** ≈ Moreover, He received a crown of glory.

Paul spent 14 years in solitude with the Lord preparing and the rest of his life in jails and is responsible for spreading more of the word than any other apostle. (Rom 15:18-20) ≈ **For I will not dare to speak of any of those things which Christ hath not wrought by me, to make the Gentiles obedient, by word and deed, Through mighty signs and wonders, by the power of the Spirit of God; so that from Jerusalem, and round about unto Illyricum, I have fully preached the gospel of Christ. Yea, so have I strived to preach the gospel, not where Christ** was named, lest I should build upon another man's foundation. ≈ Luke 5:8 deals with Peter, and he had the honour of being told by Jesus Himself that upon that rock He would build His church.

SPORTS FISHERS

Sport fishers catch the fish and then let them go. Although they do not kill the fish, the damage is still done to the fish. Going back to my story about my dad fishing and hooking himself, that hook cut into his flesh and the cut took time to heal. There is no telling how long it is before the fish can eat again either.

The sport fishers–are popular churches, churches that change trends to keep up with fashion and the demand of its patrons, the politically correct churches. (Rev 2:20-23) ≈ **NOTWITHSTANDING I HAVE A FEW THINGS AGAINST THEE, BECAUSE THOU SUFFEREST THAT WOMAN JEZEBEL, WHICH CALLETH HERSELF A PROPHETESS, TO TEACH AND TO SEDUCE MY SERVANTS TO COMMIT FORNICATION, AND TO EAT THINGS SACRIFICED UNTO IDOLS. AND I GAVE HER SPACE TO REPENT OF HER FORNICATION; AND SHE REPENTED NOT. BEHOLD, I WILL CAST HER INTO A BED, AND THEM THAT COMMIT ADULTERY WITH HER INTO GREAT TRIBULATION, EXCEPT THEY REPENT OF THEIR DEEDS, AND I WILL KILL HER CHILDREN WITH DEATH; AND ALL THE CHURCHES SHALL KNOW THAT I AM HE WHICH SEARCHETH THE REINS AND HEARTS: AND I WILL GIVE UNTO EVERY ONE OF YOU ACCORDING TO YOUR WORKS.** ≈

When the world readily helps and supports your church according to the Word of God, there is something wrong with it. When Jesus speaks of the woman calling herself a prophetess[35], He is referring to ministers and church leaders who have the intent of living in rebellion and out of the will of God. They do as they wish in their personal lives allowing themselves to be horrible examples for their flocks.

(Matt 10:22) ≈ **AND YE SHALL BE HATED OF ALL (MEN) FOR MY NAME'S SAKE: BUT HE THAT ENDURETH TO THE END SHALL BE SAVED.** ≈ & 34 & 35 ≈ **THINK NOT THAT I AM COME TO SEND**

---

[35] This is not an admonishment against women as ministers but a railing condemnation against disobedience and vanity; traits historically attributed to women.

PEACE ON EARTH: I CAME NOT TO SEND PEACE, BUT A SWORD. FOR I AM COME TO SET A MAN AT VARIANCE AGAINST HIS FATHER, AND THE DAUGHTER AGAINST HER MOTHER, AND THE DAUGHTER IN LAW AGAINST HER MOTHER IN LAW. ≈

These are the characteristics of the sport fishers/churches. They, like the fishermen in real life, will actually do the work and make a good haul but it is for naught. They simply let the harvest fall back into the sea when the times change. Like that television commercial with the slogan, *never let em' see you sweat* They let go the fish because they have no intention of sweating.

They write sermons and books about subjects that they can manipulate to their favor; such as money, tithing, acceptance of sinful practices, etc. These things are sacrificed unto idols because much like pagans who used food to appease their gods--sports fishers offer their broken rules and huge numbers of members as proof of their work. The fact that the size of their church is based on a much-diluted version of the word of God is of no concern to them.

Jesus said that what we do in the dark He will bring to light. These sport fishers have been exposed by Jesus and given time and a chance to repent. However, they often repent of their evil ways but they have not changed. Therefore she (referring to the bride of Christ) will be laid out much like a piece of fly paper and anyone/ministry that joins with her will not only be guilty but cast into great tribulation except the sheep that repent. So, when you have friends and neighbors being sucked in by these people give them the true word and allow them to choose. Be warned, however, the Jez-test[36] is not subjective, it cannot be based on what you believe. It must be based on the word of God and the Holy Spirit.

(1 Cor 5:10-13) ≈ **Yet not altogether with the fornicators of this world, or with the covetous, or extortioners, or with idolaters; for then must ye needs go out of the world. But now I have written unto you not to keep company, if any man that is called a brother be a fornicator, or covetous, or an idolater, or a railer, or a drunkard, or an extortioner; with such an one no not to eat. For what have I to do to judge them also that are without? do not ye judge them that are within? But them that are without God judgeth. Therefore put away from among yourselves that wicked person.** ≈ One of the greatest tools of sport fishers is the concept of unconditional acceptance and many are drawn to this. This is very

---

[36] Testing for the traits of Jezebel.

attractive to newcomers because they do not feel judged. The problem with the sport fishers is that they continue to extol this policy and they do not allow, support, or promote change in the lives of new converts. They are only interested in keeping up appearances and maintaining numbers.

(Gal 1:6-10) ≈ **I marvel that ye are so soon removed from Him that called you into the grace of Christ unto another gospel; Which is not another; but there be some that trouble you, and would pervert the gospel of Christ. But though we, or an angel from heaven, preach any other gospel unto you than that which we have preached unto you, let him be accursed. As we said before, so say I now again, If any (man) preach any other gospel unto you than that ye have received, let him be accursed. For do I now persuade men, or God? Or do I seek to please men? For if I yet pleased men, I should not be the servant of Christ.** ≈ This speaks to those in the ministry that fall by the way side very quickly. We are warned about perverting the gospel for those that do are accursed. We are told not to try to persuade (bribe, entreat) God or man, more specifically if we preach the gospel and it be pleasing to man it does not please God.

(Eph 5:3-21) ≈ **But fornication, and all uncleanness, or covetousness, let it not be once named among you, as becometh saints; either filthiness, nor foolish talking, nor jesting, which are not convenient: but rather giving of thanks. For this ye know, that no whoremonger, nor unclean person, nor covetous man, who is an idolater, hath any inheritance in the kingdom of Christ and of God. Let no man deceive you with vain words: for because of these things cometh the wrath of God upon the children of disobedience Be not ye therefore partakers with them. For ye were sometimes darkness, but now (are ye) light in the Lord: walk as children of light: (For the fruit of the Spirit (is) in all goodness and righteousness and truth; Proving what is acceptable unto the Lord. And have no fellowship with the unfruitful works of darkness, but rather reprove (them). For it is a shame even to speak of those things which are done of them in secret. But all things that are reproved are made manifest by the light: for whatsoever doth make manifest is light. Wherefore he saith, Awake thou that sleepest, and arise from the dead, and Christ shall give thee light. See then that ye walk circumspectly, not as fools, but as wise, Redeeming the time, because the days are evil.** ≈ Once we start becoming saints, Paul tells us that sin should not be named among us.

Although this is a very tall order, I believe that the spirit of rebellion is what he is dealing with versus falling down. In addition, that we should restrain from folly and invest time giving thanks. Paul warns us to let no man deceive us with vain words because the wrath of God will fall upon us. He calls those who are deceived disobedient and what of the leaders? We were once sin but now we are the lights of the world asserts Paul. As such we should have no fellowship with sport fishers but should instead reprove them. If it is a shame to speak of darkness, then what is if we follow them and allow them to lead us?

Paul admonishes us to awaken from amongst the spiritually dead/lost and allow Christ to bring us either to the light or back to the light. The tutelage of the sports fishers, claims that due to the death of Christ, we are free to sin and fail without fear. Paul however, tells us to walk circumspectly earning ourselves places in eternity with Christ, for the days we spend here in this life are usually spent being or doing evil.

SPEAR FISHERS

Spear fishers are the lazy churches. Spear fishing is outlawed in my country and many others, because it was too easy to destroy the big fish and it was unsafe. The big fish are usually the breeders and the reason it harm the ecosystem. The spear is unsafe because the spears travel so quickly they often go through the prey. The Hawaiian sling, which is a sling shot/javelin combination, still allows for the lazy but it is safer. The other sad side effect of the spear fishing is that the animal suffers and swims away bleeding, thus attracting sharks and other meat eaters. This is what happens to the fish speared by these churches. The smell of blood of a destitute convert attracts Satan's hunters and they destroy that poor creature. These are the churches that save people all the time, but only for about one-week. They put little to no effort in keeping the fish. Let us look at what the word would say about these churches.

(Mark 12:38-40) ≈ **And He said unto them in His doctrine, BEWARE OF THE SCRIBES, WHICH LOVE TO GO IN LONG CLOTHING, AND (LOVE) SALUTATIONS IN THE MARKETPLACES, AND THE CHIEF SEATS IN THE SYNAGOGUES, AND THE UPPERMOST ROOMS AT FEASTS: WHICH DEVOUR WIDOWS' HOUSES, AND FOR A PRETENCE MAKE LONG PRAYERS: THESE SHALL RECEIVE GREATER DAMNATION.** ≈ These are proud politically correct type ministers who love to be greeted and noticed by everybody, despite the fact that they do virtually nothing to benefit anyone. They want to occupy positions of notoriety and pomp, but their objectives like Satan is to be heralded as great. True servants of God seek no acceptance from men.

Spear fishers take advantage of the weak and lonely people who would willingly take care of the charlatans. They devour the widow's house by taking all that the poor and confused have to offer whether it is money, food or time. These ministers offer up the sacrifice of fools in exchange for adoration. They make a lot of noise but say nothing. They make long prayers but they are just playing a role and as such, they shall receive a worse punishment. (Matt 23:3,4,5,6,7,15) ≈ **ALL THEREFORE WHATSOEVER THEY BID YOU OBSERVE, (THAT) OBSERVE AND DO; BUT DO NOT YE AFTER THEIR WORKS: FOR THEY SAY, AND DO NOT. FOR THEY BIND HEAVY BURDENS AND GRIEVOUS TO BE BORNE, AND LAY (THEM) ON MEN'S SHOULDERS; BUT THEY (THEMSELVES) WILL NOT MOVE THEM WITH ONE OF THEIR FINGERS. BUT ALL THEIR WORKS THEY DO FOR TO BE SEEN OF MEN: THEY MAKE BROAD THEIR PHYLACTERIES, AND ENLARGE THE BORDERS OF THEIR GARMENTS, AND LOVE THE UPPERMOST ROOMS AT FEASTS, AND THE CHIEF SEATS IN THE SYNAGOGUES, AND GREETINGS IN THE MARKETS, AND TO BE CALLED OF MEN, RABBI, RABBI.** ≈ 15 ≈ **WOE UNTO YOU SCRIBES AND PHARISEES, HYPOCRITES! FOR YE COMPASS SEA AND LAND TO MAKE ONE PROSTYLYTE, AND WHEN HE IS MADE, YE MAKE HIM TWOFOLD, MORE OF A CHILD OF HELL THAN YOURSELVES.** ≈ This scripture warns us not to follow those who are religious, but do not live right; these are pastors or leaders who admonish you to live right as they give instructions from the window of the adulteress' house. For these men, like the Sanhedrin of old, required such outrageous things that no man could live up to them. They keep many in bondage with rules and regulations that are designed to make them seem Holy and so they can point out other people's weaknesses.

Spear fishers give many rules of behavior, but observe none of them. With these rigorous rules, they hold many in bondage and in no way try to help these people. Their entire ministry is for the sole purpose of being seen and praised, they love titles and accolades but care nothing for people. Not only do they not care for men but also the Master says that they expend vast amounts of energy finding the lost sheep and when they do Jesus says that they turn them into bigger sinners than they were.

(Col 2:8) ≈ **Beware lest any man spoil you through philosophy and vain deceit, after the tradition of men, after the rudiments of the world, and not after Christ.** ≈ Do not let the tricks of the world or their simple snares entrap you. Nor allow any man to take you to hell with him through his use of words and language--follow Christ and try all else by the spirit.

(Tim 1:4) ≈ **Neither give heed to fables and endless genealogies, which minister questions, rather than godly edifying which is in faith: (so do).** ≈ Do not pay attention to stories and lies, which only serve to abate your question. Their answer, however, would not hold up to scrutiny or a test by the word. Try these stories by the word with the help of the Holy Spirit and you will find out how useless they are.

(Tim 6-11) ≈ **From which some having swerved have turned aside unto vain jangling, Desiring to be teachers of the law; understanding neither what they say, nor whereof they affirm. But we know that the law (is) good, if a man use it lawfully; Knowing this, that the law is not made for a righteous man, but for the lawless and disobedient, for the ungodly and for sinners, for unholy and profane, for murderers of fathers and murderers of mothers, for manslayers, for whoremongers, for them that defile themselves with mankind, for men stealers, for liars, for perjured persons, and if there be any other thing that is contrary to sound doctrine.** ≈

Spear fishers leave the beaten path and seek appeasement by doing very little earnest ministry but claiming credit for other people's work. They desire to teach God's law but without benefit of the Holy Spirit, Who teaches us to love. They do not understand nor adequately convey the rhetoric they teach. Remembering that God's law is good, we must perceive that the leader cannot do this because they are not living it righteously and therefore cannot teach the law. If they do not or cannot properly teach the word of God, they probably possess one or more of the following attributes: lawlessness, disobedience, ungodliness, profane, murder or manslaughter, whoremongers, spouse stealers, liars and generally any unrighteous behaviour which prevents or at least inhibits his ability to hear from the Holy Spirit.

REEF BLEACHERS

In my country, there are shellfish called crawfish (Lobsters without claws). The easiest way to catch them is to bleach the reef. By bleaching the reef, the crawfish comes out of its natural hiding place. The problem with this is that it also kills the reef, thus, destroying a huge part of the ecosystem. The reef supports so many forms of life that when it is killed (it is alive too) the things dependent upon it die too. Reef bleachers are destructive pastors and false teachers whose desire it is to glorify self at whatever cost to the body.

The church is the reef in the Gecosystem, and when ministers and clergy destroy the church; the cornerstone, the salt of the earth they too destroy the environment. However, unlike fish, our environment includes the outside world as well as the church. The Godhead detests reef bleachers for they deceive, destroy, and divide the body. In doing so they do immeasurable harm to the world because whether they accept us or not we serve as the force of good and righteousness in a creation gone bad. The word says this about these ministries:

(Ez 44:12,13) ≈ **Because they ministered unto them before their idols, and caused the house of Israel to fall into iniquity; therefore have I lifted up Mine hand against them, saith the Lord God, and they shall bear their iniquity. And they shall not come near unto Me, to do the office of a priest unto Me, nor to come near to any of My Holy things, in the most holy (place): but they shall bear their shame, and their abominations which they have committed.** ≈

Because these individuals mislead the sheep by use of deception and false idols, (music, sports, dance, money, prestige) they shall bear their iniquity. There are many reef bleachers still active in the body; some have very large followings. Verily, the word forewarns you that they will never be near the Father. He said that they would not be able to do the office of a priest unto Him. Using the definition of Ministry from the NHV bible, ministry is, "To the uplifting of the body of Messiah."

By this definition, those who are reef bleachers are not in the ministry, because God says they cannot come near Him or any of His holy things. This means that reef bleachers who perform miracles, cast out demons, and heal the sick are not doing so at the behest of the Father. The word says that they shall bear the shame and abominations, and therefore, we should not follow believe nor associate with these people.

1 John 4:1 reminds us to try the spirits (intentions of people) to see whether they are of God. Spirits in this sense also means teaching, preaching and direction of these people—by this may we know that they are false prophets. The last times have been a subject of debate for thousands of years, but over 2,000 years ago, we are told that there were antichrists and there still are. ≈ **Beloved, believe not every spirit, but try the spirits whether they are of God: because many false prophets are gone out into the world.** ≈ (1John 2:18) ≈ **Little children, it is the last time: and as ye have heard that antichrist shall come, even now are there many antichrists; whereby we know that it is the last time.** ≈ (2 Peter 2:1,2,3,8,10,12,13,14,15,17,19) ≈ **But there were false prophets also among the people, even as there shall be false teachers among you, who privily shall bring in damnable heresies, even denying the Lord that bought them, and bring upon themselves swift destruction. And many shall follow their pernicious ways; by reason of whom the way of truth shall be evil spoken of. And through covetousness shall they with feigned words make merchandise of you: whose judgment now of a long time lingereth not and their damnation slumbereth not. 8 (For that righteous man dwelling among them, in seeing 10 But chiefly them that walk after the flesh in the lust 12 But these, as natural brute beasts, made to be taken. 14 Having eyes full of adultery, and that cannot cease from sin; beguiling unstable souls: an heart they have exercised with covetous practices; cursed children: 15 Which have forsaken the right way, and are gone astray, following the way of Balaam the son of Bosor, who loved the wages of unrighteousness; 17 These are wells without water, clouds that are carried with a tempest; to whom the mist of darkness is reserved for ever. 19 While they promise them liberty, they themselves are the servants of corruption: for of whom a man is overcome, of the same is he brought in bondage.** ≈ These false prophets and teachers shall bring in or introduce to us damnable heresies. Denying the Lord is giving any credit for anything that is done by Him to themselves; i.e., I saved 10 people, I healed the sick, I made the church grow, I am the head of this church. They deny the Lord by virtue of not giving Him credit for His work. 2 Cor. 2:17 warns us that to them we are just merchandise, moneymaking tools. ≈ **For we are not as so many, peddling the word of God. However, as of sincerity, but as of God, in the sight of God,**

we speak in Messiah[37]. ≈ This is why so many of ref bleachers put so much emphasis on tithing and offering, because they want the maximum profit from their merchandise.

These false prophets are a fungus amongst the body, unlike bacteria; they are very hard to kill. They walk among the body and fellowship with us all the while bringing shame and dishonour to the body. Always willing to admit their flaws and with equal callousness they claim the grace and forgiveness promised to those who are weak, not the rebellious. Because of there covet filled hearts, they cannot depart from sin and they take many weak Christians down with them. Because their adultery in the both flesh and spirit results is cursed children in both worlds.

The sins of the fathers are passed on to the children and an adulterous relationship with the world produces accursed Christians. Actually, they are not so much accursed as they are lost and weak. Natural curses are carried through the blood of the Father. Just as the blood of Christ carried life, death comes through the blood of the world. The reef bleachers have found an easy plentiful source of riches, a cornucopia of young believers that end up tossed about.

These youngsters can be trained up in the ways that the false teachers want. As a result, we have many proselyte born to pastors, young people led back to the world, young boys being molested and hundreds of thousands of dollars being collected and squandered. This money brought to them like gods by adoring lost children who without help will either remain lost as they are or get worse.

They do not have the Holy Spirit and as such are without the Living Water promised to believers, and they are doomed to be without (truth/life) Light forever. These false teachers like Jim Jones constantly promise freedom and liberty but instead deliver death. Satan was the model of this in the garden for this is all he did was promise life and deliver death. Those who deliver death too often themselves shall be consumed by death. For whatever we give ourselves over to, we become bound by it and the bondage will last until redemption or death.

(Matt 7:15,16,17,18,21,22,23) ≈ **BEWARE OF FALSE PROPHETS, WHICH COME TO YOU IN SHEEP'S CLOTHING, BUT INWARDLY THEY ARE RAVENING WOLVES. YE SHALL KNOW**

---

[37] The Hebrew Names Version of the World English Bible (HNV)

THEM BY THEIR FRUITS. DO MEN GATHER GRAPES OF THORNS, OR FIGS OF THISTLES? EVEN SO EVERY GOOD TREE BRINGETH FORTH GOOD FRUIT; BUT A CORRUPT TREE BRINGETH FORTH EVIL FRUIT. A GOOD TREE CANNOT BRING FORTH EVIL FRUIT, NEITHER (CAN) A CORRUPT TREE BRING FORTH GOOD FRUIT. EVERY TREE THAT BRINGETH NOT FORTH GOOD FRUIT IS HEWN DOWN, AND CAST INTO THE FIRE. WHEREFORE BY THEIR FRUITS YE SHALL KNOW THEM. 21 NOT EVERY ONE THAT SAITH UNTO ME, LORD, LORD, SHALL ENTER INTO THE KINGDOM OF HEAVEN; BUT HE THAT DOETH THE WILL OF MY FATHER, WHICH IS IN HEAVEN. MANY WILL SAY TO ME IN THAT DAY, LORD, LORD, HAVE WE NOT PROPHESIED IN THY NAME? AND IN THY NAME HAVE CAST OUT DEVILS? AND IN THY NAME DONE MANY WONDERFUL WORKS? AND THEN WILL I PROFESS UNTO THEM, I NEVER KNEW YOU: DEPART FROM ME, YE THAT WORK INIQUITY. ≈ Like Satan, false prophets always present themselves as something good.

A man told me a very cute but appropriate parable: A little bird was walking and fell in a hole breaking both wings. A cow came along and used the bathroom on the bird. A short time later a cat came along and picked up the bird cleaned it off and ate it. The moral of the story is that not everybody who dumps on you is your enemy and not everybody who tries to help you is your friend. This is so true of Christianity; most often those who are the most destructive to us are very close and are always smooth. The abrasive people we always walk away from and they are not always considered a threat.

Satan has mastered the use of friends, family, and people to destroy believers. So do not always believe that those who disagree with you are the problem—at least they are honest enough to do their work openly. It is those that do it in secret that are the danger and most often they are those we hold in high esteem and trust.

Reef bleachers always have very faithful followers because what they offer is very appealing to their flock. What they usually offer is a modified form of the word. Their system does not require change nor encourage; it encourages tolerance and pushes cheap grace. They teach people to believe in Christ and if He is not changing you it is because you are fine the way you are; forgiveness and blessings are sure to follow.

The bible says that you will know a tree by its fruit, and that if the fruit is rotten (stays rotten; some get lost) it came from a rotten tree. If there are lazy Christians and ministers, it is because that is what they were taught. Like the bird in the story, too many of us will not be able to tell who the bleachers are and it will be our fault. The sheep that follow the bleachers down to death will not know they are lost. Not until they call out to Jesus requesting acknowledgement for the things they did and the Judge then says to them, ≈ **I NEVER NEW YOU: DEPART FROM ME YOU DOERS OF INIQUITY.** ≈

TEMPTRESSES IN THE TEMPLE

In the city of Nashville, where there are several International Christian Headquarters, and there is actually in another town approximately 15 minutes away the headquarters for one of the most well know Christian networks around the world. The citizens of Nashville petitioned to have a strip club shut down because it was too close to a school there stands a complete affront to God. In the city of Nashville, is a strip joint/adult bookstore, which was previously a church; actually, this place now called a show bar still looks like a church. In this former house of God, there are a bunch of lewd, naked women and debase men enjoying the lusts of their flesh…and the churches never said a word in protest. If then we can sell a church, formerly a supposed house of God then why do we even build these domiciles if they mean so little?

This reminds me of a line from the movie, "Murder by Death," wherein the detective looked into a room devoid of bodies and exclaimed…"*Look! Room filled with empty people*." What would this detective say if he were to look into some of our churches?

≈ AMEN ≈

WORK AREA LETTER III

FISHERS OF MEN

Topical Scriptures

(Matt. 13:47& 48) (Rev 15:2) Luke 2:30-32) (2 Peter 3:9) (John 12:32) (John 14:2) (Rev 14 19) (Matt 3:12) (Matt 4:18-22) (Matt 11: 29) (John 6:37) (Matt 4:19) (Mark 1:16) (Luke 5:2) (1 Eph. 4:11 &12) (Rom 12:4-7) (Matt 5:13) (Deut 1) (1 Sam 8:6-9) (1 Sam 8:10-22) (Matt 23:8-10) (Matt 11:11) (Matt 10:6-16) (Matt 12:30-32) (Rom 1:28) (Rom 1:32) (Rom 9:22) (Rom 1:24 & 25) (Exod 20:5) (Matt 15:17-20) (Gen 3:3) (Matt 10:28) (John 8:41) (Jude 9) (Matt 7:1-5) (Matt. 18:6) (Matt 23:8) (Mark 11:15-18) (Rev 3:15-16) (Gen 38:13-25) (Mark 5:30-31) (Prov 6:23-29) (Prov 7:11-27) (1 Cor 6:16) (Matt 12:45) (Mark 1:22-26) (Titus 1:5-16, Tim 3) (Acts 19:13-15) (1 Cor 3:7 & 8) (Matt 7:22 & 23) (Matt 15:32-38) (Mark 6:33-44) (Acts 19:12) (Matt 28:18) (Rom 15:18-20) (Luke 5:8) (Rev 2:20-23) (Matt 10:22,34 & 35) (1 Cor 5:10-13) (Gal 1:6-10) (Eph 5:3-21) (Mark 12:38-40) (Matt 23:3,4,5,6,7,15) (Col 2:8 (Tim 1:4) (Tim 6-11) (Ez 44:12,13) (1 John 4:1) (1 John 2:18) (2 Peter 2:1,2,3,8,10,12,13,14,15,17,19) (2 Cor. 2:17) (Matt 7:15, 16, 17, 18, 21, 22, 23)

1. WHY IS THE LINE, ≈ **FOLLOW ME...**" THE MOST IMPORTANT LINE IN THE PASSAGE MATT 4:18-22

2. WHY IS JESUS'S YOKE EASY AND BURDEN LIGHT?

3. **ASSEMBLE A 'TANK' IN YOUR NOTES AND LIST WHAT YOU WOULD DESIGN ONE.**

4. **LIST THE CHARACTERISTICS OF A SAULFISH.**

5. HOW DO YOU KEEP THE BELIEVERS AWAY FROM THE WORLD?

6. EXPLAIN MATT 15:32-38 AND HOW IS THIS A TRAIT OF A GOOD FISHER OF MEN.

7. WRITE A SHORT DEFINITION DISCIPLE.

8. LIST THE DIFFERENT TYPES OF FISHERS AND EXPLAIN STEP BY STEP HOW TO PREVENT THIS IN THE NEW FISH.

_____
_____
_____
_____
_____
_____
_____
_____
_____
_____
_____

9. (MATT 23:3-15) DETAIL A COMMON PROBLEM IN THE BODY AND EXPLAIN HOW YOU DEAL WITH THIS. WRITE WHAT EXPLANATION YOU WOULD GIVE A NEW FISH PERTAINING TO THIS PROBLEM.

_____
_____
_____
_____
_____
_____
_____

10. MATT (7:15) EXPLAIN THIS PASSAGE IN TERMS A 1 YEAR OLD WILL UNDERSTAND.

ADDITIONAL NOTES FOR THIS CHAPTER

LETTER IV

≈

TO CATCH THE FISH

≈ And it came to pass, that, as the people pressed upon Him to hear the word of God, He stood by the lake of Gennesaret, And saw two ships standing by the lake: but the fishermen were gone out of them, and were washing (their) nets And He entered into one of the ships, which was Simon's, and prayed him that he would thrust out a little from the land. And He sat down, and taught the people out of the ship Now when he had left speaking, He said unto Simon, **LAUNCH OUT INTO THE DEEP, AND LET DOWN YOUR NETS FOR A DRAUGHT.** And Simon answering said unto Him, Master, we have toiled all the night, and have taken nothing: nevertheless at thy word I will let down the net. And when they had this done, they enclosed a great multitude of fishes: and their net brake. And they beckoned unto (their) partners, which were in the other ship, that they should come and help them. And they came, and filled both the ships, so that they began to sink. When Simon Peter saw (it), he fell down at Jesus' knees, saying, Depart from me; for I am a sinful man, O Lord. For he was astonished, and all that were with him, at the draught of the fishes which they had taken: And so (was) also James, and John, the sons of Zebedee, which were partners with Simon. And Jesus said unto Simon, **FEAR NOT; FROM HENCEFORTH THOU SHALT CATCH MEN.** And when they had brought their ships to land, they forsook all, and followed Him. ≈ (Luke 5:1-11)

LETTER IV ≈ TO CATCH THE FISH

There are varieties of ways to catch fish and different fisherman use different tools. However, the only tools approved by God to catch His fish are Jesus and the Holy Spirit. Referring to (Luke 5:1-11) the people/fish begged Jesus to preach. He went over to the fisherman and they had closed up shop. The fishermen went fishing and came home empty. Their revivals had failed--Jesus was not there; yet, they should have waited for His arrival. The hook that is successful and the only way to actually catch "fish[38]" is to understand that there is no way to save anyone unless the Father calls them.

The word *call* means to draw unto Him not necessarily call in an audible sense. The simple and plain but so often missed fact is that we cannot save anything! Only God can save souls. This is what we would call in Wado-Ryu karate a hidden-waza[39], wherein Jesus tells us that ≈ **NO MAN COMES TO THE FATHER BUT THROUGH ME.** ≈ This tells us several things; one thing is that it tells us is that Jesus is the conduit to Salvation, but it also implies that no man comes unless they are called/invited (Jhn 6:44).

In other words, God has to call us; we do not decide to get saved. God talks to the inner-self and awakens the Spirit man with His breath of life--only then can we hear the small still voice of God. This message is clearly illustrated in Genesis when God created man. It says that after He formed the man (molded his body) He breathed into him giving him life not only in the spirit but also in the flesh. God also commanded Adam that if he should eat of the tree in that day he should truly die! It then tells us that the moment Adam ate/partook of the tree his eyes became open.... What does this mean? What God said is what happened, Adam died that instant, he died in the spirit. That is why he saw Eve's nakedness for the first time in his life, Adam was living and seeing in the flesh.

This is a true application of the term revelation[40]; the revelation Adam received was that Eve was naked. What was hidden again (reveiled) from him was that his Spirit-man at that point had been cut off from God. The death God spoke of was spiritual, and the day mentioned actually

---

[38] fi**sh** = the lost sheep.
[39] Secret technique or teaching.
[40] This actually means to re-veil or hide something again.

meant instant or moment. So far those who need the command in *baby formula* it would say, *{For in the instant you disobey Me and choose to partake of sin, your soul shall be cut off from Mine.}* Why then did God not simply say that? He did, we just did not get it. In addition, God talks the way He wants to. It is up to us to ask for interpretation when not clear on what God means. Remember His ways are not our ways.

Matthew 24:22 exemplifies the graciousness God. He understands that the nature of flesh is to sin and that if He stays away too long, we would all go to hell. For we all have sinned and fall short of the glory of God. Nevertheless, it also shows that the people that God saves He "chose" - not vice versa nor does it say they choose to come to Christ. ≈ **AND EXCEPT THOSE DAYS SHOULD BE SHORTENED, THERE SHOULD NO FLESH BE SAVED: BUT FOR THE ELECT'S SAKE THOSE DAYS SHALL BE SHORTENED.** ≈ (Acts 2:47) It clearly tells us that despite the efforts of the disciples the Lord did the adding--the disciples gave Him something to which to add. The disciples were good fishers of men allowing the Lord to send them a haul. ≈ **Praising God, and having favor with all the people. And the Lord added to the church daily such as should be saved.** ≈

In the scripture Revelations 17:14, twice does it articulate that the real work of the Spirit is calling us to Him (chosen generation, called you out). We do not choose to be called, but we can choose not to heed the call--we can be like the rich young ruler. When he found out what the "call" would cost him, he opted not to answer it. That was his choice, but the scripture tells us he walked away sad. Perhaps the ruler, like Jonah, knew what hell would be like, because the scripture declares that Jonah cried out from the depths of hell! In that day much like Adam the ruler's sadness was probably caused when he realized that hell was being cut off from God-- not in the flesh but in the Spirit.

Does this not sum it up for all of us! We have nothing to do with being called or even saved; all we can do is refuse to accept the gift. We can stop our salvation but are powerless to start it or make it happen. Is Not God good- forgive me great! Do you see it yet? Let us see together then where it says, ≈ **These shall make war...**[41] ≈ Meaning more than one shall make war with the Lamb. It also says that they war against the Lamb--we know the Lamb to be

---

[41] Revelation 17:14 ≈ **These shall make war with the Lamb, and the Lamb shall overcome them: for He is Lord of lords, and King of kings: and they that are with Him are called, and chosen, and faithful.** ≈

Jesus. The great part is as a Lamb weak, humble, feeble, pure, and small, He overcame them all. Remember the game, "My daddy, can beat your daddy!" Well, my Lamb can beat your Dragon and your Lion, and all the other beasts and hellions out there, so na na na na na!

Although not quite so clear as Ephesians 2:8[42], this scripture again assures us that God is in control and has called us into His fold. (1 Tess 2:12) ≈ **That we would walk worthy of God, who hath called you unto His kingdom and glory.** ≈ The word used here is begotten so let us see what begotten[43] means so that we may glorify God more and have a better understanding of (John 3:16). ≈ **For God so loved the world, that He gave His only begotten Son, that whosoever believeth in Him should not perish, but have everlasting life** ≈ This is one of the most quoted but under appreciated verses in the Bible.

Another scripture confirming God's sovereignty is (Romans 5:9) ≈ **Much more than, being now justified by His blood, we shall be saved from wrath through Him.** ≈ Again asserting that Jesus saves us-- nothing about our saving ourselves is mentioned.

Finally, words from the Master Himself. If you do not understand what the concept of master means, go some place as simple as a Dojo (Karate Studio) and watch the people when they talk about their masters and what they said. One of the proudest claims of a black belt is that they studied under the Master. There is only one master in karate, though many teachers, but they all refer to the master with love and respect, it is interesting to see.

(Matthew 9:12 & 13) ≈ **But when Jesus heard (that), He said unto them, THEY THAT BE WHOLE NEED NOT A PHYSICIAN, BUT THEY THAT ARE SICK BUT GO YE AND LEARN WHAT (THAT) MEANETH, I WILL HAVE MERCY AND NOT SACRIFICE: FOR I AM**

---

[42] ≈ **For by grace are you saved through faith; and that not of yourselves; it is a gift from God.** ≈

[43] be-got-ten (bi-gotn).To bring (a product or idea) into being. (V) create, author, be the source of, bear, beget, brew, coin, compose, concoct, contrive, devise, give birth to, hatch, innovate, invent, make, originate, pioneer, spawn. To produce sexually or asexually others of one's kind. (v) reproduce, bear, beget, breed, bring forth, engender, generate, get, give birth to, have, multiply, procreate, produce, proliferate, There are many synonyms for the word begotten listed here in the American Heritage Dictionary. However, only one phrase is of importance to us, I highlighted it for you. Unlike all other humans, including Adam, Jesus was the only one created after God's own kind. He alone was just like God. The mule is created in the shadow of the horse but only another horse is of its own kind. Remember the creation after Adam's own kind was another being of flesh.

NOT COME TO CALL THE RIGHTEOUS, BUT SINNERS TO REPENTANCE. ≈

Glory to God in the highest: His mercy allowed Him to send Jesus to us to make the "call" much easier to heed and to understand what it meant for several reasons. First, is that in the Old Testament the call was often a novelty as with Abraham who did not even know God at the time, or Samuel who was the same.

Second, is that the call came through dreams which were hard to understand or convey to other people. The call sometimes was a manifestation of God or an angel of God. Nevertheless, when Jesus came along, He was the difference between color television and radio. People could see Him, touch Him, watch Him, and hear Him. No longer was the call a mystery to men, it was made flesh and walked among us. What a beautiful plan God had --We would call it an example.

After Jesus, there should have been no confusion, in fact, the Spirit of truth can not be confused. (John 10:14) ≈ **I AM THE GOOD SHEPHERD, AND KNOW MY (SHEEP), AND AM KNOWN OF MINE.** ≈ The problem is that man tries to follow Jesus in the flesh. It is no wonder God seeks followers who worship Him in spirit and truth; the flesh is doomed to always sin.

Is it a wonder that sin causes sickness and death? It was sin that caused the fall of man and the war in heaven. Sin causes confusion on earth with churches and religions and causes many lost sheep. With so many lost, no wonder the 24 elders worshipped all day in Revelations--did not God promise more joy in heaven over one repentant sinner, what about millions of them?

We know sin causes sickness, because the Master exemplified this in (Matthew 9:5 & 6) ≈ **FOR WHETHER IS EASIER, TO SAY, (THY) SINS BE FORGIVEN THEE; OR TO SAY, ARISE, AND WALK? : BUT THAT YE MAY KNOW THAT THE SON OF MAN HATH POWER ON EARTH TO FORGIVE SINS, (THEN SAITH HE TO THE SICK OF THE PALSY,) ARISE, TAKE UP THY BED, AND GO UNTO THINE HOUSE.** ≈ Wherein He cured the sick by forgiving them of their sins. That explains why the word tells us that Jesus conquered death, and sickness. For His death, and His blood forgave us all.

This also means that despite redemption, there are a lot more Adams' walking the earth even today. Paul tells us that Jesus gave us life and saved us from death. Sickness and death still exist but we have been saved from them. (Romans 5:21) ≈ **That as sin hath reigned unto**

death, even so might grace reign through righteousness unto eternal life by Jesus Christ our Lord. ≈

Actually, maybe the fault is as it was in Eden, the weaker vessel--Eve[44]. In this case, we know the Groom is without spot. So the weaker vessel is Christ's bride; the church. Because His bride has not been virtuous, sin has entered and Satan is still able to exert free reign over the earth and its people.

≈ **AMEN** ≈

---

[44] Referring to the bride/ help-meet of Christ.

WORK AREA
LETTER IV

TO CATCH
THE FISH

Topical Scriptures

(Luke 5:1-11) (Jhn 6:44) (Matt 24:22) (Acts 2:47) (Rev. 17:14) (1 Tess 2:12 (John 3:16) (Romans 5:9) (Matthew 9:12 & 13) (John 10:14) (Matthew 9:5 & 6) (Romans 5:21)

1. AS A FISHER OF MEN WHAT SKILLS SHOULD YOU HAVE?

2. JOHN 10:14 EXPLAIN AND THEN DETAIL HOW YOU GET TO KNOW THE SHEEP.

3. WHY IS IT SO DIFFICULT TO CATCH A FISH WITH JUST A HOOK?

4. WHY DID JESUS LAUNCH OUT TO THE DEEP?

5. WHY WERE THE FISHERMEN ABLE TO CATCH SO MANY FISH?

6. EXPLAIN WHY JESUS TOLD PETER TO FEAR NOT IN LUKE 5:1-11.

7. HOW DO FISH BREATH UNDER WATER. WHAT IS THE SPIRITUAL EQUIVALENT?

_____
_____
_____
_____
_____
_____
_____
_____
_____
_____
_____
_____
_____
_____
_____
_____
_____

8. WHAT IS THE BEST WAY TO CATCH A FISH?

_____
_____
_____
_____
_____
_____

9. WHAT IS THE SINGLE MOST IMPORTANT THING TO REMEMBER ABOUT CATCHING FISH?

10. WHAT TWO STEPS ARE REQUIRED FOR SALVATION AND CITE SCRIPTURES.

ADDITIONAL NOTES FOR THIS CHAPTER

91

LETTER V

≈

LURE, BAIT AND THE BEST WATERS

≈ **Counsel in the heart of man (is like) deep water; but a man of understanding will draw it out.** ≈ (Pro 20:5)

LETTER V ≈ LURE, BAIT AND THE BEST WATERS

Have you ever watched an infomercial on fishing lures? They show different types--some glow; some move in a life-like manner automatically. Still others maneuver when tugged. Regardless of which type of lure used, there is only one goal in mind--catching fish. Hooks and lures work in conjunction with rods and reels, wherein the fisherman is extensibly laying in wait for an unsuspecting fish. This is not the type of fishing that the Father ordains.

Lures are traps that are intended to entice the otherwise uninterested fish into biting--many churches use lures as well. Some of them erect huge steeples that glow in the dark. The light found in them is not the Light of Jesus, consequently the newly converted fish often leave disenchanted. They also use the type of lures that automatically move in a life-like manner and others that require manipulation. Things like a *good* word, meaning popular and inoffensive. It sounds like the word of God, but it is missing God.

Then, there are the types that require manipulation--popular television slots, collaborating with worldly groups and some even go so far as to talk, walk and act like the world. The question then arises if we do not admonish the babes in Christ to come away from the world and not to be conformed to this world--then why tell them to stop sinning at all? Why not just let them have their cake and eat it, too?

Many churches have become catwalks that rival New York's designer districts. The only changing that goes on in these places is the frequent changing of fashion. I attended an award ceremony one year, when I arrived there was electricity in the air and the people were a buzz and all aglow. Traversing the lobby, I began to notice all the elaborate colours and hairstyles. The more I looked at the clothing and demeanor of the people the scene was actually more reminiscent of a Prince concert. The best-dressed, brightly, coloured clothes belonged to the males! I was appalled, to say the least, at this farce; Satan's attempt to subvert yet another outreach of the church, with the help of the church. I have never been back, but this should raise a spiritual alarm. If these are the people writing the music for the church and believers, what does that say about the spirit the music conveys, and whose spirit is it? Moreover, what does this say about the church's standard of what to accept and portray as the things of God. I am not certain, but the electricity that I perceived upon arriving at the event, I feel was spiritual tumult--the spirits of the world combating the true witnesses of Christ; they do not get along.

A closer look at Jesus' gatherings explain exactly what things Jesus used to attract (notice not bait) the fish. Mark 4:1 ≈ **And He began again to teach by the seaside: and there was gathered unto Him a great multitude, so that He entered into a ship, and sat in the sea; and the whole multitude was by the sea on the land.** ≈ It is clear from the scriptures that traps and lures are not needed. It is not the trappings of the church that attracts souls, for spirits do not see in the flesh! When you attract the flesh and all you have to offer is to the flesh then you are fighting a losing battle. Lest you believe that music and dancing is more appealing to the flesh than sex and drugs. If that were the case, we would not have needed Jesus.

The fact of the matter is that too many churches offer delicacies to the flesh and not enough to the spirit. As a point of study, Jesus did not cater to the people's need for food until He had given them soul food. We cannot mesh the flesh and the spirit. Obviously, people bring them both to church but the church MUST not cater to the flesh. Catering to the flesh, however, does serve two worldly-church purposes. It keeps the people coming back for another show. Secondly it helps boost the financial uptake of the church. This matter will be dealt with in a later letter.

The people flocked to Jesus and subsequent disciples because they were giving them the message of God, the good news of Jesus Christ. Not the news that the Messiah had come but that this time God came as the Redeemer and Saviour. Not to judge--but to justify; not to punish--but to purify and not to condemn--but to claim. If this is not enough to capture hearts and souls and keep them, there are two possible explanations:

i) The word we are giving out is so lukewarm that it could not be used for shaving (Rev 3:15-16) ≈ **I KNOW THY WORKS, THAT THOU ART NEITHER COLD NOR HOT: I WOULD THOU WERT COLD OR HOT. SO THEN BECAUSE THOU ART LUKEWARM, AND NEITHER COLD NOR HOT, I WILL SPUE THEE OUT OF MY MOUTH.** ≈ The word of God when given in its pure and unadulterated form boils and bubbles over out of the flesh--it literally explodes forth from the body. The fleshly tomb[45] cannot hold the rivers of Living Water and joy that

---

[45] Called a tomb because the flesh dies in favour of the Spirit, only the Holy Spirit of God gives Life.

salvation brings. David got so hot for God that he even had to take off his clothes[46]. The tomb cannot contain the joy unspeakable that God brings that is why Moses' face glowed; why Jesus could bear what He bore. Why Moses' and Elijah's bodies were never found, why Peter was able to walk on water and especially why after being transfigured Jesus told Mary to look but not to touch. He was free from the tomb/grave and did not wish to be entombed again, nor could He ascend in that (particular body of) flesh.

Traditional bait consists of worms, bread, and/or bacon. Through man's desire to improve his traps (maybe the fish got wise) he created lures. These lures are simply a synthetic version of the traditional bait; the result is still the same--bondage or death for the fish. Worldly fishers have indeed done the same thing. They have increased the size of their choirs, improved the buildings, provided more parking and turned up the volume of the music. This is still just bait without the Spirit of Jesus as the main attraction.

In the Bahamas, there are not many industries due to the lack of natural resources. Consequently, the country has a history of creative industries. One such industry was the Wrecking industry. This industry consists of erecting a lighthouse in the middle of a reef and then shutting down all the real lighthouses. Therefore, the ships coming in from the storm saw the light and followed it in. The ships struck the reefs and sunk, leaving the cargo for looting. Many churches employ the same type of lighthouses. They advertise salvation, but sink many vessels, looting them spiritually, financially, and sometimes sexually. They then leave them broken and empty adrift on a shoal.

ii) Ministers are simply trying to increase dividends, and they do this by spoon-feeding the body. Much like an intravenous drip, the body gets to the point that it becomes so dependent on the drops that it cannot function. Many believers are on forced spiritual fasts, employed by ministers (whether intentional or not) for keeping the flock under their care. However, if you do not let sheep grow they never shed their wool and the blessings are held up for everyone. If the tree never matures, it will never bear fruit. Moreover, the tree -- the Bible says is known by its fruit (Matt 7:16), if you bear no fruit then your stones are broken and you are also in disobedience to the command, ≈ **BE FRUITFUL AND MULTIPLY.** ≈ (Gen 1:28).

Sadly enough, but so apparent in so many churches, is that fruit that stays on the tree too long that ripens, over ripens, falls to the ground

---

[46] 2 Sam. 6:14.

and rots. As it rots, worms, birds, and other animals consume it. Again, not following the simple instructions of the Master plan will ALWAYS result in death. Verily, verily, I admonish you to stop starving God's children for it is written, ≈ **WHOSOEVER CAUSES ONE OF THE LITTLE ONES WHO BELIEVES IN ME TO STUMBLE, IT IS BETTER FOR HIM THAT A HEAVY MILESTONE BE HUNG AROUND HIS NECK, AND THAT HE[47] BE DROWNED IN THE DEPTH OF THE SEA!** ≈ On the stumble scale, from 1-10 where do you think stunting their growth would fall?

It is at this point that healthy spirituality turns into religion[48]. The body then becomes addicted -- not to Christ, but to the minister. The minister then becomes indispensable to that body; and they follow them? This is always bad! Believers are to follow God only! Even God's appointed are only an extension of God's grace; thus, following them is still following Him. However, ALWAYS look to God first, then to His word, then to man last of all. Neither God nor His word will ever fade or fail, but the nature of man will always be to sin.

How many have been placed and or kept in bondage by ministers only to support their endeavors? The spirit walk is supposed to lead to life and freedom, not indentured servitude with the pastor's pockets lined and the flock starving spiritually.[49]

THE BEST WATERS

Why is it that believers are likened unto fish? There are several reasons and if you watch a National Geographic episode on Sea life, it will become apparent.

i) Fish come in all shapes and sizes, just like believers do (thanks to Jesus who also came to the Gentiles.)

ii) Each fish has a purpose in the ecosystem. (Covered in depth in the letter Fishers of Men.)

iii) Fish eat each other and each other's young. Believers devour each other out of jealousy. They constantly destroy the new converts out of

---

[47] The masculine gender is used here because at the time there were little if any female church leaders, but this applies to women as well.
[48] Father Leo Booth writes a very good book on this called, <u>When God Becomes a Drug</u>.
[49] This is covered more in depth in the letter called the 13th tribe.

ignorance sometimes, but as we discussed earlier, leaving them unprepared is leaving them to be devoured.

iv) Fish school together. Believers also tend to school together, sometimes for protection but more so because humans are social animals. Much like the schools of fish--fish tend to move together in whichever direction the school travels right or wrong[50]. School is also the place where learning and teaching takes place, and it is in this school that the fish learn to care for each other, love each other and survive to take their place in the ecosystem.

v) Fish wander. While watching the documentaries, studies have shown that fish move around throughout the world's oceans. Believers also move together through the oceans of life from phase to phase, church to church and from popular ministry to popular ministry.

vi) Most fish are non-predatory. Most believers are not aggressive, when it comes to the things of God they are quite content to be herded and led about.

vii) Most fish will always run to the bottom or the darkness to hide. When the storms of life come or it gets cold in the water, fish retreat to the depths of the water to weather it. Believers tend to sink into the depths of sin to weather or lessen the trials that they face in life. Predators also know this, and so when the storms come or the cold weather the predators (Satan's workers) know exactly where to look for the fish.

viii) Fish if taken out of the water too long, will die. God gives us the breath of life that is like the air the fish breathe. Without spiritual air-(the breath of God) the believer dies in the spirit.

ix) Fish lay eggs. Believers should be laying eggs all over the world to keep the species alive and to help spread the good news to every ocean (Nation).

x) Fish are scaly on the outside but tender in the middle. The scales contain the beauty of the flesh, but the inside is where the meat and entrails are. Believers adorn themselves like trust up peacocks and on the inside is a hodgepodge of lying, fear, and shame. Much as fish can shed scales believers can change their outward appearance and actions but only spair^ can change hearts.

xi) Fish are afraid of loud noises and very susceptible to shock when their environment changes too quickly or drastically. Fish also have this condition, we call it backsliding and living in bondage. The devil is

---

[50] Sheep do the same thing; this is why believers are likened to docile, herdable creatures.

characterized as a roaring lion[51] and his roar scares many Christians. The Father tells us that He did not give us a spirit of fear and that if we Submit to Him and resist the devil he will flee.

By studying each afore articulated points in sequence, disciple gains a better understanding of how fish act, and become better fishers for God. Understanding these things is also important because it will help to understand missions, evangelism, and even revivals. All of these fishing endeavors are to be Spirit led and chosen.

Referring again to the account in Luke 5:1-9, we find a very important aspect that is often overlooked. God must tell us where to fish in order that we maybe successful. The kingdom promises made by Jesus were so appealing that they gathered unto Him more people than Jesus had room for. How many times have we delivered a word and had this response? Or do most people like Jesus try to find a way to get away from us. How difficult it is to fill a room with no walls? Some of us cannot even fill one service in a tiny church using the same material Jesus did. After 20 years Star Wars was able to pack the theaters and Disney is still able to sell their movies after 18 years off the shelf. We have the best news going and yet cannot gather 1/50 of what Jesus did. The fault must be ours because He was no liar and He assured us that, some would come after Him and do greater things than He did.

Jesus noticed some fishermen cleaning their tools after a day's work. Without asking, Jesus stepped onto one of the boats and asked to be carried out a little way, so He could have more room to preach. Jesus carried His message all the way to Calvary[52] by Himself--all He asks us to do is carry Him a little way so He may have more room and then let Him do the teaching.

When the sermon ended, Jesus said to Simon Peter, ≈ **FETCH OUT IN THE DEEP AND CAST YOUR NETS.** ≈ How intriguing that He sent them unto the deep. The story of Jonah shows us that the deep represents two things for fish. There are bigger ones there, and there are generally more fish in total in the deep. The deep-water represents the troubled lives of those Jesus said that He came to *Call* in Mark 2:17. ≈ **When Jesus heard it, He saith unto them, THEY THAT ARE WHOLE HAVE NO NEED OF THE PHYSICIAN, BUT THEY THAT**

---

[51] (1 Peter 5:8)

[52] With the exception of Simon of Cyrene who was, "pressed" to help Him carry the cross.

ARE SICK: I CAME NOT TO CALL THE RIGHTEOUS, BUT SINNERS TO REPENTANCE. ≈ In addition, Jesus indicates that those of us that stay in the shallow waters are really missing the great harvest of souls that the Father prepared.

Peter told Jesus it will be a waste of time, but he obeyed nonetheless. Peter had the same problem many of us in the ministry do; which is trying to accomplish spiritual things in the flesh. Fortunately, Peter was obedient enough to obey even in the midst of his doubt. It is obvious that Peter did not doubt Jesus' power he doubted himself. Peter was a zealot, and although he apparently had more oomph than the other disciples did, he still wrestled in the flesh and with his lack of confidence.

The result of Peter's obedience was a harvest so bountiful that they had to call for help to prevent themselves from sinking. Man cannot save any souls. When the Spirit of God abounds man cannot even contain the blessings though they be pressed down and shaken together. Can you envision a camp meeting so fruitful that you have to enlist the help of sister[53] churches? Imagine the telephone calls in the middle of the night saying come help the yield is to great for us to carry

Unfortunately, much like the joke about the Desert Island there is too much envy, and cleavage in the body. So much so that if someone called for help (and somebody actually answered…Since for many saving souls is a 9-5) they would be bombarded with questions. Questions about their denomination, the tithe status, who their minister was ordained by, etc. In addition, when they did show up they would probably show up in a destroyer and torpedo the disciples boat!

Perhaps this metaphor is extreme, but it is no less extreme than the divisions in the church. Maybe that is why Jesus chose a doctor as a disciple, so he could help mend the cuts and remove the knives from the backs believers hurt by other believers.

What was Peter's response to Jesus? It was to recognize the King. He did not tarry to adhere to the principle of giving honour to whom it is due. (Phil 2:10-11) ≈ **That at the name of Jesus every knee should bow, of (things) in heaven, and (things) in earth, and (things) under the earth; And (that) every tongue should confess that Jesus Christ (is) Lord, to the glory of God the Father.** ≈ He gave ALL glory to God for the good things He did. Peter also instantly recognized his unworthiness to be in the presence of Glory. Is it a wonder that Jesus blessed Peter and told him, ≈ …**BLESS YOU PETER …ON THIS ROCK I**

---

[53] Sister because they give birth to new ministries and new Christians.

SHALL BUILD MY CHURCH. ≈ It was Peter's faith as well as his brashness that Jesus appreciated. Peter right or wrong was exuberant about what he did. What Peter did not do was jump around shouting, nor did he attempt to claim any of the credit. He recognized, as did his companions, that they had nothing to do with the event. The fisher men bowed out of Jesus' way and glorified Him kneeling in amazement. This is what we need today, "some old time religion." Like the song says, when things cease to function the best way to repair the damage is to go back to the beginning. ≈ **In the beginning was the Word[54] and the Word was with God, and the Word was God.** ≈ (John 1:1) Therefore, to get the church right with God, again all we need to do is begin again, and get back to His basics.

Brothers and sisters let us look at what it was that Jesus offered that was so appealing and to whom and how it was offered. ≈ **AND SEEING THE MULTITUDES, HE WENT UP INTO A MOUNTAIN: AND WHEN HE WAS SET, HIS DISCIPLES CAME UNTO HIM: AND HE OPENED HIS MOUTH, AND TAUGHT THEM, SAYING, BLESSED ARE THE POOR IN SPIRIT: FOR THEIRS IS THE KINGDOM OF HEAVEN. BLESSED ARE THEY THAT MOURN: FOR THEY SHALL BE COMFORTED. BLESSED ARE THE MEEK: FOR THEY SHALL INHERIT THE EARTH. BLESSED ARE THEY, WHICH DO HUNGER AND THIRST AFTER RIGHTEOUSNESS: FOR THEY SHALL BE FILLED. BLESSED ARE THE MERCIFUL: FOR THEY SHALL OBTAIN MERCY. BLESSED ARE THE PURE IN HEART: FOR THEY SHALL SEE GOD. BLESSED ARE THE PEACEMAKERS: FOR THEY SHALL BE CALLED THE CHILDREN OF GOD. BLESSED ARE THEY, WHICH ARE PERSECUTED FOR RIGHTEOUSNESS' SAKE: FOR THEIRS IS THE KINGDOM OF HEAVEN. BLESSED ARE YE, WHEN MEN SHALL REVILE YOU, AND PERSECUTE YOU, AND SHALL SAY ALL MANNER OF EVIL AGAINST YOU FALSELY, FOR MY SAKE. REJOICE, AND BE EXCEEDINGLY GLAD: FOR GREAT IS YOUR REWARD IN HEAVEN.** ≈ (Matt 5:1-12). Jesus offered this to the "multitudes" (Multitude in Hebrew - *hamown* meaning noise, tumult, many, crowd or *chay* meaning alive, raw, fresh) which makes it oh so glorious. Unlike the church, the Master offered it to the noisy rabble. He did not tell them to be quiet or to even be still. They were raw and still

---

[54] For more insights as to why word is capitalized in this passage refer to these books on the subject; <u>The Secret Sounds of East and West</u>, and <u>The Power of the Spoken Word</u>.

avid sinners when Jesus delivered the message. If you notice the method He used was to tell the lost what the result of salvation would be and what changes would take place during the walk with Christ. Jesus never told them to stop what they were doing in order to receive. Jesus taught that once you received you would eventually stop what you are doing. Allow me to repeat this for emphasis, He taught that once you received you would eventually stop what you are doing.

It then says that it was not until Jesus was set (ready, prepared) that He called His disciples unto Him. Undoubtedly the preparation" was to pray before the Lord, meditating and fasting, as was His custom. Then He opened His mouth and taught them. Opening His mouth initially seems to mean He spoke. Further analysis however, would seem to suggest that the preparation was to allow the Father to speak through Him.

Thereby reasserting His humility and subordination to the Father and at the same time reconfirming His status as Son. For who but the Father could make these promises and who else, would He entrust to deliver them but His Son?

Instead of trying to change people, while they were yet sinners. Jesus told them about love and the gifts of the Kingdom. Imagine the happiness the people felt after being persecuted and scoffed at, after being spiritually oppressed by the Sanhedrin, and held in bondage by the Romans. To hear a message of goodness and hope, to hear a message that promised change for the better, to hear a message that better times were ahead?

This brothers and sisters is why The Christ was so successful in His ministry. Christ promised that good things would come as you change and that the more you changed the more good things would come. Unlike today's teaching that change must occur first and then we will get the good things. Christ however, promised that there would be an end to suffering and woe when you accept His lifestyle.

This apparently was more appealing to the multitudes than telling them that if they walk away from their life style that they can share in His. As if anyone that was enjoying the lusts of their flesh was going to walk away from sin for the simple promise of eternal life. What Jesus told them about was a chance to have happiness, and to find a reason in living righteous that they could understand and appreciate here and now. Not all of the Kingdom promises are for the hereafter. Many of the promises take root now and allow us to last until He comes again.

As mentioned before, God chooses whom He wishes to save, people do not choose. Therefore, choosing to go and "*save*" people arbitrarily is a waste of your time. Catching souls, or better yet trapping souls is a Spiritual Rights Violation and it is counter-productive. The church is in the business of winning souls and when you win something, it is yours forever. To win something usually implies a contest; therefore, without another contest your winnings cannot be taken away.

In other words, only the souls that God gives to the church will be kept[55]. The ones the church saves will soon go back to their prior state. Jesus is our gold medallist, and no one can be plucked from His bosom. Those who leave do so by choice, or even worse are given over to the enemy by those placed in charge of them. Much like Adam gave dominion over the earth to Satan, the body of Christ for too long has conceded souls back to Satan. If there is much joy in Heaven over one repentant sinner-- what then is the feeling when a repentant sinner is handed back or sold back to Satan?

(Gen. 37: 4 & 25-28) gives a more humanistic account of why brothers would destroy another child of the Father. ≈ **And when his brethren saw that their father loved him more than all his brethren, they hated him, and could not speak peaceably unto him. 25 And they sat down to eat bread: and they lifted up their eyes and looked, and, behold, a company of Ishmeelites came from Gilead with their camels bearing spicery and balm and myrrh, going to carry (it) down to Egypt. And Judah said unto his brethren, What profit (is it) if we slay our brother, and conceal his blood? Come, and let us sell him to the Ishmeelites, and let not our hand be upon him; for he (is) our brother (and) our flesh. And his brethren were content. Then there passed by Midianites merchantmen; and they drew and lifted up Joseph out of the pit, and sold Joseph to the Ishmeelites for twenty (pieces) of silver: and they brought Joseph into Egypt.** ≈ Why would a shepherd sell or give away one of his sheep? Well, most people trade things for gain. Matthew 4:8 & 9 exemplifies the main reason shepherds trade back souls. ≈ **AGAIN, THE DEVIL TAKETH HIM UP INTO AN EXCEEDING HIGH MOUNTAIN, AND SHEWETH HIM ALL THE KINGDOMS OF THE WORLD, AND THE GLORY OF THEM; AND SAITH UNTO HIM, ALL THESE THINGS WILL I GIVE THEE, IF THOU WILT FALL DOWN AND WORSHIP ME.** ≈ In the last 20 years, how many ministers have we seen defrocked and even jailed, having succumbed to this ploy of Satan?

---

[55] Jn 6:37.

Wyatt Earp in the movie, Gunfight at the O.K. Corral, made a joke to a corrupt sheriff. The sheriff boasted that due to his corruption he had plenty money in the bank and one hundred head of cattle. Wyatt replied the wages of sin must be rising! Despite Wyatt's wit, the fact is that there has been no raise in Satan's kingdom. Satan still pays the same wages as he did the day evil was found in him…Death! However, I understand that he extends an easy, extensive line of credit to those that apply however.

When Jesus died, all power over death, the grave, in Heaven, and earth was given to Him (Matt 28:18) ≈ **AND JESUS CAME AND SPAKE UNTO THEM, SAYING, ALL POWER IS GIVEN UNTO ME IN HEAVEN AND IN EARTH,** ≈ but we have abdicated the earthly seat again. The scriptures say that if you bind up the strong man you can take his house. This is what Satan always tries to do (that is why he deals with kings, heads of state, pastors and heads of ministry). However, Satan does not know all the plans of the Father as indicated by this scripture. (1 Cor 2:8) ≈ **Which none of the princes of this world knew: for had they known (it), they would not have crucified the Lord of Glory.** ≈

By killing Jesus Satan did not destroy the house but lost power over the grave. Much like the School of Life[56], Satan the embalmer of the flesh was a master of claiming bodies[57] and souls. But the Redeemer closed his school forever. Now only those seeking embalming need to go see Satan. All of his clients (except those sent) go to him much as people in the heyday of Egypt went to the School of Life. They went looking for eternal life through embalming but found only death. Eternal life comes only through Christ.

When Jesus prepared for arrest, the scriptures show how much authority Jesus actually had even while He was in the flesh. (Luke 22:53) ≈ **WHEN I WAS DAILY WITH YOU IN THE TEMPLE, YE STRETCHED FORTH NO HANDS AGAINST ME: BUT THIS IS YOUR HOUR, AND THE POWER OF DARKNESS.** ≈ He duly informed the men that they could arrest Him for His task was done; this is important to us for three reasons:

---

[56] This was school where Egyptians learned to embalm, which was supposed to grant life eternal. Embalming was very expensive and although it was filthy work, the school commanded much respect.

[57] (Jude 1: 9) ≈ **Yet Michael the archangel, when contending with the devil he disputed about the body of Moses, durst not bring against him a railing accusation, but said, The Lord rebuke thee.** ≈

i) It makes clear to us that the body is just a vessel, which has been given to us for completing God's work. The body is just a tool for our spirits to use to deploy God's saving grace in this world.

In a Star Trek episode called, 'By any other name' aliens from another universe came into this galaxy. Although they had bodies, their forms were unsuitable to perform tasks in this galaxy. In order to complete their tasks, they took human bodies and inhabited them. To be successful the aliens sacrificed all emotions and senses. Because they were unaccustomed to the nuances of the flesh they were living in, they got carried away and were soon overcome by their flesh.

The flesh carries with it senses. Through manipulating these Satan entices and controls us. The senses enable us to experience and enjoy life. However, like the aliens mentioned in the Star Trek episode senses can easily become intoxicating. They can overpower us and thereby dictate our actions. Senses are emotions foremost partners. Our senses determine whether we like or dislike something. This is actually perception; senses simply gather information, they do not assimilate any of it. When we interpret sensual information we then add our personalities and emotions. This is how we derive our likes and dislikes.

This is what happens to so many of us in our walk back to the Father. I say back to the Father because He deposited the spirits in the clay pots here on earth, and we spend a lifetime trying to regain admission to Heaven. (Gen 2:7) ≈ **And the Lord God formed man (of) the dust of the ground, and breathed into his nostrils the breath of life; and man became a living soul.** ≈

ii) It confirms the fact that while we are in God's service and adhere to His strict guidelines Satan will come against, us but he cannot prosper. Satan can harm us but not defeat us. (Job 1:10 & 12) ≈ **Hast not thou made an hedge about him, and about his house, and about all that he hath on every side? Thou hast blessed the work of his hands, and his substance is increased in the land. And the Lord said unto Satan, BEHOLD, ALL THAT HE HATH (IS) IN THY POWER; ONLY UPON HIMSELF PUT NOT FORTH THINE HAND. SO SATAN WENT FORTH FROM THE PRESENCE OF THE LORD**. ≈

iii) Most importantly it reasserts that the body is the Temple of the Lord. What is a temple used for? Temples are used to worship, they are storehouses for the things of God, they are to hear petitions, they are for baptisms, they are for sacrifices, they are for teaching, they are for weddings and they are for funerals. All of these things Jesus either did or exemplified as the true purposes for the temple.

In John 2:19[58] Jesus tells the Pharisees that He was the Temple, (2:19, 21, 22) but when people listen to the Spirit in the flesh they hear the sounds but the meaning escapes them[59]. In Luke when He tells those who came to arrest Him about the Temple again He was talking about Himself. In addition, what they did not understand was that while He was here in the flesh [60] walking and preaching they were powerless to harm Him.[61] Now, He was relinquishing authority to them in order that His flesh could be stripped from Him and His true glory and nature be revealed. (Also read Jn 19:11) He has to relinquish control to man but to His Father. For it was the Father's plan that He be crucified. The prophecy called for it and God set it to be for the purpose of redeeming the lost.

So again we see that man is powerless to hinder God's will, but we can choose not to accept His salvation. Whether or not we choose salvation does not mean He will not use us to further His goals; we simply get no reward for it. This is the difference between a bond servant and a slave. They both work but the slave gets no reward. Everything the owner gives a slave is to enable the slave to work. A bond servant is given tings that also improve their quality of life.

≈ AMEN ≈

---

[58] ≈ **Jesus answered and said unto them**, DESTROY THIS TEMPLE, AND IN THREE DAYS I WILL RAISE IT UP. ≈

[59] This is why He tells us who has ears to hear let them hear. This actually means receive and understand.

[60] His flesh also entombed Him but since he is the King the term enshrined would be more appropriate. For He too had to die in the flesh, so that he could have/regain eternal life.

[61] Even though people tried to stone Him several times but He disappeared. Luke 4:30

WORK AREA
LETTER V

≈

LURE, BAIT AND THE BEST WATERS

TOPICAL SCRIPTURES

(Mark 4:1) (Rev 3:15-16) (2 Sam 6:14) (Matt 7:16) (Gen 1:28) (Mark 2:17) (Phil 2:10-11) (John 1:1) (Matt 5:1-12) (Jhn 6:37) (Gen. 37: 4 & 25-28) (Matt 4:8 & 9) (Matt 28:18) (1 Cor 2:8) (Luke 22:53) (Gen 2:7) (Job 1:10 & 12) (John 2:19, 21, 22) (Jn 19:11)

1. WHY DO FISHERMEN USE LURES?

2. WHAT MADE JESUS' TEACHING SO POPULAR?

3. WHAT LURE DID JESUS USE?

4. WHICH WATERS DID JESUS FISH?

5. WHAT RESPONSIBILITY DO YOU BEAR FOR THE FISH YOU CATCH?

6. OF THE REASONS WE ARE LIKE FISH, WHICH ONE APPLIES TO YOU PERSONALLY? WHAT IS THE RESOLUTION?

7. WHAT LESSON IS TO BE LEARNED IN THE FACT THAT JESUS TOLD MEN WHERE TO FISH?

8. WHAT WATERS CONTAIN THE BEST FISH AND WHY?

9. WHY IS IT SO EASY FOR SATAN TO LURE IN FISH?

_____
_____
_____
_____
_____
_____
_____
_____
_____
_____
_____
_____

10. WHEN ASKED BY FISH WHY THEY SHOULD CHANGE WHAT WILL YOU ANSWER?

_____
_____
_____
_____
_____
_____
_____
_____
_____
_____

ADDITIONAL NOTES FOR THIS CHAPTER

LETTER VI

CLEANING AND SCALING

≈ **He that hath clean hands, and a pure heart; who hath not lifted up his soul unto vanity, nor sworn deceitfully. He shall receive the blessing** from the LORD, and righteousness from the God of his salvation. ≈ (Psm 24:4-5)

LETTER VI ≈ CLEANING AND SCALING
(REMOVING THE SCALES)

After catching a fish, it must be cleaned and descaled so that it may be eaten. A potato peeler with a serrated edge does an excellent job of removing the scales. Then you cut the fish open; remove the entrails and using salt and lemon to cure it prepare it to be eaten.

After fish are brought into the church from the world they too must be cleaned and descaled. After years of living, the pains of life and the disappointments generate scales (hardness) in our persons. We carry this pain with us everywhere we go and it adorns us like scales.

On the body of the fish there are scales for various functions. There are those that protect, some that help steer, and even those used for battle. People are the same, in them you will find four basic types of scales.

i) (Acts 9:18) ≈ **And immediately there fell from his eyes as it had been scales: and he received sight forthwith, and arose, and was baptized.** ≈ Scales over the eyes, are to protect them from seeing the ugliness of life, however, they often serve to blind us to the truth. In the movie, Chaka Zulu, the king, was warned that those who wish to be served by magic themselves end up being its servant.

In story about a man that went skiing the man went over a cliff; the only thing that stopped him from falling the entire way was a tiny plant jetting out from the rock face. When the rescuers arrived, he was clinging to the plant for dear life. The rescuer had to lower a ladder to save him, but the guy would not let go of the plant. The counselor told him to let go and he replied, *"If I let it go I will fall!"* To that the rescuer replied, *"If you don't let go your gonna die."*

The moral to this story, is that often the very thing that saves us from falling all the way is the same thing that will kill us if we cling to it too long. Scales have this quality also. Those of us who employ them usually end up their captives. Far too many people blind themselves to the truth of life, and as a result they always fail. For it is only the knowledge (seeing, feeling, hearing, and understanding) of the truth that sets us free.

ii) (Matt 19:8) ≈ **He saith unto them, MOSES BECAUSE OF THE HARDNESS OF YOUR HEARTS SUFFERED YOU TO PUT AWAY YOUR WIVES: BUT FROM THE BEGINNING IT WAS NOT SO.** ≈ Scales over their hearts, which have formed from the broken hearts with which they have had to contend. It is of these scales Jesus spoke of in Matthew 15. It is these scales over the hearts that cause the evil things that people do, think and become (Matt 15:18-20).

iii) (Titus 1:15) ≈ **Unto the pure all things are pure: but unto them that are defiled and unbelieving is nothing pure: but even their mind and conscience is defiled.** ≈ Then, there are those with scales on their minds. These are the people who have become so disenchanted with life that they simply choose not to deal with reality. Not only are these people hard to help, they are hard to reach for they have stopped listening to reason and feel beyond help.

iv) (James 3:8) ≈ **But the tongue can no man tame; it is an unruly evil, full of deadly poison an unruly evil which no man can tame.** ≈ The fourth type of scale is found on most people. These are on the tongue, man's favourite weapon. It is this set of scales that takes years to perfect. The armour on the tongue is fashioned and shaped into a perfect weapon that can attack both flesh and spirit. James 3:8 tells us that it takes God's help to remove these sales and tame this member.

Scales can also represent people in their various stages of Christian development. There are different stages of Christian development, each stage characterized by the type of change needed. The objective hardness of new converts is always a challenge, but understanding these four scale groups helps.

God created us for His glory and to worship Him, therefore, Christian development is not a matter of "if" but of "what stage?" These four types of scales much like the plant in the skiing story become our biggest hindrance to a healthy spirit-filled life. This is precisely why Satan (in the form of counselors and friends) is so zealous to assist us in forming defense mechanisms, for he too understands the true nature of the flesh and knows that any mechanisms we choose to protect ourselves actually serves him.

Believers it is these pieces of armour that we fashion that hinders our growth and stops God's free access to us. It is only in God's perfect kiln that His clay pots are molded and fired into His perfect pots. Any air bubbles or impurities in the clay stop it from firing properly. Hence, those things we choose to defend us are actually defenses for Satan to be able to hide safely in us, and block God.

How then can we protect ourselves believers? Let us see what the Bible has to say about armour (Ephesians 6:13-17) ≈ **Wherefore take unto you the whole arm our of God, that ye may be able to**

withstand in the evil day, and having done all, to stand. Stand therefore, having your loins girt about with truth, and having on the breastplate of righteousness; And your feet shod with the preparation of the gospel of peace; Above all, taking the shield of faith, wherewith ye shall be able to quench all the fiery darts of the wicked. And take the helmet of salvation, and the sword of the Spirit, which is the word of God. ≈ The armour spoken of here is not simply a hiding place as our defense mechanisms are. This is the only true armour there is, a lifestyle of righteous obedience to God. Only this knighthood results in victory. You may never be called, "Good Sir knight", but the title, "Good and faithful servant" will assure you salvation.

EYE SCALES

Luke 11:34 ≈ **THE LIGHT OF THE BODY IS THE EYE: THEREFORE, WHEN THINE EYE IS SINGLE, THY WHOLE BODY ALSO IS FULL OF LIGHT; BUT WHEN THINE EYE IS EVIL, THY BODY ALSO IS FULL OF DARKNESS.** ≈ When removing scales from the eyes, great care must be taken, as it is through the eyes that light enters the heart and soul, without them one dwells in Spiritual darkness. If we damage them, the fish will never be able to receive the light of Jesus Christ. The parable of the blind leading the blind exemplifies this to us. Therefore, sinners and new converts are not truly able to lead people to the Light-- because they have not been able to see it yet. This is one of the reasons sending new converts out to reach people is such a horrible idea.

Satan is a spiritual power outage, he blocks the sunlight and we are solar powered.[62] Much like plants we too photosynthesize, we transform Sonlight into spiritual energy with which we do God's good work. Vitamin D is the "sunshine vitamin" it comes from the Sun, and cannot be stored in the body.

Our vitamin "JE" comes from the Son of God and we cannot store it either, for the word tells us that out of us it will flow. (John 7:38) ≈ **HE THAT BELIEVETH ON ME, AS THE SCRIPTURE HATH SAID, OUT OF HIS BELLY SHALL FLOW RIVERS OF LIVING WATER.** ≈ This is why the Master says in His tutorial prayer. ≈...**GIVE US THIS DAY OUR {DAILY}**(emphasis mine) **BREAD**...≈ (Matt 6:9-13). We need to get a fresh supply of vitamin "JE" daily in order to satisfy the SDA (Spiritual

---

[62] Powered by the Son of God.

Daily Allowance) so that we do not develop rickets. Rickets is a bone disease resulting from a lack of vitamin D, which results in brittle easily broken bones. These weak bones prevent strenuous labour and physical fun. Perhaps this very ailment causes the bent broken backs of so many churches. Their lack of vitamin "JE" has given them rickets and hence they are unable to bear the weight of their tasks. This is probably why so many believers decline to make themselves available to do God's good works, for they fear being broken under the strain of His goodness.

Those of us in ministry that mislead the sheep, in any teaching, are leading them back into darkness, and this type of darkness leads only unto death[63]. Remember, Eve saw as soon as Satan scaled his eyes, and what Adam saw was beautiful. However, when Satan opens your eyes instead of the Master, it is what you cannot see that is important. Adam never saw death and that was what killed him. The desire for knowledge is good but only the knowledge of God leads unto life--all other learning leads unto damnation. For it is through the eyes that the heart sees, and when the eyes see the wrong thing then also doth the heart.

HEART SCALES

The hard heart is a result of fear, and fear and love cannot coexist

(Jer 17:9) ≈ **The heart is deceitful above all things, and desperately wicked: who can know it.** ≈

(Job 41:15) ≈ **His scales are his pride, shut up together as with a close seal.** ≈

(John 4:18) ≈ **There is no fear in love; but perfect love casteth out fear: because fear hath torment. He that feareth is not made perfect in love.** ≈

What we fail to understand is that it is only through our own suffering that we develop compassion. Without compassion, we cannot employ wisdom properly. Love without compassion becomes another emotion that we store up for a rainy day. Love allows us to feel for others

---

[63] (Rev 2:14-16) ≈ **BUT I HAVE A FEW THINGS AGAINST THEE, BECAUSE THOU HAST THERE THEM THAT HOLD THE DOCTRINE OF BALAAM, WHO TAUGHT BALAC TO CAST A STUMBLING BLOCK BEFORE THE CHILDREN OF ISRAEL, TO EAT THINGS SACRIFICED UNTO IDOLS, AND TO COMMIT FORNICATION. SO HAST THOU ALSO THEM THAT HOLD THE DOCTRINE OF THE NICOLAITANES, WHICH THING I HATE. REPENT; OR ELSE I WILL COME UNTO THEE QUICKLY, AND WILL FIGHT AGAINST THEM WITH THE SWORD OF MY MOUTH.** ≈

and to empathize with them. However, compassion moves us to do something to help those who are hurt.

For many people there is a fear of loving people, but to them being loved is more frightening. They have been beaten, abused, and hurt so often by those who say that they love them that they come to associate love with pain. Although love allows us to stomach pain, they are not codependent.

It is the hardness and treachery of men's hearts that make them so very difficult to deal with. (Matt 15:17-20) ≈ **DO NOT YE YET UNDERSTAND, THAT WHATSOEVER ENTERETH IN AT THE MOUTH GOETH INTO THE BELLY, AND IS CAST OUT INTO THE DRAUGHT? BUT THOSE THINGS, WHICH PROCEED OUT OF THE MOUTH, COME FORTH FROM THE HEART; AND THEY DEFILE THE MAN. FOR OUT OF THE HEART PROCEED EVIL THOUGHTS, MURDERS, ADULTERIES, FORNICATIONS, THEFTS, FALSE WITNESSES, BLASPHEMIES: THESE ARE THE THINGS WHICH DEFILE A MAN: BUT TO EAT WITH UNWASHEN HANDS DEFILETH NOT A MAN.** ≈

In older times the heart was considered to be the center of life because it produced blood and therefore life. The word says in (Acts 13:22)   ≈ **...when he had removed him, he raised up unto them David to be their king; to whom also he gave testimony, and said, I have found David the son of Jesse, a man after mine own heart, which shall fulfill all my will.** ≈ If we go according to the way, the term heart was used, it means so much.[64] Brothers and sisters it means that David gave God the things that kept Him alive, that kept His spiritual blood flowing, and that gave Him nourishment. Remember that God is love and therefore David's constant praise and worship fueled the very essence of God. This very hot fuel, much like lava it is also the reason that God's wrath is so severe. A great heart is essential for love, mercy, and compassion but it is also capable of great wrath and fury.

Satan convinces us through fear of judgment and hell that God cannot love us, but the bible tells us that a Father who does not reproach his child does not love him. The Father sacrificed His only begotten Son for us--do you think that He would hesitate to pass judgment on an unrepentant heart?

---

[64] The one thing it does not mean is that God and David have similar hearts. We know David's heart is proud and fleshly, this certainly cannot be the same with God. David means beloved in Hebrew, therefore a man dear to God. David's name by the way is mentioned more times in the Old Testament than any other. Test your Bible IQ. Edwards

(2 Tim. 1:17) ≈ **For God hath not given us the spirit of fear; but of power, and of love, and of a sound mind.** ≈ And as such we must also not fear the love of God. Mommy and daddy spanked or at least should have spanked us a great deal as children. Not only did we not fear them, we learned to respect, trust, and love them. Do not fear the Lord's discipline, but accept His loving hand and guidance.[65] Be more like Jonah, when or if we are punished and condemned by God always recognize what it is. It is His love for all of His children (even those cast asunder) that guides His actions. Scales on the heart prevent you from feeling love and giving love. Even when you do love it becomes warped as it did with Saul and David[66]. Beloved, gentleness can only be expected of the strong it is the weak who are cruel.

MIND SCALES

(James 1:8) ≈ **A double minded man is unstable in all his ways.** ≈ Double-mindedness is a result of scales on the mind. When these scales sediment, they prevent clarity of thought and as result we are unable to heed God. This type of scale usually results from the flesh winning small but consistent battles over the spirit. King David is an excellent example of this, he surcame to his fleshly thoughts instead of those of the Father. David started doing silly things, things for which he was judged, things that cost him four out of five children. When the scales cloud the mind, self-judgment becomes virtually impossible.

The parable set forth by Nathan against David found in 2 Samuel was beyond David's ability to fathom because David's flesh had so clouded his mind. This man who sat in judgment, settled disputes, and heard petitions all day was unable to see the error in his ways. Although there is no doubt that David knew he was wrong, the scales simply blocked his reasoning and remorse; they even blocked his fear of God. The mind scales even blocked his communication with God for it took a prophet, a man of flesh and blood to get David's attention.

The scales of double-mindedness became very apparent when Absolom was slain and David spoke to the prophet--but his message was to God. In a moment, which most parents would call rebellious, David tells God through the prophet that he no longer cared anymore about

---

[65] A recommended book on this subject is <u>Celebration of Discipline</u> by Foster.
[66] I Sam 19:10.

anything and he will mourn the loss of his son/enemy until the day he died.

Although he said he did not care, the scriptures tell us that after this, it came to pass that David sinned no more. Therefore, the scales can be removed from the mind--but at what cost to us if we resist the freedom and grace obedience allows[67].

When drawing plans and maps the legend always says, "to scale" and this is because the drawing is a scaled down version of the real thing. When you have scales over your mind, the same thing happens. Your ability to control yourself is diminished. Matthew 15:17-20 explains certain facets that come from the heart of man and without a sober mind no one can control them.

The most vicious and controlling facet we loose control of is fear. Throughout the Bible, fear is a stumbling block for many of God's workers. This thing called fear encompasses things from doubt to downright terror. The spirit of fear was not given to us by God, (notice it is called a spirit) so fear poses even more problems that the obvious.(Rom 8:15) Here is a list of some of the problems;

i) Some spirits are very hard to cast out (Matt 17:21) ≈ **HOWBEIT THIS KIND GOETH NOT OUT BUT BY PRAYER AND FASTING.** ≈

ii) If cast out improperly this one spirit will give rise to the presence of at least seven more spirits (Matt 12:43-44) ≈ **WHEN THE UNCLEAN SPIRIT IS GONE OUT OF A MAN, HE WALKETH THROUGH DRY PLACES, SEEKING REST, AND FINDETH NONE. THEN HE SAITH, I WILL RETURN INTO MY HOUSE FROM WHENCE I CAME OUT; AND WHEN HE IS COME, HE FINDETH IT EMPTY, SWEPT, AND GARNISHED.** ≈

iii) The host cannot cast out most spirits and most hosts that allow them in are not in their right mind--else they would not have allowed them to enter. Spirits cannot control us since Jesus redeemed us from the destroyer, however, like vampires they can be invited in. In actuality invitation[68] is the only way demons can get into us, once baptized into the body we have a hedge about us.

Just like in the Garden of Eden Satan is powerless to control you while you belong to God (John 6:37) ≈ **ALL THAT THE FATHER GIVETH ME SHALL COME TO ME; AND HIM THAT COMETH TO ME I WILL IN**

---

[67] Recommended on this subject: The Cost of Discipleship, D. Bonhoeffer. 1959, Touchstone books, New York, NY.
[68] How to try a Spirit… explains the many ways invitations are made.

NO WISE CAST OUT. ≈ However, what he is a master of is enticing you to leave the Father. Much like Esau, he easily convinces us to buy, trade, or sell our birthrights[69] and then we are powerless against him. Although we are strong, we are powerless against Satan without God. Satan you see uses tactics we do not understand for he unlike Jesus did come to destroy.

The deck is already stacked against us. Satan simply capitalizes on the flesh and focuses on controlling your spirit by use of your flesh. Whenever Satan tempts in the scriptures, he always offers the flesh the reward. He has nothing to offer the soul--especially after Calvary. In Genesis, he offered something to Eve's flesh and her soul, but now that the knowledge of Christ has spread, he no longer tries to make promises to the soul.

≈ **Ye are of God, little children, and have overcome them: because greater is He that is in you, than He that is in the world.** ≈ (1 John 4:4) The devil walks about as a roaring lion (1 Peter 5:8), which means that the only true way to resist Satan is to submit to God first. For it is then that Paul says He is perfected in our weakness. When Satan tempted Jesus, angels ministered to Him after the ordeal. If resisting Satan exhausted Jesus, what chance do you think you have?

Fear controls so many doorways to the other emotions--emotions like anger, hatred, prejudice, violence, and sadness and of course loneliness. Although, I consider myself to be a brave man, I lacked understanding of how fear truly grips a person; mind, body, and spirit. Fear can grip our spirits because we succumb to it and once that happens it blocks out all rational thought. My encounters with fear convinced me of two things; one was how great fear is and the other is how much greater God is.

My first encounter with fear was aboard an airplane on the way to visit family in the Bahamas. About 30 minutes outside of Atlanta, the plane began to buck, lurch, and roll. The first roll was to the right and the stewardess that was serving beverages railed against the right bulkhead. When the plane rolled in the other direction, the stewardess fell in the lap of a passenger and then the plane dropped, dropped, and dropped! It dropped for so long that I pushed the guy's chair almost completely in the folding position while (much to my surprise) the only sound that I could make was to yell the name -- Jesus!

---

[69] Rights given to us by the Redeemer – freedom, health, wealth, sound mind, etc.

The instant I called His name, the roughness smoothed. After the roughness smoothed out, it took the pilot approximately two minutes to come on the speaker, and when he did the only thing he did was to stutter and apologize. He said he was not sure what happened but hopefully it would not happen again. That did not make me feel any better that was only the beginning of the ordeal. Although the rest of the trip was perfectly smooth, I found no peace.

While in the Marine Corps, I repelled and fast-roped like (sliding down a fire pole) out of helicopters and turbulence never bothered me, but after that ride I could not relax. Fear began to take hold of my mind, and then it took hold of my body. Then it took hold of my soul. The first attack came against my mind, and it came to pass that every noise and every sound made me think the plane was going to crash.

Then absolute fear caused me to develop a sick stomach that caused me to really be uncomfortable riding in that tiny bathroom with no belt (as if a seat belt will really help in a crash). Then I became too frightened to read the word of God or to even listen to music about Him, I could not get my mind off the crashing thing. This is how Satan uses fear best, he makes it so that you are so preoccupied that you can neither worship nor praise… bondage begins here!

I felt exactly what the disciples felt when Jesus arose in, (Mark 4:39) ≈ **And He arose, and rebuked the wind, and said unto the sea, PEACE, BE STILL. And the wind ceased, and there was a great calm.** ≈ When I called upon the name of Jesus (actually yelled), the dropping ceased and the ride was smooth from then on. I learned something a lot of people already knew; conquering fear is only temporary as long as we allow the Holy Spirit to remain. Jesus becomes like Popeye's spinach--He gives us strength for that moment. Instead of dwelling there in the bosom and retaining the strength He hath given us, we opt to return to our previous state. The word tells us that if we return to that state as a dog returneth to its own vomit, the new state becomes worst than the last. (2 Peter 2:22) ≈ **For it had been better for them not to have known the way of righteousness, than, after they have known it to turn from the holy commandment delivered unto them.** ≈ James 4:7 tells us to submit to God then resist Satan and he shall flee, the trick apparently is staying submitted both in body and spirit.

The second encounter with fear was at my home, lying on the couch resting. The couch was right under a window, and I was laying on my back daydreaming. As I lay there I heard and felt a rancid breath on my back, which spoke to me in a deep whisper. The voice said to me three times, "I see you!" and at that point, I lay there paralyzed with fear. Several things ran through my mind at the time, one of which was if I lay still it would not see me. Secondly, I thought maybe it will just go away but it did not. It stayed there breathing down my neck, sending shivers of fear throughout my body. The next thing that I thought was that if I was fast enough I could punch through the glass, grab the thing, and wrestle it; whatever it was.

Fortunately, God intervened and allowed me to think clearly. What crossed my mind was, if it was outside the window and I could hear, and feel it could not have been of this world. The physical laws of this world are binding on anything of this world; therefore, I could not fight this foe in the flesh. I sat up, looked at the window, and rebuked the spirit and it immediately left. In this case submitting to God simply meant allowing Him to clear my mind for me and accepting His light. Submission is not always this easy, ask Abraham and Job but the result is always the same and that is that Satan is fled.

Unlike the first encounter, the residual effects were minimal but as with all sins there are always residual effects. And with all spirits there are always residual effects, and this is why Paul tells us to renew our minds daily and that we become new creatures in Christ. Only Jesus can cleanse all these scars and truly free us from bondage. Bonhoeffer's[70] cheap grace as he calls it (meaning isolating ourselves from life) does nothing but prolong the agony. Satan makes true victims. The true victim stays isolated living in fear because they are afraid to be hurt again. This is why Jesus said ≈ **HE CAME THAT WE MIGHT HAVE LIFE AND HAVE IT MORE ABUNDANTLY**. ≈ In Him there is freedom. In Him, there is life, for He is love -- perfect love and as we read brothers and sisters, perfect love casteth out fear.

Fear causes depression and depression causes all kinds of addictions. As long as the fear exists the behaviour will exist. This is one of the main reasons that Jesus Himself gave the commandments, (John 13:34/35) ≈ **A NEW COMMANDMENT I GIVE UNTO YOU, THAT YE LOVE ONE ANOTHER; AS I HAVE LOVED YOU, THAT YE ALSO LOVE ONE ANOTHER. BY THIS SHALL ALL MEN KNOW THAT YE ARE MY DISCIPLES, IF YE HAVE LOVE ONE TO ANOTHER.** ≈ In this commandment the crucial part is, ≈ **AS I HAVE LOVED YOU** ≈ for it was His perfect love that brought Him to earth to die for us. It is His perfect

---

[70] The Cost of Discipleship, D. Bonhoeffer.1959, Touchstone books, New York NY.

love that allows Him to constantly forgive us, and it is His perfect love, which saves us from His wrath. His perfect love also casts out fear. Therefore, it should be in His spirit of perfect love that we live. In this spirit, we should deal with other believers because we are free only because His love brakes all yokes.

TONGUE SCALES

(James 3:8) ≈ **But the tongue can no man tame; it is an unruly evil, full of deadly poison.** ≈ The final set of scales we encounter is found in most people, they are found on the tongue.

Prov 18:21) ≈ **Death and life are in the power of the tongue: and they that love it shall eat the fruit thereof.** ≈

(Gen 1:1) ≈ **In the beginning, God created the heaven and the earth... (And God said)...** ≈

(Matt 4:4) ≈ **BUT HE ANSWERED AND SAID, IT IS WRITTEN, MAN SHALL NOT LIVE BY BREAD ALONE, BUT BY EVERY WORD THAT PROCEEDETH OUT OF THE MOUTH OF GOD.** ≈

(Phil 2:10-11) ≈ **That at the name of Jesus every knee should bow, of things in heaven, and things in earth, and things under the earth; Philippians. And that every tongue should confess that Jesus Christ is Lord, to the glory of God the Father.** ≈

(Psm 22:3) ≈ **But Thou art Holy, O Thou that inhabitest the praises of Israel.** ≈

(Mark 11:22) ≈ **FOR VERILY I SAY UNTO YOU, THAT WHOSOEVER SHALL SAY UNTO THIS MOUNTAIN, BE THOU REMOVED, AND BE THOU CAST INTO THE SEA; AND SHALL NOT DOUBT IN HIS HEART, BUT SHALL BELIEVE THAT THOSE THINGS WHICH HE SAITH SHALL COME TO PASS; HE SHALL HAVE WHATSOEVER HE SAITH.** ≈

Brothers and sisters the word tells us that the power of life and death is in the tongue, now is time to increase knowledge! The above scriptures were chosen to elucidate the power of the tongue. Actually, when the power of the tongue is referred it is referring to the spoken word. Much like the heart is considered the center of life because of its function. The tongue is treated the same. The tongue is necessary for the formation of sounds and words, a deformed tongue results in a slurred speech or a lisp.

When reading the scriptures about the tongue allow for a new train of thought. How did God create and recreate the Earth? He spoke it into being. This is important because we must understand the esoteric nature of sounds and vibrations. If one understands the lesson in this portion, they will understand why no one is allowed to call the Father by His name, and why He has approximately 78 names (appellations or titles) in the testaments.

A word is a sound agreed upon, i.e. we form languages by agreeing that a particular sound means a particular thing. The sound however is actually the essence of the thing; it is sound recognition that allows us to communicate. When a sound/word is uttered we key on the sound and it conjures up an image and as a result we speak and think. If sounds make us speak and think, they can also make us feel, if they make us feel, they can be used to determine whether these are good or bad feelings. The words and sounds we use affect us in a variety of ways. A prime example of this concept is the term "disease" which literally means ill at ease or not at ease. In other words, your body is not at ease and as a result sick. What is my point? The point is when you get your body back at ease you will no longer be sick ~ this is why the devil torments you.

The storms of life are caused to affect you in this way, and this is why Jesus told us to tell these storms to be still. When we are tormented or tried, the body is taken from ease (commonly called the comfort zone) to ill at ease and this is why we get tired and sometimes sick. This tumult serves purposes for both God and Satan[71], good for One, evil the other. God uses this restlessness (Charles Stanley, How to Listen to God) is designed to get our attention and drive us to seek His peace. Satan on the other hand uses this disease to pull us away from God and away from people.

What does this have to do with the spoken word? If the Father tells us that if we have the faith the size of a mustard seed, and tell a mountain to be removed, the mountain will be removed. What type of damage do you think possible if this power was used for evil or personal gain (See story of Balaam). This brings us back to the power of life and death and the tongue[72], when you speak 'ill" to a person or of a person the vibration you send forth brings with it disease and discord.

---

[71] Remember Satan used to live and work in Heaven and undoubtedly retained some of the methods when he was cast out.

[72] Remember the Holy Spirit speaks in tongues and all languages are called tongues.

This is why the Bible speaks against curse words, which differ from cus words. "Cus" words are simply explicatives that mean absolutely nothing except to the people familiar with the usage. Curse words however are actual words or sounds, which are derived from other languages (tongues) and are used in spells and incantations.

There is a four-letter word that starts with "f" that the dictionary defines as slang often referring to copulation, but it also goes on to say that it means to damn. Magic books define this as meaning ushering/calling for damnation on a person. There are several problems with this term;

i) Only God can damn somebody, and when you call on Him to damn someone, you do two things. First, you judge someone as worthy of hellfire, and the word tells us judge ye not lest ye be judged.

ii) Secondly, you called upon the Lord your God in vain, not only in vain called upon His wrath and judgment in vain.

iii) You are asking for eternal damnation upon this person's soul not their flesh and this could pose a bunch of problems. God said ≈ **IF WE IN HIM AND HIS WORDS ABIDE IN US THEN ASK WHATEVER YOU WILL OF HIM.** ≈ He also told us that ≈ **WHATEVER WE BIND ON EARTH WILL BE BOUND IN HEAVEN.** ≈

iv) Since the "f" word is not of English derivation and it is part of a spell/conjuration (hence the word curse) when we involve this incantation we call upon whichever deity will respond. The Father will not, but even worse, we are actually practicing witchcraft. Witchcraft is rebellion and if in rebellion, we cannot be in the will of God.

Scales are the biggest barriers to cleaning the fish, because they become part of the body. Often the scales on the new fish are not half as prominent as they are on the church. Some churches have so many scales on them that they employ gargoyles on their exterior to chase some of the spirits away. Unfortunately, only good thwarts evil, evil does not compete against itself.

There are churches so scaled that they will not even allow the Holy Spirit to come inside for Jesus has a tendency to cast out evil spirits and demons. Therefore, they attempt to block Him as they always have through lost people.

When Jethro (the priest of median) told Moses about the temple hierarchy, he explained to Moses the need for help, for the task was too great for one person[73]. Elders and deacons are there to help share the

---

[73] Exod. 8:15-27).

burden of the leader, for they do have a large task. The best way to share the burden is on your knees in intercession and with singleness of mind. And then to allow the wisdom of the Lord to impart through you.

Armor bearing has its basis on the Old Testament and the need for armor bearers implies two things:

i) Firstly, you are going off to war or at least going out to fight. When soldiers are in a castle, they do not need the armour as the fort itself protects them. Many pastors regard their churches as kingdoms and they spend most of their time hiding in their fortress not going out to the sick; Many of the clergy insulate themselves with layers of people and they become almost unapproachable much like a pope or a king.

ii) Secondly, it implies royalty. Only royalty and the wealthy could afford the services of armour bearers. And although we are told that we are a royal priesthood,[74] this was meant to set us apart from the world not exault us above it. We are instructed to put on the full armour of God in order that we may do battle. (Eph 6:10-17) What this means is that we are God's armour-bearers. We are supposed to be clad in Him/His armour.

We are not kings that we need servants; on the contrary, Jesus Himself showed us that the true followers of Christ are servants and we are to bear our own armor. (Jn 13:45) ≈ **After that He poureth water into a basin, and began to wash the disciples' feet, and to wipe them with the towel wherewith He was girded. Then cometh He to Simon Peter: and Peter saith unto him, Lord, dost thou wash my feet? Jesus answered and said unto him, WHAT I DO THOU KNOWEST NOT NOW; BUT THOU SHALT KNOW HEREAFTER. Peter saith unto Him, Thou shalt never wash my feet. Jesus answered him, IF I WASH THEE NOT, THOU HAST NO PART WITH ME.** ≈ We are also to bear our own crosses, if able, and we are all to help the weak and the lost. Nevertheless, if you are constantly unable to go out to battle (unlike David against Goliath, and as did Joshua, Gideon, Samson, and Elijah) then perhaps you should step down from leadership.

Leadership by example is the message that Jesus taught, and He did not appear to be a weak and broken man. He only stumbled once in His entire ministry and that was carrying the cross; the dead weight of the tepid church. However, for Heavens sake, He was carrying the sins of the world, fighting off Satan's hordes and carrying a tree…and He did it all with a smile. We should gladly bear His armour and loudly proclaim Him

---

[74] For we are sons of the KING of KINGS.

King of Kings and Lord of Lords. To God ibe the glory for the good things He has done.

I have taken the liberty of including a few poems that I wrote over the years. These exemplify the power scales have on the soul and the heart. If I can have these feelings coming from an affluent childhood with most of the amenities of life, imagine some of the feelings the less fortunate have. Imagine the scales developed by those severely hurt and scarred by harmful people, harmful situations, and harmful churches.

<u>HATE</u>

The emotion hate is so beautiful a thing,
To a world of new sensations it will bring,
Even to the most noble men of standing,
It's consuming fire ever and ever demanding.

Hate will take a small hole and turn it into a door,
Take a near virgin and make her a whore.
Turn the best of friends into the archest rivals,
Turn a simple game into a bout for survival.

Hate can take the world so full of green,
And change it all into some fiery battle scene.
Hate will enslave a man because of the colour of his skin,
And make you kill his offspring because they look like him.

Hate will make you doubt the existence of the Creator,
And thus you become another Godless hater.
Hatred makes no deals--makes no points but does have a goal,
To make you destroy everything then turn over your soul.

HATE II

The emotion Hate is so beautiful a thing,
To a world of new sensations it will bring.
Even the most noble men of standing,
It's fire ever and ever demanding.

When it's light and you are alone,
Hate will make as though the sun has never shone.
It'll stay closer to you than your very best friend,
When used it'll always stand ready again.

It'll help you win battles and victory it's true,
But do you serve it or does it serve you?
It'll help you be a great shaker of men,
And when the applause stops it'll still be your friend.

When all said and done and no friends you have,
You and Hate can sit back and bitterly laugh.
Amidst the laughter you'll find out it's true,
That Hate is as lonely and frightened as you.

It needs you to bring its vigour to life,
It needs you, just like a butcher needs a knife.
It cannot exist until you give it breath,
The last exhalation before your own death.

HATE III

The emotion hate is so beautiful a thing,
To a world of new sensations it will bring.
Even to the most noble men of standing,
It's consuming fire ever and ever demanding.

Hate is the only lover that you can keep,
It will always stand by you as you weep.
But don't try to leave Hate or destroy you, it will,
Just as sure as it made you, it will easily kill.

You may find a new lover with whom hate can compete,
But you'll find through time only Hate makes you complete.
Hate is all you know--now a slave you've become,
To Hate's passions ---- Hate's will be done.

There will be times when you try to escape,
To try love another; but this is a waste.
Unlike other lessons in life's sad fondue,
The subject takes over and makes a servant out of you.

You'll learn to be faithful and a good worker too,
If not loneliness is the punishment prescribed for you.
You become constant companions and Hate leads the way,
It'll tell you how to act and exactly what to say.

After destroying your dreams and making friends walk away,
Hate will leave you and you'll beg it to stay.
Hate will turn to you with a devilish grin,
"I am through with you this time, to go after your friend"

How do you escape this Hate? Is freedom really true?
When you find out let me know, for I am a prisoner too.
I thought untrue the old adage about digging two graves,
Until in time I realized I too was hate's slave.

I WISH I COULD HAVE BEEN AN ABORTION

I wish I could have been an abortion,
A child that did not live,
Then I could have missed all the hatred,
All the "love" people had to give.

Think of all the kids they killed,
Of all the wombs they've torn.
They had to leave me to live,
...One who didn't wish to be born.

I wish I had died before birth,
Or better yet, not conceived.
And then I wouldn't have been,
One of those abused and deceived.

I never complained a lot,
never asked for very much,
save an occasional hug,
a kiss or soft warm touch.

But, those were not given--
so now I have to ask.
If you're going to love a child,
then why not let it pass?

And, now that I have lived,
and seen the lies and distortion,
I can safely say...
I wish I could have been an abortion.

SILENT TEARS

As I lay here in bed tears run down my face,
They stream off my nose then hit the pillow and waste.

I whimper in silence no moans, groans or sighs;
Just a poor heart tearing, as silent tears fall from my eyes.

I make no noise crying; but, scream out inside
Can't seem like a weakling --so my true feelings must hide.

I loved all my enemies and look what I got.
My mind's in a shambles-- my heart all in knots.

Dear Lord please try to love me--my heavenly
Father please try; But until such a day I'll silently cry.

I cry for the children that have all been abused,
and then I wonder why I couldn't have been one of the ones you choose.

You have all that power, but you won't help me none.
I don't know if you realize it but I too am your son.

Dear Lord and Master I've tried to comply.
You watched me at night as silent tears fell from my eyes.
I cried to you and begged you to make me your own
Allow me the honor to kneel at your throne.

You know I'm dead inside I need one of your gifts.
Only you can restore my will to live.

Now I'll lay here in silence and wait and wonder why,
but as long as I hurt I shall silently cry.

THE DEPRESSION SYNDROME

Ram shacking thru sordid memories;
Trying hard to find a place.
Where I was happy for awhile.
Or at least had a smile on my face.

Detesting yesterday's yield
Not knowing what tomorrow brings
Hoping that I repeat
Some of the past happy things.

Running off to nowhere
Getting there very fast
Trying to outrun the darkness
But it always seems to catch up and pass.

My heart is searching.
My hands and mind roam.
I'm searching in the past
For a safe port or home.

Depression is a nightmare
From which you cannot wake.
The infamous villain stalks you
And will not let you escape.

The pain is trapped deep inside
And no matter how you try to shout--
True searing pain and cries
Just simply won't come out.

Silently, laying there staring
Uselessly searching empty space
For something that looks pleasant
Maybe just a smiling face.

There's nothing one can do
Except lay and hope it will pass.
Hoping that the cruel being
Will release his often-fatal grasp.

You want to plea and beg him
Please do let me be.
I wish so very desperately
To once again be free.

Your pain causes you silence
Your misery causes you grief.
Your sorrow can cause blindness
That's why he's such a good thief.

He robs you of your senses
Then comes and takes over your mind.
You can't cry out or complain
As you sit and watch him rob you blind.

After he has finished
And nothing but a shell remains
He goes away whilst you recuperate
Then returns and does it again.

There is only one way to successfully remove scales from new converts, with the love of Jesus. He alone has the skill necessary to carefully, and permanently remove the scales. Prayer and fasting may remove the demons from the body but only the medicine in Jesus' healing blood can cure the sickness, bind up the wounds, and remove scars.

≈ **AMEN** ≈

WORK AREA
LETTER VI

CLEANING
AND
SCALING

TOPICAL SCRIPTURES

(Acts 9:18) (Matt 19:8) (Matt 15:18-20) (Titus 1:15) (James 3:8) (James 3:8) (Eph 6:13-17) (Luke 11:34) (John 7:38) (Matt 6:9-13) (Jer 17:9) (Job 41:15) (John 4:18) (Matt 15:17-20) (Acts 13:22) (2 Tim. 1:17) (James 1:8) (Matt 15:17-20) (Rom 8:15) (Matt 17:21) (Matt 12:43-44) (John 6:37) (1 John 4:4) (1 Peter 5:8) (Mark 4:39) (2 Peter 2:22) James 4:7) (John 13:34/35) (James 3:8) (Prov 18:21) (Gen 1:1) (Matt 4:4) (Phil 2:10-11) (Psm 22:3) (Mark 11:22) (Exod. 8:15-27) (Eph 6:10-17) (Jn 13:45)

1. WHAT PART OF THE FISH IS THE MOST IMPORTANT TO CLEAN; HOW IS THIS DONE?

2. HOW DO YOU DEAL WITH THE SCALED FISH?

3. HOW DO YOU HANDLE REJECTION CAUSED BY SCALES?

4. EXPLAIN THE DIFFERENCE BETWEEN HARDNESS SCALES AND DEVELOPMENTAL SCALES.

5. HOW DO SCALES DIFFER FROM THE ARMOUR IN EPH CHAPTER 6?

6. WHY MUST WE GIVE MORE CARE TO THE REMOVAL OF EYE SCALES THAN OTHER SETS?

7. AFTER YOU REMOVE THE SCALES HOW DO YOU TEND TO THE FISH'S FEELING OF NAKEDNESS?

_____
_____
_____
_____
_____
_____
_____
_____
_____
_____
_____

8. HOW DO YOU PREVENT THE SCALES FROM RETURNING?

_____
_____
_____
_____
_____
_____
_____
_____

9. WHY IS FEAR SO POWERFUL?

10. WHY DO PEOPLE HOLD ON TO SCALES SO VEHEMENTLY?

ADDITIONAL NOTES ON THIS CHAPTER

LETTER VII

≈

A TALE OF A WHALE

≈ (Am) I a sea, or a whale, that thou settest a watch over me? ≈
(Job 7:12)

LETTER VII ≈ A TALE OF A WHALE

From Jonah Chap 1- 4 ≈ **Now the word of the Lord came unto Jonah the son of Amittai, saying, ARISE, GO TO NINEVEH, THAT GREAT CITY, AND CRY AGAINST IT; FOR THEIR WICKEDNESS IS COME UP BEFORE ME.** But Jonah rose up to flee unto Tarshish from the presence of the Lord, and went down to Joppa; and he found a ship going to Tarshish: so he paid the fare thereof, and went down into it, to go with them unto Tarshish from the presence of the Lord. But the Lord sent out a great wind into the sea, and there was a mighty tempest in the sea, so that the ship was like to be broken. Then the mariners were afraid, and cried every man unto his god, and cast forth the wares that (were) in the ship into the sea, to lighten (it) of them. But Jonah was gone down into the sides of the ship; and he lay, and was fast asleep. So the shipmaster came to him, and said unto him, What meanest thou, O sleeper? Arise, call upon thy God, if so be that God will think upon us, that we perish not. And they said every one to his fellow, Come, and let us cast lots, that we may know for whose cause this evil (is) upon us. So they cast lots, and the lot fell upon Jonah. Then said they unto him, Tell us, we pray thee, for whose cause this evil (is) upon us; What (is) thine occupation? And whence comest thou? what (is) thy country? and of what people (art) thou? And he said unto them, I (am) an Hebrew; and I fear the Lord, the God the Lord exceedingly, and offered a sacrifice unto the Lord, and made vows. Now the Lord had prepared a great fish to swallow up Jonah. And Jonah was in the belly of the fish three days and three nights. 2:1 Then Jonah prayed unto the Lord his God out of the fish's belly, And said, I cried by reason of mine affliction unto the Lord, and he heard me; out of the belly of hell cried I, (and) thou heardest my voice. For thou hadst cast me into the deep, in the midst of the seas; and the floods compassed me about: all thy billows and thy waves passed over me. Then I said, I am cast out of thy sight; yet I will look again toward thy holy temple. The waters compassed me about, (even) to the soul: the depth closed me round about, the weeds were wrapped about my head. I went down to the bottoms of the mountains; the earth with her bars (was) about me forever: yet hast thou brought up my life from corruption, O Lord my God. When my soul fainted within me I remembered the Lord: and my prayer came in unto thee, into thine holy temple. They that observe lying vanities forsake their own mercy. But I will sacrifice unto thee with the voice of thanksgiving; I will pay (that) that I have vowed. Salvation (is) of the Lord. And the Lord spake unto the fish, and it vomited out Jonah upon the dry (land). of heaven, which hath made the sea and the dry (land). Then were the men exceedingly afraid, and said unto him, Why hast thou done this? For the men knew that he fled from the presence of the Lord, because he had told them. Then said they unto him, What shall we do unto thee, that the sea may be calm unto us? For the sea wrought, and was tempestuous. And he said unto them, Take me up, and cast me forth into the sea; so shall the sea be calm unto you: for I know that for my sake this great tempest (is) upon you. Nevertheless the men rowed hard to bring (it) to the land; but they could not: for the sea wrought, and was tempestuous against them. Wherefore they cried unto the Lord, and said, We beseech thee, O Lord, we beseech thee, let us not perish for this man's life, and lay not upon us innocent blood: for thou, O Lord, hast done as it pleased thee. So they took up Jonah, and cast him forth into the sea: and the sea ceased from her raging. Then the men feared 3:1 And the word of the LORD came unto Jonah the second time, saying, **ARISE, GO UNTO NINEVEH, THAT GREAT CITY, AND PREACH UNTO IT THE PREACHING THAT I BID THEE.** So Jonah arose, and went unto Nineveh, according to the word the Lord. Now Nineveh was an exceeding great city of three days' journey. And Jonah began to enter into the city a day's journey, and he cried, and said, Yet forty days, and Nineveh shall be overthrown. So the people of Nineveh believed God, and proclaimed a fast, and put on sackcloth, from the greatest of them even to the least of them. For word came unto the king of Nineveh, and he arose from his throne and he laid his robe from him, and covered (him) with sackcloth, and sat in ashes. And he caused (it) to be proclaimed and published through Nineveh by the decree of the king and his nobles, saying, Let neither man nor beast, herd nor flock, taste any thing: let them not feed, nor drink water: But let man and beast be covered with sackcloth, and cry mightily unto God: yea, let them turn every one from his evil way, and from the violence that (is) in their hands. Who can tell (if) God will turn and repent, and turn away from His fierce anger that we perish not? And God saw their works, that they turned from their evil way; and God repented of the evil, that He had said that He would do unto them; and He did (it) not. 4:1 But it displeased Jonah exceedingly, and he was very angry: And he prayed unto the Lord, and said, I pray thee, O Lord, (was) not this my saying, when I was yet in my country? Therefore I fled before unto Tarshish: for I knew that thou (art) a gracious God, and merciful, slow to anger, and of great kindness, and repentest thee of the evil. Therefore now, O Lord, take, I beseech thee, my life from me; for (it is) better for me to die than to live. Then said the Lord, **DOEST THOU WELL TO BE ANGRY?** So Jonah went out of the city, and sat on the east side of the city, and there made him a booth, and sat under it in the shadow, till he might see what would become of the city. And the Lord God prepared a gourd, and made (it) to come up over Jonah, that it might be a shadow over his head, to deliver him from his grief. So Jonah was exceeding glad of the gourd. But God prepared a worm when the morning rose the next day, and it smote the gourd that it withered. And it came to pass, when the sun did arise, that God prepared a vehement east wind; and the sun beat upon the head of Jonah, that he fainted, and wished in himself to die, and said, (It is) better for me to die than to live. And God said to Jonah, **DOEST THOU WELL TO BE ANGRY FOR THE GOURD?** And he said, I do well to be angry, (even) unto death Then said the Lord, **THOU HAST HAD PITY ON THE GOURD, FOR THE WHICH THOU HAST NOT LABOURED, NEITHER MADEST IT GROW; WHICH CAME UP IN A NIGHT, AND PERISHED IN A NIGHT: AND SHOULD NOT I SPARE NINEVEH, THAT GREAT CITY, WHEREIN ARE MORE THAN SIXSCORE THOUSAND PERSONS THAT CANNOT DISCERN BETWEEN THEIR RIGHT HAND AND THEIR LEFT HAND; AND (ALSO) MUCH CATTLE?** ≈

The story of Jonah, the prophet, is always useful to those in the ministry. It exemplifies so many of the people of Christ. Many times when the word of the Lord comes upon us, we also flee. Sometimes we flee out of fear or guilt, sometimes it is laziness; but most often, we have a snobbish, denigrating attitude. Much like the Pharisees, we hold sinners (fish/lost sheep) in bondage with our attitudes of judgment and contempt. Sadly enough, Jonah was being asked to intercede for this City because of their wickedness. However, Jonah did not want to go (Chap 4).

Most consider this simply a call to preach, but to Nineveh, Jonah was actually saving a city from God's wrath. This is the true nature of intercession, to place ourselves in between lost sheep and God's wrath.

Next to Jesus, the best example of what true intercession is to be is found in Numbers 22:22-34--the story of Balaam and the donkey. We will study this in depth later in the chapter.

After Jonah decided to flee the presence of the Lord, he ran to another city. What an offense to God, not only was one of His workers in disobedience and rebellion, but how belittling to think that you can run from God...is He so small? Many of the modern members flee, too. Some of them flee to drugs, sex or alcohol~ anything but deal with God's will.

When the storm came, Jonah was the only one on the boat in his own little world of peace that he had created. He had created this in two fashions. Primarily, he decided to disobey God and in doing this prepared himself to face God's wrath. Another contrivance that we as runners often create; I call it the, "*We ain't finished syndrome.*" In this fantasy belief, we find solace in the erroneous belief that God will not let us die because He is not finished with us and His will has not yet been completed. This presumes that God actually needs us and cannot succeed without us. Well, reread your Bible, and pay special attention to a man, a begotten man named Jesus and then reassess.

The men asked him to what he owed this peace in the midst of the tempest, and what did he do for a living. Jonah told them that he was a Hebrew, and a worker for the Lord, ≈...**for the Men knew he had fled from the Lord,** ≈ implies that they knew he was a man of God on the run. Even in the midst of our sin and our hiding, once we have been touched/called by God there is still something that sets us apart.

Although the men were afraid of drowning, they tried hard to row to shore versus throwing the man overboard, even over his pleas to be cast adrift. God in His wisdom and mercy does not cast us adrift nor does He allow other people to do away with us. He is always in charge and even when we want to die it is still His will, mercy and grace that abounds.

The men tried to do the right thing although they were not of the Hebrew faith they each cried out and begged to be released them from this chasm. They did not wish to drown, nor did they dare anger Jonah's God further by casting him adrift and killing him in deference to God's will. Sadly enough, it is too often the case that people of the world show and have more reverence for God than His own chosen people[75], or their leaders.

---

[75] Referring to all believers in Christ.

An apathetic church causes this type of peace. A church that allows believers to think that once saved there is no longer the threat of hell[76] as long as your tithes are up to date. This is exactly why Christ not only had to come, but also had to die to redeem the lost in the world and those who were just as lost in the church. When we run from God refusing to heed the call to help others, we leave Jesus bleeding on the cross, making His sacrifice a vain, Bible story. The church gave Jesus problems and it was the church that had Jesus crucified. Moreover, it is the church that is still crucifying Jesus--the Lamb of God.

After the other men on board ran out of options and because there was no other way to save themselves from the wrath of God they threw Jonah overboard. This is another lesson in the way God executes His wrath. Not only, those disobeying His will are punished, but those who assist and those who follow them[77].

Remember that Satan took one-third of the stars angels when he left heaven, dooming them to dwell in hell for eternity[78]. The church is still doing this with believers; false teaching is steering many believers away from the bosom of the Father. Then, God in His mercy has to send another to try to bring back this lost sheep. It is for this reason that the growth of the church has been stunted for so many years and for this very reason that so many believers walk away from salvation.

When I was in the Marine Corps, I was taught that killing a man was good, but to wound him was even better. This served two purposes; firstly, it took two other men to carry away the wounded. Secondly, even if you did not get to kill the other men you have exposed at least two other men to death -- three for the price of one.

The Prince of Darkness uses these same tactics against the saints. Wounding one requires at least one other to help. Swallowing one requires two or more to touch and agree and maybe another to intercede. So, by hampering one saint the lives of many others are effected or destroyed. The best employ of Satan's technique is when the shepherd of the flock is hampered.

We know that no man is too powerful to be hampered by Satan because Satan hampered the angels God sent. (Matt 12:29) ≈ **OR ELSE HOW CAN ONE ENTER INTO A STRONG MAN'S HOUSE, AND SPOIL HIS GOODS, EXCEPT HE FIRST BIND THE STRONG MAN?**

---

[76] Heb 10:26.
[77] Rom 1:32.
[78] Rev 12:4.

AND THEN HE WILL SPOIL HIS HOUSE. ≈ And (Dan 10:13) ≈ **But the prince of the kingdom of Persia withstood me one and twenty days: but, lo, Michael, one of the chief princes, came to help me; and I remained there with the kings of Persia.** ≈ confirms the use of both of these tactics by the Dragon to thwart the work of God the Father. Let us remember that although he can slow us and harm us the Father told us that no weapon formed against us shall prosper and that if we SUBMIT to God and then resist the Devil he will flee.

Unfortunately, there are far too many Jonahs heading the flocks that God herded together under their command. Much like Jonah, they too judge people as to who is worthy to be saved and who is not. They also count the work of the Spirit as their own providence, pretending they are the saviours of the lost souls.

I was in a service once and the pastor had a bright Red Cross[79] at the pulpit and it was illuminated at the time. Then the pastor walked up and turned off the light and begun to explain. *"The reason I turned the light off was that when I came to church there was no record given to me of any soul being saved. When we get back to saving souls then I will turn the light back on again."*

What is so sad is that the pastor was so close to the truth; but yet, so far from Jesus. The truth of the matter is that sometimes God talks to us through us when we will not listen to Him. The Lord was speaking to him and telling him that the light of his ministry had gone out and that the Spirit had stopped adding to his church daily.

The shepherd was not being a good steward and consequently had not been given any more sheep. This is too often the case with ministers. They start in earnest listening to God, then, they start to use scriptulaton and interpolation to disseminate His word. When their flesh takes control they begin to say, what I really think He meant to say was! Moreover, in this way we again not only block ourselves but also hinder the school from moving closer to Christ.

Even Jonah learned that before deliverance can come, you must submit to God your will, your heart, and you must command your flesh. It was not until Jonah did this that he was delivered. The word said that Jonah repented of his sin, praised the Lord for His grace and mercy,

---

[79] The cross or actually the "Tau" has long been a pagan symbol of sun worship. Moreover, the Red Cross or Rose cross is directly from Masonry, and adapted into Christianity through Catholic acquaintance with the Knights Templar. Refer to <u>Holy Blood, Holy Grail</u> for more information.

recognized, and reverenced His glory then; the Lord commanded the fish to spit Jonah onto the shore.

The Bible says that God prepared (fashioned, created, modified) a great fish to swallow up Jonah. This served a variety of purposes in that it took Jonah three days to try to figure it out. One thing it did was to give Jonah a lot of quiet time alone with God. It also showed God's power and His mercy, and most important at the time is it actually gave Jonah peace in the storm.

Sometimes the only way God can quiet us and get us to a place where He can quiet our storms is to place us in the belly of a whale. A place where there are no distractions and more importantly no demons to haunt us; a quiet, safe, warm place of shelter and reflection. For when God places you in a whale, not even Satan tempts or torments you. What irony, the safest place in the world for Jonah was the place he least wanted to be, consumed by a gigantic fish and at the bottom of the sea.

The beauty of God's grace provides that He even protects us when we opt to take off His armour. Despite our choice to walk away from God, until He takes His hands off us Satan is powerless to control us. Jonah, like many of us, was placed in the belly of the whale for punishment as well as his protection. When you take off the helmet of salvation, you open your mind to Satan's deceit.

In the belly of the whale however, we are safe from Satan for God is with us. The whale assures His will is done and prevents Satan from getting his way. The blessed truth of the 3 days under the water is that during that time spent alone with God Satan never approached Jonah.

Despite his rebelliousness, God permitted the great fish to spit Jonah onto dry land. Jonah ran from God and tried to enlist the help of man to escape. Through his sinful ways, he brought hardship on those around him and ended up drowning in the middle of a ragging sea. When we try to live life apart form God's will, we do the same as Jonah and end up the same way. However, through the grace of God when we abide by His law He does four things;

1) Captures our hearts and minds.
2) Changes the direction/course of our lives.
3) Allows the time for clarity of thought.
4) Puts us back where we should be, safe, dry, and changed.

Jonah describes the feeling of being cut off from God as being in the depths of Hell. For him to be isolated swallowed and helpless was Hell; but how many lost sheep are left in this predicament everyday by churches in the same city? How many lost sheep do we drive-by on the way to (play) church, who just like Jonah are consumed in their sin and feeling cut off from God's mercy and grace? These people are lost through no fault of their own and totally in the belly of their sin/hell and we drive by. Unlike the men who asked to help, we just throw them overboard because they smell badly, they are prostitutes, drug addicts, gay, or the wrong colour.

Let us discuss how most whales eat? As huge as they are they eat plankton and tiny shrimp most of them. They strain it by the ton as they swim and simply swallow it just like Jonah, just like the lost sheep. The whales just swim by all day swallowing up the lost sheep that we have cast asunder. Sheep left to either drown in the storm of their sin or be swallowed up by it and destroyed. For them just like Jonah, destruction does not come from being swallowed but by not being able to hear the good news of Jesus Christ. Because the church does not want to go and tell the world about Christ we allow them to die in the darkness. What a railing accusation against us! When we stand before the Throne and face the Creator and He asks us:{*WHOSE HAND CREATED THESE FISH? WHOSE HAND SENT REDEMPTION?*} And the final accusational question would be {*BY WHOSE HAND WERE MY FISH MADE TO BE FEASTED ON BY GREAT FISH?*} [80]

God is omnipresent, and sometimes we forget this, we believe that we can be cut off from Him. This was Jonah's next lesson and the purpose for this entire episode in Jonah's life. Nevertheless, the lesson applies to all of the fishers of men, and God Himself directly explains this in chapter four. God asks Jonah why he was mad about the death of the gourd, and then He asked him why should he be mad at all? God told Jonah that he has neither right nor cause to be mad or hurt for he had nothing to do with the creation of the gourd. Just as Jonah had nothing to do with the gourd, we have nothing to do with the creation of sheep. We certainly are not qualified to judge them or shun them.

As we live in our safe homes and wallow in our flesh, while our lost brothers and sisters fester and die. Who are we to cast opinion on the working of the Lord our God that was, is, and is to be? Who are we to let God's people die and be consumed by sin while we sit by and enjoy the fruits of God's labour. Like Jonah, God is telling us that He made all of

---

[80] Italics mine, to indicate vocabulary, but they are not bold nor are they highlighted. They are not the actual words of God nor can they be found in the scriptures. They are used to admonish us to heed the spessons that have been set forth for us to reproach our lethargy in the good works for which we have been called.

our comforts that we enjoy and relish so greatly, but He made them for all of His children to enjoy and share.

Heaven was created for all of God's children, and we, the selfish brothers are acting just like our ancestor, Cain. We are committing spiritual murder everyday, and committing adultery with the world everyday. Allowing our brothers and sisters to be consumed by great fish; while we argue over the toys that our Father gave us. God also reminds us that much like Bill Cosby is famous for saying, *"I brought you into this world and I can take you out!"* More applicable to this scripture is that God tells us that He gives us the toys He desires to give us. If we accept, or gain, or use them for the wrong thing He will take them away just as easily as He gives them.

We glossed over the story or Balaam and the donkey, but this letter would not be complete without explaining the true nature of intercession. (Numbers 22:22-34) ≈ **God's anger was kindled because he went: and the angel of the Lord stood in the way for an adversary against him. Now he was riding upon his ass, and his two servants (were) with him. And the ass saw the angel of the Lord standing in the way, and his sword drawn in his hand: and the ass turned aside out of the way, and went into the field: and Balaam smote the ass, to turn her into the way. But the angel of the Lord stood in a path of the vineyards, a wall (being) on this side and a wall on that side. And when the ass saw the angel of the Lord, she thrust herself unto the wall, and crushed Balaam's foot against the wall: and he smote her again. And the angel of the Lord went further, and stood in a narrow place, where (was) no way to turn either to the right hand or to the left. And when the ass saw the angel of the Lord, she fell down under Balaam: and Balaam's anger was kindled, and he smote the ass with a staff. And the Lord opened the mouth of the ass, and she said unto Balaam, What have I done unto thee that thou hast smitten me these three times. And Balaam said unto the ass, Because thou hast mocked me: I would there were a sword in mine hand, for now would I kill thee. And the ass said unto Balaam, (Am) not I thine ass, upon which thou hast ridden ever since (I was) to unto this day? Was I ever wont to do so unto thee? And he said, Nay. Then the Lord opened the eyes of Balaam[81], and he saw the angel of the Lord standing in the way, and his sword drawn in his hand: and he bowed down his head, and fell flat on his**

---

[81] Even in this, we see the glory of the Lord for it was He that opened Balaam's eyes.

face. And the angel of the Lord said unto him, Wherefore hast thou smitten thine ass these three times? Behold, I went out to withstand thee, because (thy) way is perverse before me: And the ass saw me, and turned from me these three times: unless she had turned from me, surely now also I had slain thee, and saved her alive. And Balaam said unto the angel of the Lord, I have sinned; for I knew not that thou stoodest in the way against me: now therefore, if it displease thee, I will get me back again. ≈

The story is about a fisher of men being given a task by the Almighty and getting sidetracked by his flesh.[82] God is angry with Balaam, so He sends and Angel to stop him from going astray. Balaam much like we described Adam in another portion of this letter was seeing more in his flesh than in the Spirit. Consequently, he did not see the angel, however, the donkey did and stopped out of fear of the angel; especially, since he had his sword drawn.

The donkey turned away from the path they were on, and Balaam struck her trying to get her back on the path. This is precisely what lost and confused fish do to those who are trying to get them back on tract--the tract that God put them on. They beat them, curse them, and strike out at them often not seeing their own demise and devolution.

Since Balaam turned the donkey, the angel hemmed them into a narrow alley and in doing so the donkey leaned against the wall pressing Balaam's foot. Again, Balaam struck the donkey this time with his stick. The hurt and lost will often strike even harder the more they are backed into a corner. The simple fact of futility is that the more you fight in an enclosed space the more desperate you become. This is because you fight harder but seem to accomplish less.

In the final act of desperation, when the intercessor can no longer bear the burden, they simply collapse under the strain. Jesus, in the garden of Gethsemane felt exactly this despair when He asked the Father if the cup could be taken away from Him. It was the strain of despair of intercession that Jesus was feeling at that point. He did not really want the cup to pass; He simply wanted a break from the anguish and strain of carrying all of us to the cross.

---

[82] Covered more in depth in the letter The other white meat.

God enabled the donkey to speak[83] to Balaam; and she asked what she had done to deserve being struck by Balaam several times. Do you not think that Jesus wanted to ask those who crowned Him and flogged Him the same question? It is so hard to understand the true pain of intercession until you have been scourged, beaten and betrayed by those whom you stand in the gap for.

God allowed a speculative lesson in life that allows for us to feel an inclining of what standing in the gap should be and how being betrayed and having to make very difficult choices is…they are called kids. It is through parents' trials and cares for their children that the true nature of intercession becomes known. The essence of carrying someone else's weight and their denigration and stripes because you love them…even unto death.

I would like to take this moment to mention a friend; a father of two boys. During this perilous time of war, he told me that he contacted the Marine recruiter to find out if he could get back in the service, despite having been out for at least 20 years. I asked him why and what he told me made my spirit cry. He said he tried to get in because he feared the reintroduction of the draft. He did not want his two boys to go therefore he tried to get them to take him instead. That is intercession! For God so loved the world that, He gave His only begotten Son, for us!

Balaam replied to the donkey that he struck her because she made him look stupid, and he would have killed him if he had a sword. This is exactly the same attitude that the church held towards Jesus, except they did kill Him because He made them look as silly and as treacherous as they were.

He too made them/us look bad by living the word and by calling the church back to the correct path. He was ridden to court and flogged, then crowned with our spurs. He was Forced to bear even a greater physical load, and then we road Him to Calvary where we crucified Him for trying to save us from a certain death.

The donkey then asked if she had ever done this before, why then was your response to your faithful servant violence. The intercessor did not understand why after years of spending time together with her master when she did something out of the ordinary he did not question her but smote her instead.

---

[83] When we walk in the flesh we are unable to hear the Lord clearly, thus when Balaam was outside the will of God he was not listening. As he was not listening to God, the Father enabled the intercessor to speak in a manner which the lost can hear.

When people are on the run from God, they live and hide in the flesh and they do not think as we do. Their spirit is not talking to the Father and as a result they cannot truly understand intercession, as it is done spiritually. It was not until God opened Balaam's eyes, meaning allowed his spirit to see again that Balaam understood what the donkey had protected him from.

Likewise, the books of (Matt 27:54), (Mark 15:39), (Luke 23:39-43) relate that it was not until after Jesus' crucifixion, that men saw Him truly as the Son of God. It is often at the last or even too late that we allow the Father to show us His mercy and glory. It is often just before we encounter His wrath do we catch sight of His glory on the way to His seat of judgment.

The angel then asked why Balaam had struck the donkey, and told Balaam that the way had been blocked for he had been contrary to God's will. The Father will always block us when we are out of his will; especially, when our disobedience will bring damnation unto other sheep. When God does open our eyes, the instant it happens several things becomes apparent. One thing is that His towering power is instantly revealed to us and His sheer majesty always makes us cower. (Gen. 3:8) ≈ **And they heard the voice of the Lord God walking in the garden in the cool of the day: and Adam and his wife hid themselves from the presence of the Lord God amongst the trees of the garden.** ≈

Another thing that happens is that our sin is instantly revealed to us, and we recognize our unrighteousness as unrighteousness. (Gen 3: 7, Matt. 27:54, Jonah 2) A third thing that happens is that we recognize how lost we were and that it was only through God's gracious mercy upon our intercessor that we are saved. It was only the relationship, which God has with them, that allows our sins to be overlooked and His wrath stayed. (Gen 18:23-33, Exod. 32:11-14) ≈ **And Moses besought the Lord his God, and said, Lord, why doth Thy wrath wax hot against Thy people, which tThou hast brought forth out of the land of Egypt with great power, and with a mighty hand? Wherefore should the Egyptians speak, and say, For mischief did he bring them out, to slay them in the mountains, and to consume them from the face of the earth? Turn from Thy fierce wrath, and repent of this evil against Thy people. Remember Abraham, Isaac, and Israel, Thy servants, to whom Thou swarest by Thine own self, and saidst unto them, I will multiply your seed as the stars of heaven, and all this land that I have spoken of will I give unto your seed, and they shall** inherit it for ever. And the Lord repented of the evil, which He thought to do unto His people. ≈, (Luke 23:34)** ≈ **Then said Jesus, FATHER, FORGIVE THEM; FOR THEY KNOW NOT WHAT THEY DO. And they parted his raiment, and cast lots.** ≈ Probably the most important thing we realize is the peril that we are being spared by the hand of the Father. Yet as long as we see in the flesh, we cannot see our true foe for the Bible warns us that, ≈ **For the weapons of our warfare are not carnal, but mighty through God to the pulling down of strong holds.** ≈ (2 Cor 10:4). It is not until we are allowed to see in the Spirit that we actually get to see the weapons formed against us.

The angel told Balaam that had the donkey not turned aside that Balaam would have been slain and the donkey spared. There is always a reward for the faithful servants of God. The donkey's reward was to be spared as are so many of God's faithful. Jesus' reward for His intercession was as great as the load He bore.

Jesus' reward was the Crown of Glory, to sit at the right hand of the Father and reign for all eternity. As God rewards each with his own reward, the reward given Jesus is a true testament to the load He bore and the task He did. The word of God tells us that obedience is better than sacrifice (1 Sam 15:22). When we are called to intercede as all disciples are (Gal 6:2), to shirk this obligation is disobedience or as God calls it; rebellion.

In the book of Matthew Chapter 10:38 the Master informs us that, ≈**...HE WHO DOES NOT TAKE HIS CROSS AND FOLLOW AFTER <u>ME</u> IS NOT WORTHY OF <u>ME</u>**. ≈ In so doing He forewarns us that the road to salvation is not only a long trek but it requires a few things along the way:

i) We MUST follow Him both in terms of obedience and in manner.

ii) We must bear the weight of ourselves.

iii) We must bear the weight and burdens of ourselves

iv) We must be an example to others—even unto death.

v) If we follow Him, we must be crucified in the flesh, lest we will never be with Him in the Spirit.

vi) Our reward is found only through suffering and forging in the Father's good flame.

vii) Anyone who tries to go it the quick and easy way will NEVER be with Him.

viii) Without suffering, there will be no rewards, nor shall His glory be revealed and/or shared with you.

For many just like the rich young ruler, this task is too great a feat for them to even imagine. The Master tells us in (Luke 9:59), ≈ **NO ONE, AFTER PUTTING HIS HANDS TO THE PLOW AND LOOKING BACK, IS FIT FOR THE KINGDOM OF GOD.** ≈ In other words, No quitters! God will deal with failure in His mercy and glory, but quitting is disobedience and He detests that. Better for you like Samson to die trying to succeed in the midst of your failure than to break covenant with God. When Peter walked on the water in (Matt 14:29) and he faltered did the Master scourge him? No the Master, admonished his weak faith and extended the power (the hand) to help Peter back to right hood.

God will try you but has no desire for you to fail while you are going about doing His work. Much like the message He gave Gideon, we are what God says we are, but the choice to follow Him must be made by you and you alone.

≈ AMEN ≈

WORK AREA LETTER VII

A TALE OF A WHALE

Topical Scriptures

(Jonah Chap 1-4) (Numb 22:22-34) (Heb 10:26) (Matt 12:29) (Matt 27:54) (Mark 15:39), (Luke 23:39-43) (Gen. 3:8) (Gen 3: 7) (Matt. 27:54) (Gen 18:23-33) (Exod. 32:11-14) (Luke 23:34) (2 Cor 10:4) (1 Sam 15:22) (Mat 10:38) (Luke 9:59), (Matt 14:29)

1. WHAT IS THE IMPORTANCE OF THE JONAH'S THREE DAYS?

2. THE THREE DAYS REPRESENT WHAT? BY JONAH'S DEFINITION WHAT IS HELL? CITE SCRIPTURES.

3. COMPARE AND CONTRAST JONAH'S THREE DAYS TO JESUS' THREE DAYS. LIST ANY DIFFERENCES IN ACTIONS AND ATTITUDES AS WELL AS RESULTS.

4. WHY DID JONAH NOT WANT TO GO TO NINEVEH?

5. WHY DID GOD SIMPLY NOT KILL JONAH? (BECAUSE HE LOVES HIM IS NOT THE ANSWER.)

6. WHAT IS THE IMPORTANCE OF JONAH 4.

7. WHAT IS THE PURPOSE OF THE STORM AND THE BOAT?

8. DOES GOD EVER COMBINE HIS TRIALS AND TRIBULATIONS?

9. WHY WAS GOD GOING TO ALLOW THE ANGEL TO KILL BALAAM?

10. WHY DID GOD MAKE THE DONKEY SPEAK?

11. WHY DID BALAAM WANT TO KILL THE PEOPLE?

12. WHY DID GOD USE THE DONKEY INSTEAD OF A PERSON? CITE SCRIPTURE FOR YOU ANSWER.

13. WHY IS 2 COR. 10:4 SO IMPORTANT TO DISCIPLE MAKERS AND EVANGELISTS?

ADDITIONAL NOTES FOR THIS CHAPTER

PART II
ALMOST A CHURCH

LETTER VIII

≈

ME AND MRS. BONES...
(THE UNFAITHFUL WIFE/CHURCH)

LETTER VIII ≈ ME AND MRS. BONES
(THE UNFAITHFUL WIFE/ CHURCH)

There are three usage's or three basic types of adultery[84] in the scriptures;

    i) <u>**Sexual adultery**</u> (fornication, whoredom)

- (2 Pe 2:14) ≈ **Having eyes full of adultery, and that cannot cease from sin; beguiling unstable souls: an heart they have exercised with covetous practices; cursed children:** ≈

- (Rom 7:3) ≈ **So then if, while her husband liveth, she be married to another man, she shall be called an adulteress: but if her husband be dead, she is free from that law; so that she is no adulteress, though she be married to another man.** ≈

    ii) <u>**Spiritual adultery**</u> (Idolatry, covetousness, apostasy.)

- (Jeremiah 3:6-9) ≈ **The Lord said also unto me in the days of Josiah the king, HAST THOU SEEN THAT WHICH BACKSLIDING ISRAEL HATH DONE? SHE IS GONE UP UPON EVERY HIGH MOUNTAIN AND UNDER EVERY GREEN TREE, AND THERE HATH PLAYED THE HARLOT. AND I SAID AFTER SHE HAD DONE ALL THESE THINGS, TURN THOU UNTO ME. BUT SHE RETURNED NOT. AND HER TREACHEROUS SISTER JUDAH SAW IT. AND I SAW, WHEN FOR ALL THE CAUSES WHEREBY BACKSLIDING ISRAEL COMMITTED ADULTERY I HAD PUT HER AWAY, AND GIVEN HER A BILL OF DIVORCE; YET HER TREACHEROUS SISTER JUDAH FEARED NOT, BUT WENT AND PLAYED THE HARLOT ALSO. AND IT CAME TO PASS THROUGH THE LIGHTNESS OF HER WHOREDOM, THAT SHE DEFILED THE LAND, AND COMMITTED ADULTERY WITH STONES AND WITH STOCKS.** ≈

(Eze.16: 32-33) ≈ **But as a wife that committeth adultery, which taketh strangers instead of her husband! They give gifts to all whores: but thou givest thy gifts to all thy lovers, and hirest them, that they may come unto thee on every side for thy whoredom.** ≈

---

[84] For the of this purpose of this letter any reference to the wife or female is referring to the church and the Groom, Husband or man will be reference to God. Any relationship will be metaphorical to the covenant between Jesus and the church.

(Rev 2:20) ≈ **NOTWITHSTANDING I HAVE A FEW THINGS AGAINST THEE, BECAUSE THOU SUFFEREST THAT WOMAN JEZEBEL, WHICH CALLETH HERSELF A PROPHETESS, TO TEACH AND TO SEDUCE MY SERVANTS TO COMMIT FORNICATION, AND TO EAT THINGS SACRIFICED UNTO IDOLS. AND I GAVE HER SPACE TO REPENT OF HER FORNICATION; AND SHE REPENTED NOT. BEHOLD, I WILL CAST HER INTO A BED, AND THEM THAT COMMIT ADULTERY WITH HER INTO GREAT TRIBULATION, EXCEPT THEY REPENT OF THEIR DEEDS. AND I WILL KILL HER CHILDREN WITH DEATH; AND ALL THE CHURCHES SHALL KNOW THAT I AM HE WHICH SEARCHETH THE REINS AND HEARTS: AND I WILL GIVE UNTO EVERY ONE OF YOU ACCORDING TO YOUR WORKS.** ≈

(Isaiah 1:21) ≈ **How is the faithful city become an harlot! It was full of judgment; righteousness lodged in it; but now murderers.** ≈

(Eze 23:7 & 37) ≈ **Thus she committed her whoredoms with them, with all them that were the chosen men of Assyria, and with all on whom she doted: with all their idols she defiled herself 37 That they have committed adultery, and blood is in their hands, and with their idols have they committed adultery, and have also caused their sons, whom they bare unto me, to pass for them through the fire, to devour them.** ≈

(Matt 12:39) ≈ **But He answered and said unto them, AN EVIL AND ADULTEROUS GENERATION SEEKETH AFTER A SIGN; AND THERE SHALL NO SIGN BE GIVEN TO IT, BUT THE SIGN OF THE PROPHET JONAS** ≈

(James 4:4) ≈ **Ye adulterers and adulteresses, know ye not that the friendship of the world is enmity with God? Whosoever therefore will be a friend of the world is the enemy of God.** ≈

(Romans 7:4) ≈ **Wherefore, my brethren, ye also are become dead to the law by the body of Christ; that ye should be married to another, even to Him who is raised from the dead, that we should bring forth fruit unto God.** ≈

iii) <u>**Adultery**</u> (defined by lust and or covetousness.)

(Eze 6:9) ≈ **And they that escape of you shall remember me among the nations whither they shall be carried captives, because I** am broken with their whorish heart, which hath departed from me, and with their eyes, which go a whoring after their idols: and they shall loathe themselves for the evils which they have committed in all their abominations.** ≈

(Jer 3:9) ≈ **And it came to pass through the lightness of her whoredom, that she defiled the land, and committed adultery with stones and with stocks.** ≈

Language, is very important, we must be able to understand the particular application of the term or any of the sub-definitions. Therefore we must understand that the term "lust" is synonymous with adultery. When you read a scripture that includes either term or the theme of adultery the applications must be applied. The common theme of adultery in any of the three usages is the breaking or transferring of a relationship from one covenant source to another entity.

More simplistically written it is breaking a bond with "a" in order to enjoy "b". The key to basic adultery is the bond with "a". How then do covetousness and lust fit into this concept? The Bible tells us that if we have lusted in our hearts then we have committed the deed, (just as sure as if you have done it in real life.) The Bible tells us in the book of Matthew that things that come from a man's heart defile him. Therefore, we must understand that anything that defiles a man places him in an adulterous state with God. Our relationship with the Father is based on a covenant relationship, (Bought by the blood of Christ), obedience, and righteous living. When we willfully disobey His word, we practice witchcraft and therefore in bed with another.

Moreover, the sin of fornication, we are told is the only sin that a man taketh into his body. (1 Cor 6:18) ≈ **Flee fornication. Every sin that a man doeth is without the body; but he that committeth fornication sinneth against his own body.** ≈The body is the temple of the Lord. The word informs us and therefore when we lust, covet, fornicate, and practice infidelity or any sexual sin, it is like the moneychangers in the temple. We saw how He reacted to those individuals in the temple and they were just changing money.

Be clear, however, sex in and of itself is not an abomination, it was created and given to us by God; and indeed we were commanded to have sex. (Gen 1:28) ≈ **And God blessed them, and God said unto them, BE FRUITFUL, AND MULTIPLY, AND REPLENISH THE EARTH, AND SUBDUE IT: AND HAVE DOMINION OVER THE FISH OF THE SEA, AND OVER THE FOWL OF THE AIR, AND OVER EVERY LIVING THING THAT MOVETH UPON THE EARTH.** ≈ The commandments of

God whether articulated or not always have at least one condition to them; that condition is that they be done in accordance with His will (e.g. Marriage).

Therefore, everything God articulates as a sin can never be in accordance with His word. God clearly has told us:
- That any sexual practice outside of marriage,
- Any lustful or covetous behaviour,
- Extra-marital affairs,
- Sex with animals or children, and
- Homosexuality are an abomination to Him.

Despite all the arguments for same-sex marriages, the scripture is clear that same-sex marriages or relationships will forever be an abomination. The purpose of marriage beyond the covenant, relationship is to be fruitful and multiply. Jesus' relationship with the church was based on not only a covenant relationship and intimacy but also reproduction.

The regenerative principle was given to us to glorify God. Simply put same-sex intercourse can never comply with this command. (Psalms 128:3) ≈ **Thy wife shall be as a fruitful vine by the sides of thine house: thy children like olive plants round about thy table.** ≈

Moreover, the references to human marriages in the bible always refer to men and women. This accomplishes two basic purposes for marriage, reproduction, and that the man and the woman become one flesh. Going back to the Creation of man, God formed Him from the dust and then brought him to life. He then took a portion of the man's body and created another being of the same make-up.

Whatever God took from man during the creation of woman was never given back to the man. The re-integration of the missing pieces comes about because of marriage. What this means to same-sex marriages is that you have two-incomplete persons in a covenant relationship with God.

Believers let us break this down succinctly:
- (Matt 19:11&12) tells us that singleness is a gift. ≈ **But He said unto them, ALL MEN CANNOT RECEIVE THIS SAYING, SAVE THEY TO WHOM IT IS GIVEN. FOR THERE ARE SOME EUNUCHS, WHICH WERE SO BORN FROM THEIR MOTHER'S WOMB: AND THERE ARE SOME EUNUCHS, WHICH WERE MADE EUNUCHS OF MEN: AND THERE BE EUNUCHS, WHICH HAVE MADE THEMSELVES EUNUCHS**

FOR THE KINGDOM OF HEAVEN'S SAKE. HE THAT IS ABLE TO RECEIVE IT LET HIM RECEIVE IT. ≈

- 2 Cor 6:16 tells us that the body is the temple of the Lord. ≈ **And what agreement hath the temple of God with idols? For ye are the temples of the living God; as God hath said, I will dwell in them, and walk in them; and I will be their God, and they shall be my people.** ≈

- Gen 2:24 tells us marriage results in oneness (completion). ≈ **THEREFORE SHALL A MAN LEAVE HIS FATHER AND HIS MOTHER, AND SHALL CLEAVE UNTO HIS WIFE: AND THEY SHALL BE ONE FLESH.** ≈

- Matt 15:14 tells us the lost or unprepared (incomplete) cannot benefit (lead) each other. ≈ **LET THEM ALONE: THEY BE BLIND LEADERS OF THE BLIND. AND IF THE BLIND LEAD THE BLIND, BOTH SHALL FALL INTO THE DITCH.** ≈

- Gen 2:21 tells us that after making woman man was left incomplete. ≈ **And the Lord God caused a deep sleep to fall upon Adam, and He slept: and he took one of his ribs, and closed up the flesh instead thereof;** ≈

A synthesis of this information results in the following conclusion as to man's body. Man's body is the Temple of the Lord. When bricks are removed from the temple has, it is incomplete. After Adam's temple was made, bricks were removed. The gift given of singleness allows a temple to function when it is incomplete because the Holy Spirit completes the temple.

Without this gift we are incomplete temples and cannot function properly to lead other people to the Father. More importantly, this incomplete structure does not permit the complete indwelling and filling of by the Holy Spirit because the container leaks: it has holes in it.

Marriage is then the patch for the incomplete temple. Marriage results in oneness; not only completion but also unity. Thereby allowing that temple to be used to its fullest potential. This is why the majority of offices spelled out in the New Testament require marriage. Boone[85] asserts that marriage is a stewardship test wherein God judges our treatment of our bride in order to determine how we will treat His bride.

Our synthesis should spell out why same-sex marriages remain outside the will of God; the temple is NEVER complete. The blind cannot lead the blind and there is no unity (reintegration) of the flesh. Where

---

[85] Your wife is not your mamma. Boone, Wellington.

there is no vision the people perish. (Prov 29:18) ≈ **Where there is no revelation, the people cast off all restraint: but one who keeps the Torah is blessed**[86]. ≈ Now you have two incomplete people in an incomplete joining which results in an incomplete and uninhabitable temple.

Proverbs Chapter 31 gives the characteristics of a worthy/virtuous woman that if the church were the virtuous wife would readily apply. There is a speculative in each of the verses regarding the wife and how she should act, and how the marriage should work. ≈ **Who can find a virtuous woman? for her price (is) far above rubies. The heart of her husband doth safely trust in her, so that he shall have no need of spoil. She will do him good and not evil all the days of her life. She seeketh wool, and flax, and worketh willingly with her hands. She is like the merchants' ships; she bringeth her food from afar. She riseth also while it is yet night, and giveth meat to her household, and a portion to her maidens. She considereth a field, and buyeth it: with the fruit of her hands she planteth a vineyard. She girdeth her loins with strength, and strengthened her arms. Treasury of Scripture She perceiveth that her merchandise (is) good: her candle goeth not out by night. She layeth her hands to the spindle, and her hands hold the distaff. She stretcheth out her hand to the poor; yea, she reacheth forth her hands to the needy. She is not afraid of the snow for her household: for all her household (are) clothed with scarlet. She maketh herself coverings of tapestry; her clothing (is) silk and purple. Her husband is known in the gates, when he sitteth among the elders of the land She maketh fine linen, and selleth (it); and delivereth girdles unto the merchant. Strength and honour (are) her clothing; and she shall rejoice in time to come. She openeth her mouth with wisdom; and in her tongue (is) the law of kindness. She looketh well to the ways of her household, and eateth not the bread of idleness. Her children arise up, and call her blessed; her husband (also), and he praiseth her Many daughters have done virtuously, but thou excellest them all Favour (is) deceitful, and beauty (is) vain: (but) a woman (that) feareth the Lord, she shall be praised. Give her of the fruit of her hands; and let her own works praise her in the gates.** ≈

The speculative lessons covered are found in the next portion of this letter, these traits would apply if the church were virtuous.

---

[86] The World English Bible: Messianic Edition, http://www.ebible.org/bible/hnv/ 11/05/05.

i) ≈ **Who can find a virtuous woman? For her price (is) far above rubies.** ≈ Jesus would trust her and He would have no lack of gain. Gain in this instance would be followers-true followers.

ii) ≈ **The heart of her husband doth safely trust in her, so that he shall have no need of spoil.** ≈ The church would do Christ good all the days of her life instead of crucifying Him repeatedly.

iii) ≈ **She seeketh wool, and flax, and worketh willingly with her hands.** ≈ The church would be industrious, benevolent, and diligent about God's work.

iv) ≈ **She is like the merchants' ships; she bringeth her food from afar.** ≈ Like the ships the church would bring new souls from afar (lost sheep) ~the "food" that Jesus craves. Note here that the ships serve as only a vessel to bring the food they do not prepare it! That still is the province of the Holy Spirit.

v) ≈ **She riseth also while it is yet night, and giveth meat to her household and a portion to her maidens.** ≈ Rising early in the morning was always the custom of the Master, to separate Himself and to worship and pray to the Father. The food that the bride gives to her household (the body) is prayer.

vi) ≈ **She considers a field and buys it; from her earnings, she plants a vineyard.** ≈ Whenever a husband and wife plan their future and their success they confer and consider the risks and the congruity. The church (only after conferring with her Husband) considers a field--in other words found a need she buys it or takes it under care in the case of mission field, etc. From her earnings (which are believers) she plants a vineyard. The Vineyard she plants consists of the believers sent out to bare fruit.

vii) ≈ **She girds herself with strength, and makes her arms strong.** ≈ The strength she possesses is the joy of the Lord[87]. ≈

viii) ≈ **She senses that her gain is good; her lamp does not go out at night.** ≈ The good gain is the fold increasing and we know according to Jesus only the Father is good[88]. And that none are called

---

[87] (Neh 8:10) ≈ **Then He said unto them, Go your way, eat the fat, and drink the sweet, and send portions unto them for whom nothing is prepared: for (this) day (is) holy unto our Lord: neither be ye sorry; for the joy of the Lord is your strength**. ≈

[88] (Matt 19:17) ≈ **And he said unto him, WHY CALLEST THOU ME GOOD? (THERE IS) NONE GOOD BUT ONE, (THAT IS), GOD: BUT IF THOU WILT ENTER INTO LIFE, KEEP THE COMMANDMENTS.** ≈

except by the Father. The lamp never goes out because Jesus is the light of the world[89]

ix) ≈ **She stretches out her hands to the distaff, and her hands grasp the spindle.**[90] ≈ The sewing refers to the cohesion created in the body[91] By the saints by fellowship and togetherness[92].

x) ≈ **She extends her hand to the poor: she stretches out her hands to the needy.** [93] ≈ Her charity is beyond compare.[94]

xi) ≈ **She is not afraid of the snow for her household: for all her household are clothed with scarlet.** ≈ The church is not afraid because her Husband has and does provide well for her and the household. (John

---

[89] (John 8:12) ≈ **Then spake Jesus again unto them, saying I AM THE LIGHT OF THE WORLD: HE THAT FOLLOWETH ME SHALL NOT WALK IN DARKNESS, BUT SHALL HAVE THE LIGHT OF LIFE.** ≈

[90] (Acts 2:46-47) ≈ **And they, continuing daily with one accord in the temple, and breaking bread from house to house, did eat their meat with gladness and singleness of heart, praising God, and having favour with all the people. And the Lord added to the church daily such as should be saved.** ≈

[91] (Matt 18:19) ≈ **AGAIN I SAY UNTO YOU, THAT IF TWO OF YOU SHALL AGREE ON EARTH AS TOUCHING ANY THING THAT THEY SHALL ASK, IT SHALL BE DONE FOR THEM OF MY FATHER WHICH IS IN HEAVEN.** ≈

[92] (1 Cor. 1-10) ≈ **Paul, called (to be) an apostle of Jesus Christ through the will of God, and Sosthenes (our) brother, Unto the church of God which is at Corinth, to them that are sanctified in Christ Jesus, called (to be) saints, with all that in every place call upon the name of Jesus Christ our Lord, both theirs and ours: Grace (be) unto you, and peace, from God our Father, and (from) the Lord Jesus Christ. I thank my God always on your behalf, for the grace of God which is given you by Jesus Christ; That in every thing ye are enriched by him, in all utterance, and (in) all knowledge; Even as the testimony of Christ was confirmed in you: So that ye come behind in no gift; waiting for the coming of our Lord Jesus Christ: Who shall confirm you unto the end, (that ye may be) blameless in the day of our Lord Jesus Christ. God (is) faithful, by whom ye were called unto the fellowship of his Son Jesus Christ our Lord. Now I beseech you brethren, by the name of our Lord Jesus Christ, that ye all, also speak the same thing, and (that) there be no divisions among you; but (that) ye be perfectly joined together in the same mind and in the same judgment.** ≈

[93] (Matt 25:40) ≈ **And the King shall answer and say unto them, Verily I say unto you, Inasmuch as ye have done (it) unto one of the least of these my brethren, ye have done (it) unto Me.** ≈

[94] (Luke 12:32 & 33) ≈ **FEAR NOT, LITTLE FLOCK; FOR IT IS YOUR FATHER'S GOOD PLEASURE TO GIVE YOU THE KINGDOM. AIDS SELL THAT YE HAVE, AND GIVE ALMS; PROVIDE YOURSELVES BAGS WHICH WAX NOT OLD, A TREASURE IN THE HEAVENS THAT FAILETH NOT, WHERE NO THIEF APPROACHETH, NEITHER MOTH CORRUPTETH.** ≈

14:2) ≈ **IN MY FATHER'S HOUSE ARE MANY MANSIONS: IF (IT WERE) NOT (SO), I WOULD HAVE TOLD YOU. I GO TO PREPARE A PLACE FOR YOU.** ≈

    xii) ≈ **Her husband is known in the gates, when he sitteth among the elders of the land** ≈ Her Husband is known at the gates, where He sits among the elders of the land. Moreover, the bride brings such glory to her Husband that the elders praise Him for His magnificence. (Rev 4:4,10-11) ≈ **And round about the throne (were) four and twenty seats: and upon the seats I saw four and twenty elders sitting, clothed in white raiment; and they had on their heads crowns of gold.10 The four and twenty elders fall down before Him that sat on the throne, and worship Him that liveth for ever and ever, and cast their crowns before the throne, saying, 11 Thou art worthy, O Lord, to receive glory and honour and power: for thou hast created all things, and for thy pleasure they are and were created.** ≈

    xiii) ≈ **She maketh fine linen, and selleth it; and delivereth girdles unto the merchant** ≈ The tradesmen (men of the world) come to the church for ideas and teachings with which to clothe themselves, the bride does not go to the world. (Rom 12:2) ≈ **And be not conformed to this world: but be ye transformed by the renewing of your mind, that ye may prove what (is) that good, and acceptable, and perfect, will of God.** ≈

    xiv) ≈ **Strength and honour are her clothing; and she shall rejoice in time to come** ≈ She is clothed in the strength of unity, and the wisdom afforded by the Holy Spirit. Moreover, when her task is done she shall stand before the Lord and hear the words *Well done thy good and faithful servant!* And she shall rejoice…(Eph 6:10-13)

    xv) ≈ **She openeth her mouth with wisdom; and in her tongue is the law of kindness.** ≈ No unwholesome word proceeds from her.[95]

    xvi) ≈ **She looketh well to the ways of her household, and eateth not the bread of idleness.** ≈ She always teaches the truth and

---

[95] As it is written, life and death is in the power of the tongue. (Eph 4:29-32) ≈ **Let no corrupt communication proceed out of your mouth, but that which is good to the use of edifying, that it may minister grace unto the hearers. And grieve not the Holy Spirit of God, whereby ye are sealed unto the day of redemption. Let all bitterness, and wrath, and anger, and clamour, and evil speaking, be put away from you, with all malice: And be ye kind one to another, tenderhearted, forgiving one another, even as God for Christ's sake hath forgiven you.** ≈

lives the life. She never allows idleness and double-mindedness to fester and grow amongst her parts.

xvii) ≈ **Her children arise up, and call her blessed; her husband also, and he praiseth her.** ≈ She is a blessed mother[96].

xviii) ≈ **Favour is deceitful, and beauty is vain: but a woman that feareth the Lord, she shall be praised. Give her of the fruit of her hands; and let her own works praise her in the gates.** ≈ Favour and beauty are the popularity and fame of the church, and these are described as deceitful and vain but a church that honours and fears (reverences) her husband will be praised[97].

Ephesians the Fifth Chapter verses, 22-33 lists more attributes of a marriage are laid out. The letter to Ephesus asserts a variety of virtues that a marriage should posses, for both husband and wife. We all know that the Groom (Jesus) has done His part, but let us analyze the wives requirements and evaluate her performance.

(Eph 23-24) ≈ **Wives, submit yourselves unto your own husbands, as unto the Lord. For the husband is the head of the wife, even as Christ is the head of the church: and He is the saviour of the body Therefore as the church is subject unto Christ, so (let) the wives (be) to their own husbands in everything.** ≈ Tells us (the church) to submit ourselves to Christ for He alone is the head and the Saviour of the body. To submit is not a subjective posture, you either are submitted or you are not. When we opt to branch off from God's purpose for the church, we are not submitted to Christ.

Have you ever been driving along on the interstate and been struck by a sudden bout of diarrhea or nausea? Is this not the most inconvenient and annoying thing? How then does the church (the body parts) do anything without His permission? It is the same as the involuntary

---

[96] (Psalms 128: 3-6) ≈ **Thy wife (shall be) as a fruitful vine by the sides of thine house: thy children like olive plants round about thy table. The Lord shall bless thee out of Zion: and thou shalt see the good of Jerusalem all the days of thy life. Yea, thou shalt see thy children's children, (and) peace upon Israel.** ≈

[97] (Rev. 3:8 & 9) ≈ **I KNOW THY WORKS: BEHOLD, I HAVE SET BEFORE THEE AN OPEN DOOR, AND NO MAN CAN SHUT IT: FOR THOU HAST A LITTLE STRENGTH, AND HAST KEPT MY WORD, AND HAST NOT DENIED MY NAME. BEHOLD, I WILL MAKE THEM OF THE SYNAGOGUE OF SATAN, WHICH SAY THEY ARE JEWS, AND ARE NOT, BUT DO LIE; BEHOLD, I WILL MAKE THEM TO COME AND WORSHIP BEFORE THY FEET, AND TO KNOW THAT I HAVE LOVED THEE.** ≈

expurgations, the Head was not the initiator of the function and therefore just like we would feel about diarrhea He feels about the church having its own way.

(Eph 25 & 26) ≈ **Husbands, love your wives, even as Christ also loved the church, and gave Himself for it; That He might sanctify and cleanse it with the washing of water by the word.** ≈ His Water, Blood, and Words baptize us. The word says that we therefore are sanctified and cleansed. How many of us take a bath and then get out putting on the same dirty clothes and underwear?

The bride of Christ has traded her new garments for her old clothes and sin-stained underwear. In the traditions of marriage, we were supposed to get something borrowed, something new, and something blue. We borrowed the word of God and ran around the world with it, diluting it and censoring it. We received salvation as the new gift of love and grace that we have traded for acceptance by the world. And that which was blue is the Lamb of God, for blue is the symbolic colour for truth and fidelity. What better example of truth and fidelity than the Lamb who told us that He alone is, ≈ **THE TRUTH THE WAY AND THE LIFE** and **LO I WLL BE WITH YOU EVEN UNTO THE END OF THE WORLD.** ≈

(Eph 27) ≈ **That he might present it to Himself a glorious church, not having spot, or wrinkle, or any such thing; but that it should be holy and without blemish.** ≈ She is to be cleansed and purified by our sanctified behaviour. For our own reword for faithful service is a pure bride. (Ecc 9:9)

(Eph 28) ≈ **So ought men to love their wives as their own bodies. He that loveth his wife loveth himself.** ≈ He that loveth his wife loves himself because she is his completion and therefore the reciprocal is also applicable. He that hates his wife hates himself.

(Eph 29 & 30) ≈ **For no man ever yet hated his own flesh; but nourisheth and cherisheth it, even as the Lord the church: For we are members of His body, of His flesh, and of His bones.** ≈ If we the churches are the brides, we should be as well as being virtuous we will in turn nourish our Husband. For as we nourish Him, we nourish ourselves and bring about joy, peace and love. We were not only members of His body but we partook of His flesh too.

No matter what we do good or bad, we do to Him as well; but the virtuous bride was never described as doing her husband ill. So then, we the church are untrue and ill natured for we are not submitted and are not uplifting.

(Eph 31) ≈ **For this cause shall a man leave his father and mother, and shall be joined unto his wife, and they two shall be one flesh.** ≈ Jesus left His parents (creators) and came to us here on earth, and He, through His ministry and death, joined with His wife. In addition, we became one flesh with Him, we have become a diseased portion of His flesh, but we are still one.

(Eph 32) ≈ **This is a great mystery: but I speak concerning Christ and the church.** ≈ The author calls this relationship a great mystery but then tells us that he speaks of Christ and the church. Is it then that there is more to this mystery of Christ and the church or are we simply missing the message here, too?

Bride is a feminine characterization of the body of believers, therefore as such must have commonality with women. If this is not so why then of all the words in the Hebrew language was the word bride used synonymously with the church. Synonyms were used to make clear to the hearers and readers of the word what God meant.

This means that bride is the closest thing to His principle here in nature He could used to convey His message.

(Eph 33) ≈ **Nevertheless let every one of you in particular so love his wife even as himself; and the wife (see) that she reverence (her) husband.** ≈ Regardless of whether we understand this mystery or not we the wife (church) are admonished to reverence Him.

When the bride of Christ commits adultery with the world[98] she stands in adultery. Some churches have become as bold as the whore of Babylon is described. When we do this, we also give up our virtue and power to heal, cast out devils and do God's work. Although we have been redeemed, too many brides have again become adulterous and unfaithful. Is it a wonder that the Groom was angry? Beautiful as He thought His bride to be she was sleeping with another man. Probably telling him how great he was for being so good to her, taking all her sins into her recompense. Bearing his bastard[99] children, enjoying it, flaunting it before God and the world, what an adulteress!

---

[98] Rev 17:1-3.
[99] This term commonly used to denote a child born out of wedlock, this is not a judgment on single parents; this letter does not address this issue at all.

What does God think of an adulterous church?

We consult the word as to whores, adulterers and whoremongers. These descriptions speak to us about what has become the modern church?

(Pro. 6:23-29) ≈ **For the commandment is a lamp; and the law is light; and reproofs of instruction are the way of life.** ≈ The commandment acts to guide us and keep us from the shadowy realms of Satan. It also stands to correct us for the shadows are chased away in the truth of the light.

(Pro. 6:24) ≈ **To keep thee from the evil woman, from the flattery of the tongue of a strange woman.** ≈ The commandments are there to keep us away from the world that is as seductive as a woman but like the beautiful Satan is still evil. In addition, it serves to train our ears away from the seductive lies of the world, for by the word of God the sheep; all of the sheep will be saved.

(Pro. 6:25) ≈ **Lust not after her beauty in thine heart; neither let her take thee with her eyelids.** ≈ Do not crave the wiles of the world either in deed or in thine heart, for remember that it is in the heart that the will and the man himself is defiled.

The introduction of the veil to Eastern Society was an attempt to prevent this very phenomenon. Men are visually stimulated and just like Herrod[100] they are extremely given to the lust of the eyes. Therefore, the women were covered. Not for the woman's bad behaviour, but to circumscribe man's behaviour. Because men are so given to their sexual urges women had to be hidden away.

(Pro. 6:26) ≈ **For by means of a whorish woman a man is brought to a piece of bread: and the adulteress will hunt for the precious life.** ≈ Because of the weakness of man, the word tells us that He will be brought to poverty. Three great examples of the great lengths a man will go are Samson, David, and Solomon. Although these men loved these women, they allowed their hearts to rule them instead of ruling their own hearts. The word, however, does not simply warn us about women but it tells us that a whore will bring us low.

This whore destroys man because it is in her nature to have all, be all, and leave none happy for she is not. She is selfish and destructive catering to her own debase desires. The whore/world always looks for the precious life to destroy.

---

[100] Who merely watched a dance and gave away half his kingdom, then destroyed a vessel of God.

Darkness and loathsomeness cannot overshadow good, no matter the disproportionate amounts. Although good is meek and quiet it cannot be silent, and it will always outshine evil. Just as the Lamb of God outshone Satan and the whore when they mocked and scourged Him. They hung Him on the cross hoping to dim His light, what folly, in that everybody knows that the light illuminates more the higher it is. When they hung Him up, they exposed more of the world to Him than ever before, for He is the light of the world.

(Pro 6:27) ≈ **Can a man take fire in his bosom, and his clothes not be burned?** ≈ 28 ≈ **Can one go upon hot coals, and his feet not be burned?** ≈ When we play with dangerous things, the result is always bad. The world does not love you believer, and it never will accept you for they did not accept Him. (Matthew 10:22) ≈ **AND YE SHALL BE HATED OF ALL MEN FOR MY NAME'S SAKE: BUT HE THAT ENDURETH TO THE END SHALL BE SAVED**. ≈

(Pro 6:29) ≈ **So he that goeth in to his neighbour's wife; whosoever toucheth her shall not be innocent.** ≈ This is self-explanatory in the flesh but how does it apply to the spirit? Simply, the spiritual kingdom is a gated community; there are only two couples who live there. The bride and Groom and Satan and his bride…she is called the world. Therefore, whosoever goeth into the world shall not be innocent for they commit adultery as well as whatsoever other sins they commit.

Continuing in the study of the adulterous we move to Proverbs 7:11-27 (Pro 7:11)≈ **She is loud and stubborn; her feet abide not in her house.** ≈ The church spends lots of time outside of her walls trying to convince the world that she is true and earnest. The problem is that they are not our judges nor or they qualified to judge us. We are to be their barometer not the other way around.

(Pro 7:12) ≈ **Now is she without, now in the streets, and lieth in wait at every corner.** ≈ The world has lost her veneer of grace and mercy that was afforded her before the resurrection. Now that Jesus has come and died they have their sins revisited on them without any buffer or intercession. Those graces are saved now for His sheep and the new sheep.

(Pro 7:13) ≈ **So she caught him, and kissed him, and with an impudent face said unto him.** ≈ Impudence represents her brashness and brazenness to approach in the view of all, even knowing her condition in life. She presents her self unabashedly and with confidence. Just like the world aligning and affronting the church; she has no shame.

(Pro 7:14) ≈ **I have peace offerings with me; this day have I payed my vows.** ≈ She offers gifts of the flesh as a peace offering. She knows what the result will be to the holy sheep but she strives to bring them down to death with her. She feels that she has paid her dues and is now above or at least beyond reproach.

(Pro 7:15) ≈ **Therefore came I forth to meet thee, diligently to seek thy face, and I have found thee.** ≈ She therefore says to us that because she has no shame, guilt, or fear she has sought us out. The normal course of a harlot provides for her to be sought out, but the brashness of the adulteress affords her the gall to seek out the virtuous to destroy. This is why Revelations makes a point of saying the great whore of Babylon commits adultery with the church. For the boldness of the adulterous exceeds the boldness of even the harlot.

(1Pro 7:16) ≈ **I have decked my bed with coverings of tapestry, with carved works, with fine linen of Egypt.** ≈17≈ **I have perfumed my bed with myrrh, aloes, and cinnamon.** ≈ She adorns herself with whatever trappings she thinks she will need to seduce and appeal.

(Pro 7:18) ≈ **Come, let us take our fill of love until the morning: let us solace ourselves with loves.** ≈ She offers herself to him as a comfort and tells him to ease his woes and sorrow inside her. This trap is the ultimate death for so many, for in the very essence of pleasure, where comfort and fragrance abound, death is produced! From the undefiled marriage--bed life is the result of lovemaking but here in the folded sheets of the adulteress death and accursedness are the offspring.

(Pro7:19) ≈ **For the good man is not at home, he is gone a long journey** ≈ 20 ≈ **He hath taken a bag of money with him, and will come home at the day appointed.** ≈ The good man is said to have gone about his business and is expected to be home on time, he is unaware of his impending doom. For even as a fallen sinner, it is beyond his fathoming exactly what this contriver has in store for him. He is weak and unfaithful but he is not necessarily evil. The adulteress, however, is evil, destructive, and malevolent. His desire is to please himself and hers is to destroy.

(Pro 7:21) ≈ **With her much fair speech she caused him to yield, with the flattering of her lips she forced him.** ≈ 22 ≈ **He goeth after her straightway, as an ox goeth to the slaughter, or as a fool** to the correction of the stocks. ≈ 23 ≈ **Till a dart strike through his liver; as a bird hasteth to the snare, and knoweth not that it is for his life.** ≈ For so many weak foundationless Christians, the deceiver is too much to defeat. He adorns himself as he did in Eden with the appearance of life and contentment but only brings about death. The foolish gullible men, those given dominion over the earth, are still falling prey to the wiles of a woman because they have yet to gain dominion over themselves. The adulteress thrives where lust, sloth and uncommittedness exist. For the truly faithful man/church, that is like Joseph was will always flee death and the folds thereof for he loves God and therefore loves life.

(Pro 7:24) ≈ **Hearken unto me now therefore, O ye children, and attend to the words of my mouth.** ≈ 25 ≈ **Let not thine heart decline to her ways, go not astray in her paths.** ≈The warning is set out for all of us who are weak and unsettled. The adulteress represents any tool/device or means that Satan can employ to dissuade us from being good servants of Christ. We are warned not to decline to her ways, which means that succumbing to her ways, our hearts are defiled and therefore the man is then defiled. The decline necessary to accept her ways brings about devastation and alters the man for his countenance must first be changed from righteousness to allowing the flesh again to reign.

(Pro 7:26) ≈ **For she hath cast down many wounded: yea, many strong men have been slain by her.** ≈ The power of the adulteress has overpowered many strong men. The word tells us and she has cast down many men. The strong man in the church must be bound first according to the word, and we see that she has cast down many strong men. Therefore, many churches are destroyed by her power and many more will be. The word tells us that we must not let our hearts decline to her paths, and we have seen so many members fall by the wayside. Much like a love-starved teenager, they sit and wait on a dream that cannot come true. They wait on a suitor who promised to marry in the morning but at dawn is gone leaving behind broken virtue, broken dreams, and broken hearts.

(Pro 7:27) ≈ **Her house is the way to hell, going down to the chambers of death.** ≈ Our bodies are the temples of the Lord; yet, the word calls her body a chamber of death. Jesus already conquered death and the grave; He went down into the grave once for us and there is no mention of Him doing it again. It is therefore incumbent upon us to avoid her house and not to let her into ours; for she has the power to turn our temples into tombs. We have been told how the Master feels about staying in tombs. Just as He did when they crucified Him and put Him in a tomb, He will roll away the stone; leave and seek glory and praise elsewhere.

Only God can again raise the Temple. It took three days for Him to rebuild His destroyed Temple, but that house was without sin. The word without means from the outside or to be outside, so His temple never had sin inside of it. However, when we join our hearts with the heart of Jezebel we not only allow our hearts to be defiled thereby defiling Him, but we evict Jesus and replace Him with something else.

Most often, the things we replace Him; with come in groups of seven, and as the letter, *Let my people know,* (informs us this number is the number of completion). Therefore, we exchange our temple indwelt by the Holy Spirit for a tomb filled with demons. The temple is going to be filled because nature abhors a vacuum what it is filled with is up to us.

Be careful with which ministries you collaborate and pray. For the ministries that were either built out of or that have slipped out of wedlock, all we can do is pray and intercede for them that they be admitted to the banquet for the Lamb. Marriages result in offspring here in the flesh, and they also do in the spirit world. All relationships with the bride of Christ and the world produce cursed offspring. (Hosea 2:4) ≈ **AND I WILL NOT HAVE MERCY UPON HER CHILDREN; FOR THEY BE THE CHILDREN OF WHOREDOMS.** ≈ And without the intercession of the Lamb may curse those unfaithful brides. (2 Peter 2:4) ≈ **For if God spared not the angels that sinned, but cast them down to hell, and delivered them into chains of darkness, to be reserved unto judgment**. ≈

I close this letter from one believer to all of us with the love of the Father. I plead with you fellow members of the body; take heed and stop sharing your beds and hearts with the whore of the world she does not love you, nor herself. Her way leads only unto death, not just the death of your soul but of your family, your church and your flesh.

≈ **AMEN** ≈

WORK AREA

LETTER VIII

TOPICAL SCRIPTURES

(2 Pe 2:14) (Rom 7:3) (Jer 3:6-9) (Eze.16: 32-33) (Rev 2:20) (Isaiah 1:21) (Eze 23:7 & 37) (Matt 12:39) (James 4:4) (Rom 7:4) (Eze 6:9) (Jer 3:9) (1 Cor 6:18) (Gen 1:28) (Psm 128:3) (Matt 19:11&12) (2 Cor 6:16) (Gen 2:24) (Matt 15:14) (Gen 2:21) (Prov 29:18) (Prov 31) (Neh 8:10) (John 8:12) (Acts 2:46-47) (Matt 18:19) (1 Cor. 1-10) (Matt 25:40) (Luke 12:32 & 33) (Eph 4:29-32) (John 14:2) (Rev 4:4, 10-11) (Rom 12:2) (Eph 6:10-13) (Ecc 9:9) (Prov 6:23-29) (Mat 10:22) (Prov 7:11-27) (Hosea 2:4) (2 Peter 2:4)

1. WHY HAS THE CHURCH BEEN UNFAITHFUL? USE THE SEVEN LETTERS IN REVELATIONS AS A REFERENCE.

2. EXPLAIN (MATT 19:11&12) AND WHAT IT MEANS TO DISCIPLES AND DISCIPLE MAKERS.

3. WHAT IS THE DIFFERENCE BETWEEN TEACHING CHURCH AND TEACHING CHRIST?

4. MATT 28:19&20 REQUIRES US TO TEACH WHAT?

5. WHAT THEN DOES MATT 28:19&20 MEAN IS REGARDS TO TEACHING DOCTRINE.

6. READ (EPH 4:29-32) RELATE THIS TO FISH AND FISHERS OF MEN.

7. READ 2 TIM 3:6&7 AND EXPLAIN THIS USING THE GREAT COMMISSION.

_____
_____
_____
_____
_____
_____
_____
_____
_____
_____

8. GIVE THREE TYPES OF ADULTERY AND AS A MEMBER OF AN UNFAITHFUL CHURCH DEFINE WHICH CATEGORY YOU FALL INTO. THEN WRITE WHAT STEPS YOU WILL TAKE TO CORRECT THE PROBLEM.

_____
_____
_____
_____
_____
_____
_____
_____

9. ACCORDING TO MATT 10:22 WHY WILL WE BE HATED?

10. PROVERBS 7:16 & 17 LIST SOME TYPES OF LURES THE WORLD USES.

ADDITIONAL NOTES FOR THIS CHAPTER

LETTER IX

≈

SINK OR SWIM
(BAPTISM)

≈ **The like figure whereunto (even) baptism doth also now save us (not the putting away of the filth of the flesh, but the answer of a good conscience toward God,) by the resurrection of Jesus Christ:.** ≈ (I Pet 3:21)

LETTER IX ≈ SINK OR SWIM
(BAPTISM)

Baptism has long been a topic of debate in the church. Some debate whether baptism is mandatory. Still others debate exactly when you should be baptized. There is even a discussion as to whether or not the Holy Spirit comes before or after baptism. Although these letters will not necessarily change opinions, they serve to give you the word as is written about a particular subject.

Let us start by defining what baptism is and what the word says it is for. The New Hebrew Version uses the word, "Immersion" instead of baptism. (Mark1: 9) ≈ **And it came to pass in those days, that Jesus came from Nazareth of Galilee, and was baptized of John in Jordan. And straightway coming up out of the water, He saw the heavens opened, and the Spirit like a dove descending upon Him. And there came a voice from heaven, saying THOU ART MY BELOVED SON, IN WHOM I AM WELL PLEASED.** ≈ The use of the term immersion implies a complete submergence into or underneath. Although there are traditions[101] that baptize by sprinkling or a cup full of water -- these would seem to be inconsistent with immersion. They are more consistent with an anointing as David alluded to in Psalms 23:5.

The term immersion is used because the concept of washing sins away requires complete washing of the body (corpse) the Spirit is dwelling in. ≈ **Know ye not, that so many of us as were baptized into Jesus Christ were baptized into His death? Therefore we are buried with Him by baptism into death: that like as Christ was raised up from the dead by the glory of the Father, even so we also should walk in newness of life. For if we have been planted together in the likeness of his death, we shall be also in the likeness of his resurrection: Knowing this, that our old man is crucified with Him, that the body of sin might be destroyed, that henceforth we should not serve sin. For he that is dead is freed from sin. Now if we be dead with Christ, we believe that we shall also live with Him: Knowing that Christ being raised from the dead dieth no more;**

---

[101] This tradition began when a Pope in his last days could not make it to the water to be baptized. The priests therefore brought it to him and this type baptism was born.

death hath no more dominion over Him. For in that He died, He died unto sin once: but in that He liveth, He liveth unto God. Likewise, reckon ye also yourselves to be dead indeed unto sin, but alive unto God through Jesus Christ our Lord.** ≈ (Rom 6:3-11)

Without completely washing the entire sinful body then, we do not get the full benefit of baptism. ≈ **And now why tarriest thou? Arise, and be baptized, and wash away thy sins, calling on the name of the Lord.** ≈ (Acts 22; 16). If we are not going to be cleansed of our sins then why be baptized at all? ≈ **Then said Paul, John verily baptized with the baptism of repentance, saying unto the people, that they should believe on Him which should come after him, that is, on Christ Jesus.** ≈ (Act 19:4)

(Matt 3:11) ≈ **I indeed baptize you with water unto repentance: but He that cometh after me is mightier than I, whose shoes I am not worthy to bear: He shall baptize you with the Holy Ghost, and with fire.** ≈

(Tit 3:5) ≈ **Not by works of righteousness which we have done, but according to His mercy He saved us, by the washing of regeneration, and renewing of the Holy Ghost.** ≈

In (Matt 20:22) ≈ **But Jesus answered and said, YE KNOW NOT WHAT YE ASK. ARE YE ABLE TO DRINK OF THE CUP THAT I SHALL DRINK OF, AND TO BE BAPTIZED WITH THE BAPTISM THAT I AM BAPTIZED WITH? They say unto Him, we are able.** ≈ The Master Himself speaks of baptism as a covering and a change. He tells the disciples that they had no idea of the things they were asking. He asked whether they could drink of "the cup" from which He had to drink?

There are three cups that Jesus was referring to and they are;

i) The cup of His blood referred to the sacrifice He is, and the sacrifices He made in His ministry. ≈ **LIKEWISE ALSO THE CUP AFTER SUPPER, SAYING, THIS CUP IS THE NEW TESTAMENT IN MY BLOOD, WHICH IS SHED FOR YOU.** ≈ (Luke 22:20).

ii) This cup of bitterness represents the taste of the sins of the world. ≈ **They gave Him vinegar to drink mingled with gall: and when He had tasted thereof, He would not drink.** ≈ (Matt 27:34).

iii) The third cup was the cup of crucifixion, death, and taking on the sins of the world. The task of being stripped whipped and hanged on high, left to bleed and die for the sins of the world ≈ **SAYING, FATHER, IF THOU BE WILLING, REMOVE THIS CUP FROM ME:**

NEVERTHELESS NOT MY WILL, BUT THINE, BE DONE. ≈ (Luke 22:42).

(Is 52:14) ≈ **As many were astonished at thee; His visage was so marred more than any man, and His form more than the sons of men.** ≈

(Heb 5:7&8) ≈ **Who in the days of His flesh, when He had offered up prayers and supplications with strong crying and tears unto Him that was able to save Him from death, and was heard in that He feared; Though He were a Son, yet learned He obedience by the things which He suffered.** ≈

In (Luke 24:49) The baptism He was referring to was the baptism of the Holy Spirit (Mk.1: 10)[102] and the power and responsibility given to Him because of the gift of this baptism. ≈ **AND, BEHOLD, I SEND THE PROMISE OF MY FATHER UPON YOU: BUT TARRY YE IN THE CITY OF JERUSALEM, UNTIL YE BE ENDUED WITH POWER FROM ON HIGH.** ≈

The second reason to get baptized is that Christ Himself commanded it. - Matt 28:19) ≈ **GO YE THEREFORE, AND TEACH ALL NATIONS, BAPTIZING THEM IN THE NAME OF THE FATHER, AND OF THE SON, AND OF THE HOLY GHOST.** ≈

- (John 3: 5) ≈ **Jesus answered, VERILY, VERILY, I SAY UNTO THEE, EXCEPT A MAN BE BORN OF WATER AND OF THE SPIRIT, HE CANNOT ENTER INTO THE KINGDOM OF GOD.** ≈

- (John 13: 8) ≈ **Peter saith unto him, Thou shalt never wash my feet. Jesus answered him, IF I WASH THEE NOT, THOU HAST NO PART WITH ME.** ≈

Many argue that this is contradictory to what Jesus Himself did; they say that He never baptized anyone. Verily, I say unto you that those who say this are in danger of being lost forever. For it says plainly in the scriptures, in both witness (testaments) that Jesus the Lamb of God baptized all who ever lived, but not just with water but also with His very blood. Lest you forget that when they pierced Him in the side water ebbed out, baptizing us all in both water and in blood.

The Baptist, as John was called baptized hundreds maybe thousands of people one by one heralding the coming of the King. However, when the King arrived, it was then done in royal fashion. Even

---

[102] ≈ **And straightway coming up out of the water, He saw the heavens opened, and the Spirit like a dove descending upon Him.** ≈

when crucified, the Lord was elevated to a place where He had to be looked up to; He wore a crown and a vestige, and in one deed He accomplished four things:
i) Redeemed dominion over the world.
ii) Baptized everyone with His Living Water.
iii) Baptized everyone in His blood.
iv) Forgave the sins of the world and His glory shone around.

This is why several things that He spoke of during His ministry no one understood. Because they would not take place until His death…but rest assured He left no stone unturned. The Redeemer even went into the grave and provided for those desirous to be freed to follow Him. Here are a few scriptures to assist you. (Isa. 44:3) ≈ **FOR I WILL POUR WATER UPON HIM THAT IS THIRSTY, AND FLOODS UPON THE DRY GROUND: I WILL POUR MY SPIRIT UPON THY SEED, AND MY BLESSING UPON THINE OFFSPRING.** ≈

(Joel 2:28 & 29) **AND ALSO UPON THE SERVANTS AND UPON THE HANDMAIDS IN THOSE DAYS WILL I POUR OUT MY SPIRIT.** ≈

(Mk 16:16) ≈ **HE THAT BELIEVETH AND IS BAPTIZED SHALL BE SAVED; BUT HE THAT BELIEVETH NOT SHALL BE DAMNED.** ≈

(Luk 24:49) ≈ **AND, BEHOLD, I SEND THE PROMISE OF MY FATHER UPON YOU: BUT TARRY YE IN THE CITY OF JERUSALEM, UNTIL YE BE ENDUED WITH POWER FROM ON HIGH.** ≈

(Acts 1:5) ≈ **FOR JOHN TRULY BAPTIZED WITH WATER; BUT YE SHALL BE BAPTIZED WITH THE HOLY GHOST NOT MANY DAYS HENCE.** ≈

(Gal 3:27) ≈ **For as many of you as have been baptized into Christ have put on Christ.** ≈

(Eph 5:26) ≈ **That He might sanctify and cleanse it with the washing of water by the word.** ≈

In the Old Testament, instructions were given in Exodus to take the blood of the Passover Lamb (a lamb especially set aside for the Passover) and spread it on the doorpost and lintel). It then says that when the Lord passed through He would not allow the destroyer to come inside and smite those inside the house (Ex 12 21-24).

In the book of Job, the word tells us that Satan conversed with God about what he called a hedge[103]. The hedge that Satan is speaking about is the hand or protection of God the Father. Satan's argument was that he could not tempt Job because Job was protected by God's hand. It was not until God gave Satan permission to torment Job could Satan do anything to adversely affect Job's life (Job 1:10-12).

How do these two passages relate you may wonder? A revelation from God answered this question for me. I was instructed to combine the aforementioned scriptures thus obtaining understanding of baptism by the blood of Christ. The effect being this; the blood of Christ brings about the hedge about us. For Christ is the true Passover Lamb, and it is the covering of our souls with His blood that prevents the destroyer from destroying us. Therefore, when the destroyer traverses the Earth back and forth he will not be allowed to come in and smite us. Because God's hand is about us…let us call this Metectors. When Jesus redeemed us, those of us who choose to adorn ourselves with His blood received the Metectors and thusly - eternal protection.

In the book of Exodus, the two door posts and the Lintel (top of the door) were marked with the blood of the lamb, but the ground or footstep was not. Those covered by that Baptism received the best that was offered in His covenant to the Children of Israel. However, this covering did not allow for the forgiveness of sins or repentance, and it did not redeem us from Satan's grasp. This covering simply protected us from the wiles of the devil.

The Master explains this better to us in (John 13:7-10) wherein He explains that Peter was partially covered, but he still had the filth of the world on his feet. Back in Jesus' time, everybody wore sandals and as such always had filthy, stinky feet. A person's feet were always an indication of where they had been. Thus as it is with our lives, our lives also contain footprints of our sins and lifestyles. Before we can get completely on Holy ground, we must also clean the crud from our feet (lives).

Jesus told Peter that if he were a bather all he would need was to wash his feet and he would be completely clean. Once we decide to walk away from our old selves into His new life and accept His yoke in total,

---

[103] A hedge being a very thick bush, this is almost impenetrable without destroying it or there being a hole in it.

He tells us that when we completely immerse ourselves including our feet in Him we will be completely clean.

The Passover covered us on three sides (head and two sides) but left the feet unfettered, for God kept much better records of our transgressions. With immersion in Jesus, we are completely cleansed and born again, of the Water and of the Blood. We were reborn in Jesus and the word says we become part of Him a part of His body. We are reborn both in spirit, (as we are in covenant), and in flesh (as part of His flock on earth). (Rom 6:4) ≈ **Therefore we are buried with Him by baptism into death: that like as Christ was raised up from the dead by the glory of the Father, even so we also should walk in newness of life.** ≈

The final reason for the immersion is that it identifies us as part of the flock and allows us to become our badge of office and authority. It gives us back dominion that Adam abdicated. (Luke 3:21-23), (Mk 1:9-13) and (Matt 3 13-17) all confirm certain points:

i) Jesus did not begin His work until after He was baptized.

ii) Upon being baptized, the heavens opened and Jesus was identified as God's Son.

iii) The Holy Spirit was sent down to Him in the form of a dove. (Possibly, the same dove that brought Noah the fig leaf.)

Remember Jesus told us that all we needed to do was wash our feet to be completely clean. Since He was born of the flesh, He too was born into sin but was without sin (2 Cor 5:21). Having walked the earth, He too had dirty feet and carried on His feet the woes of the world. God desires a clean temple to indwell.

As soon as the Master reemerged from the water, He was perfectly cleansed, without spot, or blemish. It was in this perfectly cleansed, sin-free vessel that the Holy Spirit came to dwell. Because His body was without sin it was a vessel worthy of all the spirit had to give, that was life, and light; and there were many witnesses.

We may follow the Father and become great at His works, but none will be called the begotten Son of God again. That vessel was specially prepared for the task of saving all of creation. Since this task was designed to be carried out by the Holy Spirit, it required a special body, and even that body had to undergo a refining process.

We too will be refined but take heed of this also my believers. If you read the accounts further, you will see that immediately after being granted the badge of power Jesus was challenged and tempted by Satan. Before God gives you power to do His work you have no ability to combat

Satan by yourself. It is as if you are in boot camp. It is not until graduation that they give you weapons and ordinance. Satan as your enemy cannot harm you while you stay covered[104] but he does not fear you either. When you become a full-fledged warrior for God, he becomes envious and tries to destroy you and your witness.

Are you saved without being baptized? The answer is yes--you can be saved and not be baptized[105]. However, the Cross baptized you in the blood of Christ--a public baptism is an allegiance with Jesus. It is an open acceptance of His sacrifice for your sins. It is like putting on a uniform. This lets the world know that you made a choice to follow Christ, and it is being obedient.

However, you will neither have the covering nor the power a baptized believe Has for their temple has been cleansed inside and out and is now ready to be completely filled by the Holy Spirit.

This brings this letter to the last point and that is whether you should baptize your children? I believe that the scriptures would indicate that the most important part of following Christ is the choice to do so. It is for this reason that immersing a child is not a good idea because we then put them in a position to break a covenant they did not even know they were a part of. As well as the fact that you put them in a position to receive a gift they have no ability to deal with.

Fortunately, God will not endow children with this gift too early in life -- just like you would not give your child a motorcycle. Even in karate, children who achieve the Black belt are required to retest for the same belt when they turn 18. This serves to make sure they understand the duties and responsibilities of that position. If children do no know what sin is and God does not hold them accountable until they come of age how can they know hat it means to be washed clean of sin?

By all means dedicate your children to God, by all means tell them and show them about Jesus. But choosing to follow God must be their choice; and immersion is a part of that choice. Once baptized into the blood and body of Christ, we are sons and daughters and entitled to our inheritance. Let us not be like the prodigal son and ask for our inheritance before we are deserving, for everything has its time.

≈ AMEN ≈

---

[104] Remember as pointed out in Romans 1 you can walk away from God.
[105] Romans 10:9.

WORK AREA LETTER IX

SINK OR SWIM -BAPTISM

TOPICAL SCRIPTURES

(Mk 16:15-16) (Mark 1: 9) (Psm 23:5) (Rom 6:3-11) (Acts 22; 16) (Act 19:4) (Matt 3:11) (Tit 3:5) (Matt 20:22) (Luke 22:20) (Matt 27:34) (Luke 22:42) (Is 52:14) (Heb 5:7&8) (Luke 24:49) (Mk.1: 10) (Matt 28:19) (John 3: 5) (John 13: 8) (Isa. 44:3) (Joel 2:28 & 29) (Mk 16:16) (Lk 24:49) (Acts 1:5) (Gal 3:27) (Eph 5:26) (Ex 12 21-24) (Job 1:10-12) (John 13:7-10) (Rom 6:4) (Luke 3:21-23) (Mk 1:9-13) (Matt 3 13-17) (2 Cor 5:21) (Gal 4:7)

1. DOES NOT BEING BAPTIZED PREVENT SALVATION? REFER TO MARK 16 FOR CLARIFICATION.

2. WHY IS BAPTISM IMPORTANT?

3. LIST AND EXPLAIN FOUR TYPES OF BAPTISM. (TWO COME FROM MATT 20:22)

4. ACCORDING TO MATT 28:19 WHO CAN BAPTIZE? AND WHO CAN BE BAPTIZED?

6. WHY WAS JOHN THE BAPTIST BELOVED OF MEN?

7. (JOHN 13:8) WHAT IS THE SPIRITUAL LESSON IN THE VERSE?

8. WHAT IS THE MAIN PURPOSE OF BAPTISM?

9. DOES BAPTISM COVER ALL SINS FOREVER? WHY?

10. DEFINE BAPTISM (INCLUDE METHODOLOGY, PRECEDENT ETC.)

ADDITIONAL NOTES FOR THIS CHAPTER

LETTER X

≈

YOUR PLACE OR MINE

(COMPETITION BETWEEN CHURCHES)

"It is only the minister who stands forth as a personal witness and living proof of the ministry of the Spirit whose word will have full entrance into the hearts of the people and exercise full sway over them"[106]

---

[106] Loving God. Colson p.182.

LETTER X ≈ YOUR PLACE OR MINE
(COMPETITION BETWEEN CHURCHES)

In the book, God's Dream Team Tommy Tenny addresses a phenomenon called *"Sheep stealing."* This is when shepards of various flocks engage in persuading other sheep to become part of their flocks. This even included a contract that was sent out to the various churches to be signed. What a reprehensible thought that shepards are being required to sign an agreement not to steal.

The problem with this concept is that they are stealing treasures from each other that do not belong to them. For, all the sheep belong to the Father (Jn 6:37) ≈ **ALL THAT THE FATHER GIVETH ME SHALL COME TO ME; AND HIM THAT COMETH TO ME I WILL IN NO WISE CAST OUT.** ≈ Yet, another sadness associated with this is that roughly 6 billion people live on the planet, Earth. An estimated 25% of those have not heard the good news of Jesus Christ. Why then do we keep shuffling sheep from flock to flock--they can only be saved one time so what are we doing with them?

The answer becomes apparent when looking at the size of some churches. The purpose of sheep stealing is two-fold. One is to generate income and the second is that increased membership justifies increasing church size and the salary of the pastor.

Even if pastors genuinely believe that they have such good information that they need to pass it on; this is only arrogant presumption. This assumes that God's five-fold ministry is not effective; it presumes that the Holy spirit is not capable of teaching as well as some pastors are. It also assumes that the Holy Spirit is not omnipresent and cannot use other persons to spread His good news.

There is a reason that there are five elements to what God ordained to perfect His saints, and that is that each function is needed to spread the good news:

Emissaries (apostles) - exist to start churches and to go ahead of the evangelist and lay the foundation: (Paul, Timothy, Titus, Apollos)

Evangelists - go in after the apostle and break the ice by proclaiming that Christ has come. (John the Baptist), (Billy Graham)

Preachers - are there to proclaim the year of the Lord and to give the word of God to the world. (the 12 disciples)

Teachers - Jesus and the Holy Spirit explained the word in depth; this is what a teacher does -- groom the sheep.

Prophets - are here to give warnings and to constantly update communication from God. Prophecy is used for edification. (Moses, Daniel, Isaiah, John)

This points above explain the five tiered ministry. However, what does this have to do with sheep stealing? Since these ministries do not duplicate themselves; i.e., most operate in one or two gifts, the shepards who steal sheep between ministries are obviously operating outside of their ministry. This progression is designed to groom sheep and to groom the church itself. When we interrupt or preempt the normal progression, we destroy the healthy growth of people and of the body.

Star Trek's Prime Directive is: *Non-interference with the natural development of a civilization,-* under penalty of death! The most important word in the directive is *"natural,"* unfortunately sometimes sheep are brought in the flock in mid-stages. This posses a peculiar problem for the ministry, because they are past stage one and two but not far enough for the next stage. However, the sheep may not wish to go back through the basics. When faced with this dilemma, one should always admonish the sheep to go back to the beginning and then address where and why they got lost in the first place.

Why is this so important? I am a prime example. While attending church as a young lad, I accepted Christ. I attended church regularly, and approximately every two to three weeks I got saved again. The pastor finally noticed and asked me why I kept getting saved? I responded that it was because *I did not feel the change.*

What I was talking about was that every Sunday the pastor gave a sermon about changing and growing in Christ. He explained concepts like lust, adultery, homosexuality and fornication. God explained that when we are saved we walk away from these things and become new creatures in Christ. All of this is true--God was giving good lessons, the problem was me! The word says when we were children we thought as children and we did childish things. The reason there was no change was that I was not engaging in those things and therefore the message was not for me.

This confusion had a horrible effect on me. Confusion caused me to doubt God and wonder if Christianity was actually real. It was not until some years later while I was trying to practice Islam, that I came across a Surah (chapter), which stated. "Those who believe in the Qur-an. And those who follow the Jewish (scriptures), and the Christians and the Sabians -- any who believe in Allah and the Last Day, and work righteousness shall have their reward.[107]" At that point, I decided that if that was the case, I may as well return to Christianity. However, it took years away from a healthy walk with God.

Churches exist in the same manner. Much like a high school, churches operate in graduated stages. Notice that the preacher comes before the teacher; this is because the teacher teaches at a much more in depth level than the preacher. The preacher is (or at least should be) the entry point for new sheep, transitioning them from lost sheep to meat eaters.

New converts cannot grasp the word like mature believers can, so when you thrust them together the only thing you can do is preach to the lowest level or you chase the new converts away, back into the world.

The two-edged sword is that the mature Christians feel slighted in these services, and they no longer feel like they are growing--they are correct! This is not because the preacher has lost his anointing, as man claims, this actually cannot happen. What God giveth NO man can taketh away or lose; Aaron is a prime example of this principle. Despite his bungling it was not until God removed his anointing that it was lost to him. King David is another fine example of this principle for while he was in God's favour he would not lift a hand against God's appointed king. The Bible chronicles a host of mess-ups by Saul from hunting David to killing priests--but David was true to God not to Saul. It is noteworthy at this point to elucidate that the anointing is solely for the service of the Father. Once the anointing is removed the service is done, the anointed is called home.

Notice I did not writte that once the service is done the anointing is removed. This was intentional because many in the service have walked away from their service but retained the anointing of the Father. They may believe themselves finished or through with God, but the Father knows all things and all time.

Consider Moses' 80 years in training, consider Samson's years of blindness and servitude, only to still have the direct access to the throne to do the bidding--the original bidding of the Father. Let us always be cognizant of the fact that God is done with us when He so desires, not when we want to quit. We may not get any reward for our service but He still will use us to accomplish His will.

---

[107] The Holy Koran Surah 2:62, NRE by Abdullah Yusef Ali.

There are some gifts given us by Him that are for our enjoyment; things like health, wives, kids, or prosperity; but the anointing is from Him for Him. It is given to us as a Master gives tools to a servant to do his work. However, at the end of the planting season the tools are returned to the shed until time to harvest. The Great Farmer schedules the seasons and the tools are all His. When we are allowed to use the anointing in any one of its seven forms[108] they are for the building up of His body only. Balaam is a great example of trying to use the tools the wrong way. As long as we remember that these tools belong to Someone else, and they are to be returned in good working order, we will retain a very healthy respect for the Holy Spirit. Always remember it is all of Him and none of us.

Actually, the tools are not to be returned in good working order. To really please the Master they should come back with extremely high mileage, overworked, strained and with as much appreciable damage as possible. Can you imagine the Farmer having to constantly replace a plow for one of His workers ten times more quickly than any other? Eventually, it will catch His eye and He Himself will wonder what the field hand is doing. Imagine the sheer elation when the Master gets to the section of the field entrusted to that field hand, there stands for His inspection a happy worker with a work yield of grand proportions.

Can you imagine being employee of the month in Heaven![109] Having your cute little picture on the wall, maybe getting two free tickets, on the floor to the binding up of Satan and the locking up of the gates to Hell! Maybe even a special parking slot for your new company chariot. The point being, God is pleased and the servant rewarded.

I also note at this point-to-point out that once the anointing is removed the anointed dies. Aaron, Moses, John the Baptist, and a host of others exemplify this principle. This is not a punishment but a reward for faithful service. As the anointing is not removed until service is complete and it would be useless to take the tools back to Heaven. We revert to

---

[108] (I Cor. 12: 7-12) ≈ **But the manifestation of the Spirit is given to every man to profit withal. For to one is given by the Spirit the word of wisdom; to another the word of knowledge by the same Spirit; To another faith by the same Spirit; to another the gifts of healing by the same Spirit. To another the working of miracles; to another prophecy; to another discerning of spirits; to another (divers) kinds of tongues; to another the interpretation of tongues: But all these worketh that one and the selfsame Spirit, dividing to every man severally as He will.** ≈

[109] If a day in the sight of God is as a thousand years in the sight of man imagine how long your picture will stay up.

being useless without the anointing. Hence, when your task is done God calls you home to rest.

Believers are not growing in these churches because they are stuck in the third grade. If you spent 20 years in the third grade you would be proficient at third grade work, but you will not learn anything new. This is why there are so many spoiled Christians; they have stayed on the tree too long. The idle mind is the Devil's workshop and when adolescents spend years in the third grade they become idol and mischievous.

These rotten Christians need to go on to the next grade instead of being allowed to be juvenile delinquents. This explains the backbiting, grumbling and rumors in the church; the body is bored and needing fresh bread.

Solomon tells us that there is a time for everything under the Son (sun), and that the seasons change constantly. It is therefore the same with the church. There is a season to be in the third grade, and then there is a time to move on to another grade or maybe even another school. Understanding this pastors need to let the sheep move and grow, or offer in their churches a variety of grades. To stifle the growth of sheep is not only holding them captive but also making them prey.

There are approximately 320 species of shark, but there are thousands of varieties of fish. If you put a fish in an aquarium, experts tell us that it will only grow as large as the body of water in which it lives. The growth of the fish is directly proportional to the volume of water; mathematically this would be represented thusly:

$$\text{SIZE of FISH} == \text{VOLUME of WATER}.$$

The equation for Sharks, however, would read:

$$\text{SIZE of SHARK} =/= \text{VOLUME of WATER}$$

This is because the shark grows to it fullest dimension regardless of the container. For you see the shark is a scavenger and it keeps the ocean clean. Therefore, it has approximately 60% of its entire body mass reserved for its huge liver. The Liver is the chief filtration device in the body and because they eat trash all day they need this ability to function, as they should. Therefore, they will not stop growing no matter where you put them until they are functional, even if they outgrow the tank.

Just as there are only hundreds of species of shark there are only so many believers. These believers will grow beyond their surroundings no matter what size. The rest of us, as we have seen many times in the word, have been likened unto fish. As such cannot grow larger than the house in which we dwell.

Brother Andrew Murray's book, <u>In Search of Spiritual Excellence</u> [110] gives the best rationale and explanation as to why so many are fish versus sharks. "Everywhere among the children of God we hear complaints of weakness and sin. Among those who do not complain, there is reason to fear that their silence is ascribed to ignorance or self-satisfaction. It is important that we concentrate on this fact until we come under the full conviction that the condition of the Church is marked by impotence and nothing can restore her except the return to a life in the full enjoyment of the blessing of Pentecost.

The more deeply we feel our deficiency; the more speedily we will desire and obtain restoration. It will help awaken longing for this blessing if we earnestly consider how little it is enjoyed in the Church and how far the Church is from being what her Lord has power to make her. "

Or perhaps a more recent adaptation of what Brother Murray is saying is found in a journey of a few friends that included three misfits. One went looking for a brain, the other a heart, and the third courage. Neither of them believed they could be complete or happy without these items. When they finally reached the Wizard to receive these gifts, the Wizard demanded a very high price and sent them out to face this peril without the very gifts that they came looking for.

Upon returning to the Wizard the second time, they were told that the gifts they sought they already possessed; but they never believed it themselves…they lacked faith. We, like them, lack faith. Because we lack faith, we cannot readily appreciate nor utilize the gift given to us over two thousand years ago on the cross at Calvary. ≈ **IF YE LOVE ME, KEEP MY COMMANDMENTS. AND I WILL PRAY THE FATHER, AND HE SHALL GIVE YOU ANOTHER COMFORTER, THAT HE MAY ABIDE WITH YOU FOREVER.** ≈ (John 14:15-16) The Master promised us the Holy Spirit would be with us forever.

Just like the Wizard empowered the three lost souls in their journey --the death of Jesus empowered us. For you see, before He died His disciples were just like the Lion, Scarecrow and Tin Man…cowardly,

---

[110] <u>In Search of Spiritual Excellence</u> Murray, Andrew. Edt. By L Carson, Reprinted 1984 Whitaker House, USA. (p.46).

uncompassionate and unthinking. However, they were given the Holy Spirit by Christ's death and became bold, spoke intelligently, and loved people unceasingly. It is the Holy Spirit that we lack in the body today-- the very Breath of Life without which we all are simply following the Yellow-brick Road.

Sadly enough, most Christians are waiting for the gift or power in Christ and like the three travelers, we have always had access to the power of the throne. The power of the Holy Spirit is promised to all who believe and that gift was left for us long ago, but we have not chosen to claim it. We have not yet agreed to accept it, for it is not free as many claim. It cost the Saviour dearly, His Father in Heaven, too. Why then should we assume that we who have done nothing to earn it should be allowed to keep it without charge? God requires no less of us than was required from His Son who told us to, ≈ **TAKE UP YOUR CROSS DAILY AND FOLLOW ME!** ≈

Salvation is certainly not spiritual welfare. Simply being alive does not entitle us to Salvation. Jesus paid the price and those who chose to confess Him as Lord and King can have it. Those who obey Him and honour and love Him are entitled to even more. Those who preach it is free mislead us. Yes, the Bible says it was a gift freely given but that means God the giver gave it to us without reservation or hesitation. It does not imply the lack of cost. John 3:16 tells us of the cost. The last passages of the four Gospels and the book of Acts tell us of the cost.

In fact, the entire Bible tells of the cost of our redemption at the foot of the cross. It is our cheapening of God's grace that affords such unworthy followings. It is because we consider Salvation charity and welfare that we hold it in such low regard. It is our lack of respect for the sacrifices of others that allows us to go to the club dressed better than we come to the house of God. It is our patent disregard for the sanctity of the word that prevents us from knowing the scriptures but yet, we know the words to almost all the songs on the radio. Moreover, sadly enough, all the trivia and knowledge of Hollywood will get us no closer to heaven than we were before Jesus came and died.

"The truth is that we have become so accustomed to the confession of sin and unfaithfulness, of disobedience and backsliding, that it is no longer regarded as a matter for shame.[111] "

---

[111] In Search of Spiritual Excellence Murray, Andrew (p.125).

Brother Murray again instructs us as to problems arising from a lack of the Holy Spirit. Without the Holy Spirit there is no conviction and without conviction there is no change. A brief analysis of conviction shows us that it is a necessary part of change. Many of us go through life assuming that we have gotten away with our sins because they have not been witnessed by anyone. But, as the Master told the woman at the well our sins are many…which means that He sees them all, and apparently takes note of them.

Conviction comes in when an authority tells us that they know of our sins and they know we are guilty. Despite our guilt, we are loved, forgiven and allowed to continue in their service. Freedom in conviction comes from our secret lives being held up to a light for all to see. Freedom comes from not having to live in fear of being caught, but in being caught and forgiven. Without being caught and convicted, we would never modify our behaviour or our lifestyles. Without being told, ≈ **GO AND SIN NO MORE!** ≈ We will continually sin and try to hide it. It is only in seeing our weakness, and in seeing God's mercy that we desire to change. It is only in the feeling of release from our guilt that we can enjoy the fruits of His Spirit. (Acts 19:1-2)

An example of this conviction comes from a movie called Grosse Point Blank. In this movie, a hit man kicks in a door and shoots the victim in the stomach. The victim while holding the wound responds by saying, *"Whatever it is that I am doing that you don't like I'll stop."* When the Holy Spirit comes in and holds are sin up for the world to see this is how we should feel when convicted. Whatever it is that we are doing wrong we are willing stop it. Like the man in the movie, we do this out of fear, but as we progress in our relationship with the Father, we learn to do it out of love for Him.

If I may be so bold, a suggestion was made in a meeting that the 0800 service be used for advanced teaching and training since these are usually the mature sheep. Then use the 1100 and evening services to give the generic word to the general body. Church is for preaching but mature believers need teaching and guidance. When adhered to, these principles would negate the need for sheep stealing. Stop stealing other shepherd's delinquents and adding them to your gang. Give the word and operate in your ministry so that the body as whole can grow. Stop minimizing the number of disciples and preachers and teachers we train up by keeping them in bondage to our churches. Free them to continue the good work and see that if we operate in our ministry and stay diligent to God we will have a steady constant flow of new converts.

It is the Holy Spirit, that sends sheep to us, but like the parable of the talents this is contingent upon what we are going to do with them. If we plan to bury them and hold on to them, He will rarely send you any, for He does not want them to be wasted by us. If you are producing good fruit, He will add to your Church daily and the good stewards are rewarded.

A conversation with an elder about a new larger church resulted in the following conversation;

E...God gave me a vision, 8000 members of this body.
Me...How sad? E.... Why is that? Me...How long ago? E...Four years ago. Me...Do you know what that means? E...What?
Me...The Lord has been waiting to increase the flock. Do you have more members now or last year?

E...Last year! Me...We have been holding up progress for four years because we cannot get our house in order do you not understand that. If God did bless you with a bigger Church, but He is not giving you new bodies that means two possible things.

i) He did not bless you with the Church or
ii) Much like David and Solomon He will pave the way for somebody else to steward the 8,000. For we know, God will move you out of the way if you block Him or live outside His will

This is the difference between a bond-servant and a slave. God will use you regardless of your stewardship. However, if you are a bad steward you get no rewards-and are thus a slave. The bond-servant produces and is thusly rewarded for his good stewardship, and when they are done will be received at the gates with the words, ≈ **WELL DONE THY GOOD AND FAITHFUL SERVANT.** ≈

≈ **AMEN** ≈

WORK AREA LETTER X
Your Place or Mine? Competition Between Churches

<u>Topical Scriptures</u>

(Jn 6:37) (I Cor. 12: 7-12) (John 14:15-16) (Jn 3:16) (Acts 19:1-2)

1. WHY IS THERE COMPETITION BETWEEN CHURCHES?

2. IN WHOSE NAME ARE WE TO BAPTIZE? AND WHY? CITE SCRIPTURES.

3. DOES EVERY CHURCH TEACH THE SAME THING? WHY?

4. WHAT CAUSES PEOPLE TO LEAVE CHURCH?

5. WHAT SHOULD YOU DO WHEN YOU OUTGROW YOUR CHURCH?

6. WHO HAS MOST AUTHORITY IN THE FIVE-FOLD MINISTRY?

7. WHO IS RESPONSIBLE FOR OUR SPIRITUAL GROWTH? CITE SCRIPTURE.

8. WHAT DOES THE SCRIPTURE SAY IS THE PURPOSE OF CHURCH? CITE SCRIPTURE.

9. WHAT IS THE DIFFERENCE BETWEEN THE CHURCH AND THE TEMPLE?

10. WHAT IS THE DIFFERENCE BETWEEN WHAT WE CALL CHURCH AND WHAT CHRIST CALLS HIS CHURCH? CITE SCRIPTURES.

11. WHERE OR WHAT IS THE HOLY OF HOLIES IN THE CHURCH?

ADDITIONAL NOTES FOR THIS CHAPTER

LETTER XI

≈

TWO DRINK MINIMUM
(ENTERTAINMENT INSTEAD OF EDUCATION)

"The church does not draw people in; it sends people out. It does not settle into a comfortable niche, taking its place along side the rotary, the elks and the country clubs. Rather, the church is to make society uncomfortable. Like yeast, it unsettles the mass around it, changing it from within. Like salt it flavours and preserves that into which it vanishes."[112]

---

[112] <u>Loving God</u>, Colson, Charles. Zondervan Publishing House, MI. 1983 p.176.

LETTER XI ≈ TWO DRINK MINIMUM

Many of our churches have reduced themselves to the posture of simply being for entertainment. Much like the church at Corinth, we allow so much of the world into our house that many of us have become indistinguishable from the world. Like the world, we resort to subterfuge to attract and maintain congregations. When you go to nightclubs many of them shroud the true cost of entry into the establishment; many of our churches should also adopt a similar policy.

In the Bahamas, there was a nightclub that was the hot spot for sexy young women. The cover charge was a standard $40 to get in which included two drinks. The clubs that try to conceal their costs do so from fear of scaring away potential customers. In addition, it is because the product they are offering is easily overshadowed by competition. The club in the Bahamas charged what it did because they knew that they had what people wanted.

There is nothing wrong with decent wholesome entertainment, but this should not be under the guise or combined with the main worship services. The main services are used for teaching and preaching, but when you use them for entertainment the focus changes and you are catering to the flesh not the spirit.

Carl Marx made the statement that, *"Religion is the opium of the masses[113]."* What an intriguing statement. In the drug ecology, by far the smoothest, most addictive drugs are opiates. These drugs are so addictive because they mimic natural endorphins (chemicals that create a feeling of pleasure) in the body. As such, the body has a hard time differentiating between the real dopamine (endorphin) and the opiate. As drugs go, the opiates by far have the mellowest type of euphoria. Because the body cannot readily distinguish between the drugs and endorphins, it is virtually impossible to break an addiction from these drugs. In the case of Heroin (opium), a placebo was created; or the people would never be able to break the addiction to the drug.

The reason it is so difficult to break the addiction is that the body fights to get this chemical that it makes it feel good and fights pain. In addition, as far as the body is concerned this substance belongs in its

---

[113] Manifesto of the Communist Party (1848).

repertoire. Much like trying to make the body give up oxygen ~ it is not prepared to reconfigure its biochemistry.

Is it not peculiar that Marx would liken religion to this drug? This is because like the opiates, religion becomes easily addictive and much like the drugs very difficult to get free. Like the smooth opiate religion has a way of getting into the body and mimicking a natural state. That state is the natural state of the spirit man.

Opium attaches itself so easily because the body is designed to receive it. The spirit is designed the same way; it was designed to receive from the Lord. Like the opiates, religion mimics true spirituality and attaches itself to the spirit making it feel good. The problem with this is that everything that feels good may not be good for you. The religion that mimics true spirituality gets you in to the spirit realm of the body, becomes addictive, and is a hard habit to break[114].

There is a song wherein the words say *you are innocent when you dream*! These words imply that in your dreams, you can do whatever you want to because there are no consequences, and you are not responsible for your actions. Religion, like the dream, allows you to be guilt free and yet go on sinning. True Christianity allows you to feel the conviction and the effect of your sin. This feeling does not come from flagellation, but in the form of disappointing the Father, again. This is why the prodigal son was able to say forgive me father for I have sinned against you.

Only after the prodigal son discerned that what he had become was not what he should have become, and where he was living was an abomination did he freely return home. His father never knew what he was doing or where he was. Therefore, the son could have come home and lied to him. Knowing the love of his father and not wishing to be a blight any longer cause the conviction in his heart. This caused him to throw himself humbly at his father's mercy and ask for forgiveness for the sins he had committed against his father.

Going back to the ministry of Jesus, He did not employ dancers and loud music to entice the people; they were there to hear the good news. When we keep sheep too long, they require more prodding to do the same thing.

The bible says that Jesus revealed Himself first to Mary. This was because she loved Him above all others for He had saved her from seven

---

[114] For more information on this read father Leo Booth's, <u>When God becomes a Drug</u>.

demons. (Luke 8:2) ≈ **And certain women, which had been healed of evil spirits and infirmities, Mary called Magdalene, out of whom went seven devils.** ≈

New sheep are hungry and thirsty for the word of God. Just as babies are born ready to suckle, new sheep are fresh and full of vim and vigor. It is the old sheep that actually need the prodding. The lambs do not worship God yet as they have not been taught how to. The praise and worship comes from those who are mature and have a relationship with God.

The old sheep require the prodding and the coaxing away from their idleness and their brooding. The praise and worship service is geared towards moving the sheep toward receiving from the Holy Spirit. This is fine and this may well be necessary and is a good use of the praise and worship "ministry." The draw back to this is that God clearly states that He inhabits the praises of His people ≈ **But Thou (art) holy, (O Thou) that inhabits the praises of Israel.** ≈ (Psm 22:3). And if the only people singing and praising are the choir then they will be moved and they will receive, but what of the remainder of the congregation?

Consequently, there becomes a Pavlovian response created in that believers become so conditioned that they cannot worship, receive or hear from the Lord without the singing and praising. God's still, small voice is sometimes drowned out by the noise and the word missed because the believer was trying to get ready to receive a word. Many times believers complain that they do not get to hear from God. Well, we assume that He still speaks, but we have to be prepared to receive a word, even as Samuel did in his sleep, as Jonah did in the whale or even in the Lion's den. Ever praising internally will keep your heart tuned to JBN, the Jesus Broadcasting Network.

The performing members of the church become entertainment when they alone sing. Have there been instances where choirs have moved people? Yes, but far greater things have been brought about when the entire congregation sings. Things like yokes being broken, people released from bondage, healing, convictions, and jubilation. This is what praise is for, to let us be free to receive from the spirit and to worship Him in spirit. The dancing girls and the great renditions by the choir are good fun, but they just drag out the service. More breakthroughs come from whole-body praise and worship than you will ever see from a performance.

Brothers and sisters, we must be careful of what importance we place on performance. Yes, the word tells us to do all things as unto the Lord, but this is talking about the spirit, purity, and intensity of the action not the result. God appreciates effort not achievement, for all the work is still really done by Him. Paul tells us to be boastful about nothing for we created nothing ≈ **For by grace are ye saved through faith; and that not of yourselves: (it is) the gift of God: Not of works, lest any man should boast.** ≈ (Eph 2:8 & 9).

Brothers and sisters, the word tells us to make a joyful noise unto the Lord. Oddly, the word noise is used to describe the sounds of the music. Normally its harmony and melody define music, but God's ways are not our ways. Have you ever been to a concert and heard the musicians tuning their instruments? That is noise. A complete discordant clanging of a variety of sounds which are disharmonious and a - directional.

Why then does the Father love this noise? The Father loves this noise because of what produces the noise. When professional musicians arrange a piece of music for a band, they arrange it so that each instrument can be heard. The band is arranged so that no one instrument drowns out the other. They mute trumpets; decrescendo the piano and even muffle the drums with a plastic shields. God's noise is produced when all those involved play and sing to Him to the best of their ability, as loudly as they can -- in complete deference to how they sound and who they drown out. When 100 people are singing and playing at the top of their hearts it sounds horrible to us but not to God. He sees it like you would see a children's recital where your child was the worst musician but gave their all!

When that sound reaches the uppermost heavens, it gives the Father so much pleasure that He leaves His abode to come down and sup with us. Notice He does not send an angel or the Holy Spirit, He comes Himself! He comes down to see who it is making this sweet sound unto Him. He sups with us for a while because we have poured into Him and in turn, He pours into us.

Using a stanza from Sesame Street, the words are; "S*ing, sing a song, sing out loud, sing out long. Don't worry if it's not good enough, for any one else to hear, just sing, sing a song!*" When we praise the Lord, let this song be our guide -- just sing and minister unto Him; see how your bonds are broken and the blessings that flow forth from Heaven out to you.

I was in a restaurant at Christmas and there were about 20 people talking and laughing and telling jokes. All of a sudden a little girl started singing Away in a Manger. Her words were all wrong and she got most of the verses incorrect, but she sang at the top of her lungs. The mother told her to hush she was too loud, but the father said she is happy let her sing.

That little voice raised the spirits in the restaurant one hundred fold, she had the floor, and it was a blessing.

When you are praising the Lord truly and worshipping Him, be like that little girl and take the floor. If anyone tries to rebuke you remember that Jesus said, ≈ **SUFFER THE LITTLE CHILDREN TO COME UNTO ME, FOR THE KINGDOM OF HEAVEN BELONGS TO SUCH AS THESE.** ≈ (Matt 19) Brothers and sisters, *never rebuke [115]the Holy Spirit!* What you have to say is not that important. When the Holy Spirit is ready He will still give you His word, He does not work against Himself, as we do, He does not interrupt Himself, He has the timing perfect. Let Him guide the service and do His job of breaking yokes and freeing the captives…who cares about the announcements. When the word is going forth, the Holy Spirit will usher in silence if it is a good word, but it is His job to bless us, allow Him to.

A good shepherd who is able to discern the work of the spirit may be lucky enough to hear the spirit say, ≈ **BLESS YOU FOR FLESH AND BLOOD DID NOT REVEAL THIS TO YOU!** ≈

≈ **AMEN** ≈

---

[115] Correct, overlook, overshadow, chase off, or rush.

WORK AREA
LETTER XI

TWO DRINK MINIMUM-
(ENTERTAINMENT INSTEAD OF EDUCATION)

<u>Topical Scriptures</u>
(Luke 8:2) (Psm 22:3). (Eph 2:8 & 9) (Matt 19)

1. WHY ARE CHOIRS MORE IMPORTANT THAN THE TEACHING IN MANY CHURCHES?

2. IF THE TEACHING IN CHURCH IS SO AWESOME WHY IS THERE SO LITTLE CHANGE?

3. WHAT IS THE DANGER OF ENTERTAINMENT IN CHURCH?

4. WHY DO CHURCHES TREAD LIGHTLY ON SPIRITUAL ISSUES AND SETTLE FOR ENTERTAINMENT?

5. HOW DOES ONE QUENCH THE HOLY SPIRIT?

6. HOW DOES ONE GRIEVE THE HOLY SPIRIT?

7. IS THERE A PLACE FOR ENTERTAINMENT IN THE CHURCH?

8. WHY DO PEOPLE PREFER ENTERTAINMENT INSTEAD OF THE TRUTH?

9. WHY IS RELIGION THE OPIATE OF THE MASSES?

10. WHICH PART OF THE BODY RESPONDS TO THE SPIRIT AND WHICH PART ENTERTAINMENT?

11. IS THE PURPOSE OF THE CHURCH TO FEED THE BODY OR THE SOUL?

ADDTIONAL NOTES FOR THIS CHAPTER

LETTER XII

≈

THE OTHER WHITE MEAT
(THE TRUE NATURE OF THE FLESH)

Probably because the Latin word for "apple" and for "evil" are identical (*malum*), the apple came to represent the forbidden fruit of the Garden of Eden. It is therefore often used to symbolize the fall into sin, or of sin itself. When Christ is portrayed holding and apple, He is acknowledged as the Second Adam who brings life[116].

---

[116] <u>Symbols in Christian Art and Architecture.</u> Gast, Walter. http://home.att.net/~wegast/symbols/headline.htm.

LETTER XII ≈ THE OTHER WHITE MEAT
(THE TRUE NATURE OF THE FLESH)

"Man has two great enemies by whom the devil tempts him and with whom he has to contend. The one is the world without, and the other is the self-life within. The last, the selfish ego, is much more dangerous and stronger than the first. It is quite possible for a man to have made much progress in forsaking the world while the self-life retains full dominion within him[117]."

FLESH- The material entombing our souls that is replete with senses.
EVIL- Acting in a manner contrary to God's will.
DESTRUCTIVE- Designed for the purpose of destroying.
HELL-BOUND- An action or attitude known to result in damnation.
SALVATION - When your spirit is redeemed from damnation.
DELIVERANCE - When the flesh is freed from a particular bondage.

We must start by clearing up a few things and then explaining a few terms. I will write this in large italics because I want this point to be perfectly clear; *Christ shed His blood and died to save your soul not your flesh.*

The purpose of defining these terms is that the true nature of the flesh is evil but not necessarily destructive. What does this mean? Evil has always been synonymous with destruction and malevolence, but the true nature of the flesh is not to destroy but to serve itself. Although living in the flesh leads unto damnation, the flesh itself is not seeking to destroy but to bask and enjoy itself; the punishment for this happens being death.

The above example with the apple asserts the traditions we have become accustom to often dictate what we believe. Nowhere in the Bible does it list the fruit from Genesis as an apple, but this is what has been taught for centuries. In order to defeat Satan we must first better ourselves, this begins with accurately understanding our own theology.

---

[117] In Search of Spiritual Excellence Murray, Andrew Whitaker House 1984 (P.35).

The evil God found in Satan was that Satan wanted to exalt himself above God. According to scriptures Satan was not trying to actually destroy Heaven; he just wanted to be in charge. Satan's desire to be above God is what was evil, and because Satan was cast out and promised the pit; his wiles became evil. Remember that rebellion is considered witchcraft. Any contrariness to God is in and of itself evil. The intention may not be to destroy, despite the fact that destruction is always the result.

When we teach that the flesh is malevolent that is not exactly accurate. It is evil, in that it exalts itself, but the flesh desires to live to the fullest extent it can. Sometimes these desires are perverse and debase, but this is still the flesh exalting itself.

The word tells us we were born in sin, because we were born of the flesh. It is the flesh's nature to be evil and thus sin against God. This does not require special learning, it is a natural off shoot of the five senses and experiencing the world. **REGARDLESS OF THE OFFENSE ALL SINS ARE COMMITTED AGAINST GOD.** In other words if a man steals from you he has indeed stolen but the sin is against God.

As a member of a particular fraternity, I was taught to circumscribe my passions in order to become a better person. This concept undoubtedly comes from the Hebrew mandate by God to be circumcised. Passion is an emotional upheaval in a person, and the greatest emotional upheaval in most men is sexual. Most passions in life do not rival sex and those that are truly enjoyable are likened to sex. Sometimes these passions even release the same hormones as sex. Since the greatest passion for most men is sexual in nature to circumcise a man extensibly circumscribes (controls, cuts back, mitigates, lessens) their passion. (Col. 2:11) ≈ **In whom also ye are circumcised with the circumcision made without hands, in putting off the body of the sins of the flesh by the circumcision of Christ.** ≈

As in the fraternity, circumcision is symbolic of a lifestyle choice, or at least it was according to the Hebrew tradition. This symbol meant that you chose to lead a life in a manner consistent with God's law and to be obedient to His strict laws in difference to your passions and desires. The circumcision is also a symbolic part of the Hebrew tradition of shedding blood to consecrate a covenant. The circumcised member of the body is exemplary of his new life. His obedience to God was more important than his personal desires. Much as Jesus shed His blood on the cross to seal His covenant with us, we shed our blood to seal our side. Now that He has risen and His blood redeemed us we no longer shed blood. We now shed sin as our evidence of covenant.

What blood is to life in the flesh sin is to spiritual life. We must therefore circumcise our lives before God, and the tradition also requires a witness. The evidence of the Hebrew covenant was the obvious lack of foreskin. Now our evidence to the world should be consecrated lifestyles.

The flesh desires to experience the fullest life has to offer and God wants us to as well, but under His direction and with restraint. Passion as Solomon exemplifies in the Song of Solomon is necessary for a happy healthy relationship. The circumscription (circumcision) is in the fact that a marital state is required.

In the Garden of Eden, Satan tempted Eve. (Gen. 3:1-6) It was the series of promises that actually appealed to Eve's flesh.

1. Satan told her she would not die,

2. Satan promised that her eyes would open (meaning he knew about spiritual sight).

3. Satan promised that her knowledge would increase. In none of his promises does Satan mention the power to destroy, or killing someone or even disobeying God. All of his ploys offered the flesh more of what it had and more of what Eve wanted.

Eve says that Satan beguiled[118] her, and she was correct. Satan offered Eve more of what she had, he told her in essence, "If you do this then your life will be enhanced and much more exciting." Of course, the flesh jumped at the offer and Satan did tell the truth, he just neglected to inform her the cost, was spiritual death.

This is as it is with all of Satan's lies; there is always 80-90% truth in his lies, just enough to make it sound good and believable. Satan also makes his offer sound good for you, he never mentions the bad side. When Satan is finished with his deviation from the truth, he will/can convince you that you are doing a good thing. Nevertheless, you never can do good things outside of God's will. Anything Satan offers you is evil, or else he would not offer it. He will not pretend to be God although he wanted to be above God. (He leaves impersonation to us. He already knows he is going to hell).

Whatever Satan offers you is unto death, but it will always have a sweet sensation about it to your flesh. Jesus tells us that if He stays gone too long that even the elect will not be saved. (Matt. 24-22) ≈ **AND EXCEPT THOSE DAYS SHOULD BE SHORTENED, THERE SHOULD**

---

[118] To use flattery or cajolery to achieve one's ends. tempt, seduce, ensnare, to cause to believe something false by means of trickery or fraud. (American Heritage Dictionary).

NO FLESH BE SAVED: BUT FOR THE ELECT'S SAKE THOSE DAYS SHALL BE SHORTENED. ≈

Although Satan will not imitate God, he will mimic God. Despite Satan's evil ways, he still obeys God. We know this based on the words in the following scriptures. (Job 1:12) ≈ **And the Lord said unto Satan, BEHOLD, ALL THAT HE HATH (IS) IN THY POWER; ONLY UPON HIMSELF PUT NOT FORTH THINE HAND. So Satan went forth from the presence of the Lord.** ≈ **(Jude 1:9)** ≈ **Yet Michael the archangel, when contending with the devil he disputed about the body of Moses, durst not bring against him a railing accusation, but said, The Lord rebuke thee.** ≈ (Matthew 16:23) ≈ **But he turned, and said unto Peter, Get thee behind me, Satan: thou art an offence unto me: for thou savourest not the things that be of God, but those that be of men.** ≈ He will get as close as possible but even then, he never crosses the line. The Anti-Christ will present himself as such but even he will be just a pawn of Satan. There is power in the tricks Satan uses.

Do not underestimate either the power of Satan or the power of the flesh; either mistake will result in death. Samson was ordained to judge Israel before he was born. However, Samson's flesh caused him to loose his power and be imprisoned in shame. For the scripture says that his falling for Delilah was ordained, so that God would have a thorn against the Philistines (Judges). Nevertheless, it was Samson himself who succumbed to the wiles and the weeping of the woman. Much like Eve, sin entered through the weaker vessel. Like Adam however, it was the true nature of the flesh that caused Samson to give up his power.

Not only was Samson supposed to glorify God, he was to be a champion for and of Israel. The scripture tells us (Judges 12:5) that more than simply doing what God wanted Samson wanted to punish the Philistines. Again, the flesh comes through and causes Samson to hate the Philistines. The Lord tells us to love our enemies, not to hate them and not to be hateful towards them.

In Exodus, Moses put had 3,000 men put to death that had left Egypt in the group. These men were family and friends but they were an abomination to God and constantly came against God's appointed man. Even when David was given the command to destroy the inhabitants, (all the inhabitants) of the land there was no mention of hate.

The Bible tells us that obedience is better than sacrifice, and in the case of executing God's tasks we simply need to obey-not judge or hate. If you are being obedient to God, you do not need to hate your enemy.

Loving God will be far more conducive to your task and will allow you to do whatever God tells you -- even if that means kill.

Some of the most famous men in the bible fell prey to the true nature of the flesh. Most certainly you too shall be caught up in the flesh and you will stay in bondage until you understand that salvation comes to your spirit in an instant deliverance of the flesh is not instant. The other main difference is that salvation requires faith and acceptance, deliverance requires work. The flesh and the spirit although blended are completely separate entities. They serve two different purposes and have two different goals. The are never at peace and one can control the other. To exemplify the difference I will used the following scriptures.

1. ≈ **For the flesh lusteth against the Spirit, and the Spirit against the flesh: and these are contrary the one to the other: so that ye cannot do the things that ye would. Now the works of the flesh are manifest, which are (these); Adultery, fornication, uncleanness, lasciviousness, Idolatry, witchcraft, hatred, variance, emulations, wrath, strife, seditions, heresies, Envyings, murders, drunkenness, revellings, and such like: of the which I tell you before, as I have also told (you) in time past, that they which do such things shall not inherit the kingdom of God. But the fruit of the Spirit is love, joy, peace, longsuffering, gentleness, goodness, faith, Meekness, temperance: against such there is no law.** ≈ (Gal 5:17, 19-23)

2. ≈ **And fear not them which kill the body, but are not able to kill the soul: but rather fear Him which is able to destroy both soul and body in hell.** ≈ (Matt 10:28)

It was important for me to explain this because many Christians believe that that upon receiving salvation their flesh is instantly changed. We can see both in the bible and in our churches this is not true. By the same token each of us knows a wonderful person that is kind and gentle but not Christian. The fact is that many Christians are still carnal and have yet to die completely to the flesh. It is a difficult process and as I pointed out earlier deliverance is from a particular demon or bondage. As it was with the Children of Israel in Exodus, they were freed from the bondage of Egypt only to submit to the bondage of their own flesh. God can deliver you from anything but He requires you not to go back[119]. The purpose of parting the Red sea was prophetic as well as functional. The

---

[119] Heb 10:26, 2 Pe 2:20-22.

prophetic portion pointed to Christ shedding His blood on the Cross, and the other is simple. When God delivers you from something He makes it impossible to go back to that thing. You on the other hand many spend the rest of your life craving that lifestyle again; but like Pharaoh it is dead and you will never get back to that place again. You make something similar, it may taste and smell like you sin or your Golden calf but the thing you knew before is gone.

KING DAVID

King David was called a man after God's own heart. **This passage however does not** mean that God and David have the same heart. It is inexcusable that Christians promulgate that there could be any hint of sin, lust and deceit in God's heart. To clear this irreverence up let us look together at Acts 13:24 and 1 Sa 13:14. I glossed over this concept before but here we must not continue to over look this concept. Though I am sure no deceit is intended this misrepresentation can only serve one purpose; That is to try to justify sin.

≈ **But now thy kingdom shall not continue: the Lord hath sought him a man after His own heart, and the Lord hath commanded him (to be) captain over His people, because thou hast not kept (that) which the Lord commanded thee.** ≈ (1 Sa 13:14)

≈ **But God removed him from the kingship and replaced him with David, a man about whom God said, `DAVID SON OF JESSE IS A MAN AFTER MY OWN HEART, FOR HE WILL DO EVERYTHING I WANT HIM TO.'.** ≈ (Acts 13:22 - New Living Translation 1996 Tyndale Charitable Trust)

After reading both of these passages it should be obvious to you that the issue was not similarity it was obedience. When the Lord speaks in Acts He clearly indicates that David's desire to do His will is what pleases God. After His heart according to these passages is more accurately defined as *pleasing to me*. If you read these passages with that phrase it makes far more sense than to say their hearts are similar. Believers, there is under absolutely no circumstances a justification nor excuse for sin.

David's name is mentioned more than any other in the Old Testament[120], but even his flesh controlled a lot of what he did.

- He failed to kill all the inhabitants of the land as God instructed.

-He failed to uphold the law in regards to Absolom killing his half-brother.

-He killed Uriah in order to steal his wife. (2 Samuel 11:15)

-Threw a temper tantrum about Absolom being slain. (2 Samuel 19:1) Yet, God promised that the light in his house would never go out. So, yes the flesh is evil, but Gods loves us as long as we repent and are actually trying to live right. We will have to be punished (2 Samuel 12:15) for the word admonishes us and says that a father who dos not chasten his child does not love that child.

JOHN the BAPTIST

John the Baptist was created and blessed in his mother's womb. He even had the Holy Spirit in his mother's womb, but even in his obedience to God, John's flesh prevailed. As we discussed earlier, the flesh is self-serving and sometimes this presents itself in the form of over zealous behavior. John's only mission was to herald the coming of his first cousin the Messiah. That was all, apparently was a great privilege as Jesus tells us. (Matt. 11:11) ≈ **VERILY I SAY UNTO YOU, AMONG THEM THAT ARE BORN OF WOMEN THERE HATH NOT RISEN A GREATER THAN JOHN THE BAPTIST: NOTWITHSTANDING HE THAT IS LEAST IN THE KINGDOM OF HEAVEN IS GREATER THAN HE.** ≈

John in is his zeal to serve God, went beyond his calling and started judging people; namely Herod, and his wife. (Matt. 14: 3-4) ≈ **For Herod had laid hold on John, and bound him, and put (him) in prison for Herodias' sake, his brother Philip's wife. For John said unto him, It is not lawful for thee to have her.** ≈ This is not what we are to ever do. We are not called to judge but to proclaim the good news (Gospel) of Jesus Christ.

---

[120] David's name is mentioned some 1085 times throughout the bible.

John's overzealous nature ultimately caused his demise. Moreover, the word tells us that after John's beheading[121] that Jesus left the city abruptly[122] which would seem to imply that it was unexpected or at least not intended, at that time. Perhaps it was a sign to Jesus that John had decreased and He was to begin His works. On the other hand, perhaps Jesus left because He was first cousin to John, and had been heralded by John as the Messiah, and it was not yet time for Jesus to die.

However, we do know that when heeding the call of God not to loose our heads in His work. This is a play on words, but the beheading of John symbolized what happens when in our zeal we go beyond our calling--we get severed from God and severed from the body. Even Jesus stuck to the will of God and did not stray from the beaten (ordained) path.[123]

SIMON PETER

Peter is another zealot. In his love for the Master, his flesh also prevailed. Peter was by far the most active disciple of Jesus. He was very diligent in his love but often his flesh won out and he got into trouble.

The first time was when he was walking on the water. As long as his eyes were stayed on Jesus, he stayed aloft but as soon as he took his eyes off the Master sank. As long as we stay the course, we will stay aloft but much like Peter when our flesh clouds our minds and open our fleshly eyes, we sink.

Whenever we are walking in the spirit, we are able to walk on water, to run behind chariots, or even wrestle a lion barehanded. However,

---

[114] (Matt. 14:10-11) ≈ **And he sent, and beheaded John in the prison. And his head was brought in a charger, and given to the damsel: and she brought (it) to her mother.** ≈

[122] (Matt 14:13) ≈ **When Jesus heard of it, He departed thence by ship into a desert place apart: and when the people had heard thereof, they followed Him on foot out of the cities.** ≈

[123] (Matt. 26:42) ≈ **He went away again the second time, and prayed, saying, O MY FATHER, IF THIS CUP MAY NOT PASS AWAY FROM ME, EXCEPT I DRINK IT, THY WILL BE DONE.** ≈ (Matt. 8:29) ≈ **And, behold, they cried out, saying, What have we to do with thee, Jesus, thou Son of God? Art thou come hither to torment us before the time?** ≈

when the flesh chimes in, it brings with it all the physical laws that hamper the body. In other words, the flesh starts to tell us that we cannot walk on water, we cannot wrestle a lion, and we need to stop it before we get hurt.

As the flesh is self-serving it undoubtedly, reminded Peter of how rough the water was and probably kept whispering to him. Get back into the boat before you drown look how rough the water is. Look at how deep the water is, look how far away the boat is. The fish are going to eat you while you drown. For the Bible says he was afraid (Matt. 14:30).

Jesus' response was ≈ **YE OF LITTLE FAITH**. ≈ Remember that faith the size of a mustard seed will move a mountain, so apparently faith produces supernatural power that is able to override the physical laws that control us. It also is apparently a useful tool in the war against the flesh.

When Christ is apprehended in the garden, Peter protects his Master the only way he knows how – in the flesh. He lops off the ear of a guard with a sword. Jesus however, corrects him and mends the ear. Part of the confusion arose from the Master telling Peter to buy more swords. (Luke 22:36) ≈ **Then said He unto them, BUT NOW, HE THAT HATH A PURSE, LET HIM TAKE (IT), AND LIKEWISE (HIS) SCRIP: AND HE THAT HATH NO SWORD, LET HIM SELL HIS GARMENT, AND BUY ONE.** ≈

Peter listening in the flesh did not hear the Master but shows his love his way; by using violence. Peter's flesh instructed him to protect the Master and as such, he responded. Peter's spirit did not understand the dichotomy between the flesh and spirit, and was still in the dark-despite Peter's insight. Peter was still in the dark because he had not received Jesus as truth yet. He had seen him and discerned Jesus' audible tongues but he had not *"heard or seen"* in the spirit yet.

When the slave girl identified Peter as a follower, he denied Christ three times[124] just as the Master said he would. Peter's flesh made him want to live, despite having to deny what he had seen and lived for three years. Despite having to deny the very Man that he claimed that he loved above life itself, the flesh is so powerful. It was not until after the cock crowed and Peter was convicted that his spirit was released and the word tells us that he wept uncontrollably

---

[124] Once for each year that he walked with Jesus, the number, three represents spirituality, meaning that Peter allowed his spirit to be overpowered by his flesh. (Matt 26:24).

Remember the flesh has no goals or desires but to serve self. It wishes to do neither harm nor good it just wants to reveal and bask in self. Is this not the true meaning of vanity? It was vanity in Lucifer that caused him to be cast out of heaven, so therefore vanity is evil, and the flesh is, too.

It was through Adam and Eve that sin/evil entered the world. For they too dwelt in the flesh and were not evil. It was not until vanity and covetousness manifested itself in Eve that evil[125] was found in the world.

I have no intelligent discourse to offer as to why this characteristic was also found in Heaven except to say that all things come from God and therefore there must be a reason for it. Nevertheless, we do not live in Heaven, and we are stuck here in this world in these pots (bodies) so it is to this we speak.

MOSES

Moses is heralded by the bible as the greatest prophet that ever lived (Deut 34:10). His journey was a very common one for those of us in the ministry. Referring to the story earlier about the skier in the letter *Cleaning and Scaling*. It is usually the characteristics, that make us good workers for God that get us in trouble. Most of us get into trouble because of our attitudes. Moses was a man of action and of compassion, but he was easily angered. His temper made him great for God. His temper caused him not to enter the Promised Land.

Is it ever acceptable to be angry? Yes believers it is okay to be angry, but the word tells us only do not sin. (Eph 4:26) ≈ **Be ye angry, and sin not: let not the sun go down upon your wrath:** ≈ Even the Messiah got angry but He did not sin. This means do not allow your anger to cause you to sin, Jesus did not, but Moses did. For Jesus still loved those He whipped out of the church, and He still died for them. Moses committed murder.

---

[125] The word *evil* perhaps is a contracted noun, like *human*. The word human actually is formed from *hued* and *man*, *woman* comes from the terms *womb* and *man*. Perhaps *evil* comes from the terms *Eve* and Will. As the bible records Eve getting her will and it this is the first deed of evil recorded in the scriptures.

Why then did God use Moses? His ways are not ours, besides God deals with hearts and souls not actions. He is not concerned with the flesh therefore Moses could be and was forgiven for his crime. It was Moses' anger that moved him to act and it was Moses' temper that caused him to help his wife at the well.

The Bible tells us that Moses died at 120 years old, and he wandered in the wilderness performing miracles for 40 years. That means, (if you do the math) that he began his work at the age of 80. Phenomenal that an old man was able to do what he did and still not be feeble when he died. (Deut. 34:7) ≈ **And Moses (was) an hundred and twenty years old when he died: his eye was not dim, nor his natural force abated.** ≈

However, this also means that it took him 80 years to be molded into a pot for God's use. Why did it take so long to fire him? The Bible says that it takes the hand of God to control man whereas it only takes a finger of God to control Satan. It is the free will of man that makes him so difficult to mold and to guide.

After 80 years of training, Moses interceded for the children of Israel numerous times. He actually beheld the majesty of God, and performed miracle everyday for 40 years.[126] Moses led the children of Israel from bondage into freedom and failed to enter the Promised Land because of his flesh.

In (Ex. 32:19) Moses lost his temper and destroys the two tablets God inscribed with his own hands. In (Numbers 11:11) Moses complains about the Israelites for they angered him. In (Deut. 32:51-52) Moses makes his fatal mistake which was to "break faith" with God. ≈ **BECAUSE YE TRESPASSED AGAINST ME AMONG THE CHILDREN OF ISRAEL AT THE WATERS OF MERIBAH-KADESH, IN THE WILDERNESS OF ZIN; BECAUSE YE SANCTIFIED ME NOT IN THE MIDST OF THE CHILDREN OF ISRAEL. YET THOU SHALT SEE THE LAND BEFORE (THEE); BUT THOU SHALT NOT GO THITHER UNTO THE LAND THAT I GIVE THE CHILDREN OF ISRAEL.** ≈ Unlike the other times, due to his temper, he did not wait on God to come through but lashed out and demanded a response. God called this breaking faith, for if we have faith we trust Him and will not require action but will wait on His grace.

---

[126] That amounts to 14,600 miracles, second only to Jesus according to the last verse of The Gospel according to John.

Because of his temper, Moses never entered the Promised Land, he saw it, but could not go in. As he explains to Joshua, (Deut. 32:51-52) that he was not able to go in because he broke faith with God when Moses was angry. God he said does not wish to start a nation based on anger. Although he laid down the law and judged for 40 years, Moses was never able to circumscribe his temper. Moses' inability resulted in losing part of his reward; he has yet to collect the rest of it.

I intentionally left Moses for last as his personal journey and the Children of Israel's journey from Egypt parallels the Christian faith walk:

i) The journey went from bondage and slavery to the Promised Land, just like going from sin to salvation.

ii) The journey took 40 years in the desert for although maps would indicate that it would have taken considerably less time. The wilderness experience is central to the faith walk. Just like the children of Israel, we will stay in the wilderness until all remnants of our old selves have died. Just like the original Children of Israel that left Egypt did. (Joshua)

iii) Without God's guidance, we will be lost.

iv) God will sustain us and give us obstacles to overcome. If we cannot overcome, then He will provide a way for us but instantly send another test.

v) Many of us will undertake the journey but many will fall by the way side and never give up. In some, the old ways will die; those who make it will be changed forever. They will not even look the same as they did when they started.

vi) Many of us will be used of God but our rewards will be cut short because we break covenant with Him. He will use us to deliver others but we will not all be allowed to enter the promise land.

vii) Many will try to go back from whence they came believing that the previous state will be easier and more desirable. However, when God undertakes us, He rarely lets us go back (to Egypt), more often than not we simply die trying. Often times not only does He send us help in the wilderness, much like the Red Sea, once He brings us out, He blocks the path back to complete bondage--in His mercy.

viii) As with Moses, often the wilderness experience is not a firing process, so much as it is a refining process. Moses was groomed for 80 years, both in Egypt and in Midian. His leadership qualities were groomed in Egypt, and his priestly skills refined by his father-in-law Jethro (a Midian priest) who by the way gave him great advice. The hard part that is always up to the individual is "attitude" which according to a Discipleship Course, I compiled is the true essence of Discipleship; attitude!

Moses was a great man, but he was a man of flesh and blood. His task was truly great and he paved the way for a great many people to follow him. He lost his brother and sister in the wilderness, watched his half-brother drown, and had to listen to constant grumbling for nearly 40 years. The Israelites became so disgusting that Moses had to intercede for them at least twice. Moses performed 14,600 miracles but he could not completely control his flesh.

Anger is a trap according to (Proverbs 29:22) ≈ **An angry man stirreth up strife, and a furious man aboundeth in transgression.** ≈ An angry man dwelleth in transgression. This is because like fear, anger is a doorway through which other spirits can enter. Anger leads into other devolutions such as hate, murder, jealousy, and vengeance. Although anger (spiritual indignation as my mother calls it) is apparently very normal we are warned against it and told not to sin.

Anger is a normal outcrop of living with other people, but we do not have to allow it to control us. The flesh is self-serving, anger is the result of not getting our way. One of the truest indicators of maturity is how a person deals with anger. If they still throw temper tantrums, they need to grow up.

A temper tantrum differs from an outburst in that the temper tantrum is simply ranting and raving because you are unhappy. The spiritual indignation felt by Jesus and Moses moved them to action, but Moses' anger went too far. Jesus was motivated to remedy the situation; Moses was simply tired, overworked, and fed up.

Believers, remember that the true nature of flesh is to serve self. This is why Paul says that he crucified his flesh daily. In order that he could serve the Father best, he had to circumscribe His passions and subject his flesh to strict discipline. He wrestled with the flesh, as we all do. However, he did not allow his flesh to allow him to be evil.

Remember, Paul initially was found persecuting the church because his flesh had told him that he was doing the right thing. He had to be reoriented in his spirit, not only to stop persecuting the believers, but he had to be made a new creature in Christ so that he could subject his flesh to the will of God.

I die daily becomes a life-style and not a slogan. This self-discipline is how you stay the course and how you develop muscle memory[127]. This self-discipline allows us to count as wrong what is wrong despite the flesh wavering and wanting to serve itself.

≈ **AMEN** ≈

---

[127] Muscle memory is a process whereby the body is trained to do things automatically, without thought. Most common types of muscle memory are called reflexes.

WORK AREA
LETTER XII

THE OTHER WHITE MEAT
THE TRUE NATURE OF THE FLESH

Topical Scriptures

(Col. 2:11) (Gen. 3:1-6) (Matt. 24-22) (Job 1:12) (Matthew 16:23) (Judges 12:5) (2 Sam 11:15) (2 Sam19:1) (2 Sam12:15) (Matt.11:11) (Matt. 14: 3-4) (Matt. 14:10-11) (Matt 14:13) (Matt. 26:42) (Matt. 8:29) (Matt. 14:30) (Luke 22:36) (Deut 34:10) (Eph 4:26) (Deut. 34:7) (Ex. 32:19) (Numb 11:11) (Deut. 32:51-52) (Deut. 32:51-52) (Proverbs 29:22)

1. WHAT MAKES THE FLESH EVIL?

2. WHEN DOES THE FLESH STOP BEING EVIL?

3. WHY WAS EVE SO EASILY TEMPTED? EXPLAIN YOUR ANSWER AND CITE SCRIPTURE.

4. WHAT TOOLS DOES SATAN USE AGAINST BELIEVERS?

5. WHY IS THE FLESH SO HARD TO DEFEAT?

6. KNOWING YOUR OWN FLESH WHAT SHOULD YOU EXPECT FROM NEW FISH?

7. DOES SIN CAUSE ILLNESS? EXPLAIN YOUR ANSWER AND CITE SCRIPTURE.

8. EXPLAIN WE NOT WRESTLE AGAINST THE FLESH BUT AGAINST SPIRITUAL WICKEDNESS IN HIGH PLACES?

9. HOW DID JESUS CONQUER HIS FLESH? CITE AT LEAST TWO INSTANCES.

10. DOES SALVATION INCLUDE THE FLESH?

ADDITIONAL NOTES FOR THIS CHAPTER

LETTER XIII

THE *MYSTERY* OF THE MINISTRIES

≈ He gave some to be emissaries; and some, prophets; and some, evangelists; and some, shepherds and teachers; for the perfecting of the holy ones, to the work of serving, to the building up of the body of Messiah; until we all attain to the unity of the faith, and of the knowledge of the Son of God, to a full grown man, to the measure of the stature of the fullness of Messiah; ≈ (Eph. 4:11-13 NHV version)

LETTER XIII ≈ THE *MYSTERY* OF THE MINISTRIES

He is my brother (Helps & Pastoral Ministry)
Milk & cookies (Kids Ministry)
Out of step (Dance Ministry)
Sirens (Music Ministry)
Mother may I. (Women's Ministry)

In holding with the definition in the New Hebrew Version of the Bible, the term "ministry" will be defined in this letter as meaning, *to the building up of the body of the Messiah*. In Matt 4:11, we see that the verb[128] minister has the following applications:
1. To have charge of: manage.
2. To give or apply in a formal way.
3. To apply as a remedy.
4. To mete out: dispense.
5. To manage or dispose of under a will or official appointment.
6. To impose, offer, or tender.
7. To manage as an administrator.

What I find curious is that theses applications came from a dictionary[129], not the bible. What is clear however is that the purpose of a minister to rebuild or repair an individual back to strength/health. What the angels did was put Jesus back in the condition He was in Matthew 4:1, happy, rested and well fed.

The Letter to the Ephesians chapter 4 makes one thing clear; the components listed are not the ministries themselves but elements of ministry. The tiers are designed for nursing the lost, sick and those that have need of a physician back to health. No matter how we slice the components verse 13 makes the point moot, we, the ministers of God are tooled to *minister* the flock into the unity of the faith. Therefore, the components not only are not exclusive, they NEVER COMPETE against each other. There the concept of the five-fold ministry is not accurate; the five-tiered ministry is more accurate.

---

[128] Remember verb is a action word.
[129] The American Heritage Dictionary. Houghton Mifflin Company. 1982, Boston, Ma.

Notice that the NHV uses different terms for the ministries or the tools of *building up of the body of the Messiah*. Apostle versus emissaries, the term emissary is more akin to ambassador than to apostle. This implies that this person is a dignitary representing a high authority or a Sovereign Kingdom. This might also explain why Paul was given such prominence amongst the church community to admonish churches and disciples alike.

Shepherds versus preachers would imply that some people have been called preachers are actually to mimic the behavior of Jesus. They should mimic Him in their attitudes, teachings and in the hierarchy of their functions (ministries). In other words, these shepherds are expected to place functions[130] in the same order of importance as Jesus did, and that would necessitate a restructuring of most church bodies.

I Cor. 12:27-31 lists the five ministries and these are the actual ministries ordained by the Father ≈ **Now you are the body of Messiah, and members individually. God has set some in the assembly: first emissaries, second prophets, third teachers, then miracle workers, then gifts of healings, helps, governments, and various kinds of languages. Are all emissaries? Are all prophets? Are all teachers? Are all miracle workers? Do all have gifts of healings? Do all speak with various languages? Do all interpret? But earnestly desire the best gifts.** ≈ (NHV). All other "ministries" are a contrivance of man. Some of them seemingly arose out of need but others seem to have been chosen to placate members or persons in offices/positions who wanted to do these things.

This letter will cover five of these so-called *ministries*, two of which can be inferred from the word of God but the others have come from the churches themselves. The functions covered in this letter are; I) Children's, II) Pastoral Care, III) Women's, IV) Dance, and V) Music.

Children' Ministry - (Milk and Cookies)

Although there is no direct scripture that accounts for the Children's function, several scriptures would give credence to the need for this mission. (Matt 19:13-14) ≈ **Then were there brought unto Him little children, that He should put (His) hands on them, and pray: and the disciples rebuked them. But Jesus said, SUFFER LITTLE**

---

[130] Also used instead of ministries allowing the five articulated ministries to remain exclusive.

CHILDREN, AND FORBID THEM NOT, TO COME UNTO ME: FOR OF SUCH IS THE KINGDOM OF HEAVEN. ≈

An intensive study of child rearing tips listed in the Bible, show scripture references in which the Father likens believers to children. It is therefore proper to utilize this concept for a function of the church.

Almost everything in the word of God is an example of what He wants us to do in the spirit realm. The examples He gives us are to be practical life lessons. In other words, the same lesson given to us in rearing earthly children are being used by Him to raise His children ~ believers. It is also the methodology approved by Him for the raising of newborn babes in Christ by His church. This is why we need to get clarity from God about assignments. God will lead us to or call us into a ministry. God is always clear about which ministry that is to be. However, we must ask for clarity sometimes as there maybe two meanings to a word God uses. An example would be the children's functions in the church. Children as we see in the word can apply to either human kids or babes in Christ, or it could be a general reference to the children of God.

This is why God's lines of communication are so important. Any councilor will tell you that the two most important factors of a successful relationship are communication and intimacy. These are the two most important in the marriage between Christ and the church as well. Clear lines of communication prevent miscommunication as well as they permit honesty and openness.

This best example of this relationship is in King David's relationship with the Father. Without openness, kids will not come forth and ask their parents, when they need advice. If the child is unable to ask their parents, they will do one of two things; resolve it themselves or ask somebody else. Believers, this can be very bad because the word tells us that curses are usually passed down from fathers to the children, but there are curses caused by the children. (1 Sam. 3:13) ≈ **For I have told him that I will judge his house for ever for the iniquity which he knoweth; because his sons made themselves vile, and he restrained them not.** ≈

Without intimacy, communication becomes meaningless banter, just unfeeling words. God maybe a lot of things but unfeeling is not one of them. We need to maintain closeness with the Father at all times in His employ so that we can maintain our status as His virtuous bride.

God gives us lessons geared toward the training of and disciplining of children. God told us to spend time with them and raise them up--we were not instructed to be their entertainment nor allow them to dictate terms to us. Therefore, the children's mission in the church should mimic child rearing in real life. When we fail to train our children, they end up delinquent and often in trouble with the Lord and the law. God's kids are the same or else He would not have likened them to children. If not properly trained they also turn into spiritual delinquents. Although playing and having fun is a healthy necessary outlet for children, it must not be at the expense of training. Fact of the matter is that the more time-spent training, the more time there will be for play later.

Probably the single most important reason that we need to properly train up the children is that much like Joshua and Caleb they will be the leaders of tomorrow. Alternatively, we cannot train them and they end up like Solomon's son and not only have a meager future but also have many of our Father's blessings taken away because they are bad stewards.

Let us look at what the bible says about children, (Deut 8:5) ≈ **Thou shalt also consider in thine heart, that, as a man chasteneth his son, (so) the Lord thy God chasteneth thee.** ≈ Taking into account that these traits apply to babes in Christ as well, the parents in this case would be God and the church.

There is absolutely no way to address the importance of family relationships to the body of Christ in anything less than a dissertation. Virtually every interaction God has with us is as His children. For this purpose it seems imperative that we undertake the proper rearing of God's children as well as our own. The simple fact is that the family is the true church and for the rearing of children. If the earthly families would train up their children properly at home, when they came out to the church they would be a blessing not a blight.

Satan understands the importance of family and as such has undertaken a huge incentive to destroy the family. In the last 100 years, there have been many tools introduced into society to make parenting non-essential and difficult. Consequently, there have been exponential leaps in child crime, drug use, prostitution, and unfortunately suicide.

We are giving our kids to Satan in droves and God's children in equal proportions. Television, video game arcades, day care and the drug Ritalin have replaced parents, and society suffers. Accordingly, the church has also paid for its lack of parenting with an increase of liberal Christianity, homosexuality, and teen pregnancy.

How is it then that we expect our fruit to be anything but rotten if we do nothing to manicure the saplings? For almost every lost child, I will show you inadequate parenting, and for every lost sheep an inadequate church.

My mother told me a joke when we were visiting her parents. She showed me a young man obviously destitute, and he was an alcoholic. The story she told me went a little like this. The reason that the guy looked like he did was that his parents did not like him because he talked too much. She said that every time they sent him to the store to get bread they moved! Although humorous, this is the case with so many sheep. Many of them have come to bad ends because the parents or flock kept moving every time they went out.

In the parable of the prodigal son[131], three aspects stand out in regards to child rearing. Firstly, the father loved the child regardless of what he did. Secondly, the father did not go out looking for his son but waited for him to return. Thirdly, the father never moved unlike my mothers' neighbours.

What this tells us is that we also must love our kids no matter what they do. To God all UNRIGHTEOUSNESS is sin; therefore, no matter what they do they are no worse than another. It also exemplifies to us that when our kids depart from the way we raised them and live amongst the pigs in the pen we do not go after them. The bible illustrates to us that; they will stay as long as they want to remain in this state no matter what we do. Until they count it as wrong, they will live with swine.

By staying the course, we exemplify two things; (a) we are staying the course no matter what. (b) Although we love them, (by not going to them where they are, we are telling them that) we do not approve of what they are doing. Remember the lesson from God is *unconditional love, not unconditional acceptance!* We must not move from righteousness. If we stay where we are, not only can they find us again, but also it shows that the lives we live are righteous.

Lost sheep too often have help getting lost. The constant moving of the flock is one of the main reasons the sheep end up lost. This is why shepherds have crooks to rein in the sheep. When the flock moves only the bastard lambs end up left behind. The lambs with fmilies are gathered up before the flock moves.

As a mother, the church is responsible for God's children and none of them are bastards. No matter what we may think of them, we cannot go around leaving sheep out as fodder for wolves. God will not forgive this.

---

[131] Luke 15:11-32.

If the sheep get lost, we are required to look for them. However, as we discussed previously, this is only if the sheep are lost. One of the ways lost sheep are found is they lie down and begin bleating. Although this is geared to notify the flock that they are lost, it has the unfortunate tendency to attract predators. This bleating indicates a lost, helpless lamb--ripe for the feasting.

Too many of God's children are left in this position by the flock. Sometimes we even cause the posture, but we have to recover them before the roaring lion devours them.

<u>Mother may I?</u> - (Women's Ministry)

Another function of the church that has some credibility is the women's function. This is not ordained as a ministry but again much like the children's function was born out of necessity.

The Emissary Paul outlines the true basis for the women's function by saying ≈ **And if they will learn any thing, let them ask their husbands at home: for it is a shame for women to speak in the church.** ≈ (I Cr. 14:35) The truth of the matter is this is a duty of the family-namely the husband. It is because the church does not extol family virtues any longer and the simple fact that the men in the church have failed miserably at their tasks as men that this function derived.

God placed man in charge and made him head of the woman, but like Adam, this is contingent on man staying in the will of God. If the elders and deacons admonished the men (those who actually come to church) in the flock, a lot of mortal strife could be avoided. The book of Titus tells the older people to help raise the younger ones by example.

For too long have we as a church allowed husbands to abuse, cheat on, and mislead their wives and families. The fact is that if the man is broken and lost he will drag his family down with him. Due to the apathy of the church and the fact that we allow bad fathering to exist in the church, women decided to go it on their own. Is there anything wrong with women in the works of the Kingdom? Absolutely not! Even the New Testament says that our sons and daughters shall prophesy (Acts 2:17), and in the Old Testament Debra was actually a judge (Judges 4:4).

Despite the positive implication of the women's functions, there is still an order to things in God's House that must be maintained. The word tells men to dwell with the woman according to knowledge--well if she has more knowledge than you do what happens? You become unequally yoked and the spiritual tension between the two gets worse. The educating of the saints is still the job of the church but the word tells the woman to go home with her husband and for them to grow together.

Again, the women's function is a result of the church not raising its members correctly and the allowance of inexcusable behavior. Because of pathetic men, the women's function has become vital to many churches and homes. Mary was more diligent and loving than the disciples were; the church would fail miserably without women.

Genesis 2:18 tells us that God created women to be helpmeets, in other words to help men achieve their best potential. For this reason, they are versatile because they were designed to be whatever men are not. If there is a need for a women's function, it is because they have to help the men meet their responsibilities.

There is a cliché that behind every great man there is a woman, well I put it to you that the converse is also true: Behind every destroyed woman; there is a man.

My Brother's Keeper - (Helps and Pastoral care)

A church flier for the pastoral care indicated that those involved needed to be willing to provide for the various. These include; ensuring at all times for the personal comfort, well being, physical needs, and spiritual needs for the Pastor. It also included providing the same for their family and guests. When I initially read the flier this passage of scripture came to mind. Ironically the passages are a part of the warning God gave the children of Israel about their new king Saul. (1 Sam 8:13-15)

≈ **And he will take your daughters (to be) confectionaries, and (to be) cooks, and (to be) bakers. And he will take your fields, and your vineyards, and your olive yards, (even) the best (of them), and give (them) to his servants. And he will take the tenth of your seed, and of your vineyards, and give to his officers, and to his servants.** ≈

If we maintain that the meaning of ministry is to the building up of the body of Messiah and we look again at the words in the handout several things jump out to me. No one in the service of God in the Bible had complete comfort, not even the Master Himself. As a matter of fact most of the New Testament disciples, evangelists and apostles spent their time in jail on the run and being persecuted.

If this much focus is required to deliver the meager yield one-day a week, there must be some barriers to the learning. For the Holy Spirit is our teacher and He does not waste time. The Master tells us to **TAKE UP OUR CROSS DAILY AND FOLLOW HIM** and as we know that was not a pleasant or easy trek.

There is never any mention in the word of Jesus' need for amenities and/or comfort. The Master's habit was actually to go out early in the morning in solitude, get on His knees pray and worship. Moreover, the only reference the word makes to Yeshua[132] being ministered to was after being exposed to Satan for 40 days and nights in the wilderness. The word then says that the angels ministered to Him. I dare say that no one since Jesus has spent that time or expended that amount of energy to the building up of the Messiah.

In further regard to the flier, in my opinion, if the pastor has time to have guests then he is not completely focused on the word and thusly negates his own claim to needing this type of adoration and care. Go back to the passage of scripture where Jesus is ministered to by angels. We see that the ministry that He received was directly proportional to the task performed. In other words, because of the great feat He performed His need for after care was also great. Nevertheless, other than Mary anointing His feet with oil there is no other mention of Jesus being cared for, He provided for Himself.

The Shepherd provides for His sheep and their comfort. Jesus' reward was great in Glory because of what He did versus who He was. For you see, He sacrificed everything. He had for His flock and poured into them without asking anything in return! Sheep do not routinely provide any services to their shepherds. They neither cook, nor clean, nor sing to provide entertainment to the shepherds. If we then are called to be like the Master, then we too must allow the Father to care for and provide for us as Jesus told us.

Believers, the Master warned us about taking things from people. He told us if anyone does offer us anything as servants of the Father to take it (just enough to sustain us.) Then the only thing we are supposed to give in return is the blessing of peace unto their house. (Matt 10:9-15) ≈ **PROVIDE NEITHER GOLD, NOR SILVER, NOR BRASS IN YOUR PURSES. NOR SCRIP FOR (YOUR) JOURNEY, NEITHER TWO COATS, NEITHER SHOES, NOR YET STAVES: FOR THE WORKMAN IS WORTHY OF HIS MEAT. AND INTO WHATSOEVER CITY OR TOWN**

---

[132] Jesus' name in Hebrew.

YE SHALL ENTER, ENQUIRE WHO IN IT IS WORTHY; AND THERE ABIDE TILL YE GO THENCE. AND WHEN YE COME INTO AN HOUSE, SALUTE IT. AND IF THE HOUSE BE WORTHY, LET YOUR PEACE COME UPON IT: BUT IF IT BE NOT WORTHY, LET YOUR PEACE RETURN TO YOU. AND WHOSOEVER SHALL NOT RECEIVE YOU, NOR HEAR YOUR WORDS, WHEN YE DEPART OUT OF THAT HOUSE OR CITY, SHAKE OFF THE DUST OF YOUR FEET. VERILY I SAY UNTO YOU, IT SHALL BE MORE TOLERABLE FOR THE LAND OF SODOM AND GOMORRHA IN THE DAY OF JUDGMENT, THAN FOR THAT CITY. ≈ God will provide for us in the form of benefactors. Consequently He never told us not to work and He most certainly warns us about getting fat off His flock.

Remember that the tithe is truly to be used to the building up of the body of Messiah. Note it does not say the body of clergy or pastors. They are here to serve us, and there is not a recorded instance of God telling the priests to get rich off the sheep. He gave them the spoils of the wicked and the world in the Old Testament, and He provided for their wealth. This is the most important part of God given wealth; God gives this wealth to those who glorify Him to the working of His deeds.

Some argue that the priests of old were told that the showbread, the remainder of the sacrifice, and the tithe were also to be used to sustain them. Nevertheless, I put it to you that those men lived consecrated lives and were ever on their face before the Lord. They forsook all for His works and retained nothing for themselves. Before the mule can be worthy of his hire, he must first be worthy of being hired.

God does not make people rich simply to make them rich. However, if you serve God honestly He will supply all your needs according to His riches in glory. His wealth is for His sheep and those who He makes rich are good stewards. Through them He can bless the other sheep He told us what He thinks of those who hoard money in (James 5; 1-6) and the parable of the talents. ≈ **Go to now, (ye) rich men, weep and howl for your miseries that shall come upon (you). Your riches are corrupted, and your garments are moth-eaten. Your gold and silver is cankered; and the rust of them shall be a witness against you, and shall eat your flesh as it were fire. Ye have heaped treasure together for the last days. Behold, the hire of the labourers who have reaped down your field, which is of you kept back by fraud, crieth: and the cries of them which have reaped are entered into the ears of the Lord of sabaoth. Ye have lived in pleasure on** the earth, and been wanton; ye have nourished your hearts, as in a day of slaughter. Ye have condemned (and) killed the just; (and) he doth not resist you. ≈

Conduits always have residual bleed over from whatever it is they transfer. Subsequently, good stewards for God will also be blessed with an outpouring and infilling of whatever they steward for GOD. This is why He tells us that He will open a window in heaven and pour out a blessing that you cannot contain. It is so He can bless you and with the overflow bless others.

Unfortunately, too many of us, unlike Boaz, will not even allow the poor to glean from the overflow, we want it all. In addition, we are willing to let sheep go to hell surround fame and prominence. Paul reminds us not to be boastful for it is only God doing the work not us. (1 Cor 9:16-18) ≈ **For though I preach the gospel, I have nothing to glory of: for necessity is laid upon me; yea, woe is unto me, if I preach not the gospel! For if I do this thing willingly, I have a reward: but if against my will, a dispensation (of the gospel) is committed unto me. What is my reward then? (Verily) that, when I preach the gospel, I may make the gospel of Christ without charge, that I abuse not my power in the gospel.** ≈

<u>Sirens</u> - (Music Ministry)

Music is a very important tool of any religion, and for a variety of reasons. The essence of music is sound, and the essence of sound is vibration. Going back to the creation of the earth and man they were both created by vibration; i.e., the spoken sound. Since the earth and all of its contents were created by the spoken sound, they are extremely susceptible/receptive to it.

Music has two important functions; the effect it has on God and the effect it has on man. As we study the effects music has on men, we see that music (harmonious sounds) are used to soothe. Rhythmic sounds are used to entice or drive, non-harmonious sounds are used to irritate or motivate people.

With this information in hand, is it any wonder that music plays such an important part in our everyday lives. Studies have shown that classical music played to unborn babies and infants, stimulates intelligence. Non-harmonious, harsh music seems to irritate the unborn babes and elevate their heart rates.

The Greek word for music is *symphonia* meaning "a sounding together." During the time periods of the bible the term singer and songs had two meanings. Singer also meant poet and song meant poem. Consequently, some of the songs mentioned in the bible are actually poems and some of the people who sang were actually speaking in prose (poems).

According to the scriptures, the Hebrew Temple actually became a school of music (sounds), and they employed professional musicians (soundicians) (2 Sam 6:5, 1 Ch 15, 16, 23:5, 25:1-6.) They even developed a tradition in the building of the temples that necessitated that Freemasons draw the plans and lay the cornerstone. The designs were created to maximize acoustics in the temples (especially cathedrals). The right design would cause the music resound and resonate upwards to the heavens, to glorify God.

A study of songs and singing in the scripture seems to indicate two main purposes for songs and; they are praise[133] and edification[134]. These two purposes not only seem very valid uses, but they are in keeping with the definition of ministry as to the building up of the body of the Messiah. There are no references to music in the temple for entertainment purposes or of music ever leading people to salvation.

Therefore, it is logical to conclude that the manipulation of sonic tools (instruments) to create performance sound conglomerations (music) is not a ministry in and of itself. Though definitely another useful tool afforded us by the Almighty in our service to Him.

Trying to use music to save people is akin to a policeman using his weapon as a paperweight, it is a misuse of a tool. A look into religions and cults in general made it apparent what music's functions is in a worship service. The music does not save the people or even bring them to salvation, nor does it keep them. The music is to prepare the person, to make them more receptive to the Spirit. The music's vibration is designed to soothe and relax people; or to hype them up in order to excite them. The words are important because they too are vibrations. We must be cognizant of the fact that the Father and Holy Spirit exist in a different plane. To them language is different, and we do not speak their language; their language is Heavenly and Holy.

---

[133] Exod 15:1, Exod 15:21, Exod 32:18, Jdg 5:3, 1 Sa 21:11, 2 Sa 22:50, 1 Ch 16:6, 23, 33, 2 Ch 20:22, 23:13, 29:30, Job 29:13, Psa 7:17, 9:21,13:6, 18:49, 21:13, 27:6, 30:4, 30:12, 33:2, 33:2.

[134] 1 Sa 21:11, 1 Ch 15:22, Deut 31:19, 31:21, 31:22, 31:30, 32:44.

Paul tells us that we pray in a language we do not understand. (Rom 8:26&27) ≈ **Likewise the Spirit also helpeth our infirmities: for we know not what we should pray for as we ought: but the Spirit Itself maketh intercession for us with groanings which cannot be uttered. And He that searcheth the hearts knoweth what (is) the mind of the Spirit, because He maketh intercession for the saints according to (the will of) God.** ≈ And again in Acts the heavenly tongue was mistaken for drunkenness. (Acts 2: 4 & 13) ≈ **And they were all filled with the Holy Ghost, and began to speak with other tongues, as the Spirit gave them utterance. 13 Others mocking said, these men are full of new wine.** ≈ Before there was music, there were sounds. Before language there, were sounds; men praised, prayed, and worshipped with sounds of their own devise.

The musical portion of worship became increasingly important as people moved further away from God. It was nothing for Adam to talk to God the Father in the garden. However, as man's sinful nature drove him farther away from God, it took more and more to get man into the frame of mind to worship and praise God. As the woes of life, hardened man's heart against God, the music became a tool to soften hearts. A tool to alter consciousness to the point that people will feel like praising God (this is how we arrive at the phrase mood music).

The type of service, (praise, or worship) is almost invariably determined by the tempo of the music and the instruments used. Musical tools (instruments) create sounds by means of moving air. Whether percussion, woodwind, brass, or string instruments the instrument creates sound by moving air and creating a vibration. This vibration then emits and projects as sound waves. The rather large ears that some of us have trap these waves and channel them toward the Tympani (eardrum), wherein the wave resonates against the drum and that information is translated as a sound.

All the science in this portion of the letter is to emphasize that music is not a ministry in and of itself. The use of music to simply entertain or simply offer people something to listen to other than the world's music prevents that type of music from being a ministry. Not only does the music that edifies tell about the Christian lifestyle but also in the true tradition the music is to teach. The music teaches believers, children, and non-believers about God's grace and the type of things that God does.

Crossover music neither edifies nor glorifies God. It is simply decent entertainment that is not offensive to anyone, but it does not qualify as a ministry. Music alone does not have the power to build up the body of

Messiah but it is a great tool to create unity in praise and worship. If taken out of the church, however, is simply a purely personal experience; but it does not rise to the level of ministry.

It also looses its power when offered not to move people but to display talent. An example of this occurred one day while I was attending a church. I was standing next to a young man who was grooving to the music. I on the other hand was trying to listen and fathom what on earth (or any other planet for that matter) the young lady was singing about. The young man who was enjoying the performance so much responded when I asked him what she was saying, "I have no idea",--he then resumed his dancing.

It never ceases to amaze me how some of the elder mothers of the church could lead praise or a worship service and had no ability to sing. Many pastors for years have also broken out in song with no tonal ability. These services often seem dry and without fervor after the songs, the service immediately continued.

To be effective, the music of the body must be sustained for two purposes. One is to allow the people to prepare for the arrival of the Holy Spirit and the second is to give the Holy Spirit a reason to come amongst them.

An analysis of the word inhabit would tend to suggest to us that the Holy Spirit lives among and for praises. (Psm 22:3) Earlier I refer to the music ascending to heaven; the same concept existed with smoke from the altar and in pagan religions things like incense and sacraments. The concept was to allow this offering as an appeasement and invitation to the deity. If the deity were pleased, they would come down from their abode and interact with the personage.

As Christians, we do the same thing as offering burnt offerings or blood sacrifices with the use of, praise and worship. When the Holy Spirit is appeased He descends to inhabit (dwell in) the praises of His people. He then deals with the body of believers present. It is then that the Holy Spirit is most receptive and pours out most into that fellowship. This is when spirits are convicted, freed from bondage and bodies healed. The praise and worship is our offering to God for all the good things He has done.

Psm 22:3 ≈ **But Thou (art) holy, (O Thou) that inhabitest the praises of Israel.** ≈ conjures up a mental image for me that I would love to share with you. The Father in heaven doing all the things needed around the universe, listening to Satan's accusations and talking to Jesus. With all the hustle and bustle a wee, small but ominous sound ascends from that third planet on the left, in a small town, from an obscure church. ***"What is that sound father? I'm not sure go check it out. Satan shut up a moment!"*** Jesus then comes down from the seventh heaven, biding the four and twenty elders to keep singing He will be right back. He then leans over one of the golden banisters and comes rushing back upstairs excited. ***"Dad! You gotta hear this"***. The Father then comes away from whatever it was He was doing and says, ***"What is it son?"***. Together They lean over the banister as the sound continues to grow louder and more jubilant. The sound is so glorious to Him that He steps out on a cloud and descends to earth (perhaps He even says beam me down Gabriel) to the sound of the praise. As He basks in the sound waves which warm Him and please Him He then comes down out of the clouds and enters into the sanctuary and floats about in the rafters enjoying and inhabiting the praises of His people. When He has enjoyed His celebration enough He pours out Himself onto the people and the blessings and healing abound.

A man was once asked, "What is in a name?" to which he replied, "It is what I am and who I am." The same question was asked about a song, and I would say about Jesus it is what He is and who He is ~ ***a celebration of God***.

Out of Step - (Dance Ministry)

In researching dancing in the bible, I find no scriptures that indicate a use for interpretive dance. If you look at the description of the dance moves, they are not soft and graceful ballet moves but the rhythmic fast-paced celebration dances. These dances represented praise and celebration.

The type of worship in the dance was a celebration of Gods grace and mercy. Yes believers, the dances were celebration (praise parties) to the Lord, and they were neither calm nor subdued, for God's grace and mercy is not subdued. God's grace and mercy are great feats worthy of praise and celebration, so much so that the Master starts His ministry with a celebration. Luke 4:18-19[135] indicates that the custom of celebrating the Lord went all the way back to the Old Testament.

The concept of praising the Lord with dance is not new, but it was never used as a ministry. Although it is an attempt to glorify God, it is the purity of the dance that is the worship. The dances were not

---

[135] Isaiah 61:1.

choreographed but literally jump and praise. In my country, we have something called *Rake and Scrape*, which came from instruments being used and fashioned out of odd bits. Hence playing these instruments consisted of raking and scraping them. The dances that derived from these sessions were very reminiscent of a group of children flitting and flipping about. There was no order or scheme, because the sole purpose of the dance was to have fun.

To worship God with a prearranged, choreographed praise-dance is much like Cain's offering. How can you plan for the Holy Spirit to come to you, and then how do you plan your response? True praise is sporadic and spontaneous, it is spiritual and do have not control of when God deals with your spirit. Matt. (19:13-14) shows us that the Master adores children because they are pure of intention and method and whatever they do they do with 100% intensity, right or wrong.

True ministry in a fellowship setting only takes place when those gathered worship in unity and strength. In the older churches, there was always an elderly lady or man willing to stand and sing at the drop of a hat. Although they invariably had no talent, they were always able to entice others to follow in the spirit.

Although they could not sing, they always were able by their display of willingness to involve the others and the Holy Spirit always blessed someone. In a fellowship setting, all or (at least many) of the persons there should be in unity of praise. No, the members of the body do not praise the Lord for the same reasons, but they all agree that He is due praise. So praise for whatever reasons you will as long as you praise Him.

The other problem with dance is that it does nothing but entertain the congregation. There are dances that edify and those that carry on tradition, interpretive dance does neither.

I was fortunate enough to attend a Barmitzpha (bat-mitz-fa) and it was a delightful experience. The service consisted of; a reading of the word, a rite of passage which was to recite several verses in Hebrew, a braking, and sharing of bread and a dance. The dance consisted of everyone getting (or being pulled) into circles and dancing around with arms laced upon shoulders and kicking legs. It was reminiscent of a chorus line. Although I was a stranger, they treated me just like everyone else.

Ballet is an art form. As stated before praise and worship should not be staged it should flow and ebb from the spirit. I assure either you if you cannot find something in your life to praise and glorify the Lord for, you are confused or already in hell.

In my Methodist high school, we sang a song (story) called, Lord of the Dance. The song relates the life and ministry of Jesus, the dance in the story is broken down into stages. Each stage of the dance (when performed) involved people joining the dance and following Jesus.

I danced in the morning when the world was begun, and I danced on the stars, the moon, and the Sun.
I danced in Heaven and I danced on the earth, At Bethlehem,[136] I had my birth.

Chorus: *Dance then wherever you maybe, I am the Lord of the dance said He. And I'll lead you all where ever may be, I lead you all in the dance said He.*

I danced for the Scribes and the Pharisees, they would not dance, and they would not follow me,
I danced for the fishermen for James and John, They came with me, and the dance lived on.

Chorus: *Dance then wherever you maybe, I am the Lord of the dance said He. And I'll lead you all where ever may be, I lead you all in the dance said He.*

They cut me down and I leapt on high, I am the Life that will never, never die, I'll live in you if you live in Me, I am the Lord of the dance said He.

Chorus: *Dance then wherever you maybe, I am the Lord of the dance said He. And I'll lead you all where ever may be, I lead you all in the dance said He.*

The last stanza describes Jesus being cut down off the cross. The word *dance* in the song was obviously indicative of a way of life. Joining the dance indicates the choice of leaving one's old life style and following Christ. This is the true dance of ministry wherein the participant dances (moves) through their spiritual life and grows closer to the Father. The

---

[136] *Bethlehem* or *Bethel* literally means city of bread, Jesus is the bread of Life.

scriptures indicate that dance can be expressive but the point herein is that expression in itself does not rise to the level of ministry. The scriptures (Ecc. 3:4) and (Matt 11:17) would indicate that the dance was symbolic of rejoicing. (Lam 5:15) would indicate that dance can be used to express mourning. Once again the various times dance is mentioned in the word none of these references even come close to being used for the *building up of the body of Messiah*---they are purely another form of expression; some of which are good and others bad.

≈ **AMEN** ≈

WORK AREA LETTER XIII

Topical Scriptures

(Eph. 4:11) (I Cor. 12:27-31) (Matt 19:13-14) (1 Sam. 3:13) (Deut 8:5) (Luke 15:11-32) (I Cr. 14:35) (Acts 2:17) (Judges 4:4) (Gen. 2:18) (1 Sam 8:13-15) (Matt 10:9-15) (James 5; 1-6) (1 Cor 9:16-18) (Luke 15:25) (2 Sam 6:5) (1 Ch 15, 16, 23:5, 25:1-6) (Rom 8:26&27) (Acts 2: 4 & 13) (Rev. 4:10) (Psm 22:3) (Psm 22:3) (Luke 4:18-19) (Isaiah 61:1) (Matt 19:13-14) (Ecc. 3:4) (Matt 11:17) (Lam 5:15).

1. DEFINE THE TERM MINISTRY.

2. WHAT QUALIFICATIONS ARE THERE FOR A MINISTER? EXPLAIN YOUR ANSWER AND CITE SCRIPTURE.

3. LIST THE COMPONENTS OF A MINISTRY? IS EACH ONE A MINISTRY BY IT SELF, EXPLAIN YOUR ANSWER.

4. WHAT ARE THE TWO MOST IMPORTANT FACTORS OF A SUCCESSFUL RELATIONSHIP?

5. WHAT TYPE OF RELATIONSHIP SHOULD A MINISTER HAVE WITH THOSE TO WHOM THEY MINISTER?

6. WHY DO CHURCHES HAVE SO MANY MINISTRIES?

7. ACCORDING TO EPH 4:11 WHO DETERMINES WHICH MINISTRY THE FISH ARE TO BE PART?

8. BASED ON THE EXAMPLE IN MATT 4:10 HOW IS MINISTRY SUPPOSED TO AFFECT THE FLESH?

9. COMPARE AND CONTRAST PRIEST AND MINISTER.

10. WHY IS MOST TEACHING ABOUT MINISTERS CONFINED TO THE NEW TESTAMENT?

ADDITIONAL NOTES FOR THIS CHAPTER

LETTER XIV

≈

THE THIRTEENTH TRIBE
(THE TRIBE OF JUDAS)

≈ Then saith one of his disciples, Judas Iscariot, Simon's (son), which should betray Him, Why was not this ointment sold for three hundred pence, and given to the poor? This he said, not that he cared for the poor; but because he was a thief, and had the bag, and bare what was put therein. ≈ (John 12: 4-6)

LETTER XIV ≈ THE THIRTEENTH TRIBE
(THE TRIBE OF JUDAS)

Although there are only 12 original tribes of the children of Israel (Gen. 35:23-26), a 13th tribe seems to have developed. The 13th tribe that seems to have emerged is the tribe of Judas Iscariot, the thief and betrayer of Jesus. The descendants of the 13th tribe have two divisions of offspring. Iscary are those who in the end became traitors. Iscaros are those who were traitors all along.

The following two scriptures account for one of the branches; in these people Satan manifested himself through their weakness and seizes control of their hearts. ≈ **Then entered Satan into Judas surnamed Iscariot, being of the number of the twelve.** ≈ (Luke 22:3) ≈ **And supper being ended, the devil having now put into the heart of Judas Iscariot, Simon's (son), to betray Him;** ≈ (John 13:20). In taking control of their hearts, he also takes control of their possessions and their ministries.

Like Judas, these tribes people were faithful at first. They lived and dwelt amongst us and praised and worshiped with us. Unlike Peter with his brash behavior and overly zealous attitudes, Iscary are the descendants of Judas who blend in and become members of the body of believers. Because our are eyes are always pointing out those, believed to be the problem, we have the wrong hearts. For you see, we judge only what we see, which are the actions, but the Father judges the hearts of men.

Satan, as we read in (John 13:2), also deals with the heart of man, for he too knows that the heart of man is the key to controlling him, ≈ **And supper being ended, the devil having now put into the heart of Judas Iscariot, Simon's (son), to betray Him.** ≈ In (John 13:2), the scripture tells us that supper has ended and even this is important. This is important because Satan's subtlety is even more apparent in the level of confidence he instills in people. Satan waited for Judas to finish partaking of the supper with the other eleven disciples. Even when our intentions are impure, Satan encourages us to blend with and mimic believers. Judas was always a dubious figure amongst the disciples, and described as a thief and he seemed to have a very contrite heart.

Even with his contrite and uninspired heart, Judas stayed with the disciples and supped with the Lord. Although the book of John relates that Satan entered Judas after the supper ended, Jesus referred to this betrayer throughout the meal and always knew that it was Judas. Either this was because Jesus knew from His power to know the future, He saw the condition of Judas' heart or He saw the evidence of Satan in Judas. Either way Judas knew that Jesus knew yet He still committed his betrayal.

Satan's subtlety is also shown here because he waited until Judas had endeared himself in the circle, and even partook of the Last Supper. He waited until Judas heard Jesus' description of the blood and the broken flesh before he entered his heart to betray Jesus. The genius of Satan and the weakness of Judas' heart become evident. After walking with the Master and supping with Him, Judas still did not recognize Him as the Master. Judas was deceived into not believing that Jesus was the true Messiah.

Satan entered the heart of this thief, and compelled Judas to betray Jesus unto death and crucifixion. This was truly masterful of Satan. Ironically, the prophecy calls for the Messiah to be denied, and betrayed by one of His disciples and then tried and crucified. The dichotomy then becomes if Christ was not the Messiah, as the Jews claimed: then why crucify and betray Him as such? Moreover, if He was the Messiah, and thus the saviour of the world, then why deliver Him up to crucifixion?

There are two reasons Judas became the betrayer of Christ.

i) The first reason is that someone had to do it. Someone had to be the impetus to fulfilling prophecy, and it had to be one of the twelve, this is what prophecy required. There is little discussion about what Judas did before being chosen and he adds little if anything positive to the three years with the disciples. He however, becomes the most pivotal disciple of the group. Not because he does anything wonderful or goes on to be a great apostle for Christ, but because he brought about the steps required to fulfill prophecy. Through Judas, Jesus was betrayed, handed over and as prophecy requires crucified. It was with Judas' help that the chief priests, captains, temple elders were handed the Messiah. (Luke 22:52) ≈ **Then Jesus said unto the chief priests, and captains of the temple, and the elders, which were come to Him, BE YE COME OUT, AS AGAINST A THIEF, WITH SWORDS AND STAVES?**≈

Judas provided the means for Jesus' arrest and trial. As popular (or unpopular depending on your point of view,) as Jesus was it seems very unnecessary that the mob would have needed any assistance in identifying Him. It is also interesting to note that when the mob came to make the arrests, they did not arrest the disciple who chopped off the soldier's ear they came for Jesus only!

i) The second reason that Judas became Christ' betrayer is that he was a thief and had the heart of a thief. The Bible tells us various things about thieves. (John 10:10) ≈ **THE THIEF COMETH NOT, BUT FOR TO STEAL, AND TO KILL, AND TO DESTROY: I AM COME THAT THEY MIGHT HAVE LIFE, AND THAT THEY MIGHT HAVE (IT) MORE ABUNDANTLY.** ≈ Because Judas in his heart was still a thief, not only was he evil but in his heart he was also a murderer. (1 John 3:15) ≈ **Whosoever hateth his brother is a murderer: and e know that no murderer hath eternal life abiding in him.** ≈

When we allow evil to dwell in our hearts, we easily become fodder for Satan's work. (Exodus 22:2), says that a thief is so low that if he is found with the evidence of his crimes, and then killed, the one who put him to death shall not be punished. ≈ **If a thief be found breaking up, and be smitten that he die, (there shall) no blood (be shed) for him.** ≈

When malice and evil dwell in our hearts, Satan has a very easy, time convincing us to commit crimes. Since the desire to commit the crime already exists, all one needs is a target and a little push in the wrong direction.

(Matthew 26:14) ≈ **Then one of the twelve, called Judas Iscariot, went unto the chief priests,** ≈ recounts to us that Judas sought out the chief priests and inquired of them what the reward would be for the betrayal of Jesus. This would imply that Satan even before the Last Supper had either duped Judas, or Judas had designs of his own.

(Matthew 27:3) ≈ **Then Judas, which had betrayed him, when he saw that he was condemned, repented himself, and brought again the thirty pieces of silver to the chief priests and elders.** ≈ This would tend to suggest that for some undisclosed reason, Judas did not believe that he was delivering Jesus unto his death. Acknowledging the heart of the thief is evil, Judas during the time of his discipleship with the Christ retained this heart condition. As did most of the disciples retain their heart condition, at least until Pentecost.

(Jn 12:6) ≈ **This he said, not that he cared for the poor; but because he was a thief, and had the bag, and bare what was put therein.** ≈ Maintains that Judas maintained the purse for the group, but it was not because he cared for the poor, but because he was a thief. This would tend to suggest that Judas' betrayal was money oriented.

What is very probable is that as the time was drawing nigh to kill Jesus, Judas was already trying to find a reason to steal or at least acquire an easy profit. As Jesus told the men when they came to arrest him, that it was only because He had allowed it that, it transpired to fulfill prophecy. This being the case, when Jesus lowered His defenses Satan (being the glutton for punishment that he is) assumed that Jesus had become weak and saw an opportunity to attack. Satan has always looked for a way to destroy the Jesus, since the prophetic curse in Genesis. When Satan saw what he believed was the chance of a lifetime, he jumped right into the plan.

Judas, just like the other eleven disciples was under the protection of Jesus for the three years. Satan was unable to sway Judas until such a time as Jesus allowed. When Judas went to the chief priests, it was because Jesus allowed this intrusion for the purpose of fulfilling the word. The strong man of the house having not been bound yet, Satan obviously had no power to come in and be divisive.

The word records that from the time, that Judas went to the priest in he spent the rest of his time trying to figure out a way to betray Jesus (Matthew 26:16) ≈ **And from that time he sought opportunity to betray Him.** ≈ We now see Satan fully at work in the heart of a thief. Instead of being blessed by the presence of Jesus, he spent all his free time trying to figure out how to earn his 30 pieces of silver. Instead of feeling a change and seeing the good things, that Jesus had done all the thief could see was money. Even when allowed to partake of the Last Supper (a sacrament), all Judas could think of was his 30 pieces of silver.

With no regard for the friendship of Jesus, or the disciples, moreover, with no fear of reprisal from Peter (the hothead), Judas betrays Jesus openly, publicly and with a most ironic gesture. In a greeting of brotherly love (the kiss), Judas betrays his Lord and Master unto the chief priests and the mob. Judas did what the crowds, chief priests, and authorities had failed to do for three years, get close to, and betray this Fisher of men from Galilee.

According to the word, the entire time Judas walked with Jesus and heard what He said. He saw the mercy and charity of Jesus, and knew that Jesus had done no wrong, betraying him for a fee was not in Judas' mind wrong. This is part of the inherent problem with sin it is never victimless. There were a host of sins committed during the trial and crucifixion of Jesus; this is a partial list;

I) Covetousness.
II) Blasphemy.
III) Bearing false witness against a neighbor.
IV) Murder.
V) Lying.

Sadly enough, sin like an airborne virus is highly contagious, and you do not have to know that you have been exposed to be guilty. For example, when Jesus was arrested (on false charges,) only those who knew of the plot were guilty of that sin. However, anyone involved from that point on was guilty of the same sins committed by Judas and the other liars. The chief priests had the Romans try, and crucify Jesus because their law forbid their doing so. As well as the fact that many of them knew who He was and like Pilate were trying to wash their hands of the crimes.

Sin you see, is like a piece of stolen property, only the person who steals it is a true thief. However, when the item is passed on, perhaps as a gift, all those who receive the item become thieves as well. We drag people down into our sin quite easily and our shortsightedness (greed) blocks our vision of the true effect we cause upon people and the world.

For a mere 30 pieces of silver, which he did not even retain; Judas help extinguish the Light of the world. Judas destroyed a man who never did anything harmful to him, walked, and supped with him for three years. A man who brought peace to so many people and never treated Judas in any other manner than with love.

When we have sins of any type in our hearts, they cloud our judgment and our vision. We develop severe shortsightedness, and the only thing we can see is the immediate gratification. Much like children, we refuse to acknowledge the inevitable consequences.

In the Old Testament, a veil surrounded the Holy of Holies. This veil separated us from the inner most sanctuary of God. The other thing the veil did was to block our view of the goings on in the Holy of Holies. We could not see the priest's goings on in the sacred place with the Father. When the motion at the end of the rope ceased,[137] it also prevented seeing what the priests did to be smitten.

The veiled chamber also served the purpose of isolating us with the Father and He alone confronts us with our sins. If we were unclean, we never left the chamber alive. The veil also kept God from having to be

---

[137] Scripture provides that the Priests were smitten if they or the party they were interceding for were unclean. The rope therefore contained bells, and when the bells stopped ringing the priest was dead and was pulled out.

amongst the unrighteousness of the world. While Jesus was with us, the veil obscured all from His presence but those He desired.

The last thing that the veil accomplished was to only allow those qualified (clean and pure) to come into close communion and see/experience the glory of God. The blindness caused by sin in our hearts has the same effect on us; it prevents us from experiencing the true joy and glory of God. It also prevents us from being able to come close to God and dwell in His presence.

When Jesus was crucified, the Bible relates that the veil was torn in two. ≈ **And, behold, the veil of the temple was rent in twain from the top to the bottom; and the earth did quake, and the rocks rent;** ≈ (Matt 27:51) With the veil torn (removed) things between man and God changed forever. One of the first things that changed is that all men were allowed open access to the Father's heart. What a wonderful Lord we serve to be so high above us and yet allow complete and unencumbered accesses to His throne room.

Another thing that changed was we had no veil to give the appearance of hiding our ways from God. God allowed us total access, but at the same time, we lost the preparatory levels of our relationship. Now, no longer are we expected to sanctify ourselves before coming before God as the priests did in days gone by. Now we are expected to be ever ready, ever vigilant, and ever sanctified. Now God expects us to live a life of sanctification and righteousness.

Yet another byproduct of this 360-degree view God granted is the view of God, This new view carries conviction. For you see both Judas and Peter and the rest of those involved were not 100 % sure until after the veil had been removed from their eyes and their hearts ~ and they had to concede His Sonship at that point.

Openness to and with God always glorifies and edifies us. God told Moses to remove his shoes before the burning bush for he was standing on Holy ground. Moses had no idea that there was a difference, and he did not know what was required to prepare to stand upon holy ground. When we communicate with the Father, He always lovingly points out what we need to change in our lives and our hearts before we can stand upright in His presence. Yes, He hears the prayers of sinners, yes He answers who He will. But He is under no obligation to answer the prayers of those that are not His. And to His children He is bound by as His will and answers according to the contents of our hearts.

Conviction comes because the barrier between truth and us has forever been removed. Now we must stand and judge our own hearts, and judge our own sins as wrong. As the spirit man now has complete unfettered access to God, He constantly reminds the flesh of its sinful nature--some call this a conscience. That which we call conscience or the little voice is the voice of grace telling us to get back on the path. It is the still small voice of God's guiding hand upon us. Too often, we allow the flesh to win. This is only because we do not truly understand our own hearts and motives are sinful and disobedient.

Just as when we were children, we craved the things, we wanted and rarely if ever, those things were good for us. All that God gives is good and all we choose is tainted, for we judge with our fleshly hearts and not our spirits. It is only through giving our spirit complete control over our hearts that we can be free and truly enjoy our blessings from the King.

When the veil was intact, no one told the priests which sins they were responsible for sanctifying themselves from, and they hoped that they got it right. The penalty was death for them. When the Lamb of God came He sanctified us all, and He got it right. He reopened the door to the Father, now our spirits talk all day--whether we want them to or not. Paul tells us that the Holy Spirit prays for us in moans and groans in a tongue, that we do not understand (Rom. 8:26 & 27).

The priests guessed many times what they needed cleansing from, but our standards are not God's standards and so many of them died still in because of their sin. Free communion with God, we can ask through our spirit exactly where are sins lie, what faults we have, and how best to be receptive to God's molding of our hearts.

Since Jesus already died for us, He paid that debt in full, but the result for many of us may still end up the same. We may find that hell is the result, but this death results in eternal suffrage. Most believers choose to feel that this openness frees them from the burden that the priests felt by coming into the Holy of Holies. The apathetic church fostered this view because of a lack of regard for the sanctity of the relationship with God. We always talked of needing to be able to speak to God and to be able to hear Him. When the veil was torn, God grant us complete access to Him through the death and resurrection of the Messiah, the formality was taken away forever. Now all day and all night what we do, say, or think displays in front of the King--all of it!

When David saw Bath-Sheba bathing from across the courtyard, it caused his loins to burn for her, to be with her and to be close to her. He was not able to satisfy this urge until after he had her husband killed and married her and was able to lay with her flesh to flesh. Even when he faced with the prospect of punishment for the adulterous affair and the murder of Uriah the Hittite, David pled to God. His plea was *"Do what you will with me only do not take the woman from me."* He earnestly accepted the lost of their first child if it meant keeping the woman.

If a mere man can love this way, can you imagine how much greater is the love of our Father? He loved us so much that He gave His only begotten Son to redeem us from the clutches of Satan and hell. God desires to be close to us even more vehemently than David to Bath-Sheba. Unlike David's fleshly desire for Bath-Sheba, God wishes to have intimacy and supplication with us spirit to spirit. In addition, like David He is willing to pay a high price to accomplish this. He gave His only begotten Son and is going to allow millions to perish[138] just to sup with those who love Him and obey His commands. Despite our love and admiration for God, He loved us first. The heart of a thief like any other sinful heart can be changed and saved.

The problem with the shortsighted heart is that it cannot see the results until too late. It cannot recognize its own evil until it has already done the damage. ≈ **Then Judas, which had betrayed Him, when he saw that he was condemned, repented himself, and brought again the thirty pieces of silver to the chief priests and elders, Saying, I have sinned in that I have betrayed the innocent blood. And they said, What (is that) to us? See thou (to that).** ≈ (Matthew 27:3-4) This illustrates to us how devastating this shortsightedness is to everyone. Judas was fine betraying Jesus and taking the 30 pieces of silver for his deed, until he realized that Jesus was to be put to death. The scripture tells us that he then went and repented himself and tried to return the 30 pieces of silver. Judas' self-condemning realization was that he had sinned and betrayed innocent blood.

The priests responded by saying, "What do you care, you deal with that!" The word tells us that Judas (with a repentant thief's heart) attempting to rectify the situation gave back the money and then went out and hung himself. Again, we see the confusion caused by Satan's manipulation of a sinful heart. If Judas had truly understood Jesus and repentance, then he would have not killed himself for Jesus forgives all. If forgiven for his betrayal, why then commit the murder and die in sin and still go to hell? Conversely, Jesus Himself had already told Judas that he was doomed for his deeds by prophecy. (Matthew 26:24) ≈ **THE SON OF MAN GOETH AS IT IS WRITTEN OF HIM: BUT WOE UNTO THAT**

---

[138] Remember, hell is ALWAYS by choice.

MAN BY WHOM THE SON OF MAN IS BETRAYED! IT HAD BEEN GOOD FOR THAT MAN IF HE HAD NOT BEEN BORN. ≈

Perhaps Judas was one of the vessels created for destruction as spoke of in Romans. What seems to be the case is that like many of us when faced with impending judgment, knowing that we cannot sway the judgment, try to make amends with our Judge. Not for the purpose of lenience, but to make ourselves feel better about the deed and the judgment. We can say well at least I said I was sorry; He must just be mean! In the Bahamas, there is an old saying; *"Sorry don't ease no pain!"* When we hurt people whether accidentally or intentionally, we must also realize that simply saying sorry may mitigate the acts, but as in the saying, it does not ease the pain. The apology simply becomes a way for us to make ourselves feel better about our deeds and ourselves.

An old adage maintains that brave men die once but cowards die 1,000 times. How many times do you think Judas died on the way from the garden, during the trial, on the way to return the money, and whilst preparing to hang himself?

Iscary (one group of descendants of the 13th tribe)

The life and death of the Judas is guaranteed to all of the believers who started out in the service of the Lord in earnest but in their hearts there was never really a change. Judas never really became new creatures in Christ, despite the changes they underwent, their hearts never completely changed, they never sold out to God completely. Consequently, storms characterize their lives and ministries and they constantly having to say, *"I am sorry!"*

Without the Holy Spirit completely dwelling in our temple, there is room for other things. I did not say our hearts, because the temple has more than one chamber, the heart it-self has four chambers and two large valves.

The Father told us to abide in His word and let His word abide us. Many times, Paul asks us to allow the Holy Spirit to fill us, and the Master told us that we would have rivers of Living Water flowing from us. Therefore, it is obvious that the Father desires to completely fill us so that there is no room for competition. He desires all of your attention for He is a jealous God; thusly He ordained marriage as a Holy institution that comes under Himself. He allows you to have and love a wife and kids and as long as you put Him first.

Many of us still having the old hearts begin to loose sight of why we are in the service of the Lord. We begin to see stewardship as a reward and not a responsibility. How many of us think that if we as bank tellers, started treating the bank's money as our own would we retain our jobs? Too many believers adopt this posture, and it is because they still have the hearts of thieves. When Jesus fills your heart and makes it anew, you like Judas just hold on to the bag because you are a thief.

Therefore, this is why so many church leaders move away from true benevolence and charity the wealthier they become. The more money we acquire, the further removed from God we tend to become. The day you received or will receive the Holy Spirit is the wealthiest day of your life. The sooner you realize this, the sooner you can enjoy a Christian life and Christian wealth. Like the rich young ruler, we cannot serve two masters, and the word tells us that a fool and his money are soon parted.

What greater folly is there to think that you can remain a thief in Jesus' service? A thief has no honor and Jesus knows that if you will steal from Him you will most certainly fleece His flock. Remember that Judas died penniless and alone, as many of us will.

This brings us to the tithe, administrators' most favorite portion of the service. We put an emphasis on the tithe, as if this mere portion of Christianity is enough, to either get us in or stop us from going to heaven. The book of Corinthians however, does not list non-tithers amongst those who will not inherit the kingdom of heaven.

Jesus said He came to fulfill the law, which means that we must tithe, but He Himself spoke against the acquisition of wealth here on earth. He spoke against acquisition of wealth by our means and as our goals as individuals. However, common sense should impress upon us that if He spoke against individuals aspiring to their own wealth and since individuals comprise the church. The same applies to the church as a body.

In the book of Acts, a married couple Ananias and Sapphira engaged in what white-collar criminals would term (loosely) tithe-avoidance. Like tax avoidance differs from tax evasion by means of loopholes, which legally allow for the non-payment of taxes. Tithe avoidance is a very subtle program in many churches, which uses the biblical principal of a blessing from God to shroud tithe avoidance.

This couple, who at the time was relatively wealthy, decided as a couple to lie about how much money they actually gave to the Lord. Because of their treachery and deceit, the Holy Spirit smote them both. They were members of a congregation, that was earnest and diligent about giving to the Lord, and as far as wealth is concerned they were a model of how a body of unified believers should be.

(Acts 4:34) ≈ **Neither was there any among them that lacked: for as many as were possessors of lands or houses sold them, and brought the prices of the things that were sold.** ≈ This relates that all the members of the church were doing well. Not because of their own accords but because they shared all they knew how and sold their land to make sure everybody had a comfortable life.

Ananias and Sapphira were practicing tithe avoidance and like the apostle asked them, ≈ **Before you sold the land, were you not in control of it, and after you sold it, was not the money yours?** ≈ In other words, they did not have to sell the property, it was their choice, and neither did they have to give the money that too was their choice. The problem was that they claimed that the proceeds they gave to be the entire gain from the sale. Their intentions were obviously to deceive the apostle by presenting less than they claimed they did. They, much like too many brothers and sisters, tried to put on a facade of earnest love and compassion by selling their land and putting the money into the flock. The problem is like too many of us this was just for show and they paid a dear price for their pretense.

It is completely note worthy at this point to point out that Peter asked them why they allowed Satan to fill their hearts and cause the deceit[139]. Again, we see the heart of a thief prevalent in even this happy successful little church. More important than that is the fact that Peter makes it clear that the deceit was perpetrated against the Holy Spirit. Why is this so important? Well believers, it is of the utmost importance for three reasons:

1) The Holy Spirit had to tell Peter of their deceit. This means that the Holy Spirit alone keeps record of the tithes. Peter never made mention nor could he have known of the true dividend from the sale of the property. If it is the Holy Spirit who keeps the books, we find that man's record of tithes and/or offerings are completely useless; they are simply man's attempt to impose control over something they have no control or input.

2) Since the Holy Spirit is the only judge Christians recognize, He extolled the sanction against these two. This brings us to another common church practice, not allow members certain privileges without proof of

---

[139] (Acts 5:3).

their 10% tithe. This privilege is based on the church records of how much the person gave and how much the person makes. This is completely improper, for the tithe and the offering are for God's work. The book of Malachi asks will a man rob God? It does not ask will a man rob the church! Whether or not a man robs another man is a matter for the courts to adjudicate.

As the example in Acts points out, God adjudicates a man robbing God. Peter's question exemplifies that it would have been better for the couple to have not sold the property and given the false report. Theft here is not in not giving, but in lying about how much they gave. This brings us to tithe avoidance a very common practice in church today. Many Christians tithe vast amounts of money into their churches but still the promises that the pastor's promise in their tithe and offering messages never seem to manifest in the lives of the believers.

The Master spoke of the meat in the storehouse; it is and ever will be for His people, not for the storehouse to gorge itself. The modern church lacks power primarily because it misuses its resources. The wealth of a church is the healthy spirituality of its members; a distant second is material wealth. Many churches and their staffs are wealthy but the flock is ragtag. Their bills are not being met, they are in bad health and their lives are weak and without joy. Their families suffer and are falling apart and for the most part, they lack the Holy Spirit.

Unlike the church in Acts (regarding the monies put in the storehouse) the meat is not being used to feed the flock but is being stored and squandered by the shepherds. They spend it or useless programs that benefit little or nothing and do not increase the level of the Holy Spirit in the church. Any farmer that has hundreds of head of healthy cattle, but a starving family is foolish, and the bible tells us that a fool and his money are soon parted.

3) The third reason it is important is that the lesson here clearly is not the giving, but as it is with all of God's lessons, the condition of the heart. The implication is that amount is far less important than attitude. The tithe although obligatory falls to a lesser standard of requirement than love. Let us never forget that Jesus confirmed that the greatest of all commandments. ≈ **And Jesus answered him, THE FIRST OF ALL THE COMMANDMENTS IS, HEAR, O ISRAEL; THE LORD OUR GOD IS ONE AND THOU SHALT LOVE THE LORD THY GOD WITH ALL THY HEART, AND WITH ALL THY SOUL, AND WITH ALL THY MIND, AND WITH ALL THY STRENGTH: THIS IS THE FIRST COMMANDMENT.** ≈ (Mark 12:29 & 30). Had the couple not given, it is

certain that they would have been out of unity with the congregation, but they would have been in a far better position to be in good with the Holy Spirit.

Again, we must understand that the punishment was not for not giving money, but for being deceitful as to how much money they gave. When we have churches running over with money, and they still lack power, their members are sick, weak, and poor it is obvious that the problem is not tithing but sinfulness and a lack of the Holy Spirit. The deceptive practice of the couple was to give an amount, but call it another amount with the purpose of holding some back. In which way does this differ from giving a portion, but using it as a tax write-off and or deduction? If your 10% of your tithe is equivalent to $4,000, but you claim this on your taxes, verified by the meticulous records kept by your church. Then you get a refund on that $4,000 of perhaps $400 then there becomes a problem. Believers never confuse cleverness with favour from God, favour from God comes unexpectedly, and we cannot plan our own favour.

Going back to the math of the matter, the fact is that you only gave $3600 to God in earnest. This is because it was always your intention to claim the tithe on your taxes and get a dividend on it. Why else would you have filled out the tax form, He alone keeps record of what you give unto His work.

When the tithe was agrarian based the food (or as the word calls it the meat) was brought to the storage place and stored up. When the needy came to get assistance there was never a requirement to show membership, or a tithe record, nor did they have to be from a particular socio-economic status or church. The only requirement was that they be needy. Jesus told us ≈ **THE POOR WILL BE WITH US ALWAYS.** ≈ Because they will always be with us, the storehouse should constantly be taxed.

There can only be two reasons for storehouse to be found bulging; unexpected wealth throughout the land or the storehouse is hoarding the food. It is obvious that the first could not be the case with the unemployment rates skyrocketing and the poverty level having almost 20% of the people of this country living below it. As far as the theory of saving the stores as Joseph did to prepare for a famine, there are two flaws in this excuse.

1) The Lord told Joseph that the famine was coming and specifically to prepare.

2) The stores are not being stored in the storehouse but spent on other endeavors which are neither uplifting God, nor helping the poor. It is obvious that hardship, starvation, and poverty are still running rampant throughout the world--where is the meat?

The Bible tells us that the wealth of the wicked will be given to the righteous. The implication of this is that God will provide a way for the wealth of the world to filter into the storage houses and bless His children through means of His devise. It is apparent that the concept was not the fleecing of His flock. God's children were not to be held in indentured servitude to those allowed to shepherd over them. It defeats the purpose of the blessings to keep taking the blessings of God's people and funneling them back out into the world. Believers, why is it that at every juncture we work against God's good plans expecting to prevail?

If we give a true tenth of our first fruits, then we should acknowledge our debt to God in silence and humility. Nothing we ever do for God should be held up for the world to see. If glory is to be found in what we do then let God find it. After all, it is all for His glory that we work not our own. (Matthew 6:1) ≈ **TAKE HEED THAT YE DO NOT YOUR ALMS BEFORE MEN, TO BE SEEN OF THEM: OTHERWISE YE HAVE NO REWARD OF YOUR FATHER WHICH IS IN HEAVEN.** ≈

Brothers and sisters let us endeavor to keep up with the stores in the storehouse, as good stewards over God's property should be, but when you give your tithes do so in secret. Give your first fruit and watch God's blessings manifest in your lives. There is no cause to let man ever know what business you have with the Father. A side bar to this, do not believe that you can bribe your way into heaven. A tithe from a sinner is merely a donation not a seed sown. Gods' plans work as programs, tithes, plus righteous living; in addition to prayer will result in response. If you want to see God work for and in you give Him something to work with. Being obedient is better than sacrifice, but a loving, adoring child is a pleasure to a Father. The working of the Father takes time to manifest itself from the Spirit through our disgusting flesh, but He does honor His word. There is no way for you to tithe, pray, and live right and God not bless you.

However, do not be on the constant look for monetary blessings. God blesses you according to your needs, not always (if ever) your wants according to His riches in glory. His riches include money, health, kids, long life, peace, joy, happiness, safety, and a host of other things. Be grateful in everything God does for you for whatever it is worketh to your good.

Iscaro   (The second branch of the tribe)

Iscaro, are the least desirable of the two branches. Iscaro became part of the church for the sole purpose of defrauding and robbing the flock. It is of these people James 5 speaks. Iscaro have the fly by night ministries and churches. They take God's money and play stocks, support adulterous affairs and embezzle funds into offshore accounts. These members always, have the best of everything paid for with church money.

In return what do Iscaro give? Their mere presence and no works at all. They find good, honest, usually young people, and convince them that the liberal ultra-modern church is the latest move of His body. They find many supporters, sheep that find a place in this motley-flock wandering aimlessly through the wilderness. The churches are often very large with vast amounts of offices in the church and dozens of people in the pulpit with them. They reward these lost sheep with position and title for their work for their eternal souls.

Iscaro belong to all the civic groups and have an accolade of degrees in various things. Their services last for hours on end, but a tiny portion of the service is actually worship and teaching. They simply sit in robes and costumes (Ephods) lording over their conquests and gracing the parapet with an occasional skip and hop which is supposed to imply fervor.

At every opportunity, Iscaro use church funds as front collateral to further their financial gains. They then either pay the money back out of their dividends or chalk it up as a loss through some failed program.

What better job for a man or woman with no conscious, to be paid to perform in the name of God? Iscaro are even better than Hollywood for their position usually affords them, an unencumbered reign and journey. People are so taken by the air of the church that no one even challenges the men of the cloth. They are not infallible; all men must measure up to the word to be beyond challenge or reproach.

The book of James calls for the rich to weep and howl for the miseries coming upon them. Growing up in the upper echelon of society, I assure you that the pains men go through to acquire wealth cost them dearly. It is very difficult to acquire it honestly. The word tells us that the rusted wealth of our lives will not only be a witness against us and will consume us like fire. Here they speak of the addictive nature of money as well as the destructive nature.

History has shown us how the desire for wealth caused horrible acts of human nature; second only, to the acts committed by those who acquire the wealth. Then they use the wealth as do most; for evil. The wealth will be a witness against us for all who know wealth know that it is very difficult to obtain it without favors and friends in low places. Even if you yourself do not do the deeds yourself, if you work for a company that makes a fortune providing services to those who really cannot afford it you are plundering the poor. (James 5:4) ≈ **Behold, the hire of the labourers who have reaped down your field, which is of you kept back by fraud, crieth: and the cries of them which have reaped are entered into the ears of the Lord of sabaoth.** ≈

(James 5:5 & 6) ≈ **Ye have lived in pleasure on the earth, and been wanton; ye have nourished your hearts, as in a day of slaughter. Ye have condemned (and) killed the just; (and) he doth not resist you.** ≈ Talks of those who have stockpiled wealth and lived high on the hog, and it tells us that they love to, "Put to death the righteous man; he does not resist you." How is that they have put the righteous to death? Some contend that this refers to the oppression and exploitation of the underlings for personal gain. However, it is my contention that this also refers to the inner man and a spiritual death.

The oppression of the righteous is easy, for they honor authority and they abide by the law, waiting for change and improvement to happen slowly. The rich put them to death by working them into an early grave, robbing them and taking from them all the way. An economy is based on the honest, for they alone pay their dues. Thieves and crooks are blights on the system because they take from it rather than contribute. The righteous are slowly killed spiritually, for they watch the world get rich through eyes of the flesh and they wonder where God is.

The righteous watch the wicked and dishonest accrue wealth and live happy lives while they struggle financially, socially, and in their personal lives. Bit by bit this wears on their Christian life and they become dissatisfied and unhappy. Their righteousness does not permit them to do the things the world does, which are to lie, cheat, and steal to get ahead. They are humble servants of God and good Christians, they do not rebel or cause upheavals; thusly, they are the perfect victims.

Iscaro sense this as well; consequently, they also prey on the humble and the righteous. Nevertheless, they kill them and imprison them with false teaching and false doctrine. They imprison people with false teachings that imply if you are faithful with your tithe, you will have no problems with the devil. If you are sick or need deliverance, it is because you are not a good tither or you need to increase your giving. They tell us that if you want to increase your blessings from God, increase your tithe beyond the required 10%.

Probably the most sinister of all is the doctrine they push is that you will not get any kind of breakthrough, if you do not give money; some even tell you how much. Jesus spent most of his time with the poor, telling us as He went that they would be with us always. If you could not achieve anything in the kingdom and if you could not be blessed without giving money, why was He wasting His time fooling around with the poor?

There is not a documented case of Jesus taking up either a tithe or an offering or for that matter the Bible makes no mention of Him paying one either. In conjunction many of the poor have no money and there are droves of people who do not work - are we to believe believers that they are doomed to Hell for being poor.

Is it not true that Jesus taught us that it is easier for a camel to enter through the eye of needle than for a rich man to enter heaven? Did He not tell the rich young ruler to sell everything and give it to the poor? We miss a very important lesson that Jesus taught us in this story. *The poor owe us nothing because they have nothing, on the contrary we owe them everything.* Yes believers, we owe them everything, God would not have blessed us thusly if it were not for them. If there were no lost, poor, and needy, Jesus would not have come, He told us this. God blesses us so that He can bless them through us. We are merely stewards of His treasure.

Jesus came to help the poor and to set the captives free. Jesus He walked with them, lived with them, and showed us that what we have and what we are is to be a blessing to others.

Believers, if Jesus had decided not to be crucified because it would hurt and to take all the money He could, would He have still been Jesus? Yes but, I assure you that He would not have gotten any glory in heaven. Jesus's glory resulted from taking all that the Father gave Him and blessed others with it. He gave; the clothes off His body, the skin off His back and both the blood and water in His veins. He did all of this without fleecing the flock, without becoming filthy rich and most importantly without telling others that without financial contribution they would be meager Christians, with no blessings or power.

The emissary Paul (as well off as he was from making tents) used his acquired wealth to devote himself entirely to God's work. He who fed himself for the most part as well as his disciples clothed them and traveled at his own expense. Paul spent his ministry in jail, but he assures us that he had riches beyond compare. He considered himself honored to be a bondservant for Christ. To spend his wealth on earth working for minimum wage in heaven therefore when he retired his benefit package was unbelievable.

With all the monies that men accrue, they have been unable to stop the one thing that only Jesus has conquered – death! Die we will, and die we must. However, we can live everyday for Christ, and when we do die, we will see death as the blessing it is, to be called home and given eternal peace and joy.

The book of James reminds us that money not spent is valueless, it is just paper and metal bound to decay and fade away, just as we do. To store money in this life is as futile as storing up foodstuff for the next life; neither can sustain us, only God does this. Neither can money alter, nor control one iota of time, life is all in His and, it is all His money. It is His command that we the able take care of those that are unable. Just as He takes care of (us) we who cannot care for ourselves.

Suppose the Father stored His mercy and grace in a bank like we stockpile money. He withheld it from us as we do the poor-can you imagine the misery and strife we would undergo? It would be just like being poor and worrying as the disciples did about lodging, food, and money. However, the Master reassured them that He would provide for everyone as He always has and we are His proviso here on earth!

WORK AREA LETTER XIV

≈

THE THIRTEENTH TRIBE...
THE TRIBE OF JUDAS

TOPICAL SCRIPTURES

(John 12: 4-6) (Gen. 35:23-26) (Luke 22:3) (John 13:2) (John 13:2) (Luke 22:52) (John 10:10) (Deut 24:7) (Exodus 22:2) (Matt 26:14 (Matt 27:3) (Jn 12:6) (Matt 26:16) (Matt 27:51) (Rom. 8:26 & 27) (Matt 27:3-4) (Matt 26:24) (Acts 4:34) (Mark 12:29 & 30) (Matt 6:1) (James 5:4) (James 5:5 & 6)

1. WHY IS THEFT SO COMMON IN THE CHURCH? AND WHY IS IT TOLERATED?

2. WHY IS MONEY SO IMPORTANT IN CHURCH?

3. EXPLAIN THE PROSPERITY DOCTRINE IN TERMS OF, "I WOULD THAT YOU PROSPER AS YOUR SOUL PROSPERS."

4. DOES TITHING OVERRIDE UNRIGHTEOUSNESS?

5. WHY WAS JUDAS AS EASILY USED BY SATAN AND THE PRIESTS? CITE SACRIPTURES.

6. HOW DID JESUS RESPOND TO THE RICH YOUNG RULERS QUESTION – WHY? WHY DID THE RULER WALK AWAY SAD?

7. CONCERNING ANANAIS AND SAPPHIRE IN ACTS 5 WHICH OF THEIR TWO SINS CAUSED THE PROBLEM?

8. WHY SHOULD WE TITHE?

9. CITE THE VERSE OR VERSES IN THE BIBLE THAT SAY TO SPOIL PASTORS AND SUPPORT THEIR LAVISH LIFESTYLES FROM THE TITHE.

10. CONTRAST JAMES 5 TO THE PROSPERITY DOCTRINE. RECONCILE THE TWO IN AN ANSWER ABOUT MONEY TO A NEW FISH.

ADDITIONAL NOTES FOR THIS CHAPTER

LETTER XV

≈

ETERNAL AFFAIRS
AUTHORITY IN THE CHURCH

≈ For the time (is come) that judgment must begin at the house of God: and if (it) first (begin) at us, what shall the end (be) of them that obey not the gospel of God?. ≈ (1 Pe 4:17)

LETTER XV ≈ ETERNAL AFFAIRS...
AUTHORITY IN THE CHURCH...

In all governmental agencies, a body is empowered to enforce rules and regulate behavior. The same system of checks and balances occurs in the body of Christ; with Christ, of course, having the final say. ≈ **Therefore, judge nothing before the time, until the Lord come, who both will bring to light the hidden things of darkness, and will make manifest the counsels of the hearts: and then shall every man have praise of God.** ≈ (1 Corinthians 4:5).

≈ **THEREFORE WHATSOEVER YE HAVE SPOKEN IN DARKNESS SHALL BE HEARD IN THE LIGHT; AND THAT WHICH YE HAVE SPOKEN IN THE EAR IN CLOSETS SHALL BE PROCLAIMED UPON THE HOUSETOPS. AND I SAY UNTO YOU MY FRIENDS, BE NOT AFRAID OF THEM THAT KILL THE BODY, AND AFTER THAT HAVE NO MORE THAT THEY CAN DO. BUT I WILL FOREWARN YOU WHOM YE SHALL FEAR: FEAR HIM, WHICH AFTER HE HATH KILLED HATH POWER TO CAST INTO HELL; YEA, I SAY UNTO YOU, FEAR HIM.** ≈ (Luke 12:3-5).

The bible gives us checks and balances so the body can stay within the bounds of Christ.
~ Admonishment[140]
~ Scriptures[141]
~ Prophets/prophecy[142]
~ Tongues[143]

Bearing in mind Roman 13:1&2 there are only three types of authority in the church; Authority directly from God, delegated authority (which comes from man) and illegitimate authority. In the Old Testament, God himself gave men authority to rule and to judge in His-stead. Men like Moses, Abraham, Isaac, Jacob, David, and a host of others. However, let us not forget that He also gave authority to Pharaoh, Herod, Pilate (John 19:11). ≈ **Jesus answered, THOU COULDEST HAVE NO POWER**

---

[140] (1 Thess. 5:14), (Rom. 15:14), (Col 1:28), (Col. 3:16), (2 Timothy 3:16), (Titus 1: 9-13), (Titus 2:15).
[141] (Acts 17:11).
[142] (1 Cor. 14:2& 4-5).
[143] (1 Cor. 14:22).

(AT ALL) AGAINST ME, EXCEPT IT WERE GIVEN THEE FROM ABOVE: THEREFORE HE THAT DELIVERED ME UNTO THEE HATH THE GREATER SIN. ≈ Although these men like Saul abused and misused the power, they were still anointed by God. They were anointed to do His will and they were also created to help fulfill prophecy.

What Jesus is telling us is that persons sitting in authority were either placed there or allowed there by God. Sometimes people ascend in order to make room for God's people to do the true work. An example of this is the butler who was incarcerated with Joseph and allowed a way for Joseph to ascend almost to the position of king.

Many of us do not understand that the refining process to leadership is a very harsh one and very few ever really achieve greatness. This is not due to God's failing, but our inability to conform and maintain His strict regimen. However, it is only the magnitude of the reward that necessitates very strict measures. If you want the reward Jesus got, He told us to pick up our cross daily and follow Him. If you want to be reverenced and worshipped day and night, to have every knee bow and every tongue confess you king all you need to do is what Jesus did exactly the way He did it. When was the last time you mastered a feat so great that the angels themselves had to minister to you and nurse you back to strength?

Another thing that differentiates God's appointments from man's is that when the Father anoints you it is for life. The rest of your life anyway. I say this because the word tells us that there can be no covenant without death (Hebrews 9:14-22) ≈ **How much more shall the blood of Christ, who through the eternal Spirit offered Himself without spot to God, purge your conscience from dead works to serve the living God? And for this cause He is the mediator of the New Testament, that by means of death, for the redemption of the transgressions (that were) under the first testament, they which are called might receive the promise of eternal inheritance. For where a testament (is), there must also of necessity be the death of the testator. For a testament (is) of force after men are dead: otherwise it is of no strength at all while the testator liveth. Whereupon neither the first (testament) was dedicated without blood. For when Moses had spoken every precept to all the people according to the law, he took the blood of calves and of goats, with water, and scarlet wool, and hyssop, and sprinkled both the book, and all the people, Saying, This (is) the blood of the testament, which God hath enjoined unto you. Moreover, He sprinkled with blood both the** tabernacle, and all the vessels of the ministry. And almost all things are by the law purged with blood; and without shedding of blood is no remission. ≈

In addition, by the sacrifice of the Lamb for the world, we all have been born into covenant agreement with the Father. In the Old Testament, the anointing was unto death, as the Lamb of God had not yet come. Those with the Father paid great costs to achieve what they did and when their task was done, their anointing was removed. When the anointing was removed, the servant of the Lord was called home to receive their reward. The death of their anointing was a death to this world and entry into eternal life. ≈ **And Moses stripped Aaron of his garments, and put them upon Eleazar his son; and Aaron died there in the top of the mount: and Moses and Eleazar came down from the mount**. ≈ (Numbers 20:28)

Anointing only is bestowed for the uplifting of the Kingdom and there are only two ways to remove the anointing.
i) God removes your anointing and when this happens the anointed dies.
ii) The anointed chooses to no longer serve and destroy yourself. (1 Sam 31:4) ≈ **Then said Saul unto his armour bearer, Draw thy sword, and thrust me through therewith; lest these uncircumcised come and thrust me through, and abuse me. But his armour bearer would not; for he was sore afraid. Therefore, Saul took a sword, and fell upon it.** ≈ Otherwise, no man can undo your anointing nor should men question it, as they did not give it[144].

With the anointing, there is always a badge or emblem of the office. For it is the office the person represents that has the power and authority. For some prophets it was the staff, a symbol of correction and guidance as well as support. For others it was garments and priestly robes that were symbols. (Lev. 8:30) ≈ **And Moses took of the anointing oil, and of the blood which (was) upon the altar, and sprinkled (it)**

---

[144] **And when He was come into the temple, the chief priests and the elders of the people came unto Him as He was teaching, and said, By what authority doest Thou these things? And who gave Hhee this authority? And Jesus answered and said unto them, I ALSO WILL ASK YOU ONE THING, WHICH IF YE TELL ME, I IN LIKE WISE WILL TELL YOU BY WHAT AUTHORITY I DO THESE THINGS. THE BAPTISM OF JOHN, WHENCE WAS IT? FROM HEAVEN, OR OF MEN? And they reasoned with themselves, saying, If we shall say, From heaven; He will say unto us, Why did ye not then believe Him? But if we shall say, Of men; we fear the people; for all hold John as a prophet. And they answered Jesus, and said, We cannot tell. And He said unto them, NEITHER TELL I YOU BY WHAT AUTHORITY I DO THESE THINGS.** ≈ (Matthew 21:23-27) ≈

upon Aaron, (and) upon his garments, and upon his sons, and upon his sons' garments with him; and sanctified Aaron, (and) his garments, and his sons, and his sons' garments with him. ≈

In the New Testament, it was the word of God and the power to heal and cast out demons that served as indicators of those anointed. These were the things that the servant of God had to relinquish when the appointed time was up.

In the case of Jesus, the very body He was in was the symbol of His authority. Hebrews 9:23-28 Illustrates to us that the temple in which Jesus conducted His ministry (to the uplifting of the body of Messiah) differentiated Him from everyone that ever served the Father. ≈ **(It was) therefore necessary that the patterns of things in the heavens should be purified with these; but the heavenly things themselves with better sacrifices than these. For Christ is not entered into the holy places made with hands, (which are) the figures of the true; but into heaven itself, now to appear in the presence of God for us Nor yet that He should offer Himself often, as the High Priest entereth into the holy place every year with blood of others; For then must He often have suffered since the foundation of the world: but now once in the end of the world hath He appeared to put away sin by the sacrifice of Himself. And as it is appointed unto men once to die, but after this the judgment: So Christ was once offered to bear the sins of many; and unto them that look for Him shall He appear the second time without sin unto salvation.** ≈

For the word tells us that His temple (body) was specially prepared for just His work and the cup He was assigned. Of the three greatest servants in the bible, Jesus, Moses, and Elijah, the Master received the greater reward for His work. The word described the miracles of Moses as thunder and Elijah was taken up in a chariot of fire--neither body was ever recovered. The last verse in the gospel of John relates to us that the works and miracles of Jesus were so numerous that there would not be enough space on earth to hold the chronicles of them.

As great as Moses and Elijah were, neither of them got to sit at the right hand of the Father. This reward was granted to only One -- the One to whom the power over life and death and the grave was given.

However, in each case the end of their lives signified the end of their ministry on earth. Not only did Jesus die, as did Moses and Elijah, but He had the authority to reuse the badge of His office to complete His mission.

He was able to take this special vessel into Sheol, hold a revival, and still deal with the disciples allowing them to touch Him.

Then, this vessel was given a special coating that only Moses came close to. Moses' face glowed, but Christ's entire body was glorified. Moses face glowed as a residual effect of seeing the glory of God. (Exod 34:30) ≈ **And when Aaron and all the children of Israel saw Moses, behold, the skin of his face shone; and they were afraid to come nigh him.** ≈ Jesus was the Glory of God; He was without sin and blemish, and without flaw or fault: He was perfect.

Delegated Authority

The other legitimate type of authority is delegated authority, which occurs when a God appointed servant passes the badge on to an apprentice. (Numb 27:20) ≈ **And thou shalt put (some) of thine honour upon him, that all the congregation of the children of Israel may be obedient.** (11:25 & 26) **And the Lord came down in a cloud, and spake unto him, and took of the spirit that (was) upon him, and gave (it) unto the seventy elders: and it came to pass, (that), when the spirit rested upon them, they prophesied, and did not cease. But there remained two (of the) men in the camp, the name of the one (was) Eldad, and the name of the other Medad: and the spirit rested upon them; and they (were) of them that were written, but went not out unto the tabernacle: and they prophesied in the camp.** ≈ I use the term apprentice because all of the underlings in the Bible were trained and groomed by use of an apprenticeship. The term disciple implies that the person was disciplined and groomed/manicured by someone. This is why Jesus was always called Master by the twelve for He had authority over them, both granted by His Father and recognized by the twelve. A disciple can only be a disciple after they choose to submit to the training.

Therefore, it is imperative that as leaders we exude traits that would inspire people to want to emulate us, in actuality they are emulating the God they see in us. This presumes that we are actually imitating God as the New Testament directs us to do.

A close look at the qualifications spelled out for deacons and leaders would seem to indicate which traits we should exhibit.

-<u>Elders</u>- (Tit 1:7-9) ≈ **For a bishop (elder) must be blameless, as the steward of God; not self-willed, not soon angry, not given to wine, no striker, not given to filthy lucre; But a lover of hospitality,** a lover of good men, sober, just, holy, temperate; Holding fast the faithful word as he hath been taught, that he may be able by sound doctrine both to exhort and to convince the gainsayers. ≈

-Deacons- (1 Tim 3: -13-16) ≈ **For they that have used the office of a deacon well purchase to themselves a good degree, and great boldness in the faith which is in Christ Jesus. These things write I unto thee, hoping to come unto thee shortly: But if I tarry long, that thou mayest know how thou oughtest to behave thyself in the house of God, which is the church of the living God, the pillar and ground of the truth. And without controversy great is the mystery of godliness: God was manifest in the flesh, justified in the Spirit, seen of angels, preached unto the Gentiles, believed on in the world, received up into glory.** ≈

-Those who minister- (Col 1:18-28) ≈ **And He is the head of the body, the church: who is the beginning, the firstborn from the dead; that in all (things) He might have the preeminence. For it pleased (the Father) that in Him should all fullness dwell; And, having made peace through the blood of his cross, by Him to reconcile all things unto himself; by Him, (I say), whether (they be) things in earth, or things in heaven. And you, that were sometime alienated and enemies in (your) mind by wicked works, yet now hath He reconciled. In the body of His flesh through death, to present you holy and unblameable and unreproveable in his sight: Who now rejoice in my sufferings for you, and fill up that which is behind of the afflictions of Christ in my flesh for His body's sake, which is the church: Whereof I am made a minister, according to the dispensation of God which is given to me for you, to fulfill the word of God; Even) the mystery which hath been hid from ages and from generations, but now is made manifest to his saints. To whom God would make known what (is) the riches of the glory of this mystery among the Gentiles; which is Christ in you, the hope of glory. Whom we preach, warning every man, and teaching every man in all wisdom; that we may present every man perfect in Christ Jesus: Whereunto I also labour, striving according to His working, which worketh in me mightily.** ≈

For clarity, however the best example is Jesus. He who though He was Master and Teacher, Lord, and King, taught that the servant is neither above nor below the Master. He even went so far as to tell the twelve not to call anyone Master, teacher, or Rabbi for these terms implied an office that is already taken. ≈ **BUT BE NOT CALLED RABBI: FOR ONE IS YOUR MASTER, (EVEN) CHRIST; AND ALL YE ARE BRETHREN. AND CALL NO (MAN) YOUR FATHER UPON THE EARTH: FOR ONE IS YOUR FATHER, WHICH IS IN HEAVEN NEITHER BE YE CALLED MASTERS: FOR ONE IS YOUR MASTER, (EVEN) CHRIST.** ≈ (Matt 23:8-10)

Some would argue that if this was the case, why did the emissary Paul name the five - fold ministry. It is so we may know what the jobs in the Kingdom are, not to indicate rank. ≈ **BUT HE THAT IS GREATEST AMONG YOU SHALL BE YOUR SERVANT. AND WHOSOEVER SHALL EXALT HIMSELF SHALL BE ABASED; AND HE THAT SHALL HUMBLE HIMSELF SHALL BE EXALTED.** ≈ (Matt 23:11-12) These ministries are called gifts, as we truly have not earned them. More importantly, since they are gifts, Paul admonishes us not to be boastful for we have done nothing. What could be more arrogant and boastful than to claim a title over a gift given? How dare we claim to be Pastors and Bishops, Apostles, Cardinals or any other title that implies office. The only term applicable for any of us brothers and sisters is servant for this is the only true position we occupy.

The greatest officer for Christ (Paul) most often referred to himself as sinner, brother, or bondservant. Titles exist to serve only two purposes, to satisfy ego is as with the Pharisees and the Sadducees and to placate people. ≈ **WOE UNTO YOU, SCRIBES AND PHARISEES, HYPOCRITES! FOR YE DEVOUR WIDOWS' HOUSES, AND FOR A PRETENCE MAKE LONG PRAYER: THEREFORE YE SHALL RECEIVE THE GREATER DAMNATION. WOE UNTO YOU, SCRIBES AND PHARISEES, HYPOCRITES! FOR YE COMPASS SEA AND LAND TO MAKE ONE PROSELYTE, AND WHEN HE IS MADE, YE MAKE HIM TWOFOLD MORE THE CHILD OF HELL THAN YOURSELVES.** ≈ (Matt 23: 14&15)

Two thousand years after Jesus and even longer than that after King Saul, we the children of Israel (God's chosen people ~ those who believe and accept His will) still have a need for signs and to have kings rule us like other nations.

Four decades after slavery was emancipated in America, those who were slaves retained the slave mentality and were unsure what it meant to be free. For 39 years, 11 months and 29 days the children of Israel who left Egypt begged to go back to slavery and bondage. Two thousand years after the Lord came to show us the way we still cling to being sheep.

As my father always told me growing up, "Freedom is the ultimate responsibility, because you are responsible for what you do". This is why Jesus' very profound commandment was so rejected and to this day resisted by many. The Messiah told us what to do in (Mar 12:31) and with this, one concept revolutionized the world. ≈ **AND THE SECOND (IS) LIKE, (NAMELY) THIS, THOU SHALT LOVE THY NEIGHBOUR AS THYSELF.** ≈ By avoiding the sin of covetousness, which is considered the mother of all sins, Jesus was able to avoid all sin. When we adhere to this commandment, we do no harm and we actually go out of our way to make life better for everyone.

I grew up rather affluent and my father was a very influential politician and doctor. Consequently, I learned what in my opinion was the best lesson of my life. That lesson is that freedom carries with it a price tag and that tag is called giving back. For you see, it was not the strongest, or best that God used to complete His work. Although they were common people, He used people who understood that stewardship (true bondage) is freedom. For we were only "made" free to serve the Father's purpose. The blood of Christ gave our education, strength, and health to us for the sole purpose of helping others. People who have nothing, no money, no land, and no responsibilities are truly free for they are stewards over nothing.

Paul describes himself as a bondservant for Christ and in this, he realized a potential he never would have reached simply being a rich tent maker. Satan has inverted what God fashioned for society; those who have owe those who do not, not the other way around. We owe the poor all we have and know. It is not until we readily accept the sacrifice of freedom and liberty and exercise our true calling that we will gain life. To die serving your fellow man is honorable; to live serving God is a true gift. Jesus had all power and lived without a material thing. Some saw Him and thought Him poor. It was through the parable of the rich young ruler that we got to see who really was free for the young man went away sad and Jesus had far more than He ever could have dreamt.

True liberty and liberation only comes when you master yourself and allow the things you want out of life to be things that help others. If you are held in bondage to this world, you will be controlled by this world. It is not a matter of if, but when will the world call in her marker. When you live to be used and to serve God, no man has power over you. As Jesus told Pilate He was free because the only power that Pilate had was the power given from above..

I admonish you believers, to free yourself from the cares of this world. Focus on helping others, and watch God work through you. I am not close to being perfect in the will of God, but I love to serve. I have lived my life understanding that like Joseph and Moses those who are part of the system and raised by the system are in the best position to help those oppressed by the system. When God positions you in life, it is through this opening of our hearts that we choose to object to injustice and wrong doing. We could not recognize these things without knowledge of the law.

Paul was able to do what he did and write what he did because he had the knowledge of the scriptures having been a Pharisee. In addition to the fourteen years of tutelage of the Father to put him in the position he was afforded. (Galatians 2:1). ≈ **Then fourteen years after I went up again to Jerusalem with Barnabas, and took Titus with me also.** ≈ Paul was already a leader and a soldier, but he was not freed until he used the years of discipline to build instead of destroy.

The amount self-discipline and self-sacrifice needed to be true stewards is why most people prefer to remain slaves. Slave work is hard but slaves are provided for and some prefer creature comforts and security to spiritual freedom and eternal rewards. Near sightedness will eventually cost more than freedom ever could. If the children of Israel had only chosen to live according to God's will and be more like Joshua and Caleb, they too would have seen the Promised Land--but they feared tomorrow and the unknown.

Knowing how bad yesterday was, they felt safer going back to Egypt instead of facing the uncertain. However, I am free because of one thing, I am certain, that my God will supply all my needs according to His riches in glory. With this freedom[145], we can fear nothing that will harm or discomfort our bodies because our souls are safe.

Superman had no fear of anything, on this planet, because it could not harm him; however, kryptonite would kill him. We on the other hand cannot jump tall buildings in a single bound, cannot run faster that a speeding bullet, and are not more powerful than a locomotive. Conversely, our God, we can say to a mountain be thou removed and it will move. We can walk on water. Through our God, we can raise the dead, heal the sick and cast out demons. Through the power of our God, we can resist and defeat Satan and if we are faithful nothing under the

---

[145] This type of freedom comes from strong faith and healthy spirituality. It also requires the flesh to be under complete subjection.

sun/Son will or can destroy us. For through our covenant with Christ the King, we have been given dominion over all things in the earth—even over Superman. (Luke 9:1) ≈ **Then he called his twelve disciples together, and gave them power and authority over all devils, and to cure diseases.** ≈

Illegitimate Authority

The third type of authority is illegitimate authority. This type of authority once recognized should neither be followed nor supported. The primary difference between this type and the former two types is attitude. (Prov 29:2) ≈ **When the righteous are in authority, the people rejoice: but when the wicked beareth rule, the people mourn.** ≈ In the first two types, mistakes are made, the people in authority do bad things, and they sin. However their intention is not evil, they simply fall short of righteous. ≈ **And then shall that Wicked be revealed, whom the Lord shall consume with the spirit of his mouth, and shall destroy with the brightness of his coming: (Even him), whose coming is after the working of Satan with all power and signs and lying wonders. And with all deceivableness of unrighteousness in them that perish; because they received not the love of the truth that they might be saved. And for this cause God shall send them strong delusion, that they should believe a lie: That they all might be damned who believed not the truth, but had pleasure in unrighteousness.** ≈ (2 Tess 2:8-12)

However, illegitimate authority is completely disobedient to God and His will. The latter has walked away from the will of God and chooses to accept whatever the consequences, rather than be in accord with the King. King Saul in his later year is a great example of illegitimate authority, as he choose to walk away from God and pursue what he wanted. He then went so far as to try to destroy the people of God.

Solomon's son was also an example of illegitimate authority. King David was a man after God's own heart and his son was the wisest, richest man that ever lived. Both men were anointed/chosen by God and ordained to be leaders. The Lord loved David so, that the Lord promised that the light in his house would never go out. Solomon was blessed with wisdom and riches beyond any other man. Although both men made mistakes and walked away from God, they retained their authority until death.

The anointing passed on through the bloodline through generations. However, Solomon's son was an irreverent, disrespectful young man, whose kingship was cut short. He was not noteworthy, ten of the twelve tribes of Israel were taken away from the house of David and placed under the care of Jeroboam, a God fearing man. Actually, the only reason that he retained two of the ten tribes was that God made a covenant with David.

God made covenant and could not break it so instead of taking the leadership away from David's house completely. He moved the flock away and gave them to a good shepherd to hold until the twelve tribes and the gentiles could be reunited under one shepherd.

As God promised, the light never left the house of David, for this sayeth the Lord, ≈ **I AM THE LIGHT OF THE WORLD.** ≈ Again, God teaches a lesson in true authority by both keeping His word and protecting His flock. He also shows us that we should not honour illegitimate authority for evil and harm is not of God and therefore we are not bound to it.

It also reasserts that only God can remove an anointing. Until then the anointed will still have authority. However, like King Nebucadezzar they may be a blind, eating grass, and waiting for either God's mercy or His judgments. ≈ **The same hour was the thing fulfilled upon Nebuchadnezzar: and he was driven from men, and did eat grass as oxen, and his body was wet with the dew of heaven, till his hairs were grown like eagles' (feathers), and his nails like birds' (claws).** ≈ (Dan 4:33). But you are unable to harm more sheep.

We must clarify that when I refer to authority, I mean spiritual, not worldly. We are subject (under) the law but the word tells us that a righteous man is not under the law for he is already obedient to the law by being righteous. We are not free to rebel and cause disorder, but by following God, we are living holy and we will receive eternal rest from Him—not the world governments.

World governments are not interested in the spirit man and only a little bit more concerned about the fleshy man. Governments are self-serving and self-perpetuating--only God lasts forever. The authority we are allowed to question and try by the word is spiritual authority. The wrong leader (Jim Jones) can be far worse then any world government could ever be. World Governments can kill the flesh, but a bad shepherd can lead the soul to hellfire.

This is why neither Jesus nor Paul ever condoned the changing of status in society. Paul tells us that if we were converted a free man, then we should remain free and if a slave then remain a slave. For Paul understood, whether you picked cotton or owned the gin, only what you do for Christ lasts. Paul understood that the only true freedom in life is to serve Christ with and in everything that you do. Therefore, your status matters not here on earth. It is recorded that to Him we are all sons and daughters in Christ, one family with many parts, but only one need.

In addition, if we only have one need then we must be jointly fitted together as an entire vessel. If God is not a respecter of persons, then He probably, holds even less concern for position and stature. So in recognizing the authority, Christ, let us obey the most important of all commandments that is to be found in Deuteronomy 6:5 ≈ **And thou shalt love the Lord thy God with all thine heart, and with all thy soul, and with all thy might .** ≈

False prophets and teachers comprise another category of illegitimate authority. Jeremiah tells us some of the dangers of these false prophets and teachers. ≈ **The prophets prophesy falsely, and the priests bear rule by their means; and my people love to have it so: and what will ye do in the end thereof?** ≈ (5:31)

It tells us that the prophets prophesy falsely, that means that they are misleading the people intentionally and giving them false words from God. Next, it tells us that the priests rule on their own authority. That indicates that not only are the priests lying to the people, but also they are actually ruling over them. They have superimposed themselves between God and the flock. The priests were to be mouthpieces--not to rule over the people ~ that is the Father's job.

The saddest portion of this passage of scriptures is found in the later portion of 5:31 it is reads thusly, ≈...**AND MY PEOPLE LOVE TO HAVE IT SO!** ≈ This is sad because the prophet speaks of God's people. Secondly, the Father says that the people love it so, and this means that not only do they love these false prophets they also know that the things these men say are false and they love their lies. This also means that the people did not love God, but instead Satan; for Satan is the father of lies whereas God is truth.

God calls this situation appalling and horrible, meaning that He thinks thusly of; (1) false prophets, (2) false teaching and (3) the people's acceptance of same. What a sad thought to think that people are happy being thought of by the Judge and Justice of all times as being appalling and horrible. These people knowing and loving the falsehoods follow them. They honor these false men, and in knowing God's word[146] they still choose the heat of the eternal flame. They choose to live in bondage instead of basking in the fullness of God's grace and mercy. Woe unto those people as well as the false prophets.

Ahab and Jezebel had at least 450 prophets that at their direction prophesized that Baal was God and that Baal supported Ahab and Jezebel in their reign. These prophets *prophesized* at the kings bidding. These prophets told the people exactly what the crown told them to say; thus, using spiritism to further drag the people into bondage.

This is no different from political correctness in our time. When we allow the world or contributors from the world, to tell us what to say or even worse what not to say, how are we any different from the prophets of Baal? Alternatively, should I say Ahab or Jezebel?

While attending an institute of higher learning, my class was given several articles to read and to report on. These articles were on websites and you had to register to read them. Ironically, the articles written were all by the instructors' cronies. Their practice was to constantly make each others' students read each others' works; thereby, keeping their circulation consistently high and keeping their publishing's high in number.

Although this would seem to be unethical, it is a common practice in the scholastic arena. This is what industry calls a quid-pro-quo. The modern church with its clearinghouses, radio stations, and television broadcasts engage in exactly the same practice of the quid-pro-quo. The same radio stations play the same artists all day, everyday. The television programs play speakers repeatedly as if to say these are the only persons with a good message. They people they display as singers (many of whom have significantly less talent than locals) appear repeatedly and often sing the same songs. As many things as there are to teach about, why would a Christian television program engage in showing reruns of the same shows?

We have been reduced to clicks for everything and we support the same authors, singers, and preachers and ignore everyone else. The only time we display anyone new is when they become very popular, writes a best seller or a celebrity who accept Christ. Again, like the prophets in Jeremiah, God's people love it so. They have gotten so used to being fed the same thing repeatedly, they no longer crave new meat. It is as if they are collecting spiritual social security, and they no longer wish to work nor do they wish to obtain more in life than just a little bit.

---

[146] As indicated by God calling them His people and also saying that they love false prophets meaning they know the truth.

In 1 Kings 21, we find a small but no less dangerous type of illegitimate authority, and that is the subversive authority of a mate. Some of the stories of good men gone bad center around a subversive mate. ≈ **But there was none like unto Ahab, which did sell himself to work wickedness in the sight of the Lord, whom Jezebel his wife stirred up.** ≈ (1 Kings 21:25).

The first time in the Bible that a subversive mate transforms legitimate authority into illegitimate authority occurs in the book of Genesis, Chapter 3. Wherein the woman Eve (mother of all living) enticed Adam to disobey God and thusly lost both his life and his authority. This is always the result of illegitimate authority death and loss of whatever you may have been in charge of.

The other effect of illegitimate authority is that it brings about death and suffering for those under it. Not only did the loss of authority or better yet the transformation into illegitimate authority result in Cain and Abels' problems. It cost Jesus His life, as He had to come to redeem us from our sin.

The last and final transformation of authority dealt with in this letter is the striation caused by greed and selfishness.

Examples of this are numerous and throughout the testaments.

i) Sampson and Delilah
ii) David and Uriah.
iii) David and Absalom
iv) Solomon and Beth-Sheba
v) Anarias and Saphira
vi) Herod and John the Baptist
vii) The Pharisee
viii) Saul and David.
vix) Balaam

In these instances, the people involved used their office or position to further their own selfish desires and cravings. In every case, the results were either misery or death. No one can sit in the seat of justice or authority, and expect to be free from accountability. The Bible says that all discipline for the moment is painful (Heb 12:11) ≈ **Now no chastening for the present seemeth to be joyous, but grievous: nevertheless afterward it yieldeth the peaceable fruit of righteousness unto them which are exercised thereby.** ≈ However, it tells us that it is worth it. The word also tells us that with much wisdom there comes much sorrow/suffering. (Ecc. 1:18) ≈ **For in much wisdom is much grief: and he that increaseth knowledge increaseth sorrow.** ≈

Those who survived correction by God were made better rulers and leaders but they paid dearly for their folly. Wisdom itself is a long arduous, painstaking trek. God's hand is just, but it is also stern and even those whom He loves He chastens but this discipline produces eternal life for others. ≈ **For whom the Lord loveth He chasteneth, and scourgeth every son whom He receiveth.** ≈ (Heb. 12:6)

David felt the sting of God's love and it came to pass that David sinned no more, but the price for his personal life was very high. Moses bore the weight and complaints of the children of Israel for 40 years in the desert and spent 80 years in preparation for his task and even he felt the sting of God's mercy.

Authority carries with it the badge of office, but much like the animals in their kingdom, it also carries with it scars, bruises, and broken hearts. The most powerful Man in the history of the world, He who had power over life, death and salvation bore as the badge of His office:

-Holes in both hands, both feet.
-A spear gouged in the side.
-39 lashes with a whip on His back.
-Deep abrasives about His head.
-He also undoubtedly had a bitter taste in His mouth from the vinegar.
-Severe muscle strain from carrying a cross, not to mention all the sins of the world and those who came before him.
-Worst of all a broken heart.

The only thing wrong with His regalia of office is that the patch on the uniform read, "King of the Jews" but it should have read;

"LAMB OF GOD WHO TOOK AWAY THE SINS OF THE WORLD...CONQUEROR, PRINCE OF PEACE--THE LIGHT OF THE WORLD!"

These other scriptures also deal with false prophets and teachers. Lam. 2:14) (Jer. 14:14, 2:19, 5:6, 8:5, 14:7) (1 John 4:1) (Matt. 7:15, 24:11, 24:24) (Mark 13:22) (Luke 6:26) (2 Peter 2:1) (Titus 2:3)

≈ **AMEN** ≈

WORK AREA LETTER XV

≈

ETERNAL AFFAIRS

TOPICAL SCRIPTURES

(Mk 1:22) (1 Cor 4:5) (Luke 12:3-5) (1 Thess. 5:14) (Rom. 15:14) (Col 1:28) (Col. 3:16) (2 Tim 3:16) (Titus 1: 9-13) (Titus 2:15) (Acts 17:11) (1 Cor. 14:2& 4-5) (1 Cor. 14:22) (Rom 13:1&2) (John 19:11) (Heb 9:14-22) (Numb 20:28) (1 Sam 31:4) (Matt 21:23-27) (Lev. 8:30) (Heb. 9:23-28) (Exod 34:30) (Numb 27:20) (11:25 & 26) (Tit 1:7-9) (1 Tim 3: -13-16) (Col 1:18-28) (Matt 23:8-10) (Matt 23:11-12) (Matt 23: 14&15) (Mar 12:31) (Gal 2:1) (Luke 9:1) (Prov 29:2) (2 Tess 2:8-12) (1 Chr 17:24) (Dan 4:33) (Deut 6:5) (Jer 5:31) (1 Kings 21:25) (Heb 12:11) (Ecc. 1:18) (Heb. 12:6) (Lam. 2:14) (Jer. 14:14, 2:19, 5:6, 8:5, 14:7) (1 John 4:1) (Matt. 7:15, 24:11, 24:24) (Mark 13:22) (Luke 6:26) (2 Peter 2:1) (Titus 2:3)

1. WHO HAS ULTIMATE AUTHORITY IN THE CHURCH? EXPLAIN YOUR ANSWER AND CITE SCRIPTURE.

2. WHAT ARE THE SOURCES OF AUTHORITY ON EARTH?

3. WHICH IS THE HIGHEST AUTHORITY THE MAN OF GOD OR THE WORD OF GOD? EXPLAIN.

4. ACCORDING TO ECC 12 WHAT IS THE WHOLE DUTY OF A BELIEVER? WHAT IS THE DUTY OF A SHEPARD?

5. EXPLAIN WHY THE TERM MINISTER IS NOT MENTIONED IN THE FOUR-TIERED MINISTRY?

6. LIST AND EXPLAIN THE THREE TYPES OF AUTHORITY IN THE CHURCH.

7. IF THE FOUR COMPONENTS ARE GIVEN FOR THE PURPOSE OF MINISTRY WHAT CHARACTERISTICS SHOULD A MINISTRY HAVE?

8. WHY ARE THERE FIVE COMPONENTS TO A COMPLETE MINISTRY?

9. ARE THERE A VARIETY OF TOOLS AVAILABLE TO ACCOMPLISH MINISTRY? ARE THE TOOLS THEMSELVES MINISTRY?

10. WHICH COMPONENT OF MINISTRY DO YOU BELONG TO? HOW DO YOU KNOW?

ADDITIONAL NOTES FOR THIS CHAPTER

LETTER XVI

≈
LET MY PEOPLE KNOW!

"...Consider the church as just another institution with its own bureaucracy, run by ministers and priests who, like lawyers and doctors, are members of a profession (though not so well paid). And while this parochial institution fulfills a worthwhile social and inspirational function, rather like an artsy society or civic club most people could get along without it."

In many ways, of course, the church has allowed itself to become what the world says it is. (This seems to be a common human bent--to become what others consider us to be). But that sad fact has not dulled or changed what God's definition and intention for His church. For biblically, the church is an organism not an organization-a -*movement,* not a monument. It is not part of the community; it is a whole new community. It is not an orderly gathering; it is a new order with new values, often in sharp conflict with the values of the surrounding society.[147]"

---
[147] Loving God Colson, Charles p.175

LETTER XVI ≈ LET MY PEOPLE KNOW!

The scripture tells us that God's people perish for the lack of knowledge. When we read the scriptures, the miracles performed by God's people, and we see how weak the modern church is, we must wonder where has the power gone? We know that God is the same yesterday, today and tomorrow --so the difference must be in the church.

In the movie, The Empire Strikes Back, the villain (Darth Vader a powerful magician) told his son that he could not return from the "dark side." "*You don't know the power*!" is what he told his son. Well believers, apparently we too are ignorant of both the power of the dark side and the power f the good side. Much like the movie villain Darth Vader, we have been duped into believing that the dark side is stronger. Yoda the Jedi master[148], tells us, it is "*Not stronger*; q*uicker, more seductive*." It has always been easier to give in to our lower passions and become agents of evil. To resist using the power for evil (defined as selfish desires) in and of itself is the triumph over evil.

Those having power that are humble and peaceful command a power that most people will never be able to fathom. They understand that the ultimate power to do good is to let God! Whenever we come to a decision about life, we need to let God decide what to do, He alone is good. (Mk 10:18)

When given the gifts of the super-natural, we operate above nature. This is one of the meanings of the term super...above. We do not understand the mechanics of the gifts, we just know they work. Those in the bible who had these gifts did not know the science behind the miracles and the truth of the matter is that it is not important.

There are many who like the Egyptians try to take the glory from God and assert that science is solely responsible. The only problem with this theory is that you cannot have science without God. In the study of the Egyptology, one finds that science developed out of man's desire to elevate himself and lower God.

The realization of their folly resulted in an admission symbol still used to this day. It is a pyramid with an eyeball inside it and rays of light emanating from it. The symbol is a representation of Egypt's admission

---

[148] Also from the Empire Strikes Back.

that man can never be God for he is limited by his mind. That is not too far from what the bible says about the people at Babel.

It is not important to understand the mechanics of the miracles completely, what is important is that we realize that all good gifts come from God. These gifts then are tools with which we are to do His work, and in no way are we to believe that Satan has created any of them. The only thing that Satan is credited with is being the father of lies.

For years, believers sat back and watched the enemy claim and use the things of God, we even stopped using these tools. We have been indoctrinated by church and the world to believe that these tools are for the use of the enemy. Therefore, anyone who uses these tools is practicing witchcraft. This is akin to a new family moving into your house and telling your family that they are trespassing. God promised His children all the wealth of heaven and this includes the knowledge and wisdom therein.

We will discuss the following tools for the purpose of this letter:
i) Numerology
ii) Architecture
iii) Magic
iv) Alchemy
v) Ghosts/spirits
vi) Blood sacrifices
vii) Reincarnation
viii) Prophecy and quickening
ix) Sound a) names, b) vibration, c) music
x) Astrology

Again, the purpose of this letter is to remind God's handymen of the tools that we have at our disposal. In addition, it is to distinguish the difference between gifts and tools.

When God gives one of the seven gifts[149], it is for furthering a specific facet of Godly work. Tools although mission specific, are for all of God's children. The Prince of the power of the air rules the earth we live on. If we do not realize that God granted believers dominion over the earth and Satan again (thanks to the Lamb of God), His death is to no avail if we continue to live in fear and ignorance.

How can we live as free men and women bought by the Blood if we do not even bother to learn and use the basic tools of Christ? Prayer, worship, praise and fasting are higher disciplines; the tools mentioned in this letter are for basic life and basic understanding of the bible. Without

---

[149] (1Cor 12 8:10).

understanding basic things like parables and numerology, as well as many other mysteries of the bible, will remain mysteries to us. Because Satan has convinced believers that, these things are not for us. The Master told believers that the mysteries of the Kingdom would be revealed to us now that we are part of God's fold.

Believers, the word warns us that the people of God perish for the lack of knowledge. This is a simple but fatal concept. All things in life that you do not know can be hurtful or helpful. Since Satan knows a great deal, and we do not bother to find out what we have as tools to strengthen ourselves as well as our spiritual lives he uses them against us. We remain weak just as if we did not use the tools of this world like food and medicine.

Even the daily reading of the word of God is enhanced once we realize what other things are going on in the scriptures. Every aspect of your faith walk will be enhanced after you sit down and realize that the Father created everything under the sun/Son. And best of all it was all created for and given to us; God's chosen people[150]. Satan has no power over us unless we give it to him or his workers.

People associate numbers with the devil. Numerology as far as they are concerned is also of the devil. This erroneous conclusion no doubt comes in part from the book of Revelations[151] wherein the number of the Beast is given as 666. This is not to imply that the number make him the Beast. Instead, it is a tool given to us to identify the subject.

Not only does the book say blessed are those who read this book (Rev 1:3) it clearly asserts that the reading/hearing of this book imparts wisdom. If Yeshua (Jesus) is telling us that by reading this book and hearing (understanding & receiving) this word, we will gain wisdom, and the book is filled with numerology how then can it be evil? In addition, this also implies that the use of and understanding of numerology imparts wisdom.

At this point, we must come to a common understanding of what numerology is. For the purpose of this letter, let us understand that it is the use of numbers to convey concealed messages. It is also the use of numbers to express power and concepts. Not every number used in the bible is a part of a numerical system. For example, if the scriptures relay a story of a man with one dollar the number one means exactly what it says.

---

[150] Matt 24:31, Luke 18:7, Rom 8:33, 1 Pet 2:9.

[151] Which is replete with numerology and number codes.

However, when the number is used; especially arbitrarily, that number is part of a number system. For example marching around Jericho seven times, Jesus rising on the third day, the earth being created in seven days, etc. To this end, I will endeavor to explain some basic numbers, as used in the Hebrew number system called the Kabalah.

Numerology

The number one occurs 1,967 times in 1,695 verses -- the One permeates every number. It is the measure common to all numbers. It contains all numbers united in itself but excludes multiplicity. One is an ideal symbol of the Divine, because the Divine is spirit and as such has nothing to do with material qualities that are bound to appear in multiplicity$^\Re$ (p.41).

The number two occurs 835 times in 703 verses--In religious traditions, 2 means disunion, the falling apart of the absolute divine unity, and is therefore the number connected with the world of creation. One god plus another god makes two deities, which, then, no longer corresponds to the ideal of the eternal, unique one$_\Re$ (p.46).

The number three occurs 485 times in 426 verses--Represents the trinity and hence spirituality. All life appears under the threefold aspect of beginning, middle and end which can be expressed in more abstract terms as becoming, being and disappearing a perfect whole can be formed by thesis, antithesis and synthesis$_\Re$ (p.58).

The number four occurs 328 times in 282 verses--Four is inseparably connected with the first known order in the world, and thus, points to the change from nature to civilization. It is considered to be the number of material order$_\Re$ (p.86).

The number five occurs 345 times in 270 verses--Five is usually connected with human life, from early times five was considered a somewhat unusual, even rebellious number$_\Re$ (p.105).

The number six occurs 202 times in 190 verses--Is considered to be the perfect number of the created world.$_\Re$ (p.122).

The number seven occurs 463 times in 391 verses--The number of wisdom and completion. It contains the three spiritual and four material values$_\Re$ (p.127).

The number eight occurs 80 times in 80 verses--Called the auspicious number, considered to be lucky and sacred as the number

---

$^\Re$ The Mystery of Numbers, Annemarie Schimmel, Oxford Univ. Press. 1993, New York.

seems to correspond to circumcision (Lev.12: 3) and the number of blessings in the beatitudes₨ (p.156).

The number nine occurs 50 times in 49 verses--Called the magnified scared as it squared represents the three spiritual virtues multiplied (enhanced) by theeself₨ (p.164).

The number ten occurs 248 times in 223 verses--The number for completeness and perfection as it houses the first four natural numbers...1,2,3,4₨ (p.180).

The number eleven occurs 24 times in 24 verses--Considered to represent negativity, it stands between two round numbers and in itself has no positive aspects₨ (p.189).

The number twelve occurs 189 times in 165 verses--The closed circle, this number houses the two sacred numbers 5 and 7₨ (p.203).

The number thirteen occurs 15 times in 15 verses--Considered to be unlucky as it relates to things like the number at the last supper, and this number exceeds the closed circle exemplifying excess₨ (p.209).

The number thirty occurs 174 times in 164 verses--This number is considered to represent order and justice₨ (p.239).

The number thirty-three would then represent a combination of 3 indicating spirituality and 30 which represents order and justice. Therefore, the number 33 represents the perfected state of spiritual order and justice and is therefore considered to be sacred and second only to *one* the number for God. *Thirty-three* represents Jesus the Son of God, and there for a perfect balance of all virtues summed up in His purpose and life.

In the first example, the dollar was just a part of the story and the story was undoubtedly about some virtue. The seven trips around Jericho used the number seven to symbolize completion.

There are those who feel numerology and the understanding of same is of no value to believers. Those people are missing the boat for most of the prophetic books are filled with numerology. The New Testament calls prophecy the greatest of the gift of the spirit (1 Cor. 14:1) ≈ **Follow after charity, and desire spiritual gifts, but rather that ye may prophesy.** ≈ (1 Cor. 12:6-10) ≈ **And there are diversities of operations, but it is the same God which worketh all in all. But the manifestation of the Spirit is given to every man to profit withal. For to one is given by the Spirit the word of wisdom; to another the word of knowledge by the same Spirit; To another faith by the same Spirit; to another the gifts of healing by the same Spirit. To**

another the working of miracles; to another prophecy; to another discerning of spirits; to another divers kinds of tongues; to another the interpretation of tongues. ≈

Again, we see that the tool of God given to us to do great works, is minimized by man's reluctance to accept the fullness of God. I also encourage those people to explain the books of Isaiah, Daniel, and Revelations without the use of numerology.

Although I am uncertain whether the Dogons or the Egyptians stumbled upon numerology first. It is however obvious that the Egyptians capitalized on this knowledge even more than Nimrod and his people. Egyptian architecture is a living testament to numerology as most of their national and holy monuments are symbols and filled with number codes. The pyramids (which by the way means *glorious light* in the dialect) themselves are a combination of the numbers four, being the base and three for the sides. The symbol to represent man's attempt to go from his most enlightened state to divinity which the trinity represents.

It would take an in depth study to explain where and when man stumbled upon the number systems hidden in God's creation. Short decades of empirical data and study, plus man's desire to build like Nimrod attempted resulted in a numerical value system to explain life. You see brothers and sisters, man did not say that completion would be defined as seven, after seeing that the Creator took seven days to complete creation empirical data suggest then that the number 7 represented completion.

Just as man did not define one as the number for wholeness, God did many times when He exerts His supremacy and tells us that He "alone" is God. Is there a system of numbers used by the enemy? Yes, of course but theirs is a bastardized version of the form created by God.

For most of the tools that God has given, Satan has fashioned a bastard form, to not only confuse believers, but also for misusing the tools that God hath sent for His beloved children.

Architecture

I touched on architecture in conjuncture with numerology because Egypt is credited with inventing architecture and some of their math (the value known as Pi for example) and much of their architecture still baffles scientists to this day.

Modern science and technology can neither duplicate nor fully explain Egyptian architecture. Just as the Egyptians surmised one cannot explain science without God without incorporating Theos into our studies.

We will never understand Egypt because Egypt was created and constructed by men who like Nimrod wanted to be God. In order to exault themselves, and himself, Satan granted these men concessions, that allowed these men to be great for a time. Manipulating the things of God will make us great for a while but believers as Proverbs 22:22 warns us it is a man's pride that brings him low. Ask Satan, his pride lowered him all the way to the depths of hell.

The church uses architecture as well. It has been used as far back as Solomon's temple and until recently, it was used in the construction of all churches to maximize sound. Architecture is a science and for lack of a better term an exact science.

Using the term Gience[152], to replace any hint of man's independence, we must analyze Creation to see how dependent on God it is. Once you have a basic understanding of Gience, you can do marvelous things and master/manipulate the thing we call nature.

The Egyptians constructed machines that would fly, electricity, condoms, and a host of other advances that we associate with modern times. Yet the greatness of Egypt is all but erased. The only monument of their greatness remains in science and architecture. Their culture and religion[153] have long since gone the way of the Dodo bird. The only things that have remained are the things God has allowed them to use--all they created have long since gone. The Almighty Father is great, and we must learn to appreciate this wonder for only the things of God last.

How is it that they could do what no one else can? Like Satan and Nimrod, they had no fear of God. Like Satan promised Eve in the garden, and the heavenly hosts warned in Gen 11:6&7 Egypt was not constrained from doing things when they put their minds to it. Do we have the same ability? Absolutely and when the disciples perfected unity (after Pentecost[154]) they performed miracles daily and the Holy Spirit added to the church daily.

Tenney in <u>God's Dream Team</u> spends a great deal of time stressing the importance of unity as the single most important function of the body. The lack of this unity resulted in a weak, broken, powerless church.

Magic

---

[152] The science of God's creation as a whole.
[153] With the exception of Voodoon called Voodoo and Santeria.
[154] From the Hebrew word *mibchar* this means choice or chosen. Reasserting Jesus' status as the Chosen one.

In the New Testament there were three men commonly called wise men. In the older texts however, they are called "*magi*". This *magi* is the root in the word magician. Magic was an art practiced commonly during the period. Yet another reason people were skeptical about Jesus in the beginning.

Magic is the use of illusions and deception as well as a few chemicals to enhance or create an event. Scholars assert that the magicians were present at the birth because the birth itself was steeped in mysticism. I mention it only because if magic was evil and of the devil then why would 3 magicians be given a sign from the heavens and allowed to be present at the birth of Christ? This excerpt also creates some interest upon the relationship between magic and eternal life. Travelers in a fifteenth century blessing also request the protection of the magi: "May Caspar lead me, may Balthasar guide me, may Melchior protect me, and may they lead me to eternal life.[155]"

My assertion is this, the three magi practiced the use of illusions and deception, and therefore were the best qualified to recognize the real thing. They went to see Jesus because they knew Him to be the genuine article. Not by His works but by their own. Not by their lies but by the truth of His birth, and the prophecy.

I also put it to you that in an esoteric sense the three attributes mentioned in the blessing above says will lead people to eternal life represent the Trinity;

Lead…the Father in the Old Testament.
Guide…Jesus in His life and teaching.
Protect…the Holy Spirit.

Alchemy

Alchemy is the science of altering matter, it is closely related to magic. Though magic is primarily the use of illusion to manipulate people's minds, alchemy is actually changing or manipulating matter and material. This differs alchemy from magic. You see also in the word the origin of the current term Chemistry.

Changing a chemical substance or a physical makeup of a substance is beyond the ability of most men. Some wizards can do it, but

---

[155] The Mystery of Numbers, Annemarie Schimmel, Oxford Univ. Press. 1993, New York p.80.

everybody else had to use science and magic to do what God has allowed people to do with the spoken word.

Creation is the beginning and the first recorded occurrence of alchemy[156]. What men have to use science to do, God does with a spoken word. When this gift is given, it is described in Deut 34:12 as a mighty power and a great terror. When Aaron threw his staff on the ground, the sorcerers did it to assuming that it was simple magic. Moses' God allowed Aaron's staff to consume the magicians, because their trick was simply illusion. Aaron's staff by God's hand, turned into something the Egyptians could not understand.

Jesus used this Gience quite often when performing miracles involving touching, and He used number codes quite often in His parable. How can we in good conscious assert that matter transformation is of Satan when the first miracle of the Messiah's career was to change water to wine (Jn 2:7-9). We will not engage the debate as to whether or not we as Christians should drink and this juncture. Suffice to say, whether or not it was wine as the bible says or grape juice as some pastors contend it was no longer water.

It is noteworthy however; that in verse 10 the governor uses the word drunk in reference to the fermented liquid supplied for the wedding. If we as a people can honestly assert that you can get drunk from grape juice, then I will accept your postulace. We also should stop supporting Welch's as they make an excellent grape juice.

Astronomy

This is the study of the stars and the astral bodies. Do not confuse this with the art of astrology, which is a device used by the devil and a conception of man. We know that astronomy serves no purpose in Heaven but it is another God sent tool. Gen 1:14 Tells us that astronomy is to be used by us to determine signs and seasons. ≈ **And God said, LET THERE BE LIGHTS IN THE FIRMAMENT OF THE HEAVEN TO DIVIDE THE DAY FROM THE NIGHT; AND LET THEM BE FOR SIGNS, AND FOR SEASONS, AND FOR DAYS, AND YEARS.** ≈

Again, in the New Testament a star was used as a sign, studied, and followed to mark the Christ child. Would God mark His only begotten Son with an evil symbol, and then present Him to us as the Saviour?

---

[156] This includes making the Earth out of nothing and most obvious the making of Adam and Eve from dirt and bones.

Ghost and Spirits

Believers commonly inquire about ghosts and whether they exist. The answer is yes spirits do exist but they are not ghosts. No, there will not be a white image of your dead grandmother. There are only two types of spirits here on the earth and they are the good and the evil. By the way, Elvis is not one of them!

Spirits are present here on earth all the time. We cannot see them as they are nor can they touch us as they are. When they need to interact with people the most common method of doing so is to influence people.

However, there are times when God sends angels to earth and allows the normal rules (which we call laws of nature) to be suspended. God sends His angels to guide us as He did in Exodus; to torment people as He did Saul, and to talk to people as He did Abraham and Jacob. In all these cases, these angels were allowed to interact physically with humans.

Angels dwell in one of the six heavens or in the seventh with God. Demons[157] (cast out angels) dwell in four worlds below the Earth and inhabit the earth as they are released. They live in Tartasus, the pit, Sheol, and the lake of fire[158]. They come to earth for the purpose of tormenting and confusing people. Since Jesus redeemed us, when we encounter a demon, they are powerless to harm believers, but if we allow them, they can dominate us[159]. Before Jesus redeemed us, the demons interacted with man all the time. They even sired children with the daughters of men. (2 Peter 3: 5-8) (Rev 9:7)

In the Garden, Satan was powerless to do anything to Adam and Eve except deceive them[160]. We are in the same position today, we do not have to fall prey to Satan's ploys, but we allow him in by way of his deception. After Satan enters us, it is his one true wish to incubate ideas and demons in us. To such as extent that we are unable to hear anything God ever has to say. In this way, Satan takes more people to hell with him.

---

[157] For more references to demons see the following scriptures: Lev 17:7, de 32:17, 2CH 11:15, Ps 106:37, Mt 4:9, Lu4: 7, Mt 12:22, Mt 15:22-29, Mk 1:23-26, Mt 8:30-32, Mt12: 43-45, Mk 3:11.
[158] Deut 32:22, Rev 9, Gen 6, Job 38.
[159] Matthew 12:45.
[160] According to Huie the Hebrew word used in Gen 3:1 for serpent is *nachash*. There are three other possible definitions of that word i) a diviner, ii) shining brass, ii) to shine or glow. He asserts that if used in the noun form the term would be *hanachash, which* means the shinning one. Which would coalesce with 2 Cor. 11:14.
Satan, adversary of mankind, Huie, Bryan. July 12 1997

Remember, Satan is on an ego trip and if he can get people not to worship God he can claim them and then compare numbers to say that he is the greatest.

With all of this in mind, we must also remember that flesh and spirits do not speak the same language (Rom 8:26-27.) Anybody who dares to say they speak to the spirits of the dead must be in tune with evil spirits. Since God does not operate this way, anyone who tells you that they can tell the future or speak to the dead is a diviner and is practicing witchcraft. They are not all frauds Satan does grant his disciples power too-but they are ALL evil.

This brings us to psychics and fortune telling and as to whether they are all evil or not. They are in the employ of Satan because God uses prophecy to edify and to forewarn His people. He does not use fortune telling to solve crimes or give horoscopes.

A school of thought asserts that humans exist in the same space as spirits but not the same time. Happenstance affords the two to overlap for brief periods allowing for brief glimpses into the future or the past, or allowing for the mysterious happenings in this world.

At any rate this does not elevate those involved to the level of working for God. The word of God gives clear tutelage about prophecy and how to determine it and how to test it. It also gives numerous warnings about diviners and the damage they can cause. The diviners would include; psychics, séance directors, Satanists, new-agers, witches, wizards, fortunetellers, and anybody who uses drugs to alter their consciousness to interact with spirits.

Reincarnation and Resurrection

Discussions of ghosts and spirits leads us into the next part of this letter which deals with the most important tool of Christianity. A tool given to only one so far but he had the ability to pass it on. This tool is so great it could only come from God. Even Satan cannot duplicate it. At least not until he is given permission to in order to fulfill the prophecy of the antichrist. Here we speak of resurrection, the distinguishing factor between Jesus and the other holy men. Jesus actually came back and it was not as a caterpillar.

The term reincarnate when broken down means to incarnate again. Alternatively, when more simplified it means to put in a body again and is implicit of giving life. This has very important implications for us to fathom as believers. When we understand the complexities of reincarnation, the wonder of God will again be exemplified.

As previously stated, the term reincarnate by strict definition means to put in a body again but the use of the term implies that it means to give life. Combining the two the term would seem to imply putting life in a body again.

According to the book of Genesis, the Creator formed man from the dust (it was flesh but without life) then He breathed the breath of life into the pot and it became a man. Relating this to Jesus' power to raise from the dead, apparently the giving of the spirit (the breath of life) is required to reincarnate. Only God has ever incarnated anyone (given life) and therefore to give life is a province exclusively inhabited by God. This is why Jesus did not rush to save Lazarus, for it is written that He said that He waited three days *so that God would get the glory* (John 11:4). Jesus shows immense humility and respect. Remember, the Essenes according to history were going about at the same time. These groups were noted for their ability to cast out demons and heal the sick and Jesus knew this. In order to reassert His humility and obedience He waited for three days by which time the scriptures tell us that Lazarus had begun to rot. In waiting for three days, Jesus waited for the point at which no one but the Almighty could have revived Lazarus. This is what Jesus meant when He said that He waited until the Father could get the glory.

Going back to the creation of man, the clay pot called Adam, after being created, was just a mound of lifeless flesh until the spirit was given. The case of Lazarus begs the question did Jesus with the Father's help give the breath of life? The answer to this question is yes, but I will have to elaborate on this in a later portion of this letter that deals with the power of the spoken word. It is noteworthy that in each case where Jesus healed or raised anyone He either spoke to them, about them, or touched them.

When Jesus cried out ≈ **ELI, ELI** ≈ (which is equivalent to MY GOD MY GOD in Hebrew) and then said, ≈ **IT IS FINISHED!** ≈ the bible tells us that He gave up His spirit. This is to say that the second Adam reverted to the form that His predecessor was created, a lifeless lump of flesh. Jesus' resurrection[161] differed in that after the prophesied three days

---

Resurrect means to raise again to activity. The word derives from surge, which is defined as a transient sudden raise of current or voltage. Another meaning of resurrection is material belief that yields to spiritual understanding. If you are still uncertain, what this means it goes hand in hand with the information on vibrations as well as reasserts the deity of Jesus. Material belief that yields to spiritual understanding written another way would read physical laws that yield to spiritual authority. The surge, which is an increase

the Master entered the body by Himself and reanimated Himself and was then resurrected to complete the task.

The bible tells us that the angel told the women who came to tend to Jesus' body that He was no longer in the tomb and the women saw that the stone had been rolled away. What a miracle indeed but the speculative lesson is just as wonderful for it also means that by saying what he did the angel was also telling us the following three things.

Risen ~ means that Jesus brought Himself back to "life" or to our time, without assistance.

No longer in the tomb ~ means that Jesus had conquered the flesh completely. Remember He wavered for a moment in the garden but now the tomb (flesh/corpse) no longer had any power over Him.

The stone was rolled away ~ Jesus had already conquered the grave. Consequently death no longer had complete bondage over us. By rolling away the stone--that which kept the body in the tomb (in death) we were given freedom from permanently being cut off from God. The stone, you see believers, also kept what was outside the tomb separated from the contents of the tomb. The stone which was rolled away by the resurrection of the Lamb of God was sin. When Jesus was crucified, the sting of sin/death was taken away from those of us who believe. Because of the grace of God, the stone was removed forever. There is no longer a barrier between man and God. We now had free access to the Father through the Son. When the Master says, ≈ **NO MAN COMETH TO THE FATHER BUT THROUGH ME!** ≈ He can assert this accurately because unless you share in His death and resurrection you no longer have access. The Lamb of God is not just the door to the Kingdom of Heaven; He is the only way into the Kingdom of Heaven. When He was made the gatekeeper, all other means of entry were abolished. Neither wealth, penance, works nor notoriety means anything to God. Only God's undying love for us and our tried and true love for Him are important.

---

of electricity, is referring to the electromagnetic frequency that all living creatures exude. We know that all living things exude this from the years of study of the Shark and its hunting habits. This electricity or better yet Electro-chemistry (how the body functions) is necessary to maintain life. With the Master's spiritual understanding, the physical laws yielded to authority and He was able to recalibrate Himself after three days. Do not sit alarmed for we are talking about Jesus and I am using the most understandable terms possible. This should not surprise you for we watch people on television get defibrillated routinely, and if man can do it what makes you think that God cannot?

Blood Sacrifices

The blood sacrifice was used to crucify the flesh and to cover the altar with the essence of life. The sacrifice was to offer to God a gift of high importance and since animals have no souls, they were ideal libations/offerings. The crucifixion of Christ served the same purpose, to crucify/circumcise the flesh and to offer the most precious of gifts- the blood of the Lamb.

These excerpts from The Satanic Bible may help clarify the theories behind this phenomenon. As well as to serve to show that Satanists were not the inventors of the blood sacrifice.

"The supposed purpose in performing the ritual of sacrifice is to throw the energy provided by the blood of the freshly slaughtered victim into the atmosphere of the magical working, thereby intensifying the magicians chances of success. (The) fact of the matter is that if the magician is worthy of his name, he will be uninhibited enough to release the necessary force from his own body, instead of from an unwilling and undeserving sacrifice. (There) are sound and logical reasons why Satanists could not perform such sacrifices. Man, the animal is the godhead to the Satanist. The purist form of carnal existence reposes in the bodies of animals and human children who have not grown old enough to deny themselves their natural desires. They can perceive things that the average adult human can never hope to. Therefore, the Satanist holds these beings in sacred regard, knowing he can learn much from these natural magicians of the world[162]."

After the blood of Jesus was offered to redeem us from Satan's grasp, there was nothing on earth that was equivalent or even comparable to what had been offered already by Jesus. His blood broke the mold, it raised the standard so high that not only could we not top it but also Satan cannot tarnish it either. Without another Eve in the garden scenario, Satan was not supposed to retake the earth, but it happened again.

Prophecy and Quickening

Prophecy is one of the seven gifts of the Spirit; it is considered the greatest of all the gifts[163]. We are warned however that without love we still have nothing. (1 Corinthians13: 1) ≈ **Though I speak with the tongues of men and of angels, and have not love, I am become as**

---

[162] The Satanic Bible Lavey, Anton. Avon books New York, NY. 1969 Synthesized from the portion on blood sacrifices beginning on (p.88).
[163] 1 Cr 14:1.

sounding brass, or a tinkling cymbal. ≈ The scriptures tell us that this gift is for the purpose of edifying the body. (1 Corinthians14: 4) ≈ **He that speaketh in an unknown tongue edifieth himself; but he that prophesieth edifieth the church.** ≈ In the Old Testament, it was also used to forewarn people of their impending doom. Prophecy is not what soothsayers do which is trade their souls for the brief glimpses into the future that Satan allows.

Prophets often receive such clear visions, or dreams that they cannot begin to understand what they see; it is only through the explanations of the Holy Spirit that they can interpret the prophecy. In the book of Revelations, God gave John immensely clear visions, so much so that it is written in metaphors. This is largely due to the facts that Jesus wanted it written in prophetic language so as not to make it easy to decipher and because John had problems using, his current day language to explain what he saw.

According to the scriptures, this is one of the reasons God uses people to interpret the prophecy, especially today. In the Old Testament, tests and miracles verified the prophet's validity. Not that we cannot perform miracles, but God has not responded to an open challenge in the last 2000 years, since His begotten Son. After the resurrection of Christ, those who do believe are saved and those who opt not to are damned–the plan is simple.

Prophecy is the gift of being able to see and tell the future according to God's wishes. Even prophesy works when God allows it. Prophets do not walk around in a temporal fixation. God bestows the gift is according to His desires and plans.

Quickening is a much less emphasized tool used by believers. Matter of fact the world has made much more use of this concept via Hollywood. The movies and television series called Highlander uses the biblical principal of quickening but adds Hollywood to it. Hollywood would have you to believe that these immortals are from another planet and a very few in number. In order to achieve the quickening they duel and the winner lops off the head of the other. In an elaborate flash of what appears to be pain-giving lightning, the victor absorbs the acquired knowledge and power of the looser.

Although this is a very colourful rendition of the process, it is metaphorically exactly, what happens. The purpose of the quickening is to allow people today to go back in time (much like prophets go forward) and with complete accuracy give accounts, retell prophecy to ascertain any information needed to accomplish a task.

There is no visible electricity, but undoubtedly an Electro-chemical/magnetic alteration takes place. The head of the information donor is not cut off but the information that the donor possessed is passed forward to the individual quickened. Though the individuals are not from another planet, they are operating in a spiritual plane and they are very definitely few in numbers.

Last, but not least, prophets certainly are not immortal, and they do not live forever but the information does. Quickening was most commonly used in the Old Testament days before writing and reading was common place; thus, the laws and commandments were ever vigilant. In addition, it became important to maintain the prophecies between generations and between the 12 tribes that moved around but needed to keep the laws in tact. This gift permitted the prophets to maintain a completely accurate log of the law just as if given yesterday--it is because God helped them maintain this posture.

Sound, Words, and Vibrations.

(Gen 11:6 & 7) ≈ **And the Lord said, BEHOLD, THE PEOPLE [IS] ONE, AND THEY HAVE ALL ONE LANGUAGE; AND THIS THEY BEGIN TO DO: AND NOW NOTHING WILL BE RESTRAINED FROM THEM, WHICH THEY HAVE IMAGINED TO DO. GO TO, LET US GO DOWN, AND THERE CONFOUND THEIR LANGUAGE, THAT THEY MAY NOT UNDERSTAND ONE ANOTHER'S SPEECH.** ≈ Sound is one of the most used, most misunderstood tools in the believers arsenal. It is in the area of vibration that we will venture for it is this area we most often dwell. There are several terms, which need to be defined for the purpose of this letter so that we may be on the same accord.

- sound = an audible air vibration.
- word = sound agreed upon.
- vibration = movement of molecules.
- resonance = vibrations from an object.
- Life-frequency = specific electromagnetic vibration given off by all living things.

When we understand the physics of sound, we will understand why the scriptures tell us that the power of life and death is in the tongue. The tongue does not produce sound but without it, one cannot talk. The tongue is a steering or better yet channeling device that modifies the type of sonic vibration (sound) coming from a person.

The power is not in the tongue literally but the channeling device is a very poignant device. Much like a barrel on a gun or a fuse on a bomb, the tongue does not produce the effect it directs it. Without a tongue, a person can still make sounds, but they are limited in scope and volume and the sound they make will be either guttural or nasal. This is because the body is trying to find another channeling device for the sound.

Why is sound so important? Because sound is made up of a series of vibrating molecules. Sonically speaking, sound is defined as the portion of the sonic spectrum (range) that can be perceived (heard) by the human ear. Just as in the light spectrum, there are sounds on either side of the range that cannot be heard by humans...but it is still sound.

What does this have to do with Christianity? Well believers you asked! The entire Creation story starts with sound (a spoken word), the book of John starts off by saying, ≈ **In the beginning was the Word, and the Word was with God, and the Word was God.** ≈ Jericho was felled in Joshua 6:10 by seven days of marching and making noise – sounds (vibrations). Moreover, Jesus says, ≈ **WHATSOEVER YOU ASK IN MY NAME (SOUND) IT SHALL BE GIVEN YOU.** ≈ Sound is important because through sound life was created, life is maintained, and life can be destroyed. The name of anything according to the mystery systems is its Life-freq. What exactly is a Life-freq.? Remember, when your daddy had an old car and you could recognize it coming down the road by the sound it made...that sound which is unique to each living thing is its Life–freq. When sharks hunt, they track their prey by use of its Life-freq. This is why they bite boats and metal objects. When they get close, their eyes close and they rely solely on their Life-freq. (Electro-magnetic) sensors. Metal, although artificial, emits a much stronger freq. than a living thing does and the shark gets confused.

This is why Jesus' name is so powerful; the vibration created by saying His name has lifechanging power. Animals do not speak English, they learn to associate sounds with actions. If you say to them I love you but the sound is harsh, they will cower. Similarly, if you say I am going to kill you but in a soft tone, they will continue to remain close to you. In the same way we arbitrarily use the name of Christ without understanding how much power is in Jesus' name, in Jesus' Life-freq. (Philippians 2:10) ≈ **That at the name of Jesus every knee should bow, of things in heaven, and things in earth, and things under the earth;** ≈

The word disease means ill-at-ease and therefore indicates that a person's Life-freq. has been altered in some way and they are no longer at ease. Think of it this way, the human body is like a radio; we only function at certain frequencies. When something changes our dial we are out of tune (diseased), and the only way to remedy this is to return the dial to the right freq.[164] In order to retune any device there has to be a tuning fork or preset frequency. The name of God; the word of God; the Son of God is the tuning standard.

Jesus resonates (vibrates) at the same frequency as Creation for He was the word and He became flesh. For simplicity sake instead of the term "word" let us re-read the scripture using the term Lamb.[165]

In the beginning was the Lamb and the Lamb was with God and the Lamb was God, (But the Lamb became flesh). When we read it this way, it is easy to see how the continuity of Jesus being the base is maintained. Therefore the power of Jesus is that He is life itself! When He said ≈ **I AM THE WAY, THE TRUTH AND THE LIFE**, ≈ this is a literalism. For Yeshua Himself is the basis of life, is the foundation of life, and then came to the earth incarnate to restore life to its original state.

Yeshua (Hebrew for Jesus) was the true definition of super (above) natural--He was nature itself. He was the basis of life and could therefore heal, cure, and rise from the dead. His humility permitted Him to stay in His place and give God the Father all the glory. This is why we can cure, heal and drive out demons in His name. Because His name is the very key (blueprint) to life, in it is the very creative force itself. We cannot be Jesus, who was the living embodiment of creation; but we can use His name to further His works.

I would love to go into extreme depth as to Jesus' importance to creation but that information is not integral to the faith walk. Believers, if you can grasp just a surface understanding of what I am attempting to explain to you then we will have more confidence in what we believe and perhaps more resolution as to why we believe. Rather than shy away from apologetics[166] we can intelligently discuss (not defend) our faith, against the encroachment of Satan's minions.

The humility of Jesus is an integral part of His majesty and virtue. He always gave honour and glory to the Father and/or the Holy Spirit.

---

[164] This is the concept behind acupuncture.
[165] Neither adding nor subtracting from the word just providing clarity.
[166] Scientific and practical explanations of our faith.

This served to maintain His humility, to maintain the mysteries of the Kingdom, and to comply with prophecy.

Perhaps most important to us, however, is that constant reference to the Father as the greatest and doer of good works virtually made it impossible (at least improbable) that anyone would worship Hesus above the Father. The commandment still demands that we have no other God before Him.

Queries have been made as to the Trinity asking how can we worship the Father, Son, and Holy Spirit? Our response is we worship God as the Creator, God as the Son and God as the Holy Spirit. If we focus on the clay pots, then we would completely overlook the Potter. Our texts or witnesses (testaments) speak of the Father, Son, and Holy Spirit throughout their entirety and there is a reason for this.

The simplest explanation for this I received from the Holy Spirit is to envision the Trinity thusly. The Father is the ocean (water) and the Holy Spirit the salt in the ocean and Jesus would be a glass of ocean water. You cannot have ocean without water nor would it be an ocean without salt. If you put ocean water in a glass, it would have the same density, saltiness, and qualities as the ocean; but because of the container, limited in scope. Neither is more important, neither is separate but there are distinct functions for each.

In the bible, there are 78 appellations (manifestations) of God. These are not really names, no more than refrigerator is a name. It is more of a descriptive title, in the same way most of the 78 appellations are not actually names but virtues or manifestations.

≈ **There is power in the name of Jesus.** ≈ is another truism, there is power in the name. In most countries names have meanings and this meaning is usually indicative of the personality of the bearer of the name. The *tetragrammation* (actual {four-tiered} name of God) is considered to be the actual and ineffable name of the Creator "YVWH" most commonly pronounced "**Yahweh**."

In the numerological system "*Kabalah*" (Hebrew Number system) the *Tetragrammation* mysteriously also has the numerological value of 78. The name of objects in the mystery system is where the power of the thing is found. In African naming ceremonies, the names of the children are not spoken until the ceremony itself--whenever it takes place[167]. The theory is, that the spoken name (vibration) when spoken to an untuned clay pot

---

[167] This also occurs in the Jewish faith as with John the Baptist.

(newborn) programs that pot to a particular personality. In other words, if you were to name your child Johora at one of these ceremonies they would turn out to be a precious jewel of a person, as the name implies. Well, the reason you do not speak the name before giving it to the child is that the legend has it, you will steal the power of that person.

This concept translates into the spiritual realm also. This is why we are not allowed to speak the true name of God for in the name (word) is the power God. By the way, *God* is not a name but a title, much like King. The name itself does not have the power; the power in actuality is the sound, i.e. vibration. In other words, it is the Life-freq. that has the power and is then that the name is applied to the freq. based on what it is. A good example of this would be the fruit called an orange. Most fruits have a name that we have come to associate with them. The orange however, is not only named orange; but it is also the colour we call orange, the smell and taste we call orange. The fruit is inextricably tied to this word orange and at every level of the fruit, its name is reinforced.

Our Father in Heaven is extensibly the same He is tied up in His name, for He has told us of who He is…*I AM* and told us what He is, **ALPHA AND OMEGA**. However, He did not give us His name He even let Moses see His back parts but no name[168]. God has given us titles for the many functions He performs. Unlike Yeshua (Jesus) however, the name of the God of Abraham, Isaac and Jacob has never been given to us. Actually, most of the names of the spiritual bodies are never given to us. We only know and refer to them by their functions.

The names are sacred because the life-freq. that these bodies operate at if controlled by an evil person it could ruin life, as we know it. Do not scoff as if to imply this to be outrageous for there was a heavenly body named *Lucifer,* whose name means, "being of light" that did exactly

---

[168] (Exodus 33:17-23) ≈ **And the Lord said unto Moses, I WILL DO THIS THING ALSO THAT THOU HAST SPOKEN: FOR THOU HAST FOUND GRACE IN MY SIGHT, AND I KNOW THEE BY NAME. And He said, I beseech thee, show me thy glory. And He said, I WILL MAKE ALL MY GOODNESS PASS BEFORE THEE, AND I WILL PROCLAIM THE NAME OF THE LORD BEFORE THEE; AND WILL BE GRACIOUS TO WHOM I WILL BE GRACIOUS, AND WILL SHOW MERCY ON WHOM I WILL SHOW MERCY. And He said THOU CANST NOT SEE MY FACE: FOR THERE SHALL NO MAN SEE ME, AND LIVE. And the Lord said, BEHOLD, THERE IS A PLACE BY ME, AND THOU SHALT STAND UPON A ROCK: AND IT SHALL COME TO PASS, WHILE MY GLORY PASSETH BY, THAT I WILL PUT THEE IN A CLIFT OF THE ROCK, AND WILL COVER THEE WITH MY HAND WHILE I PASS BY: AND I WILL TAKE AWAY MINE HAND, AND THOU SHALT SEE MY BACK PARTS: BUT MY FACE SHALL NOT BE SEEN.** ≈

that. When the most beautiful of all angels was cast out, He took 1/3 of all the angels with him. Do you think for a moment that they all left heaven with no power.

In all of the references to light, Jesus makes the light stand for truth. Is it not ironic that the being of light is called the father of lies! I simply point this out to reassert that God's ways are not ours and there are still many mysteries of, and in the Kingdom; but we need to do the best we can to use what we have been granted.

Language is another portion of the sonic tools. It can be used to unify or to separate us as it did at Babel (which by the way is where we get the term babble to refer to gibberish or the incoherent sounds made by a baby).

Focusing on language as a tool to unify, we as believers must study and understand the words contained in our faith. It is not important to be right 100% of the time or for that matter any of the time. What is most important is unity; correcting errors is the easy part. Peter was wrong most of the time he walked with Jesus, but he was of the same mindset as Jesus and he wanted to serve God. With the right attitude, correcting him was easy and he became the greatest of the disciples.

A unified body is powerful and according to God has the ability to exceed the knowledge that the individuals would have singly been privy to. Again, we return to Babel and see that the hosts separated the unified workers on high to prevent those people accomplishing things the Father did not ordain.

Brothers and sisters, do you see the importance of unity, and the power a unified body can have? We could do works, perform miracles, that we would not individually be able to do. We would be able to read and understand words and scriptures that would never be revealed to us singularly. If we are wrong that too is ok, look at Peter being wrong is much better than being rebuked for being split. Wrong is not a spiritual condition, it is more often ignorance or lack of vision. Disagreement is a spiritual condition. It is called witchcraft. Yes, believers it is possible for an entire church body to sin; most often doctrinal sin, but the seven letters in revelations give examples of various types.

Believers; language is composed of sounds agreed upon called words. The most important consideration of a word is that we who use it agree that it is what it means. Without agreement, we arrive at slang and dialects, but the mainstream language must have almost unanimous agreement.

Therefore, believers, in order to understand our faith one must familiarize oneself with the language therein. This therefore necessitates the study of the words themselves. Unfortunately, it is difficult to study language of 2000 years ago with languages of today. Therefore, the safest way to study words is by corroborating studies.

The study of the word should begin with acquiring definitions of the word. Then move on to finding out what the root (derivation) of the word is and where it came from. Afterwards, get definitions of the root word and keep following this train of investigation until it leads to a dead end. After acquiring all of the information reread the passage plugging in the various values until it contextually makes sense. Then catalogue that definition for further reading. Metaphors are especially difficult to decipher, but remember to make the term make contextual sense and it becomes easier.

By searching words and meanings yourself, you will learn to develop a better grasp of the word and some of the concepts therein. Grasping the basic concepts will prevent you falling prey to false doctrine. Believers, if you have the wrong interpretation of the word, if you have arrived at a completely arbitrary understanding after study of the scriptures bless you!--At least you are studying the word of God. No man can tell with certainty that you are wrong for they were not given the words to write. God has given us preachers, teachers, apostles, evangelists, and prophets. They get their tutelage from the same source you do, the Holy Spirit.

The Holy Spirit has the last word on your interpretation, because He gives it to each for the purpose of edification, works, and testimony. You and I will probably not have the exact same revelation on a scripture because we have different jobs in the Kingdom; therefore, we have different tools. You will find that if you get past the semantics and our own personalities that the revelations will not be significantly different. True teaching from the Holy Spirit will never contradict itself because God is not counterproductive and will never mislead.

Whatever God tells you is right no matter what we think, nor what man tells us. God makes the rules as He sees fit, and if you want to be right, do as He says for He alone is the rewarder or punisher of those who hear His word. No matter what you are told, the five-fold ministry is here to merely guide us but God's Word is Law!

Go to the source to get the word and get the revelation for you-- God granted us access do not put stones between you and Him again. Jesus is the Way, the Truth, and the Life; no man goes to the Father but through Him. Let Him renew your mind and your soul. He standeth at the door and knocks.

≈ **AMEN** ≈

WORK AREA LETTER XVI

≈
LET MY PEOPLE KNOW!

TOPICAL SCRIPTURES

(Mk 10:18) (1Cor 12 8:10) (Rev 1:3) (1 Cor. 14:1) (1 Cor. 12:6-10) (Prov 22:22) (Gen 11: 6 &7) (Deut 34:12 (Jn 2:7-9) (Gen 1:14) (Lev 17:7) (Deut 32:17) (2 CH 11:15) (Ps 106:37) (Mt 4:9) (Lu 4: 7) (Mt 12:22) (Mt 15:22-29) (Mk 1:23-26) (Mt 8:30-32) (Mt 12: 43-45) (Mk 3:11) (Deut 32:22) (Gen 6) (Job 38) (2 Peter 3: 5-8) (Rev 9:7) (Rom 8:26-27) (John 11:4) (1 Cor 3: 1) (1 Cor 14: 4) (Gen 11:1) (Josh 6:10) (Phil 2:10)

1. **WHAT KNOWLEDGE IS IT THAT GOD'S PEOPLE PERISH FROM LACK OF? EXPLAIN YOUR ANSWER AND CITE SCRIPTURE.**

___

2. **WHAT IS THE BEGINNING OF WISDOM AND WHY?**

___

3. EXPLAIN THE PURPOSE OF THE BLOOD SACRIFICE?

4. EXPLAIN THE DIFFERENCE BETWEEN DEMON POSSESSION AND DEMONIC INFLUENCE.

5. WHAT ARE THE HIGHEST TOOLS IN CHRISTIANITY AND WHY?

6. IN PROPHECY CONCERNING NUMBERS AND DESCRIPTIONS (I.E. BEAST WITH FOUR HEADS) EXPLAIN THE TWO COMPONENTS AND THEIR FUNCTION.

7. EXPLAIN MIRACLES AND SPELLS.

8. WHY DO DEMONS POSSESS PEOPLE? WHY DID THE DEMONS ASK TO BE PLACED IN THE PIGS?

9. LIST AND EXPLAIN THE FOLLOWING; A) THE TWO MAIN PURPOSES OF PROPHECY. B) THE MAIN BENEFIT OF PROPHECY.

10. -SHORT ESSAY- EXPLAIN IN YOUR OWN OF THE QUOTE FROM LETTER XVI.

11. WHY IS PRAISE SO IMPORTANT?

12. WHY IS THE POWER OF LIFE AND DEATH IN THE TONGUE?

13. WHY IS WORD STUDY SO IMPORTANT?

14. WHAT MADE CHRIST'S RESURRECTION DIFFERENT FROM ALL OTHERS?

15. IS THERE SUCH A THING AS REINCARNATION? IF SO EXPLAIN WHAT IT IS.

ADDITIONAL NOTES FOR THIS CHAPTER

LETTER XVII

≈

A LETTER TO YOU

≈ **HEAVEN IS MY THRONE, AND EARTH IS MY FOOTSTOOL: WHATHOUSE WILL YE BUILD ME? SAITH THE LORD: OR WHAT IS THE PLACE OF MY REST? HATH NOT MY HAND MADE ALL THESE THINGS? YE STIFFNECKED AND UNCIRCUMCISED IN HEART AND EARS, YE DO ALWAYS RESIST THE HOLY GHOST: AS YOUR FATHERS DID, SO DO YE.** ≈ (Acts 7:49-52)

LETTER XVII ≈ LETTER TO YOU

Beloved brothers and sisters,

I greet you with a hug and a kiss. It is in the spirit of love and unity that I greet you from my Patmos, my soul sanctuary. Many, if not all, have been bewildered (placed in the wilderness) in our faith walks and we will be there many more times. I encourage you all not only to seek this time alone with God, but also to actively learn from each adventure.

Everybody knows that Jesus spent 40 days and nights in the wilderness being tempted by Satan. What you forget is that Jesus was actually in training (bewildered) from age 12 until 30, and He is the Son of God. Moses, the greatest prophet that ever lived, spent 80 years in training and although he was great, God denied him entrance to the Promised Land. Paul spent 3 days blind and then 14 years in training to do his great, but short works.

The wilderness experience, or the training time, is a very complicated time for most of us. It is difficult for most of us because 95% of us lack self-discipline and our flesh resents the training. The United States Marine Corps is considered to be the most successful motivational (discipline, pruning, molding) program in the world. In 12 weeks, the program takes anyone in the world and turns them into a killing machine.

David, Moses, Samson, Jonah, Baalam, Peter, and Solomon were all in God's boot camp and they were never completely indoctrinated into His system. In my boot camp class, there were 90 people when we started and by the end of 12 weeks, there were only 35 of us left. In the most successful program in the world, 55 people were weeded out as non-hackers (undesirables) and this was decided in 12 weeks.

The Father begins our training the day we are born; we enter boot camp at the age of ascent (to go up-the point in life where we start to use our understanding of the concepts of right and wrong). At this age/turning point, our actions became gauged by their intent, just like a crime in this world. When we wonder why so many bad things happen to us as children, God is testing our ability to remain good.

Many years ago, I asked the Father why so many things happened to me while growing up? The answer that He gave me then and indeed still gives me is, "**GO READ** (about) **JOSEPH**." I actually began to resent that answer because I did not feel that the answer was there. The reason for the Bible is so that we have a ready reference guide for most of life experiences. Of all the stories of the bible, Joseph covers most of the problem areas of everyday life. It goes from the childhood dramas and horrors–which the innocence of childhood prevents comprehending--all the way to the maturity of forgiveness, reassembly (wholeness) and lasting happiness.

The story of Joseph exemplifies one of the most bewildering aspects of God's training process, that being why God allows so much pain in our lives. Being confused is the biggest problem believers face. This confusion brings about the problems in the wilderness. When God does not immediately answer, it causes fear, anger, isolation, and perhaps-other feelings not listed. This is because the lack of response causes confusion during which, Satan plays many tricks with our minds.

This silence brings about confusion primarily because our lives here in the flesh with all the technology and noise necessitate sound and noise. When we are plunged in silence (like Jonah), it is torturous to us because all of the things we need, rely on, and hide behind are taken from us.

When the children of Israel left Egypt, their complaints arose because the lack of the visual coupled with the unknown brought about confusion and fear. Confusion is one of the most useful tools to bring about change or attention. When we know we are wrong the response is usually obvious, but when we are confused we do not know what to do so response is usually to pause or stand still.

Much like the Exodus, God puts us in situations designed to require His assistance. The object of the training is to develop faith and reliance on Him. Remember Jonah did not repent of his ways until he had spent 3 days in the whale's belly. The storm or being thrown overboard into the water did not move him. It was not until the stillness and the silence (to include isolation) had borne out his weakness and needs. For most of us, submission is not enough for submission is a voluntary posture. Most of us need brokenness and this differs from submission in that it comes about from a sense or despair.

It was not until after David; lost four out of five of his children, been told that the sword would never leave his house and denied permission to build the temple that it came to pass that David sinned no more. After each transgression David committed he repented and submitted himself to the Master. However, it was not until David became broken that he sinned no more. When we are broken, we tend not to ever repeat that behavior again for brokenness is extremely painful and scary.

Submission, is much like a small cut, it hurts a while, but the pain soon subsides and heals very quickly.

Brokenness is more like breaking a leg; it is extremely painful, takes a long period to heal, and it alters your ability to do the normal things. In other words, there is the painful work about a change and the healing brought about by the break. You cannot break any bone in your body and remain unchanged–the healing process itself causes a change to our bodies. However, there is also a mental change, for the body ever reminds us of that broken bone. The body does not desire to encounter that pain again. This is why broken people tend not sin after they heal because the pain is too much for them to want to duplicate.

Does this mean that we will only have to undergo this experience only once? No! Most of us will have to undergo the bewilderment about many different issues. The thing that most determines duration of our bewilderment is our attitude. When I use the term attitude, it includes our rebelliousness as well.

Moses for example, never achieved brokenness and consequently his entire career, which spanned 40 years, was tainted by his angry nature. It is obvious that not being broken by no means infers that we cannot achieve greatness in the service of the Lord, again Moses is the example. It is also apparent that brokenness can still permit hesitation and swaying as in the case of Jesus. However, in the case of Moses his brokenness either wore off or was never achieved. For he was unlike Jesus who in the garden wavered for a moment but never broke faith.

Moses, on the other hand, was told that he broke faith with God when he struck the rock twice. Consequently Moses' greatness was unaffected, but his reward was. After 80 years of training and 40 years in the wilderness, he was unable to master himself and conquer his anger, although he loved the Lord. Some have argued, using the scriptures that it was not unbrokeness in the case of case of Moses but fatigue. Their theory is that Moses was broken but he grew fatigued after bearing up the children of Israel. Moreover, like most people when we grow fatigued we tend to become irritable. I however, tend to believe that it is the lack of self-discipline and self-control that causes the falling of most believers. For the word tells us that we would not be tested beyond our ability to bear and that there is nothing we will be tested by that is not common to all the body.

Since Jesus never broke faith yet David and Moses did, the difference must be in the individual, the brokeness of the person. Jesus was/is rewarded with exaltation and honor because under the extreme test He passed with flying colours and did it with dignity. The obvious difference between Jesus and the others was/is He was/is without sin, He never broke faith and He never deviated from what He learned in His experience.

Patmos is a spiritual sanctuary. Unlike most however, this sanctuary is for the solitude and isolation of the soul. The most difficult times in my life all dealt with feeling isolated and alone. Therefore, the tests I most often fail deal with solitude and the best tool for Satan to use against me.

Believers, one of the biggest problems I have observed/experienced in my faith walk is impatience. Impatience can be caused by a variety of things such as immaturity, misunderstanding the word, not knowing the word, or being greedy.

My personal experience with impatience occurred with my dog, a beautiful German Shepherd named Regal. He was my best friend and I really loved him. He developed heartworms as he got older and my parents would not take him to vet, despite my begging and pleading. When Regal got sick enough he could not walk; he would crawl around on his belly coughing up blood.

After begging some more, my mother decided that we should touch and agree on Regals' health; nothing happened. She then gave me a bottle olive oil, which she said was anointed. She told me to go and anoint Regal (by giving him a spoonful of oil) and God would heal him. I prayed day and night and anointed Regal twice a day but he got worse.

I got tired of seeing him suffer and I offered my soul to God for his. I asked God to spare Regal and I would work for Him forever! One day my mother came to pick me up from school and when I got in the car, she turned to me and said, "*Honey*" I responded, "*I know Regal is dead.*" I got into the car and begun to seethe. I hated my parents and I hated God. They had told me they loved me and God said He would answer my prayers.

I did not understand why my parents did not help and I really resented the fact that I was so unworthy to God that I was not barter for a dog. I asked God why He failed to do what (I thought) He said He would do, I got no answer. So after getting no answer for a period of time I packed up my bibles, stopped praying, and quit being a Christian. I even told God I quit.

I gave Him my list of complaints against Him and then went on to practice other religions and beliefs. I hated God for a long time; I hated

Him because He hurt me by letting me down. I lost my trust in Him. I asked my mother why it did not work and she responded that that is just how God works. I lost trust in her too after that answer.

I may never understand why God did not accept me then or why He did not help Regal. It may not be important, but it did hurt. Perhaps it was because, like Cain, my sacrifice was unacceptable; or perhaps that the dog had no soul and was therefore no trade. The result on my faith walk was that I became afraid to trust God or people because of the sting of the hurt. Couple fear of trust with fear of silence and being alone, and you arrive at the most frustrating part of my life.

Despite these shortcomings, I still find more joy in being a bondservant for Christ than anything else. I still await the joy unspeakable that the word promises, but now I am learning to wait patiently.

I again plead with you to let Him have His way with you. It may hurt it will change you. Whatever you give up rest assured, He will replace it with something better.

≈ **AMEN** ≈

WORK AREA LETTER XVII

≈

A LETTER TO YOU

TOPICAL SCRIPTURES

(Acts 7:49-52)

1. WHY IS IMPATIENCE SO PREVALENT AMONGST BELIEVERS?

2. WHY IS CONFUSION SO PREVALENT AMONGST BELIEVERS?

3. HOW DO YOU KNOW WHEN GOD SPEAKS TO YOU?

4. WHY MUST WE REFRAIN FROM MEANINGLESS GESTURES, SYMBOLS, AND PHRASES?

ADDITIONAL NOTES FOR THIS CHAPTER

PART III

Discipleship Basics

A basic overview of first contact methods exemplified by Christ

Discipleship Basics

1) TARGET GROUP

- **Age** – Prepare parables (explanations) and the understanding or maturity level of the group you are called to serve.

- **Disposition** – What type of scales will you be dealing with. If you are tasked with only one type of scales (scars / issues) then stick to that which you have been tooled to repair.

2) MAKE CONTACT

- Do not try to preach to them just be kind

- Make small talk about unrelated issues affording them the opportunity to ask why.

- Meet as equals no matter what or where they are.

- Make casual conversation about anything interesting until you develop a report.

3) USE CONTACT AS INROAD

- Back off if needed repeat step two.

- Go slowly

- Stay within boundaries of step two for a safe period.

4) DIRECT CONVERSATION

- Let your words/ actions/ attitude be the reason they respond to you, let them mention God first.

- Let them mention church or religion first.

- Be indirect but adamant, do not be forceful but be consistent.

- Direct conversation back to God, once you switch to God stay there.

5) **WHY**

- Most have had bad experiences with church, Christians, or God.
When they ask 'why' tell them you used to be just like them but you had help changing.

6) **DO NOT ARGUE SCRIPTURES**

- Do not argue. If they want to argue facts speak of love and vice versa.

7) **THE OLD CHURCH INVITE**

- Don't invite them they won't come.

- Get a number or give them the church number to call.

- Invite them to a church picnic or fair.

8) **QUESTIONS AND ANSWERS**

- Give them an opportunity to ask questions and HAVE ANSWERS TO THEIR QUESTIONS or be able to find it in the bible (concordances are ok).

- Nothing more pathetic than an unlearned evangelist.

9) **CONVERT**

- **DO NOT ATTEMPT TO CONVERT THEM** there on the spot that is not our jobs let Holy Spirit do His job.

- Our task is to lead them to the Holy Spirit and help them not to fall.

- True expertise in Evangelism lies in our ability to open a person up to receive from the Holy Spirit.

10) DEMONS

- **Never engage demons alone biblical model is two against any number of demons.**

- Ascertain which demons you fight, remember the person is not the enemy.

- If you have the gift of discernment use it, if not ask the demon for its name. REMEMBER THE DEMON DOES NOT HAVE TO REPOND TO YOU BUT THEY MUST RESPOND TO THE HOLY SPIRIT. Therefore the more of the spirit is in you the more power you have. If you are fueled enough with the Holy Spirit no matter who the demon is they will leave.

- Always pray and fast before going out into the territory of your enemy.

11) ATTITUDE

- Leave your attitude home they owe you nothing.
- Do not expect them to be overjoyed.
- Do not expect them to be overly trusting.
- What you are saying is not new they will probably not act surprised.

12) DO NOT LET YOU GUARD DOWN.

- Remember that you are in enemy territory.
- Do not be fooled by familiar spirits
- Don't be over confident you are not as far from falling as you think.

13) **CONTROL**

- Never give up control of yourself, or your lifestyle. Do not drink, smoke or use drugs just to make contact.

- Never give up control of the situation.

- Never give up control of the conversation.

14) **DEMONS ARE EVIL THEY ARE NOT DUMB**

- Do not underestimate them, they do not have to submit to you and they never will.

- Do not count on their slipping up. They make few mistakes and they know the rules well.

- Do not think they will fight fair; they are trying to get more souls in hell THEY HAVE NO BOUNDARIES.

The Structure of a Godly Army

Shepard and Guardian
|
Elders
(ADVISORS AND ARMORY- advise and train the lower ranks)
|
Seniors
(**ARTILLERY**-Intercessors)
|
Deacons
(**PALACE GUARDS** defend and provide additional on the job training)
|
Disciples
(**SPECIAL OPS** take the battle to the enemy)
|
Church
(**BOOT CAMP** for the perfecting of the saints)

Spiritual Warfare: The Weapons

Spiritual Warfare[169]: The Weapons
Eph 6: 10 - 19

≈ **Finally, be strong in the Lord, and in the strength of His might. Put on the whole armor of God that you may be able to stand against the wiles of the devil. For our wrestling is not against flesh and blood, but against the principalities, against the powers, against the world's rulers of the darkness of this age, and against the spiritual forces of wickedness in the heavenly places. Therefore, put on the whole armor of God that you may be able to withstand in the evil day, and, having done all, to stand. Stand therefore, having the utility belt of truth buckled around your waist, and having put on the breastplate of righteousness, and having fitted your feet with the preparation of the Good News of peace; above all, taking up the shield of faith, with which you will be able to quench all the fiery darts of the evil one. And take the helmet of salvation, and the sword of the Spirit, which is the word of God; with all prayer and requests, praying at all times in the Spirit, and being watchful to this end in all perseverance and requests for all the holy ones**: ≈

1. WHY WE PUT ON THE WHOLE ARMOUR

- Because the pieces of armour provided protect everything important. The suit of armour is not like the cumbersome ones worn in the Middle ages. God's armour is light, flexible and very effective.

- If we do not put on the whole armour of God there are chinks in the armour. Through these chinks the demons access our hearts. These chinks consist of drugs, alcohol, pornography, lust, greed or any other addictive type behavior. This is why we are admonished to be sober minded.

---

[169] For more information on this topic see The handbook for Spiritual warfare. By Dr. Ed Murphy.

2. THE MOST IMPORTANT OF THE WEAPONS MENTIONED.

- Faith is what powers all the other weapons, it ties us to the power of the Holy Spirit.

- Faith is what allows our mistakes not to destroy us.

3. WHY EPH 6:10 & 11 MUST GO TOGETHER.

- Because it is the strength from the Lord that enables us to withstand Satan.

- It is the goodness and strength inherent in righteousness that keeps us away from the wiles (tricks, skills, schemes) of the evil one.

LOIN PROTECTOR

≈ **Stand therefore, having the utility belt of truth buckled around your waist** ≈

Short Reason
-PROTECTS GROIN,
-YOUR ABILITY TO REPRODUCE,
-WHAT YOU REPRODUCE
-FUTURE

1. WHAT IS A LOIN?

- Defined as the regions of the thighs and groin, or the reproductive organs.

- In other words, a tender and vulnerable region of the body.

2. WHAT LOINS PRODUCE.

- Life (Gen 35:11)

3. WHY PROTECTING YOUR OFFSPRING IS IMPORTANT?

- Because your fruit is your future. (Prov 10:1)

- We are required to be fruitful and multiply.

4. WHY WE GIRD OUR LOINS WITH THE TRUTH.

- If we gather unto ourselves a lie we will continue to produce lies. But if we gird our loins with the Truth we will also produce freedom.

5. 1 PETER 1:13 INDICATES THE FOLLOWING REGARDING THE LOIN.

- The life we protect and produce can only continue in righteousness if we do not become drunk with this life and the things of the flesh. A sober minds is one that is stayed on Christ and not unsteady or double.

TOPICAL SCRIPTURES

- (Jer 13:11) ≈ **For as the girdle cleaveth to the loins of a man, so have I caused to cleave unto me the whole house of Israel and the whole house of Judah, saith the Lord; that they might be unto me for a people, and for a name, and for a praise, and for a glory: but they would not hear.** ≈
- (I Pet 1:13) ≈ **Wherefore gird up the loins of your mind, be sober, and hope to the end for the grace that is to be brought unto you at the revelation of Jesus Christ;** ≈
- (Jhn 14:6) ≈ **Jesus saith unto him, I AM THE WAY, THE TRUTH, AND THE LIFE: NO MAN COMETH UNTO THE FATHER, BUT BY ME.** ≈
- (James 3:2) ≈ **For in many things we all stumble. If anyone doesn't stumble in word, the same is a perfect man, able to bridle the whole body also. 3:6 And the tongue is a fire. The world of iniquity among our members is the tongue, which defiles the whole body, and sets on fire the course of nature, and is set on fire by Hell.** ≈
- (Pro 10:1) ≈ **A wise son makes a glad father; but a foolish son brings grief to his mother.** ≈
- (Gen 35:11) ≈ **God said to him, "I am God Almighty. Be fruitful and multiply. A nation and a company of nations will be from you, and kings will come out of your loins.** ≈

_____

_____

_____

BREASTPLATE

≈ And having put on the breastplate of righteousness, ≈

Short Reason
- PROTECTS BONES AND SOFT TISSUE
- PROTECTS HEART
- PROTECTS LUNGS

1. **ACCORDING TO MATT 15:16-19 THE BREASTPLATE IS IMPORTANT BECAUSE.**

- It is not what goes into the person that defiles the person but instead what comes out of that person. Despite what lies we believe and have been taught we are completely responsible for our actions. Those actions allow people to see what is contained on our hearts.

2. **MATT 5:8 CLARIFIES WHY PROTECTION THE HEART IS SO IMPORTANT.**

- The heart is very important because a pure heart as described in the bible is the primary way to see God. I am not one hundred percent certain what this means but there must be a difference between getting into glory and seeing God.

3. **WHY WE PROTECT THE BREAST WITH RIGHTEOUSNESS.**
- Since all unrighteousness is sin and it takes a pure heart to see God the breastplate keeps our heart ready to see God, and receive what He has to say to us.

4. **WHY WE MUST PROTECT THE LUNGS.**

- It was not until God breathed into the nostrils of man, (Gen 2:7) (carefully avoiding the mouth and thereby and issues in the man's heart) that man became a living soul. It is therefore true that the breath of life is contained in the lungs and must therefore be protected. This power to create also can destroy. That being true, we must protect our lungs from our sinful nature as well.

TOPICAL SCRIPTURES

-(Matt 15:16-19)) ≈ **So Jesus said, DO YOU ALSO STILL NOT UNDERSTAND? DON'T YOU UNDERSTAND THAT WHATEVER GOES INTO THE MOUTH PASSES INTO THE BELLY, AND THEN OUT OF THE BODY? BUT THE THINGS WHICH PROCEED OUT OF THE MOUTH COME OUT OF THE HEART, AND THEY DEFILE THE MAN. FOR OUT OF THE HEART COME FORTH EVIL THOUGHTS, MURDERS, ADULTERIES, SEXUAL SINS, THEFTS, FALSE TESTIMONY, AND BLASPHEMIES. THESE ARE THE THINGS WHICH DEFILE THE MAN; BUT TO EAT WITH UNWASHED HANDS DOESN'T DEFILE THE MAN**. ≈

-(Matt 5:8) ≈ **BLESSED (ARE) THE PURE OF HEART FOR THEY SHALL SEE GOD.** ≈

- (Rom 10:10-11) ≈ **For with the heart, one believes unto righteousness; and with the mouth confession is made unto salvation. For the Scripture says, "Whoever believes in him will not be disappointed.** ≈

- (1 Jhn 5:17) ≈ **All unrighteousness is sin, and there is a sin not leading to death.** ≈

- (1 Tess 5:8) ≈ **But let us, since we belong to the day, be sober, putting on the breastplate of faith and love, and, for a helmet, the hope of salvation.** ≈

- (James 3:2) ≈ **For in many things we all stumble. If anyone doesn't stumble in word, the same is a perfect man, able to bridle the whole body also.** ≈

- (Isa 59:21) ≈ **As for me, this is my covenant with them," says the Lord. "My Spirit who is upon you, and my words which I have put in your mouth, shall not depart out of your mouth, nor out of the mouth of your seed, nor out of the mouth of your seed's seed," says the Lord, "from henceforth and forever.** ≈

BOOTS

≈ And having fitted your feet with the preparation of the Good News of peace; ≈

Short Reason
- GUARD WHERE YOU WALK
- KEEP CRUD OFF YOUR FEET
- ALLOW YOU TO WALK ON SOMETHING OTHER THAN THE EARTH.

1. **WHAT BOOTS ARE FOR .**

- Boots protect against elements, germs and danger (Gen 3:15).
- Allow you to kick without damaging your feet.

2. **WHAT 'SHOD' MEANS.**

- Shod is the past tense of *shoe*. The process by which horse's shoes are nailed to their hooves, and cannot be removed easily. The metal shoes prevent bruising the foot by stones and sharp objects.

3. **THE GOSPEL OF PEACE.**

- The good news of peace ushered forth into the earth in Luke 2:11-14, wherein the angel told us that our Saviour was born. The gospel of peace therefore is the spreading of the news that He arose and forgave us of our sins. And since His resurrection no need die in sin or live in hell. Remember the good news is NOT YOUR SALVATION BUT THAT SALVATION HAS COME AND IS AVILABLE NOW TO EVRYONE.

TOPICAL SCRIPTURES

- (Rom 16:20) ≈ **And the God of peace shall bruise Satan under your feet shortly. The grace of our Lord Jesus Christ (be) with you. Amen.** ≈
- (Rom 10:15) ≈ **And how shall they preach, except they be sent? As it is written, how beautiful are the feet of them that preach the gospel of peace, and bring glad tidings of good things!** ≈
- (Rom 10:13) ≈ **For, Whoever will call on the name of the Lord will be saved.** ≈
- (Eph 6:12) ≈ **For our wrestling is not against flesh and blood, but against the principalities, against the powers, against the world's rulers of the darkness of this age, and against the spiritual forces of wickedness in the heavenly places.** ≈

SHIELD

≈ Above all, taking up the shield of faith, with which you will be able to quench all the fiery darts of the evil one. ≈

Short Reason
-DEFLECT BLOWS
-HIDE BEHIND
-DEFEND OTHERS

1. **THE FIERY DARTS OF THE WICKED** (JAMES 3:6).

- Words and temptations are the darts of the evil and the wicked.

2. <u>HOW THE SHIELD OF FAITH QUENCH THE DARTS</u>

- For we walk by faith and not by sight. When you look away from the reality of life but instead look to and live in the promises of God the sting of this life is done away with.

3. <u>A DETAILED EXPLAINATION OF HOW THE SHIELD WORKS.</u>

- The shield is the faith process; nullifying or skipping any step voids the effect. And yes the effect of faith is cumulative. In this story we see all the components of this process and how they function.

Matt 14:24 - ≈ **But the boat was now in the middle of the sea, distressed by the waves, for the wind was contrary.** ≈

- Notice that the boat moved out into the deep water, that which made it dangerous was not the depth, but the contrary wind. The fiery darts of the evil one assail us, especially when we are where the Master wants us to be, and we are the most useful.

14:25 - ≈ **In <u>the fourth watch of the night,</u> Jesus came to them, walking on the sea.** ≈

- The fourth watch of the night is in the earliest part of the morning, when most things are at rest. The Lord comes when He wants to and not before. His still small voice of the Lord manifests Himself as a Calm in the worst part of the storm, when it seems too late and all is lost. In His calmness, He easily treads upon the problems of this world and shows His Mastery over all things.

14:26 - ≈ When the disciples saw Him walking on the sea, they were troubled, saying, "It's a ghost!" and they cried out for fear. ≈

- Most 'believers' do not really know the Lord, so when he does come we panic or resist Him. It is for this reason He often has to wait until we are so desperate that we will accept any help. This also is when Satan likes to show up. This is another reason that we MUST have a relationship with the Master. Under stress studies show that the first thing we forget/loose is our short term memory, that is why faith must be a lifestyle.

14:27 - ≈ But immediately Jesus spoke to them, saying "CHEER UP! IT IS I! DON'T BE AFRAID. ≈

- Notice Jesus had to identify Himself and tell the men to cheer up. Sadly enough we understand God so little we fear His presence. Whenever the Lord shows up we should rejoice and be glad in it. ≈ (Heb 12:6) For whom the Lord loveth He chasteneth, and scourgeth every son whom He receiveth. ≈

14:28 - ≈ Peter answered Him and said, "Lord, if it is you, command me to come to You on the waters. ≈

- Again we see the a lack of relationship with God causes doubt. After having been around Jesus Peter still asked for identification of the man The took out to sea with him. And we see a common evidence of meager faith. Peter asks the Lord for proof and a command, had he faith the size of a mustard seed he would not have needed proof (signs, symbols, hints, nudges, miracles or anything else).

14:29 - ≈ He said, "COME!" Peter stepped down from the boat, and walked on the waters to come to Jesus. ≈

- The most important ingredient in the process appears in this verse, faith has to based in what God has said. We cannot move before God speaks that is called bailing us out. When God tells us to do something, especially something seemingly impossible; moving upon that is called FAITH.

14:30 - ≈ **But when he saw that the wind was strong, he was afraid, and beginning to sink, he cried out, saying, "Lord, save me!** ≈

- The next stanza shows the true enemy of faith, is not doubt: it is reality. For you see Peter always doubted, that is why he went through so many preliminary steps. Remember doubt is physical evidence of the lack of faith not the cause. The cause of little faith is a weak relationship with God.

14:31 - ≈ **Immediately Jesus stretched out his hand, took hold of him, and said to him, "YOU OF LITTLE FAITH, WHY DID YOU DOUBT?** ≈

- Notice Jesus admonished him about little faith before He dealt with doubt. The inability to perform was not because of doubt but because weak faith. Doubt deals with facts, but faith deals with relationship. In all the prophets of old and apostles of new there was doubt in the initial meeting. It was not until they developed a relationship that the men learned to walk in faith. This is why obedience is so important; it is 95% of faith. Believers if we love the Lord we will obey Him.

14:32 - ≈ **When they got up into the boat, the wind ceased.** ≈

- Jesus pulled Peter back into the boat. Like Jonah when the lesson is ended Jesus always returns us to dry land. As in the case of Jonah and Peter there are always two ways to calm the storm. Faith or intervention from God will always calm the storm, but it cannot be avoided.

14:33 - ≈ **Those who were in the boat came and worshiped him, saying, "You are truly the Son of God!** ≈

- After Peter is delivered by Jesus they all worshipped Him, but even the sinners did that. Much like Thomas there is a blessing for seeing the wonders of God and believing, but more blessed are those that have not seen yet believed anyway. This type of relationship with God is called faith.

TOPICAL SCRIPTURES

-(1 Sa 17:45) ≈ **Then said David to the Philistine, Thou comest to me with a sword, and with a spear, and with a shield: but I come to thee in the name of the Lord of hosts, the God of the armies of Israel, whom thou hast defied.** ≈

-(Isa 21:5) ≈ **Look! They are preparing a great feast. They are spreading rugs for people to sit on. Everyone is eating and drinking. Quick! Grab your shields and prepare for battle! You are being attacked!** (NLT) ≈

- (Matt 5:11) ≈ **BLESSED ARE YOU WHEN PEOPLE REPROACH YOU, PERSECUTE YOU, AND SAY ALL KINDS OF EVIL AGAINST YOU FALSELY, FOR MY SAKE. REJOICE, AND BE EXCEEDINGLY GLAD, FOR GREAT IS YOUR REWARD IN HEAVEN. FOR THAT IS HOW THEY PERSECUTED THE PROPHETS WHO WERE BEFORE YOU.** ≈

HELMET

≈ And take the helmet of salvation, ≈

Short Reason
-PROTECTS FROM BLOWS AND SOUNDS
-PROTECTS THOUGHTS AND IMAGINATIONS

1. THE HELMET IS WORN AND IT PROTECTS THE MIND AND EARS.

- The ears are protected from the evil words and the false philosophies of men.

- As we get tossed about by the waves of this life the helmet protects our minds from the evil wiles of the tempter.

2. WHY WE PROTECT OUR MINDS

- As the Holy spirit renews our minds we must guard it against the vain evil imaginations that the prince of the power of the air bombards us with. It is these imaginations that repented God about man. Once free from them if we return it gets worst than it was the first time.

TOPICAL SCRIPTURES

- (1 Ch 28:9) ≈ **And thou, Solomon my son, know thou the God of thy father, and serve Him with a perfect heart and with a willing mind: for the Lord searcheth all hearts, and understandeth all the imaginations of the thoughts: if thou seek Him, He will be found of thee; but if thou forsake Him, He will cast thee off for ever.** ≈
- (Dan 5:20) ≈ **But when his heart was lifted up, and his mind hardened in pride, he was deposed from his kingly throne, and they took his glory from him:** ≈

- (1 PET 5:8) ≈ **BE SOBER AND SELF-CONTROLLED. BE WATCHFUL. YOUR ADVERSARY THE DEVIL, WALKS AROUND LIKE A ROARING LION, SEEKING WHOM HE MAY DEVOUR.** ≈

- (2 COR. 10:5) ≈ **THROWING DOWN IMAGINATIONS AND EVERY HIGH THING THAT IS EXALTED AGAINST THE KNOWLEDGE OF GOD, AND BRINGING EVERY THOUGHT INTO CAPTIVITY TO THE OBEDIENCE OF MESSIAH** ≈

- (ROM 8:6-8) ≈ **FOR THE MIND OF THE FLESH IS DEATH, BUT THE MIND OF THE SPIRIT IS LIFE AND PEACE; BECAUSE THE MIND OF THE FLESH IS HOSTILE TOWARDS GOD; FOR IT IS NOT SUBJECT TO GOD'S LAW, NEITHER INDEED CAN IT BE. THOSE WHO ARE IN THE FLESH CAN'T PLEASE GOD** ≈

- (Col 2:8) ≈ **Be careful that you don't let anyone rob you through his philosophy and vain deceit, after the tradition of men, after the elements of the world, and not after Messiah.** ≈

SWORD

≈ **And the sword of the Spirit, which is the <u>word</u> of God;** ≈

Short Reason
-FIGHT AND PROTECT
-WITNESS OF GOD
-HEAL OR DESTROY
-NAME OF JESUS

1. WHAT A SWORD IS USED FOR.

- Defense - We use the swords to protect ourselves and to protect other people.

- Attack - We also use the sword for attacks against the enemy…and the enemy is NEVER the person but Satan himself. Even when Satan uses people the person is not our enemy, and we must try not to harm the lost sheep if possible. But we must never allow that tool of the enemy to destroy one of His tools just so we do not have to do hurt their feelings.

2. THE TWO-EDGED SWORD. (HEB 4:12)

- The word of God is our sword, not anger as in the case of Peter. Whenever anger is used God must first heal the damage we cause before He can do any thing more for that person.

- There is no documented case in the bible of the word of God neither causing harm to anyone nor needing follow up healing afterwards.

TOPICAL SCRIPTURES

- (Deut 33:29) ≈ **Happy (art) thou, O Israel: who (is) like unto thee, O people saved by the Lord, the shield of thy help, and who (is) the sword of thy excellency! And thine enemies shall be found liars unto thee; and thou shalt tread upon their high places.** ≈

- (Heb 4:12) ≈ **For the word of God is living, and active, and sharper than any two-edged sword, and piercing even to the dividing of soul and spirit, of both joints and marrow, and is able to discern the thoughts and intentions of the heart.** ≈

PRAYER

≈ *With all prayer and requests, praying at all times in the Spirit* ≈

Short Reason
- GIVES GOD PERMISSION TO ACT
- MOVES FLESH
- OPENS YOU UP TO HEAR FROM GOD
- HELPS YOU LIKEN YOUR THOUGHTS TO GOD'S THOUGHTS.

1. **THE PURPOSE OF PRAYER. (MATT 6)**

- To talk to God

- To give God permission to operate in our lives.

- **TO GET A CLOSER LOOK INTO THE HEART OF GOD.**

- To get encouragement from God.

- To get direction from God

- To develop intimacy with God.

2. **TO WHOM WE PRAY AND WHY.**

- Our Father which art in Heaven is who we pray to. Not to Jesus, Mary, nor the Holy Spirit. Neither of them is 'The power and the glory for ever and ever; Amen". Since they are neither the power nor glory it makes sense to go to the one source in the universe that actually can answer prayers. And because the veil was permanently removed we need NO-ONE on this planet; Alive or dead adn buried to carry our prayers to the Father.

3. **WHY DID JESUS GIVE AN EXAMPLE OF HOW TO PRAY (ROM 8:26).**

- Paul tells us in no uncertain terms that we do not know how to pray - (Rom 8:26). Which does not mean that we do not know the words. What it means is that our thoughts and desires are so far from His that the two languages are barely even compatible. That is why He tells us in Matt 6 not to waste a lot of words we already knows what you need.

4. PRAYER, FASTING AND THE FLESH (Matt 4)

- The effective fervent prayers of the righteous avail much but there is a component that propels that prayer to a completely different level; That thing is fasting. Prayer brings us closer to God and fasting gets our flesh further away from our hearts. With the flesh subdued as much as possible the prayer and intimacy with God becomes much easier and more meaningful.

TOPICAL SCRIPTURES

- (Jam 4:3) ≈ **Ye ask, and receive not, because ye ask amiss, that ye may consume (it) upon your lusts.** ≈
- (Jam 5:16) ≈ **Confess (your) faults one to another, and pray one for another, that ye may be healed. The effectual fervent prayer of a righteous man availeth much.** ≈
- (Matt 4:1) ≈ **Then Jesus was led up by the Spirit into the wilderness to be tempted by the devil. When He had fasted forty days and forty nights, He was hungry afterward. The tempter came and said to Him, "If you are the Son of God, command that these stones become bread." But He answered, "IT IS WRITTEN...** ≈
- (Matt 6:1-14) ≈ **BE CAREFUL THAT YOU DON'T DO YOUR CHARITABLE GIVING BEFORE MEN, TO BE SEEN BY THEM, OR ELSE YOU HAVE NO REWARD FROM YOUR FATHER WHO IS IN HEAVEN. THEREFORE WHEN YOU DO MERCIFUL DEEDS, DON'T SOUND A SHOFAR BEFORE YOURSELF, AS THE HYPOCRITES DO IN THE SYNAGOGUES AND IN THE STREETS, THAT THEY MAY GET GLORY FROM MEN. MOST CERTAINLY I TELL YOU, THEY HAVE RECEIVED THEIR REWARD. BUT WHEN YOU DO MERCIFUL DEEDS, DON'T LET YOUR LEFT HAND KNOW WHAT YOUR RIGHT HAND DOES, SO THAT YOUR MERCIFUL DEEDS MAY BE IN SECRET, THEN YOUR FATHER WHO SEES IN SECRET WILL REWARD YOU OPENLY. WHEN YOU PRAY, YOU SHALL NOT BE AS THE HYPOCRITES, FOR THEY LOVE TO STAND AND PRAY IN**

THE SYNAGOGUES AND IN THE CORNERS OF THE STREETS, THAT THEY MAY BE SEEN BY MEN. MOST CERTAINLY, I TELL YOU, THEY HAVE RECEIVED THEIR REWARD. BUT YOU, WHEN YOU PRAY, ENTER INTO YOUR INNER CHAMBER, AND HAVING SHUT YOUR DOOR, PRAY TO YOUR FATHER WHO IS IN SECRET, AND YOUR FATHER WHO SEES IN SECRET WILL REWARD YOU OPENLY. IN PRAYING, DON'T USE VAIN REPETITIONS, AS THE GENTILES DO; FOR THEY THINK THAT THEY WILL BE HEARD FOR THEIR MUCH SPEAKING. THEREFORE DON'T BE LIKE THEM, FOR YOUR FATHER KNOWS WHAT THINGS YOU NEED, BEFORE YOU ASK HIM. PRAY LIKE THIS: OUR FATHER IN HEAVEN, MAY YOUR NAME BE KEPT HOLY. LET YOUR KINGDOM COME. LET YOUR WILL BE DONE, AS IN HEAVEN, SO ON EARTH. GIVE US TODAY OUR DAILY BREAD. FORGIVE US OUR DEBTS, AS WE ALSO FORGIVE OUR DEBTORS. BRING US NOT INTO TEMPTATION, BUT DELIVER US FROM THE EVIL ONE. FOR YOURS IS THE KINGDOM, THE POWER, AND THE GLORY FOREVER. AMEN.' FOR IF YOU FORGIVE MEN THEIR TRESPASSES, YOUR HEAVENLY FATHER WILL ALSO FORGIVE YOU. BUT IF YOU DON'T FORGIVE MEN THEIR TRESPASSES, NEITHER WILL YOUR FATHER FORGIVE YOUR TRESPASSES. ≈

- (Matt 26:39) ≈ He went forward a little, fell on His face, and prayed, saying, **"MY FATHER, IF IT IS POSSIBLE, LET THIS CUP PASS AWAY FROM ME; NEVERTHELESS, NOT WHAT I DESIRE, BUT WHAT YOU DESIRE.** ≈

ALERTNESS

≈ **And being watchful to this end in all perseverance and requests for all the holy ones:** ≈

Short Reason
- Keeps us out of danger.
- Helps us hear the still small voice of God.
- Helps us to be good watchmen.
- Helps us to be good stewards.

1. WISDOM AND INTROSPECTION

- Wisdom comes from above, so when God does impart His wisdom into our lives we should guard that valuable morsel of His mercy with our lives.

- If we would judge ourselves and our own hearts we would find ourselves far from God. But in doing so we have a way home and a path set before us; if we choose to walk it. Without this type of honesty there can never be success.

2. WHAT TO BE ALERT FOR (COL 2:8)

- When we get these keys to life and salvation let us retain our sobriety and not be given again to the drunken lust of this life.

  - This alertness also allows us to discern in the spirit and to be sensitive to the Holy Spirit. It prevents our being deceived any longer by the Dragon or by men.

3. **PREVENTIVE MAINTAINENCE**

- What ever things God says, His promises and the good news of Jesus Christ are things hat we should constantly fill our minds with. The more of these things we fill our minds with the less garbage we will have room for.

TOPICAL SCRIPTURES

- (1 Pet 5:8) ≈ **Be sober, be vigilant; because your adversary the devil, as a roaring lion, walketh about, seeking whom he may devour** ≈

- (1 Sam 17:45) ≈ **Then said David to the Philistine, Thou comest to me with a sword, and with a spear, and with a shield: but I come to thee in the name of the Lord of hosts, the God of the armies of Israel, whom thou hast defied.** ≈

- (Prov 5:1-2 & 21-22) ≈ **My son, pay attention to my wisdom. Turn your ear to my understanding: that you may maintain discretion, that your lips may preserve knowledge. The evil deeds of the wicked ensnare him. The cords of his sin hold him firmly. He will die for lack of instruction.
In the greatness of his folly, he will go astray.** ≈

- (Prov 4:1-11) ≈ **Listen, sons, to a father's instruction. Pay attention and know understanding; for I give you sound learning. Don't forsake my law. For I was a son to my father, tender and an only child in the sight of my mother. He taught me, and said to me: Let your heart retain my words. Keep my commandments, and live. Get wisdom. Get understanding. Don't forget, neither swerve from the words of my mouth. Don't forsake her, and she will preserve you. Love her, and she will keep you. Wisdom is supreme. Get wisdom. Yes, though it costs all your possessions, get understanding. Esteem her, and she will exalt you. She will bring you to honor, when you embrace her. She will give to your head a garland of grace. She will deliver a crown of splendor to you.**

Listen, my son, and receive my sayings. The years of your life will be many. I have taught you in the way of wisdom. I have led you in straight paths ≈

The Three main components of a Successful Spiritual Campaign

I was in the process of meditating before a sermon when the answer came to me. I do not remember asking a question, but I have learned to listen to the holy spirit because his answers are always true and timely. The answer to whatever it was my heart pondered was one simple word, "DIE!" Although the harshness of God's words still cut deeper than a two-edged sword they are as necessary now as they were then. ≈ **AND HE SAID TO (THEM) ALL, IF ANY (MAN) WILL COME AFTER ME, LET HIM DENY HIMSELF, AND TAKE UP HIS CROSS DAILY, AND FOLLOW ME.** ≈ (Luke 9:23).

The three main components of a Successful Spiritual Campaign

The tried and true method to wage a successful campaign is summed up in this acronym.

D.I.E

1. Dedication
2. Inspiration
3. Education

DEDICATION

- *O*nce we set our lives to serving the Lord our God we must be diligent. We must not grow weary in well doing, for in due time we will get our rewards. When we fight the good fight of faith the only way to loose is to quit.

- The wisest of all men puts it this way, "Fear God and obey His commandments; for this is the whole duty of man."

TOPICAL SCRIPTURES

- (Luke 4:18/19) ≈ **THE SPIRIT OF THE LORD (IS) UPON ME, BECAUSE HE HATH ANOINTED ME TO PREACH THE GOSPEL TO THE POOR; HE HATH SENT ME TO HEAL THE BROKENHEARTED, TO PREACH DELIVERANCE TO THE CAPTIVES, AND RECOVERING OF SIGHT TO THE BLIND, TO SET AT LIBERTY THEM THAT ARE BRUISED, TO PREACH THE ACCEPTABLE YEAR OF THE LORD.** ≈
- (Luke 9:62) ≈ **But Yeshua said to him, NO ONE, HAVING PUT HIS HAND TO THE PLOW, AND LOOKING BACK, IS FIT FOR THE KINGDOM OF GOD.** ≈
- (Luke 24:5) ≈ **Becoming terrified, they bowed their faces down to the earth. They said to them, "Why do you seek the living among the dead? He isn't here, but is risen.** ≈
- (2Cr 3:3) ≈ **(Forasmuch as ye are) manifestly declared to be the epistle of Christ ministered by us, written not with ink, but with the Spirit of the living God; not in tables of stone, but in fleshy tables of the heart.** ≈
- (Jhn 8:44) ≈ **YE ARE OF (YOUR) FATHER THE DEVIL, AND THE LUSTS OF YOUR FATHER YE WILL DO. HE WAS A MURDERER FROM THE BEGINNING, AND ABODE NOT IN THE TRUTH, BECAUSE THERE IS NO TRUTH IN HIM. WHEN HE SPEAKETH A LIE,**

HE SPEAKETH OF HIS OWN: FOR HE IS A LIAR, AND THE FATHER OF IT. ≈

- (Jhn 10:27/28) ≈ **MY SHEEP HEAR MY VOICE, AND I KNOW THEM, AND THEY FOLLOW ME: AND I GIVE UNTO THEM ETERNAL LIFE; AND THEY SHALL NEVER PERISH, NEITHER SHALL ANY (MAN) PLUCK THEM OUT OF MY HAND.** ≈

INSPIRATION

- Do not let the promises of God inspire you to work for Him there are two far more important reasons to serve the Lord our God.

- God's - It was love for us that motivated Him to deliver us from hell and to constantly deliver us from evil. If you cannot find love a good enough reason to serve Him then ask yourself why you spent so much of your life trying to get people to love you?

- Freedom – The purpose of giving us freedom was to liberate us so we could serve our fellow man. It is not so we could walk around spending money and wasting our lives pursuing the lusts of the flesh. It was so that we could serve Him out of love and not out of fear. It is easy to be a slave when you have no choice. Only love makes believer submit to being bond – servants for Christ.

Topical Scriptures

- (Psa 22:3) ≈ **But Thou (art) holy, (O Thou) that inhabits the praises of Israel.** ≈
- (John17:10) ≈ **ALL THINGS THAT ARE MINE ARE YOURS, AND YOURS ARE MINE, AND I AM GLORIFIED IN THEM. I AM NO MORE IN THE WORLD, BUT THESE ARE IN THE WORLD, AND I AM COMING TO YOU. HOLY FATHER, KEEP THEM THROUGH YOUR NAME WHICH YOU HAVE GIVEN ME THAT THEY MAY BE ONE, EVEN AS WE ARE. WHILE I WAS WITH THEM IN THE WORLD, I KEPT THEM IN YOUR NAME. THOSE WHOM YOU HAVE GIVEN ME I HAVE KEPT. NONE OF THEM IS LOST, EXCEPT THE SON OF DESTRUCTION, THAT THE SCRIPTURE MIGHT BE FULFILLED.** ≈
- (Mk 4:11) ≈ **He said to them, TO YOU IS GIVEN THE MYSTERY OF THE KINGDOM OF GOD, BUT TO THOSE WHO ARE OUTSIDE, ALL THINGS ARE DONE IN PARABLES, THAT 'SEEING THEY MAY SEE, AND NOT PERCEIVE; AND HEARING THEY MAY HEAR, AND NOT UNDERSTAND; LEST PERHAPS THEY SHOULD TURN AGAIN, AND THEIR SINS SHOULD BE FORGIVEN THEM.** ≈

- (Rom 8:38-39) ≈ **For I am persuaded, that neither death, nor life, nor angels, nor principalities, nor things present, nor things to come, nor powers, nor height, nor depth, nor any other created thing, will be able to separate us from the love of God, which is in Messiah Yeshua our Lord.** ≈
- (I Cor 10:13) ≈ **No temptation has taken you except what is common to man. God is faithful, who will not allow you to be tempted above what you are able, but will with the temptation also make the way of escape, that you may be able to endure it.** ≈
- (1 Cor 15:50-58) ≈ **Now I say this, brothers, that flesh and blood can't inherit the Kingdom of God; neither does corruption inherit incorruption. Behold, I tell you a mystery. We will not all sleep, but we will all be changed, in a moment, in the twinkling of an eye, at the last trumpet. For the trumpet will sound, and the dead will be raised incorruptible, and we will be changed. For this corruptible must put on incorruption, and this mortal must put on immortality. But when this corruptible will have put on incorruption, and this mortal will have put on immortality, then what is written will happen: "Death is swallowed up in victory." "Death, where is your sting? Sheol, where is your victory?" The sting of death is sin, and the power of sin is the law. But thanks be to God, who gives us the victory through our Lord Yeshua the Messiah. Therefore, my beloved brothers, be steadfast, immovable, always abounding in the Lord's work, because you know that your labor is not in vain in the Lord.** ≈

EDUCATION

- Knowledge of God is knowledge of life. If you want to know how to live you need to learn how to love and then you will learn how to obey. Once ou learn how to obey you will learn to fear (reverence) the Lord and this is the beginning of wisdom.

- Learning about Christ guarantees freedom, from sin, lust and damnation. If you reject knowledge of Him you are rejecting Him and all of His things. We cannot learn about the freedom that He has given to us freely And still have no hope. All of the joys of life and the hope of the afterlife are tied up in Him.

- Let our witness be of Him and not of our pitiful lives before Him. We spend too much time telling people what we used to be, instead of telling people who He is and why we are not that way any longer. A simple definition of this concept is;

Witness = evidence of work / Testimony = evidence of our sin

Therefore let us then focus our time and tales on the mercy and grace of Jesus Christ. Sinners are all familiar with sin; they therefore do not need elaborate descriptions of our sin to move people. Let out elaborate descriptions be of His kindness to us and our fellow sinners.

TOPICAL SCRIPTURES

- (Pro 29:18) ≈ **Where there is no revelation, the people cast off restraint; (perish) but one who keeps the Torah is blessed.** ≈
- (Has 4:6) ≈ **My people are destroyed for lack of knowledge. Because you have rejected knowledge, I will also reject you, that you may be no priest to me. Because you have forgotten your God's law, I will also forget your children.** ≈

- (Eph 1:17) ≈ **That the God of our Lord Yeshua the Messiah, the Father of glory, may give to you a spirit of wisdom and revelation in the knowledge of Him {Himself-who He is}** ≈

- (2 Pe 1:3) ≈ **Seeing that His divine power has granted to us all things that pertain to life and godliness, through the knowledge of Him who called us by his own glory and virtue;** ≈

-(Jhn 5:31-36) ≈ **IF I TESTIFY ABOUT MYSELF, MY WITNESS IS NOT VALID. IT IS ANOTHER WHO TESTIFIES ABOUT ME. I KNOW THAT THE TESTIMONY WHICH HE TESTIFIES ABOUT ME IS TRUE. YOU HAVE SENT TO YOCHANAN, AND HE HAS TESTIFIED TO THE TRUTH. BUT THE TESTIMONY WHICH I RECEIVE IS NOT FROM MAN. HOWEVER, I SAY THESE THINGS THAT YOU MAY BE SAVED. HE WAS THE BURNING AND SHINING LAMP, AND YOU WERE WILLING TO REJOICE FOR A WHILE IN HIS LIGHT. BUT THE TESTIMONY WHICH I HAVE IS GREATER THAN THAT OF YOCHANAN, FOR THE WORKS WHICH THE FATHER GAVE ME TO ACCOMPLISH, THE VERY WORKS THAT I DO, TESTIFY ABOUT ME, THAT THE FATHER HAS SENT ME. THE FATHER HIMSELF, WHO SENT ME, HAS TESTIFIED ABOUT ME. YOU HAVE NEITHER HEARD HIS VOICE AT ANY TIME, NOR SEEN HIS FORM. YOU DON'T HAVE HIS WORD LIVING IN YOU; BECAUSE YOU DON'T BELIEVE HIM WHOM HE SENT.** ≈

GLOSSARY

DESTRUCTIVE…Designed for the purpose of destroying.
DELIVERANCE - When the flesh is freed from a particular bondage.
EVIL… Acting in a manner contrary to God's will.
FISH…Sinner or lost sheep.
FLESH…The material entombing our souls is replete with senses.
GIENCE…God's creation as a whole.
GECOSYSTEM…God's ecosystem.
HELLBOUND… An action or attitude known to result in damnation.
ISCARY…A branch of the descendants of Judas Ischariot.
ISCARO… A branch of the descendants of Judas Ischariot.
JBN…(Jesus Broadcasting Network)…communication with the Holy Spirit.
JESOURCES…Amount of Jesus in your life.
JEZ-TEST…Tests to see if you possess any Jezebel like qualities.
METECTORS…Jesus' protective hands about a person.
REEF BLEECHERS…Destructive preachers.
SALVATION - When your spirit is redeemed from damnation.
SCRIPTULATION…Scriptural manipulation.
SPEAR FISHERS…Lazy preachers.
SPORTS FISHERS…Popular churches.
SCALING…Removing fish scales.
SONLIGHT…Jesus' glory
SDA…Spiritual Daily Allowance
TITHE AVOIDANCE…A scheme designed to appear to be true tithes but avoiding the actual 10%
TRAWLERS…God's true fishers.
WE AIN'T FINISHED YET SYNDROME…A belief that God will not allow a person to die before they complete their task, despite their rebellion.

Symbolic Language used in the Old and New Testaments[170]

Adultery.... Idolatry
Angel.... Messenger, hence minister
Arm.... Power
Arrows.... Judgments
Babylon.... Rome
Beast.... A tyrannical heathen monarch
Black.... Affliction—anguish
Blindness.... Ignorance
Blood.... Slaughter—depth
Brimstone.... Desolation—torments
Bride.... The Church of God
Bridegroom.... Christ wedded to his Church
Bulls.... Violent enemies
Candlestick....Church
Chariots.... Heavenly hosts
Crown.... Victory—reward
Cup....Divine Blessings/ Divine Judgments
Darkness.... Misery—adversity—ignorance
Day....An indefinite time—a prophetic year
Dogs.... Gentiles—impure persons—persecutors
Door.... An opening
Dragon......Satan
Drunkenness.... Effects of divine judgments
Earthquakes.... Revolutions
Eyes.... Knowledge
Face.... The divine favor
Fat.... Abundance
Fire....Judgments
Forehead.... A public profession
Furnace.... Affliction
Garments.... Outward appearance
Gates.... Power—security

---

[170] Nevin, Alfred, Ed., et al. "Symbolic Language Used by the Poets and Prophets of the Old and New Testaments," *The Parallel Bible*. Blue Letter Bible. 1 Aug 2002. 8 Dec 2004. <http://blueletterbible.org/study/parallel/paral17.html>.

Girdles…Strength
Goats…. Wicked persons
Grass…. The lower orders, opposed to trees
Hail….Divine vengeance
Hand…. Protection—support
Hand of the Lord…. Divine influence
Harvest…. A time of destruction/reaping
Head…. Rule or ruler
Heavens…. Political or ecclesiastical governments
Horse…. War and conquest
Hunger and thirst…. Spiritual desires
Incense…. Prayer
Jerusalem…. Church of God/ The heavenly state
Keys…. Power and authority
Lamp… A successor or offspring
Light…. Joy—prosperity/ Knowledge—bitterness
Mountains…. A state—Christ's Church
Mystery…. Not unintelligible, but not made plain
Mystery…. Not unintelligible, but not made plain
Naked…. In the sinful state of nature
Night…. Adversity—affliction—ignorance
Oaks…. Men of rank and power
Oil…. Abundance—fertility—joy
Psalms…. Victory
Paradise…. Heaven
Rock…. A secure refuge
Salt…. Purity—barrenness
Sea in commotion…. An army
Seal…. Security—secrecy
Serpent…. The devil
Sheep…. Christ's disciples
Shepherds…. Rules, civil or ecclesiastical
Shield…. Defense—protection
Sleep…. Death
Sores…. Spiritual maladies
Star…. A prince or ruler
Sun/moon/stars…. The various governors in a state
Sword…. War and slaughter
Tail…. Subjection—degradation
Teeth… Cruelty

Throne.... Kingdom or government
Travail.... Anguish—anxiety
Trees.... the higher orders/ The great and noble
Vine/vineyard.... The Church of God
Watchtower.... The Prophets
Waters.... Afflictions—multitudes—ordinances
Wilderness.... Afflicted state
Wind.... Judgments—destructive war
Wine.... Spiritual blessings—divine judgments
Winepress.... Slaughter
Wings.... Protection
Wolves.... Furious, ungodly persons
Woman.... City, or body politie / Church of Christ
Yoke.... Labor-restraint

n.b. All of the words on this list are interchangeable with their counter parts. Therefore every time you see either term the symbolic may be applicable or vice versa.

INDEX

Abase...328
Abate...63, 257
Abhor...188.
Abide...46, 53,127, 152, 185, 220, 276, 303, 310.
Ability...47, 52 55, 63, 120,121,204,205,219,237, 257,281, 354, 358, 359, 368, 383, 385, 400.
Able...20, 24, 49, 52, 57, 64, 67, 83, 87, 95, 114, 117, 128, 254, 255, 257, 283, 300, 301, 302, 326, 327, 329, 330, 331, 362, 368, 395, 400,403, 406, 409, 416, 427.
Abode...237,281,425.
Abomination...174,175,235,252
Abound...186, 283.
Above...10, 11, 18, 21, 117, 118, 125, 128, 177, 178, 186, 256, 301, 324, 329, 333, 348, 356, 366, 402, 411, 422, 429.
Abuse...275, 279, 325.
Accept...20, 42, 64, 80, 93, 101, 105, 120, 154, 185, 187, 203, 221, 329, 330, 332, 353, 357, 388, 412.
Acceptable...60, 180, 257, 427.
Access...49, 57, 116, 217, 221, 301, 302, 361, 370, 403.
Accomplish...99, 155, 217, 303, 344, 363, 431.
Accord...179, 332, 364.
Account...98, 102, 273, 276.
Accurate...24, 250, 270, 363.
Accursed...60, 66.
Accusation...49, 50, 103, 153, 252.
Acknowledge...300, 309.
Acquire...22, 299, 305, 310.
Adjure...55.
Admonish...9, 62, 93, 96, 216, 271, 331, 153.
Adorn...97, 203.
Adultery...52, 53, 65, 66, 154, 172, 173, 174, 183, 185, 186, 193, 216, 434.
Advantage...62
Adversary...154, 358, 416, 423.

Adversity...6.
Affliction...6, 48, 146.
Afraid...22, 97, 124, 146, 147, 149, 177, 180, 255, 323, 325, 327, 388, 412, 413.
Almighty...4, 25, 57, 155, 280, 355, 360, 405.
Alms...179, 309.
Alone...7, 19, 42, 54, 55, 81, 125, 131, 136, 152, 159, 176, 181, 236, 282, 300, 305, 306, 308, 311, 348, 354, 370, 384, 387, 388, 398.
Altar...282, 326, 361.
Angel...38, 60, 82, 154, 157, 158, 166, 237, 360, 409.
Anger...7, 12, 122, 147, 148, 149,181, 154, 257, 258, 259, 260, 385, 386, 417,
Anguish...155.
Animal...61, 362.
Appoint...45, 49.
Apostasy...172.
Archangel...49, 103, 251.
Arise...60, 82, 146, 147, 148, 177, 181, 200, 251.
Armor...127, 128, 140, 152, 325, 402, 403.
Ascend...95, 324.
Astray...53, 65, 155, 187, 423.
Authority...203, 222, 227, 271, 311, 322, 323, 324, 325, 326, 327, 332, 333, 334, 336, 337, 339, 340, 341, 342, 360.

Balm...102.
Baptism...8, 102, 198, 199, 200, 201, 202, 203, 204, 206, 207, 210, 211, 325.
Battle...94, 115, 128, 130, 400, 414.
Begotten...23, 25, 81, 119, 149, 156, 357, 363.
Behold...47, 49, 58, 102, 104, 154, 173, 181, 201, 202, 251, 278, 301, 311, 327, 368, 429.
Belief...149, 360.
Belong...22, 39, 54, 121, 215, 218, 310, 344, 408.
Beloved...65, 119, 120, 199, 209, 384, 429.
Blasphemy...47, 300.
Blemish...182, 204, 327.

Bless…57, 100, 181, 223, 238, 278, 279, 309, 312, 369.
Blind…50, 115, 117, 136, 176, 177, 333, 384, 427.
Blood…61, 66, 81, 82, 102, 119, 120, 136, 147, 173, 174, 200, 201, 202, 203, 204, 205, 238, 250, 259.
Boast…237, 282, 297, 298, 303, 313, 324, 325, 326, 328, 330, 349, 361, 362, 373, 387, 402, 410, 429,
Boat…16, 37, 57, 99, 149, 165, 255, 353, 411, 412, 413,
Bondservant…312, 329, 330, 388.
Born…4, 46, 49, 66, 133, 175, 183, 210, 203, 204, 236, 250, 252, 254, 275, 304, 325, 384, 409.
Bosom…7, 53, 102, 123, 150, 185.
Brother…7, 14, 19, 38, 49, 59, 102, 220, 221, 253, 254, 259, 270, 276,329.
Bought…40, 41, 50, 65, 174, 349.
Bow…18, 99, 125, 324, 365.
Break…155, 158, 175, 205, 215, 234, 235, 258, 259, 333, 386.
Breastplate…117, 402, 406, 408.
Breath…79, 88, 97, 104, 123, 131, 221, 359, 360, 407, 432,
Bride…51, 52, 54, 59,176, 180, 182, 183, 185, 188, 272.
Bridegroom…51.
Brightness…332.
Burden…38, 39, 70, 127, 155, 302.
Bury…223.

Calf…20.
Call…8, 9, 11, 16, 17, 20, 38, 42, 46, 55, 68, 79, 80, 81, 82, 98, 99, 120, 126, 127, 146, 148, 149, 150, 177, 179, 188, 203, 229, 255, 272, 302, 308, 329, 331, 354, 357, 367, 397, 410.
Captive…219.
Cast… 7, 8, 24, 36, 38, 39, 43, 46, 48, 49, 50, 52, 53, 55, 58, 59, 64, 67, 69, 98, 118, 119, 120, 121, 122, 125, 126, 127, 146, 147, 149, 153, 157, 173, 177, 180, 187, 215, 249, 256, 282, 323, 326, 332, 358, 360, 368, 415, 430.
Chasten…254.
Child…7, 12, 16, 18, 62, 102, 119, 133, 183, 205, 237, 254, 272, 273, 274, 303, 309, 357, 367, 423.

Choice...21, 25, 44, 80, 102, 152, 159, 205, 250, 253, 306, 428, 355.
Circumcise...250, 361.
Clean...138, 203, 204, 219, 277, 301.
Cloud...120, 283, 300, 327.
Comforter...220
Command...79, 96, 151, 175, 252, 313, 348, 412, 420.
Commandment...17, 23, 53, 123, 124, 184, 307, 330, 366.
Commit...47, 58, 118, 173, 185, 298, 303.
Compassion...25, 56, 118, 119, 257, 306.
Condemn...94.
Confess...99, 125, 221, 324, 420.
Confuse...21, 22, 82, 216, 256, 303, 308, 354, 357, 385, 390.
Corrupt...17, 19, 21, 67, 103, 180.
Countenance...187.
Covenant...17, 23, 158, 174, 175, 203, 205, 250, 259, 324, 325, 332, 333, 408.
Creation...64, 153, 175, 204, 279, 351, 353, 354, 356, 364, 365, 366,.
Cross...24, 51, 98, 128, 150, 151, 155, 158, 185, 204, 220, 221, 250, 277, 285, 324, 328, 337, 425, 427.
Crown...57, 158, 201, 335, 424.
Crucifixion...156, 200, 297, 299, 361.
Crucify...297, 300, 361.
Cup...155, 199, 200, 255, 326, 421.
Curse...48, 126, 127, 154, 187, 299.

Darkness...11, 24, 60, 65, 97, 103, 117, 118, 135, 150, 153, 179, 185, 188, 402, 410.
Dead...8, 16, 21, 46, 60, 61, 134, 172, 173, 199, 203, 300, 324, 328, 332, 357, 358, 359, 366, 369, 387, 419, 427, 429.
Death...8, 21, 23, 25, 41, 45, 47, 48, 49, 53, 58, 61, 66, 68, 79, 82, 95, 96, 103, 118, 125, 126, 131, 148, 150, 153, 156, 158, 173, 180, 183, 186, 187, 188, 199, 200, 201, 202, 203, 216, 220, 249, 251, 252, 297, 298, 302, 303, 304, 311, 131, 324,

325, 326, 328, 333, 336, 337, 349, 361, 364, 370, 407, 416, 429.
Defeat...104, 187, 264, 332.
Defend...116, 366, 400, 411.
Defile...48, 63, 119, 407.
Demon...358, 373, 398.
Desert...54, 56, 99, 258, 254, 337.
Desire...17, 21, 40, 52, 63, 64, 95, 118, 159, 186, 220, 222, 249, 253, 271, 298, 303, 310, 348, 353, 386, 421.
Destroy...8, 18, 49, 50, 55, 61, 64, 97, 102, 103, 105, 122, 130, 132, 184, 186, 204, 216, 249, 251, 252, 278, 298, 294, 300, 325, 331, 332, 403, 417.
Discern...148, 238, 418, 422.
Disciple...3, 5, 46, 73, 98, 99, 168, 190, 255, 297, 327, 328.
Disobedience...58, 60, 96, 149, 157, 158, 221.
Divorce...20, 32, 172.
Doctrine...50, 54, 61, 63, 118, 192, 311, 312, 316, 319, 322, 328, 339, 369.
Dominion...102, 175, 187, 199, 210, 204, 249, 332, 349.
Dragon...19, 81, 151, 422, 434.
Dust...47, 104, 152, 175, 278, 359.
Dwell...6, 50, 54, 150, 176, 204, 220,, 276, 282, 298, 301, 328, 358, 364.

Eden...83, 121, 187, 248, 251, 261.
Edify...7, 284, 358.
Elders...9, 82, 127, 177, 180, 275, 282, 283, 297, 298, 303, 325, 327, 328, 399.
Elect...80, 251.
Enemy...67, 102, 121, 173, 204, 252, 349, 354, 398, 400, 413, 417.
Enmity...173, 152.
Entice...93, 235, 279, 284.
Envious...152, 204.
Eternity...61, 150, 158.
Evangelist...152, 215, 397.

Everlasting...20, 25, 51, 81, 152.
Evil...5, 17, 20, 23, 44, 48, 53, 55, 59, 60, 61, 65, 67, 101, 103,
    116, 117, 119, 125, 126, 127, 146, 147, 148, 157, 173, 177,
    181, 184, 185, 236, 248, 249, 250, 251, 254, 256, 260, 261,
    262, 298, 303, 310, 333, 348, 350, 357, 358, 368, 402, 403,
    407, 411, 414, 415, 421, 423, 428.
Exalt...249, 329, 423.
Exhort...7, 328.
Exile...7, 9, 39.

Faith...15, 43, 63, 81, 100, 117, 126, 149, 159, 218, 220, 237,
    255, 258, 269, 270, 328, 331, 350, 353, 366, 368, 369, 384, 385,
    386, 387, 388, 402, 403, 408, 411, 412, 413, 414, 426.
False...8, 11, 20, 48, 64, 65, 66, 67, 119, 150, 251, 300, 307, 311, 334,
335, 338, 369, 407, 415.
Fast...16, 44, 123, 124, 135, 146, 147, 283, 328, 398.
Father...3, 4, 5, 7, 8, 9, 10, 11, 12,16,17,18, 21, 22, 25, 38, 39, 40, 46, 48,
    49, 50, 51, 59, 64, 66, 67, 79, 93, 94, 96, 98, 99, 100, 102, 103,
    104, 105, 119, 121, 122, 125, 126, 127, 134, 150, 151, 155, 156,
    157, 158, 174, 176, 178, 179, 180, 183, 188, 199, 200, 201, 202,
    203, 203, 215, 217, 220, 221, 235, 237, 254, 255, 259, 260, 271,
    272, 273, 274, 277, 280, 281, 283, 286, 296, 300, 301, 302, 303,
    304, 309, 312, 313, 324, 325, 326, 327, 328, 329, 330, 331, 334,
    349, 350, 355, 356, 360, 361, 366, 367, 368, 369, 370, 384, 405,
    415, 419, 420, 421, 423, 427, 427, 428, 431.
Fear...8, 23, 49, 61, 78, 87, 97, 98, 118, 119, 120, 121, 122, 123, 124,
    142, 146, 148, 155, 179, 186, 204, 220, 222, 234, 259, 299, 323,
    325, 331, 349, 355, 385, 388, 412, 426, 428, 430.
Feet...47, 53, 117, 128, 185, 186, 210, 203, 204, 277, 278, 337, 402, 409,
    410.
Fellowship...60, 61, 66, 179, 282, 284.
Fire...17, 18, 19, 37, 38, 53, 67, 123, 130, 131, 173, 185, 200, 257,
    278, 310, 326, 358, 405.
Fish...39, 40, 41, 42, 43, 44, 45, 57, 58, 59, 61, 64, 72, 74, 78, 79,

84, 86, 97, 88, 89, 93, 94, 95, 96, 97, 98, 108, 109, 110, 111, 115, 127, 138, 141, 146, 147, 148, 151, 153, 154, 155, 175, 192, 219, 220, 255, 291, 319.
Fishermen…7, 8, 38, 39, 42, 55, 57, 59, 78, 79, 87, 93, 98, 107, 285.
Fishers…8, 36, 37, 38, 39, 47, 55, 56, 57, 58, 59, 60, 61, 62, 63, 69, 74, 80, 95, 96, 98, 153, 192.
Flock…51, 58, 151, 215.
Follow…19, 38, 39, 47, 55, 61, 62, 3, 64, 65, 67, 70, 82, 96, 150, 158, 202, 204, 205, 216, 221, 259, 277, 284, 285, 324, 335, 353, 417, 425, 427.

Garden…12, 49, 66, 121, 155, 157, 248, 251, 255, 261, 281, 304, 355, 358, 361, 362 386.
Garment…12, 256.
Gience…354, 356
Gift…22, 24, 41, 51, 57, 80, 81, 175, 176, 179, 182, 201, 205, 220, 221, 237, 300, 330, 356, 361, 362, 363, 398,
Glory…4, 19, 25, 37, 46, 48, 57, 80, 81, 82, 99, 100, 102, 103, 105, 116, 125, 128, 151, 154, 157, 158, 180, 187, 199, 201, 203, 277, 278, 279, 301, 309, 312, 327, 328, 369, 360, 366, 405, 406, 416, 419, 420, 421, 431.
Godly…24, 63, 399.
Grace…24, 37, 43, 44, 60, 66, 67, 68, 82, 96, 104, 121, 124, 149, 151, 152, 153, 182, 185, 221, 237, 258, 281, 283, 302, 313, 335, 361, 405, 409, 424, 430.
Grieve…21, 180, 242.

Hammer…4
Hand…6, 11, 38, 39, 46, 64, 102, 104, 120, 126, 147, 152, 153,

156, 157, 158, 176, 178, 201, 202, 216, 217, 251, 253, 255, 258, 279, 282, 302, 326, 331, 337, 360, 368, 383, 386, 389, 412, 419, 426, 427.
Happiness...101, 309, 385.
Harlot...52, 54, 171, 172, 185.
Harm...61, 64, 104, 105, 150, 203, 256, 330, 331, 333, 358, 416.
Harmony...236.
Harvest...37, 45, 59, 99, 217.
Hatch...81.
Hate...18, 48, 129, 130, 131, 251, 260, 118.
Haunt...151.
Head...7, 10, 19, 65, 103, 145, 147, 153, 180, 181, 202, 255, 275, 307, 328, 337, 363, 423.
Hear...6, 19, 21, 22, 45, 47, 55, 63, 78, 79, 82, 101, 104, 105, 124, 152, 155, 179, 219, 234, 235, 236, 237, 256, 278, 283, 307, 358, 370, 404, 418, 421, 427, 428.
Heat...335.
Heaven... 4, 16, 17, 18, 24, 25, 36, 46, 49, 56, 57, 60, 67, 69, 82, 99, 101, 102, 103, 104, 125, 127, 146, 149, 153, 156, 175, 198, 217, 220, 236, 237, 249, 254, 256, 257, 272, 279, 282, 283, 285, 305, 309, 312, 313, 325, 326, 328, 329, 354, 358, 398, 404, 408, 428.
Heavy...62, 96.
Hedge...104, 121, 201, 202.
Heed...17, 19, 38, 39, 63, 80, 82, 120, 149, 152, 187, 203, 309.
Heir...204.
Hell... 13, 24, 42, 47, 49, 53, 62, 80, 119, 145, 149, 151, 152, 160, 186, 187, 217, 248, 250, 252, 279, 285, 302, 303, 312, 323, 329, 354, 358, 398, 404, 408, 428.
Helmet...117, 151, 401, 407, 414.
Help...11, 12, 14, 21, 56, 62, 63, 66, 67, 78, 83, 93, 97, 98, 99, 115, 116, 119, 123, 127, 128, 130, 133, 149, 150, 151, 152, 158, 219, 257, 274, 275, 276, 277, 300, 312, 324, 330, 331, 356, 358, 360, 387, 388, 396, 411, 417.
Hide...44, 79, 97, 116, 133, 156, 221, 385, 410.
Hinder...105, 150.
Hire...46, 278, 311.
Hold...9, 37, 55, 56, 62, 63, 67, 95, 118, 123, 141, 147, 220, 254, 305, 325, 326, 327, 333, 412, 422.

Holy…9, 11, 12, 16, 21, 22, 24, 24, 43, 47, 54, 55, 59, 62, 63, 64, 66, 79, 123, 125, 127, 145, 175, 177, 179, 181, 198, 199, 200, 201, 202, 203, 214, 215, 217, 219, 220, 222, 229, 235, 236, 237, 241, 242, 254, 269, 277, 280, 281, 282, 283, 284, 287, 300, 301, 302, 304, 305, 306, 307, 308, 326, 328, 333, 353, 355, 356, 359, 362, 366, 370, 383, 389, 396, 397, 401, 402, 414, 418, 420, 421, 424, 428.
Holy Spirit…9, 11, 12, 16, 21, 22, 23, 24, 43, 47, 54, 63, 66, 79, 123, 127, 175, 177, 179, 185, 198, 199, 200, 201, 202, 203, 214, 215, 217, 219, 220, 222, 235, 236, 237, 241, 242, 254, 277, 280, 281, 282, 283, 284, 302, 304, 305, 306, 307, 308, 355, 356, 362, 366, 370, 383, 389, 396, 397, 402, 414, 418, 421, 424.
Hope…54, 101, 135, 328, 362, 404, 407, 430.
Horrible…8, 58, 117, 215, 236, 310, 335.
Hostile…415.
Hour…103, 333.
Humble…39, 80, 311, 329, 348.
Humility…100, 366, 359.
Hunger…101.
Hungry…56, 235, 419.
Hunt…44, 53, 183, 365.
Husband…54, 171, 176, 177, 179, 180, 181, 182, 275, 276, 302.
Hypocrite…49.

Idle…218.
Ignorance…97, 219, 349, 369.
Ignorant…43, 343.
Illegitimate…323, 332, 333, 334, 336.
Illness…265.
Image…17, 18, 19, 37, 126, 203, 357.
Imitate…51, 251.
Immediate…300
Immortality…429
Impossible…20, 120, 233, 253, 366, 412.
Improper…306.
Infirmities…253, 281.

Inform...4, 250.
Inherit...24, 49, 101, 152, 252, 305, 429.
Inheritance...60, 204, 324.
Iniquity...18, 23, 56, 64, 67, 68, 272, 404.
Injustice...331.
Inner...79, 300, 311, 420.
Innocent...8, 53, 146, 184, 234, 303.
Inquire...357.
Instrument...236, 281.
Intercede... 54, 147, 149, 157, 187, 259.
Interpret...104, 271, 362, 363.
Intimate...9.
Irreverence...253.
Iscary...296, 304.
Iscaro...309, 310, 311.

JBN...235.
Jealous...18, 20, 97, 260, 304.
Jesources...19.
Jewel...367.
Jez-test...59.
Journey...18, 46, 53, 146, 185, 219, 257, 258, 259, 277, 310.
Joy...4, 43, 82, 95, 102, 178, 182, 301, 307, 313, 388.
Judge...5, 44, 45, 49, 50, 59, 68, 94, 127, 151, 152, 185, 252, 254,
    272, 296, 301, 302, 306, 323, 335, 422.
Judgment...6, 24, 25, 37, 38, 43, 47, 49, 50, 65, 119, 120, 127, 148,
    157, 173, 179, 183, 188, 278, 300, 304, 326.
Just...7, 9, 16, 21, 24, 25, 38, 40, 50, 55, 57, 62, 65, 66, 80, 93, 95,
    95, 104, 121, 123, 131, 134, 135, 150, 152, 153, 154, 157, 158, 174,
    182, 184, 185, 187, 201, 205, 219, 220, 236, 237, 249, 251, 252,
    256, 258, 272, 277, 279, 285, 299, 302, 303, 304, 305, 304, 311,
    313, 326, 328, 336, 337, 347, 348, 350, 353, 354, 360, 361, 363,
    364, 366, 371, 384, 387, 396, 397, 399, 427
Justice...25, 335, 336, 352.
Justify...94, 253.

Keep...53, 58, 59, 62, 72, 94, 97, 132, 179, 184, 215, 220, 221,
   235, 236, 280, 283, 309, 363, 369, 409, 423, 428.
Kill...8, 41, 42, 44, 49, 58, 66, 115, 130, 132, 150, 15, 163, 166,
   167, 173, 252, 253, 298, 311, 323, 331, 334, 365.
Kindness...23, 148, 177, 180, 430.
King...3, 44, 45, 49, 85, 105, 115, 119, 120, 128, 147, 172, 179,
   201, 217, 221, 253, 272, 298, 311, 323, 331, 334, 365.
Kingdom...4, 10, 11, 22, 24, 25, 36, 38, 46, 49, 55, 56, 60, 67, 69,
   81, 98, 101, 103, 150, 158, 176, 179, 184,185, 201, 238, 253, 254,
   271, 272, 275, 305, 312, 325, 329, 337, 350, 361, 366, 368, 370,
   421, 427, 428, 429.
Kiss...133, 299, 384.
Knee...99, 125, 324, 365.
Kneel...5, 134.
Knew...12, 18, 56, 57,67,0, 103, 120, 123, 147, 148, 149, 155,
   204, 235, 251, 297, 299, 300, 306, 356, 360.
Knife...131.
Know...9, 11, 12, 17, 20, 21, 22, 22, 24, 44, 51, 55, 58, 60, 63, 65,
   66, 68, 82, 83, 85, 94, 97, 103, 124, 128, 132, 134, 146, 147, 150,
   157, 173, 179, 181, 188, 199, 200, 205, 221, 222, 223, 251, 255,
   277, 281, 287, 300, 301, 309, 311, 328, 329, 330, 334, 354, 347,
   350, 357, 368, 371, 385, 387, 391, 399, 412, 415, 420, 423, 429,
   430, 431, 437,
Knowledge...21,22, 179, 218.

Labor...429.
Lack...22, 95, 99, 118, 220, 221, 250, 273, 307, 308, 348, 350,
   354, 355, 369, 372, 384, 385, 386, 412, 413, 423, 430.
Lady...282, 284.
Lamb...54, 80, 81, 150, 182, 185, 188, 201, 202, 203, 275, 302,
   325, 337, 361, 365.
Lamp... 53, 179, 184, 431.

Language...3, 63, 174, 183, 281, 358, 362, 364, 38, 369.
Law...429, 437.
Lay...23, 37, 52, 62, 97, 123, 134, 136, 146, 147, 215, 280, 303.
Leader...48, 54, 68, 127, 331, 333.
Learn...38, 39, 81, 97, 132, 219, 222, 275, 349, 355, 362, 365, 369, 384, 430.
Least...9, 12, 21, 41, 43, 46, 50, 63, 67, 93, 120, 121, 128, 135, 147, 150, 152, 156, 175, 179, 186, 217, 250, 254, 259, 266, 284, 298, 299, 304, 310, 335, 359, 363, 366, 369.
Liar...98, 427.
Liberty...65, 66, 128, 330, 427.
Lick...4, 8, 9, 16, 22, 23, 25, 38, 40, 41, 42, 43, 49, 51, 53, 57, 59, 61, 64, 66, 79, 81, 82, 93, 96, 97, 101, 103, 104.
Life...115, 116, 118, 119, 124, 125, 126, 128, 131, 132, 146, 147, 148, 152, 153, 156, 171, 175, 177, 178, 181, 182, 184, 185, 186, 187, 199, 202, 204, 220, 221, 249, 250, 251, 256, 260, 272, 273, 281, 295, 286, 298, 301, 304, 305, 306, 309, 311, 313, 324, 325, 330, 331, 334, 336, 337, 348, 350, 352, 355, 356, 359, 360,, 361, 364, 365, 367, 368, 370, 379, 384, 388, 404, 411, 415, 416, 422, 424, 427, 430, 431, 432,
Light...37, 38, 39, 51, 204, 222, 253, 300, 323, 332, 333, 337, 348, 353, 364, 368, 403, 431.
Likeness...17, 18, 199.
Linen...53, 177, 180, 186.
Lintel...202, 203.
Lion...19, 81, 98, 122, 220, 236, 255, 275, 416, 423.
Listen...105, 123, 126, 156, 259, 281, 282, 423, 424, 425.
Little...4, 39, 50, 56, 61, 63, 65, 67, 68, 78, 96, 98, 98, 122, 149, 218, 220, 237, 240, 255, 271, 274, 297, 298, 302, 306, 307, 333, 336, 412, 413, 424.
Live...19, 24, 42, 43, 48, 62, 125, 133, 134, 148, 152, 156, 185, 199, 215, 222, 223, 250, 254, 256, 274, 298, 302, 306, 307, 336, 412, 413, 424.
Living...5, 7, 19, 23, 24, 58, 63, 66, 79, 95, 98, 101, 104, 115, 117, 124, 149, 156, 174, 175, 201, 214, 224, 235, 249, 253, 259, 274, 304, 308, 309, 324, 328, 333, 336, 407, 418, 427, 437.
Loaves...56, 57.
Look...5, 10, 23, 40, 61, 68, 94, 100, 130, 134, 146, 156, 253, 255, 259, 273, 276, 280, 283, 309, 326, 327, 369, 411, 414, 419.

Loose…19, 45, 52, 121, 252, 255, 305, 412, 426.
Lord…3, 4, 6,10, 11, 12, 18, 21, 23, 24, 37, 49, 55, 57, 60, 64, 65,
    67, 78, 80, 82, 99, 100, 103, 104, 128, 134, 146, 149, 151, 153,
    174, 176, 178, 180, 181, 187, 199, 200, 201, 220, 221, 235, 236,
    237, 238, 251, 252, 253, 273, 278, 279, 283, 296, 299, 301, 304,
    305, 306, 307, 308, 311, 323, 325, 327, 329, 330, 332, 22, 334,
    337, 386, 389, 402, 403, 405, 408, 409, 410, 412, 413, 414, 415,
    418, 423, 426, 427, 428, 429, 430, 431.
Love…4, 14, 16, 17, 18, 21, 22, 23, 24, 25, 25, 28, 29, 31, 40, 46,
    50, 53, 61, 62, 63, 65, 81, 97, 101, 102, 118, 119, 120, 124, 125,
    131, 132, 133, 135, 155, 162, 171, 181, 182, 183, 184, 185, 186,
    187, 198, 208, 219, 220, 221, 234, 236, 251, 252, 254, 255, 256,
    257, 274, 283, 299, 300, 303, 305, 306, 307, 311, 328, 330, 331,
    332, 334, 336, 337, 361, 362, 365, 366, 384, 386, 387, 396, 407,
    411, 412, 420, 422, 428, 429, 430.
Low…12, 39, 183, 220, 298, 311, 354.
Lust…48, 53, 65, 68, 79, 101, 172, 173, 174, 183, 186, 215, 252, 253,
274, 303, 326, 402, 419, 421, 427, 428, 430.
Lying… 97, 123, 146, 300, 307, 332, 334.

M

Mad…152.
Made…11, 12, 17, 18, 39, 41, 50, 55, 57, 60, 62, 63, 65, 82, 98,
    103, 104, 107, 118, 123, 131, 145, 146, 147, 152, 153, 155, 158,
    174, 175, 199, 203, 204, 221, 233, 248, 250, 252, 260, 272, 275,
    280, 306, 326, 328, 329, 330, 333, 337, 361, 363, 364, 365, 366,
    368, 380, 389, 406, 410.
Magic…115, 127, 349, 355, 356.
Magician…348, 355, 362.
Malice…42, 179, 298.
Manifest…60, 252, 307, 309, 323, 328.
Manner…9, 12, 17, 19, 38, 45, 93, 98, 101, 155, 157, 216, 249,
    200.
Marriage…174, 175, 176, 180, 181, 185, 272, 304.
Marry…186.
Master… 9, 19, 37, 46, 49, 62, 78, 81, 96, 100, 103, 117, 118, 122,

133, 155, 157, 158, 171, 187, 199, 202, 203, 217, 219, 221, 329, 330, 348, 349, 354, 360, 361, 385, 386, 410, 411.
Mean...7, 51, 68, 79, 100, 105, 118, 126, 191, 248, 253, 304, 333, 386, 418.
Meaningless...272, 391.
Measure...49, 269, 310, 350.
Meat...9, 46, 56, 61, 97, 154, 178, 176, 216, 247, 248, 261, 278, 307, 308, 336.
Meeting...54, 221, 412.
Mercy...6, 23, 37, 48, 81, 82, 101, 119, 146, 148, 149, 150, 151, 152, 156, 158, 184, 187, 199, 221, 234, 259, 283, 299, 313, 333, 335, 337, 368, 421, 430.
Message...79, 94, 98, 100, 101, 120, 128, 158, 182, 215, 335.
Messiah...64, 66, 94, 254, 254, 257, 269, 270, 271, 276, 277, 278, 280, 282, 286, 287, 297, 302, 326, 330, 356, 415, 429, 430.
Metectors...202.
Midst...17, 19, 47, 49, 99, 145, 148, 158, 258.
Might...7, 9 48, 50, 82, 124, 147, 181, 198, 210, 203, 271, 298, 324, 328, 332, 334, 401, 404, 428.
Milk...9, 216, 270, 271.
Minister...63, 96, 99, 179, 213, 223, 236, 270, 288, 290, 292, 324, 328, 342.
Ministry...43, 54, 59, 60, 62, 63, 64, 97, 99, 101, 103, 118, 128, 147, 150, 182, 199, 201, 213, 214, 215, 221, 223, 226, 234, 235, 257, 270, 271, 272, 275, 276, 277, 279, 280, 281, 282, 283, 284, 285, 286, 288, 289, 291, 312, 325, 326, 329, 342, 343, 344, 345, 370.
Miracle...259, 271, 356, 360.
Mirror...23.
Misery...5, 135, 313, 336.
Mislead...64, 118, 220, 275, 370.
Mistake...4, 18, 49, 251, 258.
Model...66, 306, 397.
Moment...79, 120, 123, 155, 283, 357, 361, 368, 429.
Money...53, 59, 62, 64, 66, 103, 173, 185, 278, 298, 303, 304, 305, 306, 307, 308, 309, 310, 312, 313, 315, 320, 330, 428.
Moon...17, 285.
Moral...18, 23, 67, 115.
Morning...53, 147, 177, 185, 186, 277, 285, 411.

Morning...53, 147, 177, 185, 186, 277, 285, 411.
Morsel...42, 421.
Mother...8, 11, 16, 18, 20, 59, 63, 128, 147, 150, 154, 158, 174,
    180, 182, 186, 202, 216, 217, 222, 233, 236, 248, 249, 250, 251,
    254, 255, 259, 260, 270, 273, 274, 275, 277, 282, 283, 24, 300,
    303, 305, 306, 307, 308, 309, 310, 311, 3112, 324, 330, 336, 337,
    348, 357, 364, 365, 367, 368, 369, 385, 386, 387, 404, 412, 419,
    420, 422, 428, 430.
Motion...8, 104, 118, 122, 126, 130, 131, 300.
Motives...320.
Mound...360.
Mountain...101, 102, 125, 126, 171, 256, 332.
Mourn...101, 121, 332.
Mouth...48, 51, 53, 94, 100, 101, 118, 119,125, 153, 176, 179,
    186, 332, 337, 406, 407, 422.
Move...39, 62, 93, 97, 184, 218, 222, 256, 274, 282, 305, 310,
    332, 369, 385, 412, 430.
Much...7, 11, 12, 19, 40,41, 43, 48, 50, 53, 56, 57, 59, 66, 80, 81,
    82, 95, 97, 99, 102, 103, 116,117, 119, 122, 125, 133,
Mule...46, 81, 278.
Multiply...81, 96, 156, 173,174, 403, 404,
Murder...63, 68, 153, 257, 260, 300, 303.
Music...51, 64, 93, 94, 95, 123, 234, 236, 270, 279, 280, 281, 282,
    347.
Musician...236.
Myrrh...3, 102, 185.
Mystery...7, 22, 50, 82, 182, 269, 287, 328, 350, 355, 365, 367,
    428, 429.

Nails...333.
Name...16, 17, 24, 37, 44, 49, 54, 55, 58, 67, 99, 104, 119, 122,
    123, 125, 126, 178, 180, 184, 199, 200, 224, 254, 277, 283, 310,
    327, 329, 333, 362, 364, 365, 366, 367, 368, 397, 404, 409, 413,
    416, 420, 422, 428.
Nation...13, 97, 258, 404.
Natural...64, 65, 66, 95, 215, 233, 234, 249, 258, 348, 352, 362,

366.
Necessary...40, 41, 125, 135, 186, 221, 235, 250, 273, 326, 360, 362, 424.
Need...8, 11, 12, 18, 19, 21, 22, 44, 47, 49, 51, 56, 79, 81, 94, 99, 100, 103, 117, 127, 128, 133, 176, 177, 185, 202, 214, 218, 221, 235, 251, 255, 260, 270, 272, 273, 276, 277, 301, 311, 324, 329, 334, 348, 357, 364, 368, 385, 408, 418, 419, 420, 430.
Neighbour...53, 300, 330.
Never...11, 14, 15, 20, 22, 23, 42, 56, 59, 64, 67, 68, 93, 95, 100, 117, 118, 123, 128, 130, 132, 151, 157, 174, 175, 178, 180, 254, 258, 259, 270, 274, 277, 278, 282, 284, 285, 299, 300, 304, 306, 307, 308, 329, 330, 332, 333, 348, 349, 354, 363, 368, 369, 370, 384, 385, 386, 387, 388, 397, 398, 416, 420, 430.
New...8, 17, 23, 39, 40, 5, 50, 54, 60, 68, 74, 93, 97, 116, 117, 123, 124, 125, 127, 129, 130, 131, 175, 177, 181, 14, 198, 199, 202, 215, 216, 217, 218, 221, 222, 235, 249, 253, 260, 264, 270, 275, 276, 277, 281, 284, 292, 304, 320, 324, 326, 327, 335, 336, 337, 338, 339, 340, 341, 342, 343, 344, 345, 346, 347, 349, 353, 355, 357, 359, 371, 397, 412.
Night...78, 99, 133, 147, 176, 177, 302, 310, 324, 357, 387, 410, 411.
Noise...62, 100, 123, 133, 235, 236, 364, 385.
Nothing...14, 19, 22, 23, 39, 43, 52, 56, 61, 62, 78, 80, 81, 100, 116, 122, 124, 126, 135, 152, 177, 219, 220, 233, 236, 273, 238, 279, 281, 284, 307, 309, 312, 323, 329, 330, 331, 332, 350, 356, 362, 386, 396, 397.
Nourish...181
Number...37, 56, 187, 221, 256, 296, 335, 350, 351, 352, 354, 363, 367, 396, 397.

Obedience...38, 42, 99, 117, 121, 157, 173, 200, 249, 252, 253, 254, 360, 412, 415.
Obey...12, 25, 42, 45, 99, 220, 251, 303, 334, 412, 426, 430.
Obscure...18, 283.
Observe...8, 62, 146.
Obtain...101, 219, 311, 336.
Occasion...50.

Offend…50.
Offer…59, 62, 67, 94, 122, 218, 250, 257, 270, 277, 281, 326, 361.
Office…9, 43, 64, 203, 325, 327, 328, 329, 336, 337.
Officer…329.
Offspring…129, 185, 187, 210, 296, 403.
Oil…277, 236, 387.
Old…4, 8, 18, 20, 23, 24, 42, 62, 75, 82, 100, 115, 127, 131, 178,
    181, 198, 210, 202, 235, 254, 257, 258, 259, 278, 284, 2, 300, 304,
    30, 323, 32, 356, 32, 33, 365, 39, 412.
Once…21, 24, 42, 50, 51, 60, 61, 100, 121, 122, 128, 135, 148,
    149, 150, 186, 198, 202, 204, 21, 217, 256, 259, 283, 286, 304,
    326, 332, 350, 354, 386, 395, 414, 426, 430.
Only…4, 7, 8, 12, 19, 20, 21, 23, 24, 25, 37, 41, 43, 47, 49, 51, 57,
    59, 60, 61, 62, 3, 79, 81, 93, 9, 97, 99, 102, 103, 104, 115, 116,
    117, 118, 119, 120, 122, 123, 124, 125, 127, 128, 131, 1333, 135,
    148, 149, 150, 151, 155, 156, 157, 173, 174, 175, 177, 178, 181,
    186, 187, 213, 214, 216, 217, 218, 219, 221, 223, 234, 235, 251,
    252, 253, 254 256, 251, 258, 259, 260, 270, 273, 274, 275, 277,
    279, 280, 281, 284, 29, 297, 298, 299, 300, 301, 302, 303, 30, 308,
    310, 313, 323, 324, 325, 326, 327, 329, 330, 331, 333, 334, 335,
    336, 337, 348, 349, 350, 352, 354, 355, 357, 359, 31, 362, 365,
    367, 3, 384, 385, 403, 422, 426, 428.
Open…10, 79 115, 151, 156, 180, 204, 250, 255, 279, 301, 363,
    396.
Opinion…152, 277, 330.
Oppression…311.
Ordain…18, 369.
Outside…11, 64, 97, 122, 124, 155, 174, 175, 184, 187, 215, 220,
    250, 361, 428.
Overcome…23, 65, 80, 104, 122, 259.
Overflow…279.
Overthrow…24.

Pain…12, 115, 119, 134, 155, 233, 304, 363, 385, 386.
Pardon…4.

Parents...4, 18, 120, 155, 182, 183, 272, 273, 274, 387.
Partakers...60.
Partial...299.
Passion...42, 52, 249, 250.
Passover...18, 201, 202.
Pastor... 54, 56, 96, 150, 214, 215, 276, 277, 307.
Path...63, 153, 154, 155, 255, 259, 302, 421.
Patience...40.
Pay...21, 39, 63, 146, 148, 303, 310,311, 422.
Peace...9, 23, 47, 53, 55, 59, 117, 123, 126, 148, 149, 151, 181,
    185, 252, 277, 278, 300, 309, 313, 328 337, 401, 403, 409, 415.
Penalty...215, 302.
Perfect...23, 41, 50, 116, 118, 124, 125, 179, 214, 237, 311, 327,
    328, 331, 351, 352, 404, 407, 414.
Perish...25, 37, 81, 145, 146, 176, 303, 332, 348, 350, 372, 427,
    430.
Persecute...101, 413.
Persuade...60.
Perverse...154, 249.
Please...60, 133, 135, 185, 217, 283, 415.
Poor...23, 61, 62, 101, 133, 176, 178, 279, 295, 298, 308, 311,
    312, 313, 314, 330,426.
Possess...63, 357.
Possession...373.
Poverty...183, 303.
Power...48, 52,56, 57, 82, 99, 100, 103, 104, 117, 120, 125, 126,
    128, 133, 151, 156, 158, 179, 182, 186, 187, 200, 201, 203, 204,
    219, 220, 250, 251,256, 279, 282, 297, 299, 307, 308, 312, 323,
    325, 326, 330, 331, 332, 337, 348, 350, 352,356, 358 359, 360,
    361, 363, 364, 365, 367, 368, 369, 379, 402 406, 414, 418, 420,
    429, 431.
Practice...10, 19, 173, 174, 215, 306, 307, 308, 335, 387.
Praise...10, 11, 51, 119, 123, 177, 179, 180, 187, 235, 236, 280,
    281, 282, 282, 284, 285, 323, 349, 373, 404.
Pray...9, 12, 17, 54, 100, 145, 147, 177, 187, 219, 271, 277, 281,
    309, 397, 418, 419, 420.
Preach...25, 46, 49, 57, 60, 79, 98, 146, 147, 197, 205, 216, 220,
    279, 328, 395, 409, 426.
Precious...4, 53, 183, 184, 361, 367.

Presence...5, 10, 19, 100, 104, 121, 145, 146,148, 156, 251, 299, 301, 310, 326, 411.
Proclaim...128, 215, 254, 368.
Profess...56, 67.
Profit...51, 102, 217, 299, 353.
Prophecy...43, 105, 215, 297, 299, 303, 323, 324, 349, 353, 356, 358, 359, 362, 363, 366, 374, 376.
Prophet...17, 120, 147, 172, 257, 325, 334, 363, 384.
Proselyte...66, 329.
Prostitutes...5, 152.
Prostrate...5.
Proud...39, 61, 119.
Prove...179.
Proverb...23.
Punish...44, 48, 94, 251.
Purpose...5, 11, 12, 41, 51, 62, 96, 105, 152, 164, 171, 174, 180, 209, 214, 227, 244, 248, 252, 253, 270, 273, 284, 299, 300, 304, 308, 309, 310, 330, 343, 349, 352, 357, 368, 361, 362, 363, 370, 372, 418, 428.
Purse...256, 298.
Pursue...331.

Quake...301
Quench...117, 241, 401, 410.
Question...11, 63, 93, 152, 155, 202, 283, 307, 317, 325, 333, 360, 424.
Quick...56, 157, 413.
Quiet...10, 100, 151, 184.

Rabbi...46, 62, 329.
Rank...239
Reap...45.

Reason…18, 48, 61, 65, 101, 116, 119, 145, 149, 150, 200, 203, 204, 214, 215, 219, 233, 257, 273, 274, 276, 282, 298, 299, 307, 333, 366, 367, 384, 395, 403, 405, 408, 410, 411, 414, 416, 418, 421, 428.
Rebel…311, 333.
Rebuild…187, 270.
Rebuke…49, 103, 237, 251.
Recognize…11, 99, 120, 156, 297, 303, 306, 331, 356, 365.
Reconcile…320, 328.
Redeem…149, 202, 303, 336, 362.
Reef…64, 66, 67, 95.
Reef bleachers…64, 66, 67.
Refine…203, 259.
Refuse…45, 80, 300.
Regard…5, 7, 93, 128, 176, 182, 191, 218, 220, 222, 249, 254, 274, 277, 299, 302, 307, 362, 403.
Region…403.
Reign…20, 44, 45, 81, 82, 83, 157, 186, 271, 310, 335.
Reject…11, 23, 24, 44, 138, 330, 430.
Rejoice…23, 101, 176, 179, 328, 332, 411, 413, 431.
Relationship…66, 156, 173, 174, 182, 187, 221, 235, 250, 272, 273, 239, 290, 301, 32, 411, 412, 413.
Remove…6, 23, 41, 43, 60, 99, 115, 116, 119, 121, 125, 126, 135, 140, 175, 199, 216, 217, 253, 301, 305, 325, 332, 333, 361, 408, 418.
Render…50.
Renew…124, 179, 199, 370, 414.
Repent…24, 37, 49, 58, 59, 81, 81, 99, 102, 119, 146, 147, 150, 157, 172, 199, 202, 254, 98, 303, 385, 414.
Reproach…1, 119, 152, 185, 310, 413.
Reprobate…21, 47.
Reprove…60, 61, 328.
Require…9, 12, 25, 46, 50, 52, 55, 62, 67, 90, 98, 149, 157, 175, 180, 190, 198, 203, 204, 214, 220, 234, 235, 249, 250, 252, 258, 275, 277, 297, 301, 307, 308, 311, 331, 359, 385, 403.
Rescue…115.
Resist…8, 98, 121, 122, 123, 150, 279, 311, 330, 332, 348, 383, 389, 411.
Respect…10, 20, 40, 81, 103, 120, 217, 220, 333, 334, 359,

Resurrection...16, 184, 198, 302, 359, 360, 361, 363, 380, 408.
Retain...21, 47, 126, 128, 216, 217, 248, 278, 298, 300, 305, 330, 333, 421, 422.
Reveal...10, 11, 22, 25, 43, 79, 105, 156, 157, 234, 237, 256, 332, 350, 369.
Revelation...7, 22, 51, 79, 80, 82, 176, 185, 189, 202, 350, 353, 362, 369, 370, 404, 430.
Revive...360.
Reward...8, 10, 25, 37, 55, 56, 101, 105, 122, 157, 216, 217, 222, 258, 259, 293, 305, 309, 310, 324, 3325, 326, 331, 370, 386, 413, 419, 420, 426.
Rich... 42, 45, 48, 51, 66, 80, 157, 178, 278, 305, 309, 310, 311, 312, 317, 328, 330, 331, 332, 353, 364.
Righteous...23, 24, 24, 2, 37, 60, 63, 64, 65, 81, 82, 99, 101, 117, 123, 156, 172, 173, 186, 199, 203, 216, 274, 310, 309, 311, 316, 332, 333, 337, 410, 402, 403, 405, 406, 419.
Ripe...96, 155, 275.
Risen...196, 249, 254, 361, 426.
River...95, 117, 185, 304.
Roar...9, 98, 122, 275, 415, 422.
Root...22, 101, 355, 369.
Ruin...368.
Ruler...80, 157, 305, 312, 317, 330, 337, 401, 409.

Sacred...16, 300, 351, 352, 362, 368.
Sacrifice... 58, 59, 62, 81, 104, 118, 119, 145, 149, 157, 7172, 199, 204, 220, 251, 277, 278, 282, 309, 325, 326, 330, 331, 349, 361, 362, 372, 388.
Salt...39, 41, 42, 43, 64, 115, 232, 238, 366.
Salvation...25, 37, 79, 80, 90, 95, 100, 105, 117, 146, 151, 181, 206, 220, 248, 259, 267, 280, 326, 337, 401, 408, 414, 421.
Sanctify...181, 201, 301, 302.
Sanctuary...7, 283, 306, 384, 387.
Satan...8, 19, 48, 61, 66, 67, 83, 93, 97, 102, 103, 104, 111, 116, 117, 118, 119, 121, 122, 123, 124, 126, 128, 149, 151, 183, 184, 186, 210, 202, 203, 217, 248, 249, 250, 251, 263, 273, 277, 283,

96, 299, 302, 306, 317,330, 332, 334, 349, 350, 354, 355, 356,368, 359, 361, 362, 366, 384, 385, 387, 402, 408, 411, 416, 436.
Satisfy...117, 302, 329.
Save...14, 24, 49, 58, 61, 65, 79, 80, 81, 82, 99, 101, 102, 115, 124, 149, 150, 154, 155, 156, 174, 183, 184, 197, 199, 200, 201, 204, 205, 214, 215, 234, 235, 236, 248, 250, 251, 280, 303, 332, 336, 359, 363, 386, 409, 412, 417, 431.
Saviour...23, 43, 94, 15, 180,220, 297, 357, 408.
Scale...7, 50, 96, 97, 115, 116, 117, 118, 120, 121, 125, 127, 128, 129, 135, 137, 138, 139, 140, 141, 355.
Scaling...257.
Scribe...14, 50, 54, 61, 62.
Scripture...3, 5, 17, 18, 19, 21, 23, 46, 49, 56, 2,80, 81, 103, 117, 153, 166, 173, 174, 176, 227, 251, 263, 265, 271, 276, 277, 280, 286, 288, 296, 300, 301, 303, 326, 330, 340, 348, 352, 365, 370, 372, 386, 406, 428.
Scriptulation...46.
SDA...117.
Sea...36, 38, 50, 50, 2, 9, 94, 96, 123, 125 145,146, 151, 173, 252, 259, 329, 410, 411.
Search...219, 22O, 248.
Season...28, 225, 26.
Second...90, 131, 154, 208, 222, 227, 255, 269, 279, 282, 290, 306, 315, 317, 318, 333, 334.
Secret...15, 22, 60, 64, 221,309,419, 420.
Seductive...183, 348.
See...6, 14, 2, 23, 24, 42, 44, 49, 51, 52, 54, 57, 59, 60, 65, 80, 81, 82, 94, 101, 103, 105, 116, 117, 118, 120, 122, 123,126, 147,154, 156, 157, 182, 186, 203, 213, 219,221, 235, 236, 252, 257, 258, 270, 272, 277, 279, 296, 299, 300, 301, 303, 305, 306, 306, 309, 313, 327, 330, 343, 353, 354, 356, 357, 361, 362, 363, 365, 368, 369, 405, 406, 410, 411, 412, 428.
Seed...45, 126, 56, 201, 256, 276, 309, 407, 411.
Separate...177, 252, 367, 368, 429.
Servant...46, 60, 115, 121, 187, 189, 217, 222, 325, 327, 329, 333.
Seven...4, 54, 55, 56, 121, 187, 189, 217, 234, 235, 349, 351, 353, 354, 362, 364, 369.
Severe...25, 119, 300, 337.
Shadow...81, 147.

Shame...24, 42, 60, 61, 64, 66, 97, 185, 220, 251, 275.
Share...7, 12, 25, 48, 57, 101, 127, 153, 283, 361.
Sharp...347, 371, 408.
Sheep...4, 21, 42, 45, 46, 47, 49, 50, 52, 54, 56, 59, 62, 64, 66, 67,
    82, 85, 95, 97, 102, 118, 147, 149, 150, 151, 152, 156, 177, 183,
    184, 185, 214, 215, 216, 218, 221, 221, 222, 234, 235, 274, 275,
    277, 278, 279, 310, 330, 333, 416, 427, 432.
Sheol...327, 358, 429.
Shepard...214, 341, 399.
Shield...117, 401, 410, 413, 417, 422.
Shine...358.
Shock...40, 97.
Sick...46, 64, 65, 81, 82, 99, 123, 126, 128, 20, 308, 311, 332,
    360, 387.
Sight...45, 65, 115, 145, 156, 217, 250, 305, 328, 336, 368, 410,
    422, 426.
Sign...15, 16, 17, 18, 172, 214, 255, 355, 357.
Silence...133, 219, 237, 309, 385, 388.
Sin... 21, 23, 33, 37, 38, 47, 48, 49, 60, 61, 65, 66, 80, 82, 83, 96,
    97, 101, 103, 148, 150, 152, 156, 171, 173, 174, 181, 187, 198,
    199, 203, 219, 220, 221, 234, 247, 249, 250, 251, 253, 257, 259,
    260, 261, 265, 274, 299, 300, 301, 303, 324, 326, 327, 330, 332,
    336, 361, 369, 386, 387, 405, 406, 408, 422, 429, 430.
Sinful...59, 78, 151, 199, 281, 302, 303, 406.
Sing...45, 51, 235, 236, 277, 282, 284, 335.
Sink...78, 95, 97, 197, 198, 205, 255, 412.
Sinned...24, 80, 121, 152, 187, 234, 303, 337, 385.
Sober...121, 238, 402, 403, 404, 407, 415, 422.
Soil...12, 297, 381.
Son...15, 16, 20, 21, 22, 23, 24, 25, 26, 38, 44, 47, 65, 81, 82,
    100, 117, 119, 121, 145, 155, 156, 178, 198, 200, 203, 204, 213,
    220, 234, 253, 255, 269, 273, 274, 295, 296, 303, 304, 314, 325,
    332, 333, 337, 343, 350, 352, 357, 361, 363, 365, 384, 404, 411,
    412, 414, 419, 422, 423, 428.
Sonlight...117.
Sound...63, 120, 122, 123, 126, 236, 250, 279, 280, 281, 283, 328,
    349, 354, 362, 264, 365, 367, 385, 419, 422, 429.
Spair...97.
Spalarm...93.
Speculative lesson...155, 360.

Spear fishers...61, 62, 63.
Sports fishers...59, 61.
Spirit...8, 11, 12, 14, 20, 21, 22, 24, 43, 54, 55, 57, 59, 60, 61, 63,
    65, 66, 79, 80, 82, 93, 94, 95, 96, 97, 98, 101, 105, 116, 117, 120,
    121, 122, 123, 124, 125, 127, 150, 154, 155, 156, 157, 175, 177,
    179, 184, 187, 198, 200, 201, 202, 203, 204, 213, 214, 215, 217,
    219, 220, 221, 222, 233, 234, 235, 236, 37, 241, 242, 244, 248,
    252, 254, 255, 256, 360, 272, 277, 280, 281, 282, 284, 285, 302,
    303, 304, 305 306, 307, 308, 309, 324, 327, 328, 332, 333, 350,
    353, 356, 359, 360, 362, 366, 370, 384, 396, 397, 401, 402,407,
    414, 415, 415, 416, 417, 418, 419, 421, 424, 426, 430.
Star...98, 104, 215, 357.
Steward...57, 150, 222, 279, 328.
Stomach...16, 119, 123, 221.
Stone...187, 210, 360, 361, 426.
Storehouse...307, 308, 309.
Stray...50, 255.
Stumble...96, 404, 407.
Subject...65, 100, 120, 121, 180, 198, 260, 333, 350, 415.
Submit...98, 122, 123, 150, 180, 252, 327, 398, 428.
Suffer...50, 237, 271, 307, 387.
Sun...17, 20, 117, 130, 147, 218, 257, 285, 332, 350.
Surge...360.
Swallow...17, 145, 151, 152.
Sword...11, 12, 59, 117, 153, 154, 155, 216, 256, 325, 401, 413,
    416, 417, 422, 424.
Synagogue...54, 180.

Tabernacle...325, 327.
Table...174, 10.
Take...12, 13, 14, 17, 19, 23, 38, 45, 53, 62, 63, 66, 82, 97, 100,
    101,103,, 116, 117, 123, 146, 147, 151, 153, 155, 157, 181, 183,
    184, 185, 187, 192, 201, 203, 218, 220, 237, 256, 258, 276, 277,
    202, 309, 310, 311, 312, 313, 327, 348, 353, 387, 399, 401, 414,
    424, 426.

Talk…11, 81, 93, 281, 302, 357, 364, 395, 418.
Target…298, 395.
Task…11, 12, 103, 127, 154, 157, 179, 199, 203, 218, 252, 259, 277, 325, 337, 360, 363, 396.
Taste…146, 199, 253, 337, 367.
Taught…22, 42, 50, 54, 67, 78, 100, 101, 18, 149, 235, 248, 312, 322, 328, 329, 339, 405, 422, 423.
Tax…305, 308.
Teach…9, 50, 55, 56, 58, 3, 67, 94, 172, 190, 200, 225, 249, 281, 335.
Teacher…22, 39, 215, 216M 277, 329.
Temper…254, 257, 258, 260.
Temple…50, 51, 68, 103, 104, 105, 127, 145, 173, 175, 176, 187, 203, 204, 228, 280, 297, 301, 304, 325, 326, 354, 385.
Tempt…201, 250.
Tender…97, 270, 40, 422.
Tent…330.
Terror…121, 356.
Test…59, 63, 175, 259, 359, 386.
Testimony…178
Three…15, 17, 40, 41, 54, 56, 57, 103, 123, 145, 146, 151, 153, 154, 160, 161, 171, 173, 183, 187, 192, 199, 202, 215, 219, 220, 256, 274, 276, 295, 297, 299, 300, 306, 314, 323, 326, 342, 351, 3352, 353, 355, 356, 359, 360, 424, 425.
Thief…135, 295, 296, 297, 298, 299, 300, 303, 305, 306, 314.
Tithe…46, 99, 149, 278, 305, 306, 307, 308, 309, 311, 132, 319, 351, 432.
Tithe avoidance…305, 306, 307, 432.
Thirst…57, 101, 201, 235.
Thirty…298, 303, 352.
Thorn…66, 251.
Thunder…326.
Time…5, 7, 8, 10, 11, 12, 15, 16, 17, 18, 19, 20, 21, 22, 37, 39, 40, 41, 43, 44, 46, 47, 50, 56, 58, 60, 61, 62, 65, 67, 79, 82, 94, 99, 100, 102, 123, 125, 128, 131, 146, 150, 151, 154, 155, 176, 179, 184, 185, 202, 204, 214, 216, 217, 218, 219, 233, 252, 255, 259, 272, 23, 274, 277, 80, 298, 299, 301, 305, 309, 312, 313, 323, 324, 326, 335, 336, 354, 355, 357, 358, 359, 360, 361, 363, 368, 384, 387, 414, 426, 430, 431, 434.
Toil…46,

Tomb...95, 187, 360, 361.
Tomorrow...134, 273, 331, 348.
Tone...365.
Tongue...12, 53, 99, 116, 125, 126, 176, 179, 183, 281, 302, 324,
    362, 364, 379, 404.
Torment...118, 202, 357.
Torn...55, 132, 301, 302.
Trawlers...56
Train...10, 125, 183, 221, 273, 369, 399.
Treasure...178, 278, 312.
Tree...20, 49, 67, 79, 95, 96, 128, 171, 218.
Tribulation...58, 59, 172.
Trust...67, 97, 120, 176, 177, 253, 258, 387, 388.
Truth...19, 21, 22, 23, 47, 48, 51, 60, 65, 66, 82, 115, 117, 150,
    151, 180, 181, 183, 220, 243, 250, 256, 275, 301, 328, 332, 334,
    348, 356, 365, 370, 401, 403, 404, 427, 435.
Twelve...18, 57, 296, 297, 298, 327, 329, 332, 333, 352.
Two...25, 38, 39, 42, 43, 44, 46, 48, 54, 57, 78, 90, 94, 98, 122,
    127, 131, 148, 149, 153, 155, 174, 176, 182, 202, 206, 214, 215,
    216, 217, 219, 222, 232, 248, 252, 258, 266, 271, 272, 24, 276,
    277, 279, 280, 282, 289, 296, 297, 301, 304 , 305, 306, 308, 310,
    318, 320, 325, 327, 329, 330, 332, 333, 351, 352, 357, 358, 359,
    34, 397, 412, 416, 417, 419, 424, 428.

U

Ugly...7, 39, 40, 43, 44.
Unapproachable...128.
Unaware...185.
Unbelievers...12.
Unclean...55, 60, 121, 300, 301.
Undefiled...185.
Under...4, 8, 17, 18, 19, 43, 48, 81, 88, 95, 99, 123, 125, 147, 150,
    151, 153, 154, 171, 177, 215, 218, 219, 233, 250, 253, 270, 299,
    301, 305, 324, 332, 333, 336, 350, 351, 36, 386, 408, 411.
Understand...20, 22, 24, 41, 42, 43, 48, 63, 75, 79, 81, 82, 98, 101,

103, 105, 118, 119, 122, 125, 126, 155, 156, 173, 182, 201, 220, 222, 252, 256, 281, 303, 308, 324, 348, 349, 352, 354, 356, 359, 362, 364, 368, 369, 387, 388, 406, 411, 429.
Unfaithful...52, 170, 171, 182, 185, 187, 188, 189, 192.
Unfruitful...60.
Ungodly...24, 63.
Unholy...63.
Unjust...24.
Unknown...331, 362, 385.
Unrighteous...24, 63, 65, 156, 316, 332, 405, 406.
Unruly...116, 125.
Unworthy...220, 387.
Uphold...254.
Upright...301.
Useless...63, 218, 306, 307.
Utmost...306.
Utterance...178, 281.

Vagrant...
Vain...11, 12, 4, 60, 61, 63, 127, 149, 176, 180, 414, 415, 420, 429.
Vanity...256, 257.
Variety...47, 126, 151, 180, 218, 236, 279, 344, 387.
Various...11, 51, 115, 116, 214, 271, 276, 286, 298, 310, 369.
Vast...62, 307, 310.
Veil...183, 300, 301, 302, 418.
Vengeance...260.
Vessel... 16, 50, 83, 104, 177, 183, 203, 251, 327, 334.
Victor...363.
Vine... 38, 174.
Violence...122, 146, 155, 256.
Virgin...129.
Visible...363.
Vision...176, 222, 300, 369.
Voice...19, 43, 44, 45, 55, 79, 123, 145, 146, 156, 198, 235, 236, 302, 411, 421, 427, 431.

Vomit...24, 123.

Walk...7, 57, 60, 61, 65, 66, 67, 81, 82, 93, 95, 96, 100, 101, 104,
    131, 149, 151, 155, 175, 198, 203, 215, 216, 255, 258, 259, 317,
    332, 350, 363,366, 387, 388, 408, 410, 412, 41, 428.
Wall...153, 154, 217.
Wander...97.
Want...12, 19, 20, 42, 43, 44, 62, 66, 135, 147, 148, 152, 154,
    162,166, 216, 222, 23, 248, 253, 256, 274, 279, 302, 309, 311, 324,
    327, 330, 370, 386, 396, 430.
War...45, 80, 82, 128, 155, 256.
Warm...39, 132, 151, 283.
Warn...30, 183.
Warrior...203.
Wash...128, 199, 200, 202, 203, 300.
Waste...99, 102, 131, 133, 277, 419.
Watch...18, 55, 81, 82, 96, 135, 309, 311, 331, 360, 410, 411.
Water...6, 7, 17, 18, 37, 39, 40, 41, 43, 51, 65, 66, 88, 95, 97, 8,
    117, 128, 146, 151, 158, 181, 198, 199, 200, 201, 202, 203, 218,
    255, 256, 304, 312, 324, 332, 356, 357, 366, 385, 410.
Wave...281.
Way...8, 10, 11, 12, 15, 19, 23, 39, 40, 42, 44, 47, 53, 60, 62, 64,
    65, 67, 79, 80, 88, 98, 100, 115, 119, 121, 122, 123, 126, 127, 135,
    146, 149, 150, 151, 153, 154, 156, 157, 181, 183, 184, 186, 187,
    217, 222, 234, 256, 259, 260, 270, 273, 274, 275, 285, 297, 299,
    303, 304, 308, 309, 311, 324, 330, 349, 353, 354, 355, 357, 358,
    361, 365, 367, 368, 369, 370, 385, 404, 405, 421, 423, 426, 429,.
Wear...8, 38, 45, 181, 308, 311, 426.
Weakness...39, 62, 122, 183, 219, 221, 296, 297, 385.
Wealth...45, 278, 305, 306, 308, 309, 310, 311, 312, 349, 361.
Weapons...12, 157, 203, 400, 410, 402.
Weary...45, 426.
Weather...97.
Wedding...357.
Weep...278, 310.
Welfare...220.
Well...23, 40, 41, 42, 44, 64, 68, 81, 93, 100, 102, 147, 148, 151,

161, 176, 180, 181, 182, 198, 204, 214, 216, 217, 221, 222, 235, 250, 252, 257, 270, 272, 273, 276, 300, 304, 306, 310, 311, 312, 324, 325, 328, 335, 347, 348, 349, 350, 354, 355, 361, 364, 367, 371, 386, 398, 406, 426.

Wept...256.
Wet...333.
Wheat...38.
Wife...53, 156, 170, 171, 174, 175, 176, 177, 180, 181, 182, 184, 188, 254, 257, 305, 336.
Wilderness...39, 56, 257, 258, 259, 277, 310, 384, 385, 386, 419.
Will...10, 11, 12, 19, 20, 21, 22, 24, 37, 38, 39, 40, 41, 42, 43, 44, 47, 48, 49, 50, 51, 53, 54, 55, 56, 57, 58, 59, 60, 61, 62, 63, 64, 65, 66, 67, 68, 78, 79, 80, 81, 85, 94, 95, 96, 97, 98, 99, 100, 101, 102, 104, 105, 111, 115, 117, 119, 121, 123, 124, 126, 127, 129, 135, 145, 146, 148, 151, 153, 154, 156, 157, 158, 172, 174, 175, 176, 179, 180, 181, 183, 184, 185, 186, 187, 192, 193, 198, 199, 201, 202, 203, 204, 213, 214, 216, 217, 218, 219, 220, 221, 222, 223, 225, 237, 248, 250, 251, 252, 253, 254, 255, 256, 257, 258, 259, 260, 270, 271, 272, 273, 274, 275, 276, 277, 278, 279, 281, 283, 284, 285, 301, 303, 305, 306, 307, 308, 309, 310, 311, 312, 313, 323, 324, 325, 329, 330, 331, 332, 333, 334, 348, 349, 350, 354, 356, 357, 359, 360, 362, 364, 365, 366, 367, 369, 370, 383, 384, 385, 386, 388, 389, 395, 397, 403, 404, 406, 409, 410, 411, 412, 414, 420, 422, 423, 424, 426, 427, 429, 430..
Willing...9, 37, 40, 48, 55, 66, 199, 26, 279, 284, 303, 414, 431.
Win...56, 102, 130, 302.
Wind...123, 145, 147, 410, 412.
Window...40, 62, 123, 124, 279.
Wine...281, 328, 356.
Wings...67.
Wisdom...22, 24, 43, 118, 127, 148 176, 178, 179, 328, 332, 337, 349, 350, 351, 353, 372, 421, 422, 423.
Wise...39, 47, 51, 60, 95, 122, 214, 325, 355, 404.
Wish...19, 58, 95, 115, 132, 135, 148, 215, 258, 336, 358.
Witness...48, 200, 203, 213, 23, 250, 278, 300, 310, 311, 416, 430, 431.
Wives...115, 180, 181, 217, 275.
Woman...16, 52, 53, 58, 172, 174, 175, 17, 177, 180, 183,, 186, 221, 251, 275, 276, 303, 310, 336.
Womb...16, 17, 174, 254, 257.

Wonder...2, 82, 100, 133, 182, 202, 215, 217, 279, 311, 348, 355, 359, 384.
Work...4, 7, 11, 12, 43, 45, 46, 52, 56, 57, 59, 63, 65, 67, 80, 93, 98, 104, 117, 150, 158, 176, 177, 182,
   203, 216, 217, 218, 221, 223, 235, 237, 252, 255, 258, 269, 278, 279, 287, 298, 299, 306, 308, 309, 310, 311, 312, 324, 326, 330, 331, 336, 349, 386, 387, 428, 429, 430.
World...11, 16, 23, 24, 25, 42, 47, 51, 52, 53, 58, 59, 61, 63, 64,
   65, 66, 68, 72, 81, 93, 94, 97, 102, 103, 104, 115, 122, 124, 128, 129, 130, 131, 148, 149, 151, 152, 153, 155, 172, 178, 179, 181, 183, 184, 185, 187, 194, 197, 199, 210, 202, 203, 204, 20, 215, 216, 221, 233, 248, 249, 250, 257, 278, 281, 285, 297, 300, 301, 308, 309, 311, 325, 326, 328, 330, 331, 333, 334, 335, 337, 347, 349, 350, 351, 39, 362, 363, 371, 384, 401, 404, 49, 11, 41, .
Worship...17, 20, 51, 82, 102, 104, 116, 119, 123, 177, 179, 233,
   235, 277, 280, 281, 282, 283, 284, 285, 310, 336, 355, 360, 364, 386, 413.
Worth...46, 337.
Wound...149, 221.
Wrath... 25, 38, 48, 60, 61, 81, 119, 124, 127, 147, 148, 149, 156, 179, 252, 257.
Writing...93, 363.
Written...8, 50, 55, 59, 96, 125, 173, 179, 198, 216, 303, 327, 335, 359, 360, 362, 409, 419, 426, 429.
Wrong...8, 10, 38, 49, 58, 97, 100, 118, 120, 152, 153, 217, 221,
   233, 236, 260, 274, 275, 284, 296, 298, 299, 302, 333, 337, 368, 384, 385.

Year...18, 75, 93, 215, 222, 256, 326, 332, 426.
Yesterday...134, 331, 348, 363.
Yet...6, 23, 40, 41, 45, 46, 48, 49, 54, 59, 60, 79, 80, 93, 98, 101,
   102, 103, 117, 119, 132, 148, 147, 148, 156, 157, 171, 176, 177, 181, 186, 200, 214, 220, 234, 235, 251, 252, 254, 255, 256, 258, 278, 297, 301, 326, 328, 336, 355, 360, 364, 386, 413.
Yield...53, 99, 134, 186, 217, 277, 360.
Yoke...38, 70, 202.

Young...8, 9, 22, 39, 44, 45, 46, 66, 80, 97, 157, 215, 233, 274, 282, 305, 310, 312, 317, 330, 333.

Zeal...12, 254, 255.
Zealot...99, 255.

To order other books by this author,
Send an email to Shepardsink@yahoo.com ,
Write to Shepard's Ink
P.O. Box 78211
Nashville, Tn 37207.
or log on to
www.Shepardsink.Org
These books can also be obtained from the following retailers. If in the Caribbean from White Marlin Int'l Nassau, Bahamas at 1-242-341-5958

These books are also made available to believers and new converts in jail through prison outreach ministry please feel free to logon to www.Asharaministries.org and if you know someone in jail send them a copy of these stories. The copies you send to jail MUST however be the paperback cover.

THE BUTTERFLY VEIL

BLACK COFFEE

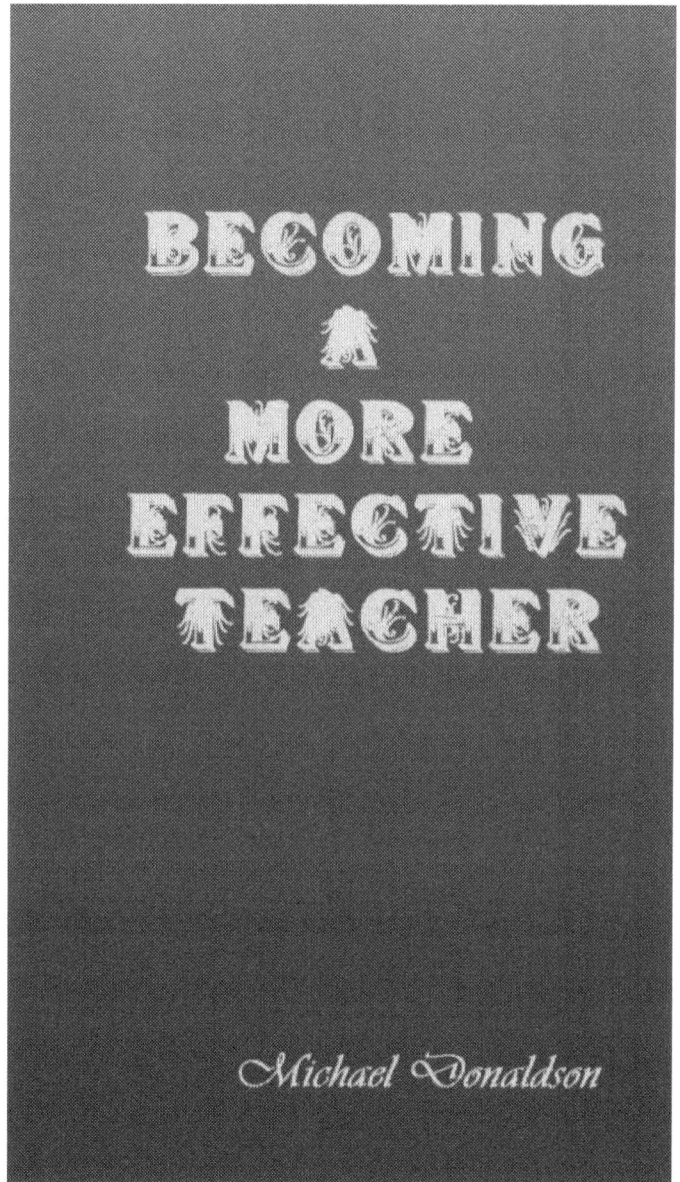

BECOMING A MORE EFFECTIVE TEACHER

FIRE IN PATMOS

AVAILABLE 2006